Literary Forms of Argument in Early China

Literary Forms of Argument in Early China

Edited by

Joachim Gentz and Dirk Meyer

BRILL

LEIDEN | BOSTON

This paperback was originally published in hardback as Volume 123 in the series *Sinica Leidensia*.

This volume received support from the "New Perspectives in Chinese Culture and Society" program, which is made possible by a grant from the Chiang Ching-kuo Foundation for International Scholarly Exchange to the American Council of Learned Societies.

Cover illustration: Wang Jie 王玠 (fl. 1331–1380), "Explanations and Commentary with Diagrams to the Wondrous Canon of the Eternal Purity and Tranquility as taught by the Supreme Venerable Sovereign" (*Taishang Laojun shuo chang qingjing miaojing zuantu jiezhu* 太上老君說常清靜妙經纂圖解註), in *Zhengtong Daozang* 正統道藏 (Taipei: Xin wenfeng chuban gongsi, 1985–1988, vol. 28., p. 839), *dongshen bu, yujue lei, shizi hao* 洞神部・玉訣類・是字號, (DZ 760, fasc. 533, following the numbering in Kristopher Schipper and Franciscus Verellen eds., *The Taoist Canon: A Historical Companion to the Daozang* [Chicago: University of Chicago Press, 2004], vol. 2, 730).

The Library of Congress Cataloging-in-Publication Data is available online at http://catalog.loc.gov
LC record available at http://lccn.loc.gov/2015023011

Want or need Open Access? Brill Open offers you the choice to make your research freely accessible online in exchange for a publication charge. Review your various options on brill.com/brill-open.

Typeface for the Latin, Greek, and Cyrillic scripts: "Brill". See and download: brill.com/typeface.

ISBN 978-90-04-33134-1 (paperback)
ISBN 978-90-04-29160-7 (hardback, 2015)
ISBN 978-90-04-29970-2 (e-book, 2015)

Copyright 2015 by Koninklijke Brill NV, Leiden, The Netherlands.
Koninklijke Brill NV incorporates the imprints Brill, Brill Hes & De Graaf, Brill Nijhoff, Brill Rodopi and Hotei Publishing.
All rights reserved. No part of this publication may be reproduced, translated, stored in a retrieval system, or transmitted in any form or by any means, electronic, mechanical, photocopying, recording or otherwise, without prior written permission from the publisher.
Authorization to photocopy items for internal or personal use is granted by Koninklijke Brill NV provided that the appropriate fees are paid directly to The Copyright Clearance Center, 222 Rosewood Drive, Suite 910, Danvers, MA 01923, USA.
Fees are subject to change.

This book is printed on acid-free paper and produced in a sustainable manner.

Contents

List of Contributors   VII

Introduction: Literary Forms of Argument in Early China   1
  Joachim Gentz and Dirk Meyer

1 A Building Block of Chinese Argumentation: Initial *Fu* 夫 as a Phrase Status Marker   37
    Rudolf G. Wagner

2 Beyond Parallelism: A Rethinking of Patterns of Coordination and Subordination in Chinese Expository Prose   67
    Andrew H. Plaks

3 On the Range and Performance of *Laozi*-Style Tetrasyllables   87
    David Schaberg

4 Defining Boundaries and Relations of Textual Units: Examples from the Literary Tool-Kit of Early Chinese Argumentation   112
    Joachim Gentz

5 The Philosophy of the Analytic *Aperçu*   158
    Christoph Harbsmeier

6 Speaking of Poetry: Pattern and Argument in the "Kongzi Shilun"   175
    Martin Kern

7 Structure and Anti-Structure, Convention and Counter-Convention: Clues to the *Exemplary Figure's* (*Fayan*) Construction of Yang Xiong as Classical Master   201
    Michael Nylan

8 *A Ragbag of Odds and Ends?* Argument Structure and Philosophical Coherence in *Zhuangzi* 26   243
    Wim De Reu

9 Truth Claim with no Claim to Truth: Text and Performance of the "Qiushui" Chapter of the *Zhuangzi*   297
   Dirk Meyer

Index   341

List of Contributors

Joachim Gentz
Chair of Chinese Philosophy and Religion, University of Edinburgh. Joachim Gentz studied Sinology, Religious Studies and Philosophy in Berlin, Nanjing and Heidelberg. He was Assistant Professor at Heidelberg (1999–2002), Juniorprofessor in Religious Studies at Göttingen (2002–2006), Visiting Professor in Tokyo (2000) and Bayreuth (2008), and has worked at the Asian Studies Department in Edinburgh since 2006. His main research focus is on Chinese history of thought. His work crosses the disciplinary boundaries of Sinology, Religious Studies, Philosophy, and Cultural Studies. His recent publications include *Keywords Re-Oriented* (2009), *Understanding Chinese Religions* (2012), and *Religious Diversity in Chinese Thought* (2013), ed. with P. Schmidt-Leukel.

Christoph Harbsmeier
Professor of Chinese, University of Oslo. Born in 1946, Christoph Harbsmeier read Chinese at Merton College, Oxford, and was awarded a PhD from Copenhagen in 1981. He is a student of classical Chinese philosophy, grammar and rhetoric with a special interest in modern Chinese illustrated literature. His books include *Wilhelm von Humboldt und die philosophische Grammatik des Altchinesischen* (1978), *Aspects of Classical Chinese Syntax* (1981), *Socialist Realism with a Buddhist Face: The Cartoonist Feng Zikai* (1984), *Language and Logic* (Science and Civilisation in China, vol. 7.1) 1998. Long-term engagements include: lecturer in Humanities, Princeton, visiting professor at University of Chicago, University of California at Berkeley, University of Michigan, Chinese University Hong Kong, Peking University, EHESS Paris, National University of Singapore, Heidelberg, Wissenschaftskolleg Berlin, Collegium Budapest, Swedish Collegium for Advanced Study, and the International Collegium Erlangen.

Martin Kern
Greg ('84) and Joanna (P13) Zeluck Professor in Asian Studies; Chair, Department of East Asian Studies, Princeton University. Martin Kern is the author of *The Stele Inscriptions of Ch'in Shih-huang*, the editor of *Text and Ritual in Early China*, and, with Benjamin A. Elman, the co-editor of *Statecraft and Classical Learning: The Rituals of Zhou in East Asian History*. He also is the co-editor of *T'oung Pao*. His work cuts across the fields of literature, philology, history, religion, and art in ancient and early medieval China, with a primary focus on poetry. He currently studies the formation of the early (Zhou through Han)

Chinese textual tradition, exploring questions of authorship, textual composition, and canonisation.

Dirk Meyer

Associate Professor in Chinese Philosophy and Fellow of The Queen's College, University of Oxford. Dirk Meyer (PhD, Leiden) read Chinese at National Taiwan University, Heidelberg, and Leiden. He took up his position at Oxford in 2007. Meyer works on the history of thought, the interplay of material conditions and ideas, orality and literacy in early Chinese philosophical discourse, argumentative strategies in early Chinese philosophy, as well as text and manuscript cultures in early China. He is the author of *Philosophy on Bamboo: Text and the Production of Meaning in Early China*. Meyer has been a visiting scholar at Princeton, National Taiwan University and Renmin University Beijing, as well as Bernhard Karlgren Fellow at the Swedish Collegium for Advanced Study.

Michael Nylan

Professor of History at the University of California at Berkeley. Books by Michael Nylan cover early Chinese urban history, pleasures in reading and classical learning, and reception of the Classics, and include two translations, with a third, the *Shangshu* or *Documents*, in progress. Her essays discuss empire, economics, forgeries and reproductions, the legalities of sex, historiography and rhetoric, and feminism.

Andrew H. Plaks

Professor of Asian Studies, Hebrew University, Jerusalem; Professor emeritus, Princeton University. Andrew Plaks received his PhD. from the Department of East Asian Studies, Princeton University in 1973, and taught in that department until 2007, when he transferred to emeritus status. Concomitantly, he has taught at the Hebrew University in Jerusalem for about twenty-five years, where he is currently Professor of Asian Studies. The main focus of his academic work in the early years of his career was in the area of the "classic" fiction and drama of the Ming and Qing periods, but for the past two decades he has concentrated primarily on issues and texts in Early Chinese thought.

Wim De Reu

Assistant Professor, Department of Philosophy, National Taiwan University. Wim De Reu studied Chinese Studies and Philosophy at the Katholieke Universiteit Leuven and National Taiwan University. He currently teaches early Chinese philosophy at the Department of Philosophy, National Taiwan University. His interests include early Chinese views on language, the theory and practice of argumentation, and cognitive linguistics. He has published articles on early Chinese paradoxes and on the role of metaphors in the construction of early Chinese philosophy (*Philosophy East and West, Asian Philosophy*). He currently runs a project that focuses on argumentation in the later chapters of the *Zhuangzi*.

David Schaberg
Dean of Humanities, UCLA. David Schaberg is professor of Chinese thought and literature and Dean of Humanities at UCLA. He is author of *A Patterned Past: Form and Thought in Early Chinese Historiography*, which was awarded the 2003 Levenson Prize for Books in Chinese Studies (Pre-1900 Category). His more recent work addresses the history of oratory and ritual speech genres in early China.

Rudolf G. Wagner
Senior Professor, Chinese Studies, Heidelberg University, Cluster "Asia and Europe"; Associate, John K. Fairbank Center for Chinese Studies, Harvard University. Rudolf G. Wagner is Senior Professor in Chinese Studies at the Cluster Asia and Europe, Heidelberg University. A recipient of the Leibniz Award, he is an intellectual historian with strong interests in the political implications of philosophical and literary works; in enhancing the precision of understanding classical Chinese texts; and in the transcultural interaction between China and the world. His recent research focus is on the transcultural framework of the Chinese press and publishing industry in the late 19th century. His relevant publications include a three-volume edition and study of Wang Bi's (226–249) *Commentary on the Laozi*.

Introduction: Literary Forms of Argument in Early China

Joachim Gentz and Dirk Meyer

Methods largely shaped by Western philosophical and philological concepts have had an enormous impact on reading strategies applied to early Chinese argumentative texts. What are commonly termed philosophical texts in the Chinese context have been analysed in terms of their so-called logical capacity. Since analytical precision has been connected to Western logical techniques alone, argumentation in Chinese philosophical texts is commonly described as ambiguous and poetic rather than systematic. As a result of this, the written texts from pre-modern China available to us now have long been treated as mere repositories of ideas. This tendency in research was furthered by the fact that many early Chinese texts are made up of distinct components, building blocks or collected episodes. Fragmentation is therefore still conceived of as a common characteristic of early Chinese written philosophy. As a result, the misconception has arisen that pre-modern Chinese texts fail to generate homogenous disquisitions of thought in treatises with a coherent outlook in which consistent literary patterns establish argumentative force.

Convinced of an identical implicit logic underlying Western and Chinese arguments, Angus Graham addressed this Western-centric misconception by differentiating two stages by which to approach Chinese argumentation. First, a stage where all argumentation appears muddled, "the few pitiful examples of Chinese 'logic' vitiated by childish fallacies, so that there seems no hope of arriving anywhere by this path unless it leads out of the mist into a world so alien that even the laws of logic reveal themselves as Western and culturebound;" a second stage is where in Chinese argumentation, as in its Western counterpart, "the gaps fill in when the questions and assumptions are rightly identified."[1] Looking at further developments in Western studies of Chinese philosophical argumentation (including Graham's own "Reflections and Replies" responding to the essays dedicated to him by students and colleagues five years later),[2] the gaps still do not seem to have "filled in," and it appears that the relevant ques-

---

1 Angus C. Graham, *Studies in Chinese Philosophy and Philosophical Literature* (Singapore: Institute of East Asian Philosophies, 1986), 1–2.
2 See Henry Rosemont, Jr., ed., *Chinese Texts and Philosophical Contexts: Essays Dedicated to Angus C. Graham* (Illinois: Open Court, 1991), 267–322.

tions and assumptions have not been rightly identified. Christoph Harbsmeier notes that "the ancient Chinese have many current forms of argument in common with their contemporary Greeks [...] but unlike in Greece, even the argumentative philosophers in ancient China did not systematically deploy the insights of the logicians and their techniques in other areas than those of formal logic."[3]

From the viewpoint of formal logic, arguments in early Chinese texts have been classified as analogical reasoning or correlative thinking, as well as arguments based on associative logic or a metaphorical method of insight. Roger Ames and David Hall explain that "Chinese thinking depends upon a species of analogy which may be called 'correlative thinking.'"[4] They hold that "The priority of logical reasoning in the West is paralleled in China by the prominence of less formal uses of analogical, parabolic and literary discourse."[5] Yet, correlative thinking, analogical reasoning, and metaphor are commonly identified with poetry[6] and semantic ambiguity.[7] Argumentation in Chinese early texts is therefore often described as ambiguous and poetic rather than systematic and philosophical. Earlier authors have often linked Chinese thinking to the Chinese language or the Chinese writing system, which they deemed to be media that is better suited to poetic expression than logical analysis.[8] This sentiment still prevails in recent publications. Michael Broschat stresses the "poetic qual-

---

3   Christoph Harbsmeier, *Language and Logic*. Science and Civilisation in China, vol. 7 (Cambridge: Cambridge University Press, 1998), xxiii.
4   David L. Hall and Roger T. Ames, "Chinese Philosophy," in *Routledge Encyclopedia of Philosophy*, ed. E. Craig (London: Routledge, 1998). URL: http://www.rep.routledge.com/article/G001SECT2 (26.10.14).
5   Hall and Ames, "Chinese Philosophy" http://www.rep.routledge.com/article/G001 (26.10.14).
6   Roman Jakobson, "Two Aspects of Language and Two Types of Aphasic Disturbances," in *Fundamentals of Language*, eds. Roman Jakobson and Morris Halle (The Hague: Mouton, 1956), 115–133. (Repr. in *On Language*, ed. Roman Jakobson, Cambridge MA: Harvard University Press, 1990, 115–133).
7   Roman Jakobson, "Linguistics and Poetics," in *Style in Language*, ed. Thomas A. Sebeok (Cambridge MA: MIT Press, 1960), 350–377, 370f.
8   This view can already be found in early Jesuit discussions and in reflections by philosophers such as Leibniz and Hegel. An early more systematic linguistic analysis undertakes Wilhelm von Humboldt in his letter to Abel-Rémusat in 1827 (transl. by Christoph Harbsmeier, *Brief an M. Abel-Rémusat über die Natur grammatischer Formen im allgemeinen und über den Geist der chinesischen Sprache im besonderen*, Stuttgart: Frommann-Holzboog, 1979). See also Joseph S. Wu, "Chinese Language and Chinese Thought," *Philosophy East and West* 19:4 (October 1969): 423–434.

ity" of Classical Chinese prose.⁹ Hall and Ames see an "aesthetic order" prevailing in Chinese philosophical thinking in contrast to a "rational order" dominating in Western philosophy.¹⁰ Jinmei Yuan refers to a "poetic logic" of Chinese thinking.¹¹

The distinction between *philosophy* and *poetry* has its firm roots in the Platonic dialogues.¹² Although Plato in the *Republic* refers to this contradiction as "an ancient quarrel,"¹³ Plato's work is nonetheless the first where we see it become conceptualised.¹⁴ Plato's definition of philosophy is in stark contrast to what he depreciates as rhetoric, art, myth, drama, and poetry, thus formulating the main criteria for philosophy basically in the sense in which we still understand it today. This gives Plato a very peculiar position in the history of Western philosophy.¹⁵ It seems all the more surprising that from the very first generation of his followers the question has been raised whether Plato's own works are actually philosophical or poetical. Starting with Aristotle who classifies the dialogues as a new type "midway between poetry and prose,"¹⁶ the poetic qual-

9   Michael R. Broschat, "Guiguzi: A textual Study and Translation" (Doctoral dissertation, University of Michigan 1985), 87–127, 98–99.
10 David L. Hall and Roger T. Ames, *Thinking Through Confucius* (NY Albany: SUNY, 1987), 16. Also emphasised in Hall and Ames, "Chinese Philosophy" http://www.rep.routledge.com/article/G001SECT1 (26.10.14).
11 Jinmei Yuan, "Analogical Propositions in Moist Texts," *Journal of Chinese Philosophy* 39:3 (September 2012): 404–423, 421.
12 Cf. for an overview with an excellent bibliography Charles L. Griswold, "Plato on Rhetoric and Poetry," *The Stanford Encyclopedia of Philosophy* (Spring 2012 Edition), ed. Edward N. Zalta, URL: http://plato.stanford.edu/archives/spr2012/entries/plato-rhetoric/ (19.2.14).
13 *Republic* 607b. For the reconstruction of such a history of that quarrel, see William Chase Greene, "Plato's View of Poetry," *Harvard Studies in Classical Philology* 29 (1918): 1–75, 6–12; Glen Most, "What Ancient Quarrel Between Philosophy and Poetry?" in *Plato and the Poets*, ed. Pierre Destrée and Fritz-Gregor Herrmann (Leiden: Brill, 2011), 1–20 refutes the existence of such a history.
14 Susan B. Levin, *The Ancient Quarrel Between Philosophy and Poetry Revisited: Plato and the Greek Literary Tradition* (New York, Oxford University Press, 2001); Most 2011.
15 Marsilio Ficino (1433–1499), one of the most influential humanist philosophers of the early Italian Renaissance and the first translator of Plato's work into Latin, referred to Plato as "sacro padre de' philosophi" in 1468 (Michael Stausberg, *Faszination Zarathustra: Zoroaster und die Europäische Religionsgeschichte der frühen Neuzeit*, Berlin: Walter de Gruyter, 1998, 106; Simon A. Gilson, *Dante and Renaissance Florence*, Cambridge: Cambridge University Press, 2005, 143–144); in a widely celebrated quote, Whitehead wrote in 1929 that "[t]he safest general characterisation of the European philosophical tradition is that it consists of a series of footnotes to Plato" (*Process and Reality*, Free Press, 1979, 39).
16 Aristotle as quoted by Diogenes Laertius who quite probably refers to a similar passage in Aristotle's *Poetics*: "But the art which employs words either in bare prose or in meters,

ity of Plato's work has been pointed out by apologists of poetry and commentators.[17] The discussion of Plato's poetical philosophy therefore provides an excellent example for the discussion of Chinese thinking. Attempts to explain the literary form of Plato's dialogues—thought of as replete with "myth, metaphor, and colourful image"[18]—consider it as "extra logical means" to draw the readers to the 'real' content of the philosophical arguments. These arguments presumably follow an entirely different rational logic and have to be regarded as separate from the autonomous literary form.[19] For this reason, some scholars explain such arguments as self-referential "implicit poetics" in the tradition of Hellenistic poetry.[20] Others hold that even after centuries of commentarial debate the inherent problem—and paradox—of relating the disparate elements of drama, philosophy and rhetoric in Plato remain due to the fact that philosophy is fundamentally an "activity of embodied individuals, constrained by both space and time, having to deal with other human beings while having

either in one kind of meter or combining several, happens up to the present day to have no name. For we can find no common term to apply to the mimes of Sophron and Xenarchus and to the Socratic dialogues." *Poetics* 1.7 (1447b) quoted in Jill Gordon, *Turning Toward Philosophy: Literary Device and Dramatic Structure in Plato's Dialogues* (University Park: Pennsylvania State University Press, 1999), 65.

17 Michael Erler, "To Hear the Right Thing and to miss the Point: Plato's implicit Poetics," in *Plato As Author: The Rhetoric of Philosophy*, ed. Ann N. Michelini (Leiden, Boston: Brill, 2003), 153–173, 154; Zhang Longxi, *The Tao and the Logos: Literary Hermeneutics, East and West* (Durham & London: Duke University Press, 1992), 39.

18 "Plato presents several views in the voices of several characters who most often disagree with one another; the philosophical conversations in which the disagreement takes place rarely, if ever, reach any single conclusion and leave thorny philosophical problems largely unresolved; Plato creates a central character who is himself not consistent in his views, and who distances himself from many of the ideas he presents; Plato constructs texts with ambiguous meaning and a vast array of possible interpretations; and finally, Plato fills the dialogues with the seemingly superfluous trappings of myth, metaphor, and colourful image. The combined effort of these strategies would lead one to the uncharitable conclusion that Plato chose the most ridiculous means of conveying his ideas and, as one would expect, he has failed to do so." (Gordon, *Turning Toward Philosophy*), 7–8.

19 Jill Gordon, for example, divides human beings into a rational part to which arguments speak and another part of the senses and the imagination to which poetic and dramatic literary devices speak. She interprets Plato as using literary forms to involve the readers into the philosophical dialogue and have them attuned to philosophy. The two realms are strictly separated and the literary forms are not creating logical arguments but induce the readers to realise them fully. Gordon even calls the literary devices "extra logical levels/ means" (*Turning Toward Philosophy*), 2.

20 Erler, To Hear the Right Thing and to miss the Point: Plato's implicit Poetics.

a private life of the mind, with some kind of access to an enduring truth."[21] Some even argue that in Plato "[p]hilosophical rhetoric seems only preliminary: it is presented as the necessary part of a mystery initiation, which culminates in something unphilosophical and unrhetorical."[22] Common to these explanations is the idea that the dramatic, poetic and rhetorical literary forms in the dialogues have to be understood as something exterior to and separate from the arguments. The distinction between poetry and philosophy is further consolidated by the fact that lately philosophers do not show a keen interest in poetry—the attempt to develop a "philosophy of poetry" is therefore still missing.[23]

Andreas Kablitz has argued that the concept of a self-referential autonomy of poetry and rhetoric as propagated most prominently by members of the Prague Linguistic Circle,[24] and still claimed in post-structuralist theories, is deeply rooted in the philosophical notion of an autonomy of the aesthetic realm, as has been developed in the European tradition of philosophical aesthetics since Kant.[25] Against the assumption of a strict division between the poetical-rhetorical and the argumentative function of language, he points out that it is one of the most basic functions of rhetorical devices (which according to Jakobson belong to the poetic self-referential functions of language) to enhance the linguistic effect of referential speech in pragmatic contexts.[26]

Many modern interpreters of Plato have come to a similar conclusion that the so called 'dramatic' or 'poetic' elements in Plato's dialogues have to be interpreted more holistically as part of the philosophical arguments laid out in the dialogues and that they provide more sharpness, depth and unambiguous-

---

21 Catherine Zuckert, "Commentary" to the contributions of Howland, Farness, and Ausland to the volume *Plato As Author: The Rhetoric of Philosophy*, ed. Ann N. Michelini (Leiden, Boston: Brill, 2003), 145–151, 151.

22 Christina Schefer, "Rhetoric as Part of an Initiation into the Mysteries: A New Interpretation of the Platonic *Phaedrus*," *Plato As Author: The Rhetoric of Philosophy*, ed. Ann N. Michelini (Leiden, Boston: Brill, 2003), 175–196, 175.

23 Anna Christina Ribeiro, "Toward a Philosophy of Poetry," *Midwest Studies in Philosophy*, 33:1 (2009), 61–77, 62–66.

24 Kablitz cites the two most prominent members Jakobson and Mukařovský, however, the "hypothesis of the distinctiveness of poetic language is the basis upon which the entire Russian Formalist method is built," see Pavel N. Medvedev (1928) quoted in Peter Steiner, *Russian Formalism—A Metapoetics* (Ithaca: Cornell University Press, 1984), 139.

25 A similar point is made by Angela Leighton in "Form's Matter: A Retrospective" in id., *On Form: Poetry, Aestheticism, and the Legacy of a Word* (Oxford: Oxford University Press, 2007), 1–29.

26 Andreas Kablitz, *Kunst des Möglichen. Theorie der Literatur* (Freiburg/Berlin/Wien: Rombach Verlag, 2013), 58–61.

ness to the philosophical arguments and are absolutely essential to the construction of Plato's philosophical discourse.[27]

This book takes a similar point of view. We believe that the method of *doing* philosophy by poetically blending the content of an argument and its literary form is also a typical feature of many early Chinese texts. Many of the 'extra-logical' elements in Chinese texts are very similar to those in Plato. Such elements include narrative prologues, setting of the scene with certain historical protagonists including indications of specific times and places of the philosophical stage, dialogical form, the extensive use of metaphors and analogies and manifold forms of parallelisms including cosmological micro-macro correlations.[28] And yet, there are obviously fundamental differences in the function of these elements in Plato and in early Chinese texts.[29]

Evidently, Plato's work is anything but unified, and even the dialogues are full of contradictory ideas and discursive strands with constantly changing themes and interlocutors. That may well be seen as an intentional part of the artistic arrangement by Plato who "avoided rather than sought a rigid technical

---

27 See the excellent analyses of Plato's *Lysis* by Francisco J. Gonzalez, "How to Read a Platonic Prologue: *Lysis* 203a–207d," in *Plato As Author: The Rhetoric of Philosophy*, ed. Ann N. Michelini (Leiden, Boston: Brill, 2003), 15–44 and of *Phaedo* by David Gallop, "The Rhetoric of Philosophy: Socrates' Swan Song," in *Plato As Author: The Rhetoric of Philosophy*, ed. Ann N. Michelini (Leiden, Boston: Brill, 2003), 113–332. See also Gabriela Roxana Carone, *Plato's Cosmology and Its Ethical Dimensions* (New York: Cambridge University Press, 2005), 2–3; Susan B. Levin, *The Ancient Quarrel Between Philosophy and Poetry Revisited*, 11; Zacharoula A. Petraki, *The Poetics of Philosophical Language: Plato, Poets and Presocratics in the 'Republic'* (Berlin/Boston: Walter De Gruyter, 2011), 9 with further references, 11–12.

28 For the latter in Plato see Carone, *Plato's Cosmology and Its Ethical Dimensions*, 153ff.

29 Evidently we do think that Plato and early Chinese argumentative texts have much in common in that the literary forms of their arguments are part of the arguments themselves and should be analysed accordingly so as to grasp more fully the complexity of those arguments. We do not think, however, that Plato uses these literary devices in his dialogues in the same way as the Chinese texts do. Both traditions face entirely different constraints to posit their philosophical ideas. Yet, the comparison with Plato proves fruitful in three ways. First, it helps to contextualise the debate on Chinese philosophy within the Western critical discourse on philosophy; second, it allows us to look at how modern Plato scholars deal with a quite similar problem in a somewhat 'holistic' approach; third, the comparison enables us to take the "extra–logical" elements of Chinese texts, such as poetical literary forms, analogies, metaphors, parallelisms and correlations, more seriously and consider them part of the logic of the textual argument. (Given the discussion on Plato's work, there is also less pressure on us to defend the application of the term 'philosophical' for these texts).

terminology, and prodigally varied the language and imagery in which he clothed his most familiar thoughts."[30] In contrast, most early Chinese argumentative texts use a great part of their literary artistry, attempting to secure the unity of the text and unveil the internal relationship and coherence of its many seemingly disparate parts.

In this volume we consider the literary forms of the analogical, correlative, associative, metaphorical and poetical as devices that serve specific argumentative functions. These literary forms are not "whatever is left over when the paraphrasable 'something to say,' message, content, subject matter, is taken away."[31] They are not regarded as disconnected 'exterior' forms into which 'pure' arguments are shaped linguistically to make them more attractive to their readers, be it for embellishment, or to make them didactically more easily accessible or memorable. Instead, we understand them as indispensable parts of the arguments themselves. One meritorious aspect of the functional approaches[32] of the Prague School in this respect is the discovery of the multifunctional dimension of language.[33] Following this idea we propose that in many pre-modern Chinese argumentative texts the literary form serves an argumentative function. It is our contention that arguments in early Chinese texts cannot be understood fully if the crucial function of their literary form is

---

30   Paul Shorey, *The Unity of Plato's Thought* (Chicago: The University of Chicago Press, 1903), 4 (130). See his vivid analysis on pp. 3 (129)–9 (135).

31   "[T]he word form, for the last two hundred years, has had an uncanny, over-protesting connection with the idea of 'nothing.' [...] poetry, more than any other genre, aspires to the condition of form as to that which escapes being about something." Angela Leighton, "About About: On Poetry and Paraphrase," *Midwest Studies in Philosophy*, 33.1 (2009): 167–176, 168–169; see also Leighton's *On Form: Poetry, Aestheticism, and the Legacy of a Word*. Leighton argues with reference to Cleanth Brooks' classical essay "The Heresy of Paraphrase," chap. 11 of his *The Well Wrought Urn: Studies in the Structure of Poetry* (London: Methuen, 1947/1968), 192–214.

32   For a discussion of five different types of the "function" approach in the Prague School see Frantisek Danes, *On Prague School Functionalism in Linguistics* (Trier: Linguistic Agency Univ. of Trier, 1984, Series A, paper no. 127), 4–5.

33   "Les magiciens des sociétés primitives produisent des actes magiques dans lesquels les fonctions magiques et esthétiques sont coordoneés avec la function médicale proprement dite en une function médicale complexe qui n'est pas fournie par la somme additive des fonctions partielles." Karel Horálek, "La function de la 'structure des fonctions' de la langue," *Recueil Linguistique de Bratislava* 1 (1948): 39–43. (Reprint in *A Prague School Reader in Linguistics*, ed. Josef Vachek, Bloomington: Indiana University Press, 1964, 421–425, 422. Cf. also Elmar Holenstein, "Einführung: Von der Poesie und der Plurifunktionalität der Sprache," in *Roman Jakobson: Poetik. Ausgewählte Aufsätze 1921–1971*, ed. E. Holenstein and Tarcisius Schelbert (Frankfurt: Suhrkamp, 1979), 7–60.

not taken into consideration and analysed accordingly. The 'poetic' form of these texts should therefore be seen as a device used to avoid one-sided reductionism, reduce ambiguity, as well as enhance argumentative complexity.

The reason why arguments were enhanced by means of literary forms can be found in the basic structural problem of language itself. On the one hand language *signifies* meaning. On the other it *embodies* meaning by using visual or phonetic forms of expressions.

The relation of and mutual dependency between the content and the body, as well as between the meaning and the form of language, have been much discussed by early philosophers. Be it in Plato's *Cratylus* or in Gongsun Long's 公孫龍 "Mingshi lun" 名實論, the question as to whether words are simply conventional arbitrary signs or have a natural intrinsic relation to the things they signify has been posed early on in both Chinese[34] and Western traditions.[35] Due to the split between signifier and signified, language has been declared a deficient mode of expressing reality in many early cultures.

Various techniques of textual enhancement have been developed to bridge the gap between content and form, thus provoking the efficacy of words for enriching the textual meaning with greater density and complexity. Literary techniques of textual enhancement appear in manifold forms in different cultures. They comprise the phonetic and semantic aspects of language but also include the aspects of its visual representation in writing.[36] In addition to the text enhancing linguistic patterns that can exist independently of writing, either as phonetic patterns (e.g., rhyme, assonance) or as semantic tropes (e.g., metaphor), features that are based on writing, typography, and layout are equally important as literary forms in argumentation. Technopaignia in all its

---

34 Cf. John Makeham, "Names, Actualities, and The Emergence of Essentialist Theories of Naming in Classical Chinese Thought," *Philosophy East & West* 41.3 (1991): 341–363; and id., *Name and Actuality in Early Chinese Thought* (Albany: State University of New York Press, 1994), chap. 3, 51–66.

35 Manfred Kraus, *Name und Sache. Ein Problem im frühgriechischen Denken* (Amsterdam, 1987). J.L. Ackrill, "Language and reality in Plato's *Cratylus*," in *Realtà e ragione*, ed. Antonina M. Alberti (Florence, 1994), 9–28. (Repr. in Ackrill, *Essays on Plato and Aristotle*, Oxford 1997), 33–52; Timothy M.S. Baxter, *The Cratylus: Plato's Critique of Naming*. Philosophia antiqua 58 (Leiden: Brill, 1992).

36 We are indebted to our most excellent anonymous reviewer for alerting us to that analytical difference. Susanne K. Langer similarly distinguishes "discursive symbolism" or "language proper" from "presentational symbolism," see id., *Philosophy in a New Key. A Study in the Symbolism of Reason, Rite, and Art* (Cambridge MA: Harvard University Press, 1979, orig. 1941), chap. 4, 97.

variants of acrostics (*telesticha, mesosticha*),³⁷ anagrams, pangrams, *abcdaria*, palindromes, lipograms, isopsephic lines, and various other kinds of play with letters or graphical components, such as the *plinthides* or the practice of dissecting characters, have precursors in Ancient Greece, Egypt, China and Babylon.³⁸ Concrete or visual poetry including calligrammes, *carmina figurata*³⁹ and micrography, pattern poems,⁴⁰ ambigrams, palindromes, word squares and many other literary figures playing with language can also be traced back to early literatures.⁴¹ Because for the most part the aspects of visual representation of arguments in writing are of a much later date than the techniques discussed in this volume,⁴² we decided not to include them in this book.⁴³

37   John F. Brug, "Biblical Acrostics and Their Relationship to Other Ancient Near Eastern Acrostics," in *The Bible in the Light of Cuneiform Literature: Scripture in Context III*, eds. William W. Hallo et al., (Lewiston, N.Y.: Mellen, 1990), 305–23; John F. Brug, "Biblical Acrostics," 283–304.

38   For examples of play on words in Greek poetry see Christine Luz, *Technopaignia, Formspiele in der griechischen Dichtung* (Leiden: Brill, 2010). For an overview on the punning hermeneutics used in Mesopotamian omens and commentaries which plays with the polysemy built in to the cuneiform writing system because of the polyvalence of many of its signs, see Marian Broida, "Textualizing Divination: The Writing on the Wall in Daniel 5:25," *Vetus Testamentum* 62 (2012): 1–13, 9–11. For palindromes in China see Christoph Harbsmeier, *Language and Logic*, 143. For the practice of dissecting written characters in China see J. J. M. De Groot, "On Chinese Divination by Dissecting Written Characters," *T'oung Pao* 1:3 (1890), 239–247

39   Ulrich Ernst, *Carmen figuratum. Geschichte des Figurengedichts von den antiken Ursprüngen bis zum Ausgang des Mittelalters* (Cologne: Böhlau, 1991).

40   Robert G. Warnock u. Roland Folter: "The German Pattern Poem. A Study in Mannerism of the Seventeenth Century," in *Festschrift Detlev Schumann* (München: Delp, 1970), 40–73.

41   Jeremy Adler and Ulrich Ernst, *Text als Figur. Visuelle Poesie von der Antike bis zur Moderne* (Weinheim: VCH Verlagsgesellschaft 1987).

42   Literary enhancements grounded in layout as seen in a number of ancient traditions also have counterparts in the Chinese literary tradition. A very entertaining and useful collection of examples of 'ludic script use' is Zhou Yuanlong 周淵龍 and Zhou Wei 周為, eds., *Wenzi youxi* 文字遊戲, 2 vols. (Beijing: Tuanjie, 1999). A brief glance suggests that most examples in these volumes are from the early medieval period or later. We are grateful to our anonymous reviewer for pointing this publication out to us.

43   Famous examples of visual text enhancement in early China include the bronze water basin that carries a text by Scribe Qiang, the "Shi Qiang" *pan* 史牆盤. The text was probably composed shortly before 900 BC. The flat surface of the vessel carries a text of 284 graphs, cast into eighteen well-balanced lines neatly divided into two halves, where the first half commemorates the achievements of the Zhou kings and the second one the service carried out for those kings by Scribe Qiang and his ancestors. As an "epitome of order and regularity," the visual representation of the text embodies "the ideal political

All these literary forms can take manifold functions, and in most cases they serve several functions at the same time. They can be used for pleasure as literary forms of entertainment,[44] as riddles or for their aesthetic value of literary embellishment, or as folkloristic ornament or for poetic effect.[45] They can serve magical purposes in the form of formulas and spells, as they purport an additional hidden meaning which mirrors the invisible body of numinous powers, and so they enhance the mysterious efficacy of the text. Moreover, such figures can be used to hide certain meanings either because of theological assumptions as reflected in early theories of manifold senses of Scripture,[46] or for purposes of safety in times of persecution.[47] Literary forms can support and further illustrate the contents they purport, like the Horatian couplets used by Alexander Pope to express his point in his "Essay on Criticism,"[48] or Scott McCloud's *Understanding Comics*, which is an introduction to the comic

---

order of the Zhou royal lineage" where "[t]he balance of the two columns ... corresponds with the balance of the eulogistic narrative." (See Martin Kern, "The Performance of Writing in Western Zhou China," in *The Poetics of Grammar and the Metaphysics of Sound and Sign*, eds. Sergio La Porta and David Shulman (Leiden: Brill, 2007), 109–174, 170.). Another example is the "Chu Silk Manuscript," dated circa 300 BC, that contains three texts, two of which deal with the creation of cosmic order and the events causing cosmic collapse respectively. Those two texts are written in reverse directions (rotated 180 degrees) to express order and chaos visually. The third text surrounding the other two presents twelve monthly guardian gods of the four cardinal directions. See Li Ling, "Discussion of the Chu Silk Manuscript and 'Shi-tu'," transl. by Jenny F. So, in *New Perspectives on Chu Culture during the Eastern Zhou Period*, ed. Thomas Lawton (Princeton University Press, 1991), 178–183.

44 See the work by Klaus Peter Dencker, especially his edited collections *Deutsche Unsinnpoesie* (Stuttgart: Reclam, 1978) and id., *Poetische Sprachspiele. Vom Mittelalter bis zur Gegenwart* (Stuttgart: Reclam, 2003), as well as his work on (international) visual poetry.
45 Dan Sperber and Deirdre Wilson, *Relevance: Communication and Cognition* (Oxford: Blackwell, 1986), 196–197, 222.
46 Cf. Henri de Lubac, *Exégèse médiévale 2: Les quatres sens de l'écriture* (Paris: Montaigne, 1959). Transl. as *Medieval Exegesis* vol. 2. *The Four Senses of Scripture* (Michigan/Edinburgh: T&T Eerdmans and Clark Publishing Co., 2000).
47 Leo Strauss, *Persecution and the Art of Writing* (Glencoe/Illinois: Free Press, 1952).
48 In his introduction—"The Design"—to *An Essay on Man*, Pope writes: "This I might have done in prose; but I chose verse, and even rhyme, for two reasons. The one will appear obvious; that principles, maxims, or precepts, so written, both strike the reader more strongly at first, and are more easily retained by him afterwards: the other may seem odd, but it is true: I found I could express them more shortly this way than in prose itself; and nothing is more certain than that much of the force as well as grace of arguments or instructions depends on their conciseness." Alexander Pope, *An Essay on Man. Moral Essays and Satires* (London, Paris & Melbourne: Cassell, 1891), 1.

genre written as a comic book. In both cases, literary forms are used to reinforce the content by enactment. In this sense they can be understood as "cognitive facilitators."[49]

Finally, such figures can also have *argumentative* functions when they provide patterns which illuminate the structure and the meaning of an argumentative text and thus reduce their ambiguity. These are the kinds of literary figures used in argumentative discourse. Starting from the above mentioned prime assumption that language is an insufficient and unreliable tool to express the complexity of epiphany,[50] many Chinese thinkers chose to do philosophy with words and shape their arguments in particular literary forms. Scholars of Chinese philosophy have assessed this rather differently. While Hall and Ames (and other defenders of what Van Norden calls "The Radical View")[51] present Chinese thinking as an alternative model of philosophical enquiry,[52] Graham, Hansen, McCurdy, Van Norden and others largely explain these modes of reasoning as belonging to the same system of philosophical logic as the Western philosophies.[53] This volume attempts to probe more deeply into the presuppositions of this debate by trying to elucidate a broader range of varieties of early Chinese modes of reasoning. Like in research on Plato, a proper understanding of the literary modes of reasoning is essential for understanding more fully any possible philosophical nuances of the argument. The approach taken here therefore does not aim at replacing philosophical analysis; rather we wish to complement it by providing further evidence for philosophical, as well as linguistic, literary, and historical analyses of early Chinese argumentative texts.

Arguments are devices of persuasion. Literary forms of arguments too serve this one goal. Whether these arguments should count as "philosophical arguments" is not our concern here. Yet, we would like to distinguish argumentative texts, which we deal with in this publication, from texts that reflect early

---

49   Ribeiro, "Toward a Philosophy of Poetry," 74.
50   Cf. Zhang Longxi, *The Tao and the Logos*, 37–55. Rudolf G. Wagner, *Language, Ontology, and Political Philosophy in China* (Albany: SUNY, 2003), 5–15.
51   Bryan Van Norden, "What Should Western Philosophy Learn from Chinese Philosophy?" in *Chinese Language, Thought, and Culture: Nivison and His Critics*, ed. P.J. Ivanhoe (Chicago: Open Court, 1996), 224–249, 233–235.
52   Hall and Ames, *Thinking Through Confucius*, 40.
53   Cf. Chad Hansen, "Should the Ancient Masters Valuate Reason?" in *Chinese Texts and Philosophical Contexts*, ed. Henry Rosemont, Jr. (Illinois: Open Court, 1991), 179–207; William James McCurdy, "Joining the Disputation: Taking Graham Seriously on Taking Chinese Thought Seriously," *Journal of Chinese Philosophy* 19 (1992): 329–355; Van Norden, "What Should Western Philosophy Learn from Chinese Philosophy?"

rhetorical traditions of persuasion in diplomatic contexts as in the dialogues of the *Zhanguoce* 戰國策, or formulate rhetorical principles for persuasive strategies as in the early chapters of the *Guiguzi*.⁵⁴ The aim of this volume is not to look at rhetorical figures in early Chinese texts,⁵⁵ but to identify the literary forms that serve as argumentative tools and that need to be recognised fully to understand the philosophical discussion in more precise terms. 'Argument' is therefore not understood as a tool to ascertain truth, as is commonly seen in Western philosophical discourse. Instead, 'argument,' as applying to the kind of texts discussed in this volume, should be described as a "pattern that, in its use, generates argumentative force."⁵⁶ By drawing attention to the philosophical relevance of form and thought in early Chinese writings, our aim is to examine the formal characteristics of a written argument in early Chinese texts that were developed not as strategic tools but as devices to convey ideas about how to regulate the self, the family, the society, the state and the world to achieve long life, prosperity, peace, harmony and perfect order. This has to be understood in the historical context of the development of written versus oral argumentation.

---

54 See for this distinction also Wolfgang Behr and Joachim Gentz, "Introduction," in "Kunstprosa in klassischen chinesischen Texten," eds. Wolfgang Behr and Joachim Gentz, *Bochumer Jahrbuch für Ostasienforschung* 29 (2005): 5–13, esp. 5–6; see also Broschat, "Guiguzi," 2–5. For an analysis of the *Zhanguoce*'s rhetoric see Paul R. Goldin, "Miching Mallecho: The *Zhanguoce* and Classical Rhetoric," *Sino-Platonic Papers* 41 (October, 1993): 1–27. (Repr. as chapter five "Rhetoric and machination in Stratagems of the Warring States," 76–89). For an analysis of rhetorical concepts in the *Guiguzi* see Joachim Gentz, "Rhetoric as the Art of Listening: Concepts of Persuasion in the First Eleven Chapters of the *Guiguzi*," in *Masters of Disguise? Conceptions and Misconceptions of 'Rhetoric' in Chinese Antiquity*, ed. W. Behr and L. Indraccolo (Berlin: De Gruyter, 2014, Special Issue of *Asiatische Studien/Études asiatiques* 68.4): 1001–1019.

55 See for this purpose Ulrich Unger, *Rhetorik des klassischen Chinesisch* (Wiesbaden: Harrassowitz, 1994); Ursula Heidbüchel, "Rhetorik im antiken China: eine Untersuchung der Ausdrucksformen höfischer Rede im Zuo Zhuan, Herzog Zhao" (PhD University of Münster, 1993); David Schaberg, "The Logic of Signs in Early Chinese Rhetoric," in *Early China/Ancient Greece: Thinking through Comparisons*, ed. Steven Shankman, Stephen W. Durrant (Albany: SUNY, 2002), 155–186; Yang Shuda 楊樹達, *Zhongguo xiucixue* 中國修辭學, Yang Shuda jiang wenyan xiuci 楊樹達講文言修辭 (Nanjing: Fenghuang chubanshe 鳳凰出版社, 2009).

56 Dirk Meyer, *Philosophy on Bamboo: Text and the Production of Meaning in Early China* (Leiden: Brill, 2012), 11.

During the second half of the first millennium BC, probably in the fourth and third centuries, there occurred a shift in the "production of philosophy"[57] when the philosophical texts of early China no longer constructed argumentations in predominantly oral ways. The first significant maturing of a manuscript culture that occurred during that period implicated a proliferation of literary texts, and with the increase of written texts in wider circulation, the pollination of various genres and text traditions. In this environment there developed a shift in the written philosophical productivity that smoothed the way for new forms of philosophical enterprise. The new forms of written philosophical communication that advanced in the context of a growing manuscript culture manifest a sophisticated attempt to facilitate direct access to the philosophical experience of what most early Chinese thinkers refer to as "*dao*" (Way). In these novel forms of written communication, authors developed philosophically sound positions that were increasingly argument-based and so less dependent on contexts of oral explanation.[58] The philosophical text thus steadily replaced the triangular relationship of meaning conveyance between master, student, and text, which previously determined the successful communication of thought. As a result, the philosophical texts gradually became direct mediators of ideas. In some cases, it may even be argued that the formal structure of the text was thought to express the philosophical insight transported in the text, which thus came to be embodied in the text itself. The result of such forms of written philosophical communication, in which the medium was simultaneously made into the matter, is that the distinction between the cognitive grasp of the philosophical thoughts and their enactment that caused so many "disputers of the *dao*"[59] considerable headache, ceased to exist. This may have worked on different levels of textual composition and text-performance, and we find a reflection of those different levels in the great variety of literary forms used to formulate and perform arguments at the same time.

It is in this context and in contrast to the 'Western' tradition that Chinese thinkers have not attempted to define an *organon* of valid logical forms. Instead, early Chinese thinkers spent some effort in generating different literary

---

57 See Dirk Meyer, "Bamboo and the Production of Philosophy: A Hypothesis about a Shift in Writing and Thought in Early China," in *History and Material Culture in Asian Religions*, eds. Benjamin J. Fleming and Richard Mann (London: Routledge, 2014), 21–38, 23.

58 Note that the division between context-dependent and argument-based texts is not absolute. Context-dependent texts may have argumentative layers and argument-based texts may contain units or elements that rely on contexts to be meaningful, see Meyer, *Philosophy on Bamboo*, 183ff., 244ff., 253f.

59 Angus C. Graham, *Disputers of the Tao: Philosophical Argument in Ancient China* (La Salle, Ill.: Open Court, 1989).

forms of philosophical reasoning, such as interlocking parallel style, overlapping structure, Janus-faced bridges, symmetrical rhyme nets, collage strategies, modular arrangements, phonetic and graphical intensification, or micro-macro structure correspondences which, however, have largely passed unnoticed by sinologists both in China and the West. This is not surprising as the various literary forms in which Western philosophy has found its expressions in epinikion songs of triumph (Bacchylidean gnomes), didactic poems (Parmenides, Empedocles), dialogues (Plato, Leibniz, Berkley, Hume), letters (Epicurus, Seneca), autobiographies (Augustine, Descartes), prayers (Anselm of Canterbury), meditations (Descartes), tractates (Spinoza, Wittgenstein), schoolbooks (Wolff), aphorisms (Lichtenberg, Nietzsche, Wittgenstein), essays (Montaigne), dictionaries (Bayle), verse (Pope, Voltaire) et cetera, have never been regarded as relevant for a philosophical analysis of the argument. Literary and philosophical (argumentative) texts are in the West dealt with by different disciplines and specialists. Literary forms of philosophical arguments as we find them throughout Chinese early literate traditions have therefore been much ignored in the field of Chinese Studies. Attempts in recent scholarship to overcome the neglected place of this philosophically productive level of compelling consent in early Chinese Philosophy by means of the literary form of an argument, are still few and far between—but not entirely absent.

With the development of structural linguistics and the performative turn in the philosophy of language, new approaches to the analysis of early Chinese argumentation have been proposed by Herbert Fingarette,[60] Rudolf Wagner,[61] Michael Broschat[62] and others which focus on the performative and structural features of Chinese arguments. A similar approach had been taken nearly two hundred years earlier already by the first generation of European sinologists who recognised parallelism as a fundamental means of constructing meaning in Chinese texts. John Francis Davis (1795-1890) was probably the first scholar in the West who, in a lecture, given at the Royal Asiatic Society of Great Britain and Ireland in 1830,[63] pointed out the importance of parallelism in Chinese poetry and its "striking coincidence" with the Hebrew forms that Robert Lowth

---

60   Herbert Fingarette, *Confucius: The Secular as Sacred* (New York: Harper. & Row, 1972).
61   Rudolf G. Wagner, "Interlocking Parallel Style: Laozi and Wang Bi," *Études Asiatiques* 34.1 (1980): 18–58; id., *The Craft of a Chinese Commentator: Wang Bi on the Laozi* (Albany: State University of New York Press), 53–113.
62   Broschat, "Guiguzi," 87–127.
63   John Francis Davis, "Poeseos sinensis comentarii: On the Poetry of the Chinese," in *Transactions of the Royal Asiatic Society* 2 (1830), 393–461 (repr. London 1970), 414–416.

(1710-1787) had defined into three classes in 1753.⁶⁴ Davis is also the first to mention the occurrence of parallelism in Chinese prose texts. In 1878, Georg von der Gabelentz (1840–1893) presented parallelism in a short analysis of an inscription as a valuable tool, which allowed clear demarcations of the non-punctuated Chinese sentences.⁶⁵ In 1892, Gustave Schlegel (1840–1903) in his translation of the Stele of Teghin Giogh also emphasised parallelism as an important tool for a correct understanding and translation of the text. He even took this 'law' of parallelism as the philological basis of his critical discussion of two translations of Zhang Yue's 張說 (667–730) preface to Xuanzang's 玄奘 (ca. 600-664) travelogue *Da Tang xiyu ji* 大唐西域記, a text composed in strict parallelisms, and provided his own translation of it.⁶⁶ However, the analytical approaches that focus on a literary form of meaning production in these texts have not yet been systematically developed beyond the mere literary form of parallelism. This might be due to the fact that parallelism has mainly been studied as a literary phenomenon in Chinese as well as in Western literary theory.⁶⁷ Although Chinese literary theories did not analyse literary forms of arguments in the first place, they have developed a substantial number of analytical concepts and terms (especially after the Song) which are also applicable in some cases to an insightful analysis of literary forms of arguments.⁶⁸

---

64   Robert Lowth, *De sacra poesi Hebraeorum praelectiones academicae Oxonii habitae* (Oxford, 1753).

65   Georg von der Gabelentz, "Ein Probestück von chinesischem Parallelismus," in *Zeitschrift für Völkerpsychologie und Sprachwissenschaft*, ed. Lazarus and Steinthal, vol. 10. Berlin (1878), 230–234.

66   Gustave Schlegel, "La loi du parallélisme en style chinois: démontrée par la Preface du Si-yü ki" (Brill: Leiden, 1896). Ironically, despite positive reviews by Legge (*Quarterly Review*) and Chavannes (*Revue critique*), von Zach, in a critical review, revealed numerous mistakes in the translation and claimed that "in der genannten Schrift auch nicht ein einziger Satz richtig übersetzt ist" (p. 3). Cf. Erwin Ritter von Zach, "Einige Worte zu Prof. Gustav Schlegel's 'La loi du parallélisme en style chinois'" (Peking, 1902).

67   Cf. Roman Jakobson, "Grammatical Parallelism and Its Russian Facet," *Language* 42.2 (1966): 399–429. (Repr. in RJ, *Selected Writings III: Poetry of Grammar and Grammar of Poetry*, The Hague 1981, 98–135); Andrew Plaks, "Where the Lines Meet: Parallelism in Chinese and Western Literatures," *Chinese Literature: essays, articles, reviews* (CLEAR) 10.1-2 (1988): 43–60. (Repr. in *Poetics Today* 11:3, Fall, 1991, 523–546); Joachim Gentz, "Zum Parallelismus in der chinesischen Literatur," in *Parallelismus Membrorum*, ed. Andreas Wagner (Göttingen: Vandenhoeck & Ruprecht; Fribourg: Academic Press. 2007), 241–269.

68   For a brilliant introduction to the terminology and central concepts of commentators in traditional Chinese fiction criticism see Andrew Plaks, "Terminology and Central Concepts," in *How to Read the Chinese Novel*, ed., David L. Rolston (Princeton: Princeton University Press, 1990), 75–123, for analytical concepts and terms relating to textual

Rudolf G. Wagner was the first to analyse parallelism as an *argumentative* form. In 1969 he published his first analysis of the argumentative figure of "interlocking parallel style" (IPS), which he further developed in later publications.[69] Further argumentative forms of parallelisms have been identified by Gentz, Meyer and Streif.[70]

One of the first systematic attempts to analyse the meaning of early Chinese texts by "determining the structures that are defining relations for the elements within a text" was proposed by Michael Broschat who applied what he called "constituent analysis" to the *Guiguzi* 鬼谷子 in 1985—to this day a much neglected work.[71] That approach was probably inspired by the linguistic methodology of "immediate constituent analysis" developed by American linguists Leonard Bloomfield (1887–1949), Rulon Wells (1918-2008), Noam Chomsky and others since the 1930s. (That tradition was in turn inspired by the Sanskrit grammar of Pāṇini, who probably flourished in the 5th–4th century BC, as Bloomfield and Wells both studied Indian languages). In contrast to earlier works, Broschat enquired into the constituents of paragraphs and whole texts rather than to the constituents of sentences. He defined his "constituent analysis" as "an analytic process in which significant constituent parts are identified, their relations to other parts are identified and specified, and the general effect of these constituents and their structural inter-relations on the meaning of the whole text is considered."[72] Broschat discusses three basic literary techniques, which serve to relate the parts of a text they demarcate to other parts, constitute structure and thereby generate meaning: rhythm, parallelism and rhyme. He differentiates the linear structure of prose texts from poetical texts and argues that many early Chinese prose texts do not follow linear structures:

---

composition and structure see esp. 85–114. An excellent introduction to earlier works of literary criticism is given by Stephen Owen in his substantial *Readings in Chinese Literary Thought* (Cambridge MA: Harvard University Press, 1992).

69   Wagner, "Interlocking Parallel Style"; id., *The Craft of a Chinese Commentator*, 53–113.
70   Joachim Gentz, "Zwischen den Argumenten lesen. Zu zweifach gerichteten Verbindungsstücken zwischen Argumenten in frühen chinesischen Texten," *Bochumer Jahrbuch für Ostasienforschung* 29 (2005): 35–56; Dirk Meyer, "A Device for Conveying Meaning: The Structure of the Guodian Tomb One Manuscript 'Zhong xin zhi dao'," *Bochumer Jahrbuch für Ostasienforschung* 29 (2005): 57–78; Christian Streif, *Die Erleuchtung des Nordens: Zum Disput zwischen Sengzhao und Liu Yimin über die Bodhisattva-Idee des Mahayana* (Wiesbaden: Harrassowitz, 2013).
71   Broschat, "Guiguzi," 87–127.
72   Broschat, "Guiguzi," 88–89.

When a piece departs from linear structure, as I would argue much of Classical Chinese prose does, it approaches the poetic, where the meaning of a piece depends more and more on the effects generated by its structures. Only when those structures, and thus their effects, are as clear as possible, can the reader presume to have a good understanding of the author's intentions.[73]

A reader should therefore

> look first at the value of the structure to avoid being incorrectly influenced by the value of the word (which can change in different contexts).[74]

In recent years the philosophical study of written arguments has gained in importance in Western and Chinese scholarship, as is further reflected in the broader interest in Chinese hermeneutics, the application of metaphor theory, the increasing awareness of integral structures of textual compositions,[75] as well as the increased number of international conferences on early Chinese argumentation.[76] The volume *Literary Forms of Argument in Early China*

---

73 Broschat, "Guiguzi," 106–107.
74 Broschat, "Guiguzi," 126.
75 A fascinating example is the analysis of the structure of the *Huainanzi* as discussed on pp. 14–20 of *The Huainanzi. Liu An, King of Huainan*, transl. and ed. J.S. Major, S.A. Queen, A.S. Meyer, and H.D. Roth (New York: Columbia University Press, 2010).
76 Attempts at analysing literary forms of classical Chinese philosophical argument were made by conference panels in 2004 ("Komposition als Konnotation: Figuren der Kunstprosa im vormodernen China") and 2007 ("Versatzstück und Montage: Antike und mittelalterliche Prosaliteratur zwischen Reproduktion, Dekoration und Innovation"), at the 29th and 30th Deutscher Orientalistentag (German congress for Oriental Studies) organised by Wolfgang Behr, Joachim Gentz and Christian Schwermann. The two panels both resulted in the publication of a selection of the contributions (*Bochumer Jahrbuch für Ostasiatische Forschung* 29, 2005; *Monumenta Serica* 56, 2008), and led to a collaboration (and publication) with scholars working on *parallelismus membrorum* in Biblical Studies (J. Gentz, "Zum Parallelismus in der chinesischen Literatur," 2007). Similar conferences on Chinese philosophical argumentation followed: Carine Defoort and Nicolas Standaert: "Argument and Persuasion in Ancient Chinese Texts" (Leuven 2005) (published in *Oriens Extremus* 45, 2005/6); Wim De Reu, Department of Philosophy of NTU: "Metaphor, Structure and Meaning in Early Chinese Philosophy" 「早期中國哲學之隱喻、結構與意義」 (Taipei 2010); Elisa Sabattini, Paul van Els and Yuri Pines: "Rhetoric as a Political Tool in Early China" (Jerusalem 2011) with publication: *Political Rhetoric in Early China*, ed. P van Els, R. Graziani, Y. Pines, and E. Sabattini (Paris: Presses Universitaires de Vincennes, 2012); Wolfgang Behr and Lisa Indraccolo: "Masters of Disguise? Conceptions and Misconceptions of 'Rhetoric' in Chinese Antiquity" (Zurich 2013) published in *Asiatische Studien / Études Asiatiques* 68.4 (2014) (Special Issue: *Masters of Disguise? Conceptions and Mis-*

further explores possibilities of the structural-analytical approach by bringing together the ideas developed both by Western and Chinese colleagues, and so construct new methods for the analysis of pre-modern Chinese philosophical texts. It investigates literary patterns and their philosophical function in pre-modern Chinese texts and analyses the correlation of form and content in Chinese philosophy.

Our approach in this volume is manifold: first, it is *formalistic* in the sense that it focuses on linguistic forms on the levels of words, utterances, paragraphs and entire text compositions. As such, it aims at generating a phenomenology of the formal patterns of arguments in early Chinese texts; second, it is *functionalist* in that it analyses multiple functional devices of the different formal patterns and enquires into the way in which they are operational in the logic of the argument; third, it is *structuralist* as the literary devices are regarded as functionalist elements within the literary whole. Textual parts are identified which gain further significance as integral parts of an overall network of structure in which the individual parts are significantly interrelated in a relationship of interdependence.

Central questions asked in this volume are: What are the formal characteristics of an argument in pre-modern China? What kind of literary figures are used to convey arguments? Does the formal pattern of a text itself contribute to the idea transmitted? Are literary patterns reflective of mapping mechanisms between conceptual domains? How do literary form and conceptual mapping shape the way in which concepts are generated?

But the focus of this volume is not restricted to the study of texts as consciously composed and philosophically coherent edifices. It also looks at the different kinds of devices of argument and argumentation in early Chinese written thought. These include the use of metaphor and other non-linear semantic utterances, different hermeneutical approaches of philosophising with texts by contemporaneous textual communities, sound correlated devices used to structure text and meaning, as well as the conscious use of paradox in written philosophical prose—but also other expressions of communicative intentions and the implementations of pragmatic effects used to criticise, ridicule, seduce, persuade, employ irony, and achieve an infinite number of other aims. Such elements of persuasion in the philosophical discourse may not only serve a function in the formal development of the argument, but also evoke ritual or abstract principles of order that reflect cosmological conceptions by contemporaneous philosophers and disputers.

---

conceptions of 'Rhetoric' in Chinese Antiquity, ed. Wolfgang Behr and Lisa Indraccolo, Berlin: De Gruyter).

The volume *Literary Forms of Argument in Early China* grew out of a three-day conference held in September 2009 at The Queen's College, University of Oxford, organised by Joachim Gentz, Dirk Meyer and Wim De Reu. Participants of the meeting came from all over Europe, North America, and Asia. The papers presented at the meeting were consistently excellent, and we decided to choose nine contributions that we thought would best represent our concern with regard to the strategies of argument construction in early Chinese discourse. The Oxford workshop was followed by a long and productive exchange between the authors and the editors where the specific dual focus on the literary form on the one hand and its argumentative function on the other was sharpened. The result is a first, tentative attempt to identify literary patterns and their specific argumentative purpose in early Chinese discourse.

In early Chinese texts, the literary form can relate to the argument of the text in various ways. Sometimes the literary form itself serves as an argument. Parallelisms suggest identity or opposition of parallel clauses,[77] enumerative catalogues suggest completeness of a set of terms covering a certain field,[78] tetrasyllables suggest didactic authority.[79] In other cases, literary forms serve as illustrative bodies that mirror the philosophical argumentation. The ways in which the ambiguous interlocked parallelisms in the *Laozi*, the playful and floating style in the *Zhuangzi*,[80] the simple, economic and clear sentences in the *Shangjun shu*, the organic metaphors in the *Mengzi*, or the artificial constructions in the *Xunzi* reflect aspects of their respective philosophies may serve as examples. Literary forms can also provide connotations that enrich the meaning of the text. Micro-macro equivalents in the composition of the text or allusive insertions add further dimensions of meaning to a text. Literary forms are often used as means of encoding and thus signifying the structure of an argument. Interlocking parallel style,[81] double directed text units,[82] overlapping structure,[83] technical terms,[84] and referential signifiers[85] are literary

---

77　See Plaks in this volume. See also id., "Where the Lines Meet: Parallelism in Chinese and Western Literatures"; Gentz, "Zum Parallelismus in der chinesischen Literatur."
78　See Gentz in this volume.
79　See Schaberg in this volume.
80　See Meyer and De Reu in this volume.
81　Wagner, "Interlocking Parallel Style," 18–58; id., *Craft*, 53–113.
82　Gentz, "Zwischen den Argumenten lesen" and his contribution to this volume.
83　Meyer, "A Device for Conveying Meaning."
84　See Wagner in this volume. See also Matthias Richter, "Cognate Texts: Technical Terms as Indicators of Intertextual Relations and Redactional Strategies," *Asiatische Studien/Études asiatiques* 61/3 (2002): 549–572.
85　See Gentz in this volume.

devices that define the units of argumentative texts and their respective relationships. Moreover, literary forms reflect basic forms of arguments such as authority-based or context-based arguments,[86] historical precedence, chain arguments, wise judgements in teaching dialogues[87] et cetera. Finally, literary forms can convey meaning through the conspicuous absence of any pattern that could support an argument. This argumentative silence of a literary form can have manifold reasons. It might give expression to the assumption that the teachings of the sage(s) are beyond our grasp,[88] or it could emphasise the claim of the independence and ahistorical truth of single textual units in a textual composition.[89]

This volume combines three dominant modes of analysis and it is structured accordingly. First is the analysis of the precise function of specific markers in argumentation as structuring devices for Chinese rhetoric and argument; second is the analysis of particular structural patterns and their argumentative function, addressing the specific function of select argumentative patterns, such as parallelism, tetrasyllables, or literary signifiers of argumentative boundaries that apply repeatedly to different texts from the classical era; third is the analysis of macro modes of persuasion in the written philosophical discourse, dealing with the question of how persuasive texts work as argumentative units where the literary form of composition as a whole becomes part of the message—either by means of absence of established argumentative literary forms or by providing meaning through (authorial or editorial) arrangements of textual units.

Rudolf Wagner heads the analysis of the literary form of argument in early Chinese discourse with a study of the initial *fu* 夫 as a phrase status marker and building block of Chinese argumentation. He notes that analytical discourse in early China is characterised by the use of rhetorical figures to mark the status of a statement as either expressing a general rule, an exception, or a side comment. Such "status markers," as Wagner likes to call them, may be silent or non-silent—that is, implicit or explicit—in classical Chinese argumentation. This adds to the difficulty in dealing with such markers, which might be part of the reason why they have been much neglected by scholarship, as Wagner laments. The result of such omission in the analysis of Chinese forms of

---

86   See Meyer, *Philosophy on Bamboo*.
87   See Kern in this volume.
88   See Kern and Nylan in this volume. See also Rudolf Wagner, "Die Unhandlichkeit des Konfuzius," in *Weisheit: Archäologie der literarischen Kommunikation II*, eds. Aleida and Jan Assmann (Munich: Fink, 1991), 455–464.
89   See Harbsmeier in this volume.

argumentation is a lack of precision when dealing with Chinese ideas, especially since in early discourse such markers are often the only device to structure an argument. With phrase and paragraph separators being widely absent in early texts,[90] a precise understanding of these markers, Wagner insists, is crucial for a precise understanding of "argumentative procedures" in early China. Wagner addresses this hiatus in learning through a detailed analysis of the initial *fu* as a phrase marker for statements of general rather than particular validity. But Wagner's analysis is fundamentally not about "mapping the bandwidth of the uses of the character 夫 during the Warring States." Instead, the study is about the rhetorical functions of *fu* in structuring texts of a philosophical nature.

Wagner's choice of analysis is that of a qualitative analysis of random phrases used by Wang Bi (226–249 AD) in his commentaries on the *Zhouyi* and the *Laozi*, from which he develops a series of hypotheses concerning the function of *fu*. The random phrase search is an important methodological choice that prevents Wagner from falling into the circularity of argument when discussing a select range of examples. In his analysis, he refutes the common perception that thinks of initial *fu* as a topical marker and concludes that its function is instead that of a marker for "statements and definitions of a general philosophical nature."

Moving on from the initial *fu* in Chinese argumentation, Andrew Plaks undertakes a re-evaluation of parallel patterns in the seminal works of classical Chinese philosophy. Plaks proposes nothing less than a revised understanding of the significance of parallelism in Chinese argumentation. 'Parallelism,' by his definition, is an overarching mode of textuality where "the paradigmatic use of parallel sequences constitutes the primary feature of a part or the whole of a given piece of prose or verse composition." Progressing from his earlier work in which he highlighted those aspects of parallelism that were specific to texts from early China in comparison to similar patterns in other literary traditions,[91] Plaks now suggests the tentative division of categories of analysis into, first, "sequences of parallel statements that culminate in the final assertion of a principal point that casts conceptual light or logical direction on a given argument"; second, "equivalent utterances that lead up to the presentation of provocative, unconventional or counter-intuitive assertions"; third,

---

90 See, however, Richter's analysis on punctuation as initiator, section terminator and separator in manuscripts from the Warring States period, especially in his "Punctuation," in *Reading Early Chinese Manuscripts*, eds. Wolfgang Behr, Martin Kern and Dirk Meyer (Leiden: Brill, forthcoming).

91 Andrew Plaks, "Where the Lines Meet," 43–60.

"pairs or strings of clauses in which a given unit serves to delineate the conditions for another unit, thus functioning as a kind of subordinate clause." While 'antiphony' or 'poliphony' in matching lines "may be considered the 'default mode' of classical Chinese expository prose," Plaks now suggests that there are "a significant number of examples" where the expected governing principle of "paratactic coordination of parallel assertions" must be nuanced by recognising a certain notion of subordination that generally goes unnoticed. By casting light on an overlooked aspect of Chinese parallelism, Plaks' work enables the student of Chinese ideas to arrive at a more nuanced assessment of the literary form of Chinese argumentation through parallel patterns and evaluate forms of argumentation in their full breadth.

Following on from parallelism in Chinese argumentation, David Schaberg discusses a subgenre of philosophical discourse from early China, which he terms "*Laozi*-style tetrasyllables." As the "single densest concentration of the specific type of gnomic verse that it contains," Schaberg notes that the *Laozi* 老子 has come to "stand for a whole distinct subgenre of philosophical discourse," with no other text relying so heavily on this form. However, assuming that to regard this form of verse as unique to the *Laozi*, or to think that parallels were found only in "Daoist" texts such as the *Zhuangzi* 莊子 would be to "ignore an important and broadly influential development in the history of Chinese philosophical argumentation," Schaberg shows that the *Laozi*-style tetrasyllables appear to have resulted from a sophistication of existing conventions for didactic verse: a type of verse that was, on the one hand, notably limited both in its lexicon and in its gamut of syntactical patterns and "figures of speech," while depending greatly upon sets of stock dichotomies and a limited set of themes, on the other.

By way of reconstructing a corpus of tetrasyllabic verse that provides the setting for the *Laozi*-style form, Schaberg notes that the genre style is typically juxtaposed with unrhymed material, most likely to mark a special aspect of speech. First appearing in texts from the late fourth century BC, rhymed tetrasyllables perform alongside unrhymed prose in passages of instruction or argumentation where they form a "distinct genre of didactic prosimetrum." Based on studies by Baxter and Wagner, Schaberg holds that the *Laozi* most likely emerged from a tradition of philosophical verse with strong oral elements and little concept of individual authorship. But while the genre was represented widely in the Warring States period, Schaberg now shows that it was surrounded by verse that had, however, very different didactic aims. Schaberg therefore assumes that "*Laozi*-style verse and this larger field of verse coexisted for some centuries."

Laozi-verse is largely concerned with representations of the *dao* 道 and the sage, including illustrations of how the *dao* works in the world and how rulers may themselves become sage users of the *dao*. Evaluating a vast range of early texts, Schaberg assumes that the tetrasyllabic verses were useful predominantly in didactic and curative contexts. While the anecdotes discussed by Schaberg are clearly delivered as fictions, the common elements in their narrative frames nevertheless allow for certain conclusions to be drawn about how *Laozi*-style tetrasyllables were used originally. Schaberg's assumption is that such verse was being performed at the courts of Warring States and Han patrons and rulers.

Schaberg's analysis brings together different aspects of the literary form of an argument in China and its sociological applications. His observations about framing and the interaction of rhymed passages with prose tally in closely with related observations made by Wolfgang Behr, Joachim Gentz, Martin Kern, Dirk Meyer, and Rudolf Wagner with regard to the marking practices of an argument in early Chinese philosophical discourse.[92]

Next comes Joachim Gentz with a close description of different examples of literary forms to show how they function as signifiers of boundaries and text relations in early Chinese written argumentation. For this, Gentz chooses three types of literary forms, namely that of the 'double-directed text units' with its subcategory of 'double-directed parallelism;' the 'enumerative catalogues;' the 'referential signifiers' and their specific function in the formulation and specification of an argument. The figure of the double-directed text units combines two unrelated parts of an argument and indicates an aspectual relationship of these elements. A subcategory to the double-directed text units is formed by the double-directed parallelism. Here, the parallel form of two sentences,

---

92   See Behr's study "Three Sound-Correlated Text Structuring Devices in Pre-Qin Philosophical Prose," 15–33; Gentz' discussion in this volume of the literary signifiers of argumentative boundaries; Kern's study of quotations the "Zi yi"; (in Kern, "Quotation and the Confucian Canon in Early Chinese Manuscripts: The Case of 'Zi yi' [Black Robes]," *Asiatische Studien/Études asiatiques* 59/1, [2006]: 293–332) Meyer's observations about structural consistency in argument-based texts (in Meyer, *Philosophy on Bamboo*) that ensure textual stability and recognisability, (id., 31, 202) signal the importance of a unit, (id., 51, 62), and mark the length of an argumentative unit in Chinese texts (id., 53); Wagner's study in this volume of the marking of an argument by means of the initial *fu*, to name but a few of the important recent developments in the study of the form of an argument in early China. See also Schaberg's earlier discussion of literary patterning that is conceived of as an image of the order that cultural achievements would bring about; (in David Schaberg, *A Patterned Past: Form and Thought in Early Chinese Historiography*, Cambridge, MA: Harvard University Asia Center [2001], 51ff.).

which can operate on the phonetic as well as the syntactical level at the same time, expresses different aspects of one and the same topic. As examples of the *Laozi* and the *Shijing* show, the double-directed parallelism may also formulate the crucial insight of an argument, and so take on a related function to that of the principal insertion discussed by Meyer in this volume. Whether the two forms of argument have a common origin or perhaps express different aspects of a related argumentative form is a question that remains to be explored.

The second form discussed is that of the enumerative catalogue. Such catalogues define groups of key analytical terms and create a particular conceptual field. The field is thereby not only defined but also structured, and a full representation of the matter is claimed. At the same time, the individual constituents mark the length of argument and act as operators within that field.

As a third category, Gentz discusses the construction of oppositional pairs of positions through contrasts, using the example of the *Xunzi* 荀子 to show how contrasting positions are being developed progressively through opposite chains of terms. As in the previous examples of argumentative figures, the literary form not only guides the argument, it also indicates the length of an argument within a text. The examples given by Gentz demonstrate the degree to which close analysis of the literary form of an argument is crucial for understanding an argument in full. The *Xunzi*, for instance, displays its rhetorical tools at the start by developing them in a strictly uniform fashion, just to weaken the rigid patterns as the text moves on and starts to shift more freely beyond those patterns. It seems as though the form of the text was key to the way in which its authors hoped their audiences would understand and use their text. One is tempted to read this in parallel fashion to the claim in the *Xunzi* about the realisation of ritual by the individual: the habituation of ritual on the part of the individual requires repetition and drill so that the individual develops a habitus of conduct where any deviation from the form would still be such that it conforms to the internalised patterns of ritual propriety.

Finally, Gentz uses the "Zhu yan" 主言 chapter of the *Da Dai Liji* 大戴禮記 to demonstrate how the different literary forms are combined and interwoven within one single text.

Moving on from coherent patterns to non-patterned literary forms of arguments, Christoph Harbsmeier discusses the literary form of the "Yucong" 語叢 1 and argues that the genre style of the text compounds to the intellectual message of the text. It is by virtue of its particular style of truncated, programmatically enigmatic propositions and theorems that the "Yucong" 1 presents itself as an "analytically pointilistic" text.

The "Yucong" 1 only occasionally organises statements into sequences of theorems. For the most part, the statements remain isolated. "Badly in need of elaborating explanations," they are obscure dicta. But they cohere. When read in context, according to Harbsmeier, they "add up to an overall vision that is intimately linked to the aphoristic form itself." A vision is created in the "Yucong" 1 where there is no such thing as a "reasoned system," but where the vision is enunciated through a succession of "analytical *aperçus*." This forms groups of "unorganised sets" where the constituents are such that they are mutually interrelated but, at the same time, "retain their semantic and rhetoric independence."

But this is not the only way by which the "Yucong" 1 is squarely out of line with tradition. Unlike known philosophical texts, the "Yucong" 1 neither references historical narrative as a point of illustration or source of authority, nor does it provide any moral advice. The rhetorical form of the "Yucong" 1 is just focused on what Harbsmeier understands as "conceptual analysis." Much in line with Wang Bi's 王弼 (226–249) understanding of the form of the *Laozi*,[93] Harbsmeier thinks of the non-form of text composition as in itself a formalistic message: that the "Yucong" 1 makes no appeal to any authoritative instance outside the text makes it speak "in its own intellectual right" where the text "is beholden to no authority past or present" the text is fundamentally, and as Harbsmeier claims, provocatively "ahistorical."

In some respect, this situation bears a resemblance to the "Kongzi shilun" 孔子詩論 (henceforth "Shilun") discussed by Martin Kern. Just as in the "Yucong" 1, the "Shilun" progresses no linear sequence of events, and there seems to be no such thing as a logical or necessary development of an argument. Although there are now some confirmed clusters to arrange the "Shilun," the links between those clusters are very loose. Just as is true of the "Yucong" 1, there is also no such thing as an explicit argument in the "Shilun." The "Shilun" has no single expository style. It is a "patchwork of various rhetorical patterns." Similar to the "Yucong" 1, the lack of a rigid progression of formalistic sequences, the 'nonform' of the "Shilun" might in fact serve as a device that points to the overall message of the text. As Kern assumes, the literary form marks it as a particular type of text, which "is defined by its particular function." However, unlike the "provocatively ahistorical" nature of the "Yucong" 1, the "Shilun" is fundamentally connected to external sanction, as signalled by the repetitive use of *yue*, "it is said," that is interceded with the lines of the "Odes," and it is closely related to the authority of Kongzi, 'Confucius.' The *yue* marks speech as an accepted voice, "sanctioned and perpetuated by tradition." It marks the absence of a "specific authorial voice" as a quality, "marking the text as an expression of traditional authority." The formulaic makeup of the text and its absence of a

---

93 See Wagner, *Craft*, 117ff.

systematic linear progression of thought therefore gives form to its "catechistic, authoritative nature." Speaking to the initiated already familiar with the anthology "Odes," it "issues pronouncements."

Kern shows that in opposition to a text such as the Mao Odes, the "Shilun" advances no historical or political interpretation of the "Odes." As is true of the "Yucong" 1, the "Shilun" is not supported by a commentary or any other means to connect it to historical anecdotes or a larger narrative framework that would situate the text.

While the "Shilun" is no guidance to the "Odes" and provides no actual interpretation, it simply confronts the text recipient with Kongzi's "exemplary judgment." But, as Kern astutely observes, the master's personal comments are fundamentally about his reactions "as the person who truly understands" the "Odes." "His structurally repetitive remarks thus stand as a model of profound insight" which is to be accepted by whoever is confronted with the "Shilun." As such, the persona Kongzi serves in fact as a chiffre for rhetorical artifice that is given form through decidedly stylised and pithy pronouncements.

The whole situation of the "Shilun" and the absence of strict forms of progression of statements in a purposeful sequence of clusters is reminiscent of the "Unhandlichkeit" (non-graspable nature or unhandiness) of Kongzi as portrayed in the *Shiji*.[94] While the *Shiji* normally captivates by its mastery of materials, the "Kongzi shijia" chapter of that anthology is surprisingly loose—not to say slack—in organisation, and the lack of coherency in the account of Kongzi and his life is striking. To think of that as a deficiency on the part of the 'Sima Qian project' in their compiling and authoring of the *Shiji* would seem too easy a suggestion in light of the consistency of the other chapters and their masterful command of handling the different materials and sources and bringing them into compelling form. The lack of consistency and stringency is in itself a masterful strategy of argumentation: you cannot handle Confucius. The sage is beyond our grasp. But while we cannot put Kongzi and his profound insight into categories of our own, he fundamentally serves as an example on which to model our conduct.

Much in line with Harbsmeier and Kern and the concept of anti-structure in early Chinese texts as developed at the Oxford meeting, Michael Nylan advances a strategy to interpret Yang Xiong's 揚雄 (53 BC–AD 18) *Fayan* 法言 (Exemplary Figures) with its lack of a consistent structure and the dual personae of "Yang-the-Master" that is so strangely at odds with Yang Xiong's masterwork, the *Tai xuan* 太玄 (Great Mystery), where much effort seems to be placed on the "exposure of an exostructure relying on *yin, yang*, and the Five Phases *qi*."

---

94   Cf. also Wagner, "Die Unhandlichkeit."

The task that is before the reader of the *Fayan*, according to Nylan, is to "interpret the multiple voices and registers" that Yang Xiong used while "fashioning this persona as master of all the phenomena worth knowing," when Yang Xiong himself signals to his readers that his texts should not be read in a literal sense.

Although the *Fayan* contains larger themes, they do not unfold easily between the chapters and they are disconnected from the literary form of the text. Syntactical units are scattered over different textual units and they are not guided by any structural principle. Different statements in the text contradict one another, and there seems to be no single consistent train of thought in the entire *Fayan*. Instead, the "stop-and-start quality" of the text bears close reminiscence with a text such as the *Lunyu*, and the lack of thematic and syntactic connections gets more and more marked as the text progresses. No line in the text sequence "yields a satisfying semantic sequence with the succeeding text elaborating, expanding, or elucidating the preceding." The only point of reference in a text without contextually joining references between the different units is the "literary Yang himself," Nylan asserts. "Yang attacks and retreats from various stances, modifying his assertions until the reader's head fairly swims." The lack of structural coherence, as well as obvious principles that would guide the text, is therefore something that compounds the difficulty in determining meaning on the part of the text recipient, making the *Fayan* much more difficult, and in fact more mysterious, than its predecessor, the *Taixuan*, and one is tempted to read this as a literary device used purposely by Yang Xiong. This being true, the non-structure seems to be a device to assist the text recipient in grasping "the subtle idea that no small part of learning and living well depends on divine insight and intuition, and cannot be grasped by strict logical forms," a point repeatedly made especially with regard to the *Zhuangzi*. At the same time, the non-structure of the *Fayan* and its constant contradiction requires a devoted reader, just as the study of the *dao* requires a devote student with a love for learning. Yang Xiong as philosophical persona therefore assumes an author function, where through his status as eminent thinker the text recipient will impute any failure in understanding the *Fayan* not to deficiencies in the text but to their own limitations. The non-form of the text, Nylan therefore concludes, brings into practice the message that "small men use to perfect themselves in small things, and the great in great." (*Fayan* 8/12)

Moving on from Nylan's discussion of the *Fayan*, the remaining two chapters of this volume discuss strategies of argumentation in the *Zhuangzi*. Much in line with Nylan's findings, the apparent non-form of textual structure is also prominent in chapter 26 of the *Zhuangzi*, the "Wai wu" (Things External), analysed by Wim De Reu. The "Wai wu" is one of the so-called *za pian* 雜篇 (miscellaneous chapters). At first sight, the text, much like the *Fayan*, seems to be lacking in consistent organisation, and the component sections appear "mutually unrelated and even trivial." It is for this reason that a common misconception has arisen that thinks of this chapter as a "ragbag of odds and ends"[95]—a view much challenged by De Reu.

Noting the lack of systematic research on the later *Zhuangzi* chapters, De Reu's analysis goes against the received perception of the "Wai wu" as something that is just "made up of scraps put together at random." Through his examination of the underlying argumentative structure of the "Wai wu," De Reu identifies three sets of explicit verbal connections in the "Wai wu" and shows that there is a coherent line of argument that connects the entire chapter into a coherent organism. For this, he divides the "Wai wu" into twelve units, all of which culminate in the final section of the chapter, which, following De Reu's analysis, must be seen as the "culmination" of the entire "Wai wu."

With his analysis De Reu calls into question the common interpretation of the chapter's well-known final section. It is usually argued that it deals with the dynamics between language and meaning. However, De Reu argues that the final section of the "Wai wu" is in fact better understood by distinguishing between two ways of linguistic engagement within a given social context, and he conjectures that the chapter as a whole possibly formulates a critique of fixed social interactions. The dominant reception of that unit is based on Wang Bi's reading of the first three lines for his exposition of the *Zhouyi* 周易 (*Changes of Zhou*). Wang Bi's de-contextualisation of this section in support of the *Zhouyi* informs the reading of this unit to the present day, stressing the relation between language and meaning and obscuring its function within the "Wai wu" as an argumentatively cohesive unit.

By showing the coherence on the chapter level of composition, De Reu invalidates the common ragbag hypothesis and demonstrates the ways in which close form analysis of a text can fundamentally change the interpretation of received wisdom as philosophically sound argumentation.

A similar situation also applies to the "Qiushui" (Autumn floods) chapter of the *Zhuangzi*, discussed by Dirk Meyer. By analysing the literary form of argument, this study casts light on the strategies through which persuasion is invoked on the level of text composition.

Although much of the *Zhuangzi* dates probably from the time of the Warring States period, the composition of the chapters in their current form is a result of Guo Xiang's 郭象 (d. 312 AD) editorial activity, through which he established a text much in line with his personal vision of the *Zhuangzi*. Meyer

---

[95]   See Angus Graham (transl.), Chuang-tzǔ: *The Seven Inner Chapters and Other Writings from the Book* Chuang-tzǔ (London: Allen & Unwin), 29; id., *Disputers of the Tao*, 173.

takes this as his starting point of analysis for the "Qiushui" and, as a working hypothesis, looks at the chapter as a whole to investigate its strategies of argumentative persuasion.

It appears that the "Qiushui" as a consistent unit, according to Meyer, formulates a coherent vision that manifests an attempt to bridge the gap between a philosophy of praxis and the attempt to communicate philosophical insight through the literary patterns of text composition. The literary patterns of the text transform the "Qiushui" into a text-performance in the sense that, when read, it makes the text recipient act out philosophical insight simply by virtue of reciting the text. The "Qiushui" therefore manifests an attempt to express the unsayable through form. The text as a whole formulates a claim to truth without ever claiming the truth in explicit terms. With the "Qiushui," Guo Xiang translates the prominent theme of skill in the *Zhuangzi* into a philosophical essay where the text itself becomes a most skilful praxis of the *dao*.

In his analysis of the "Qiushui," Meyer carries out a detailed investigation into the literary form of the argument both on the level of the micro and macro structure of composition. One might be tempted to read the "Qiushui" as a collection of mutually unrelated stories, but Meyer's analysis, like De Reu's, casts light on the literary strategies by which the different stories in the "Qiushui" are mutually interconnected in a coherent whole where a consistent vision is presented. This is much in line with argument-based texts from the Warring States period where some contain quite an elaborate architecture of text composition. Excavated texts such as the "Zhong xin zhi dao," "Qiong da yi shi" or the "Wu xing" from tomb Guodian One represent this well.[96] However, unlike a text such as the "Zhong xin zhi dao" in which each unit is given a necessary place, the "Qiushui" entertains a much more organic form of text composition. The different units in this text rather float one into the other, much in line with the overall vision of the text. The literary form of text composition therefore reduplicates the initial metaphor of the text, and Meyer feels confident in concluding that the formal composition in fact expresses the argument of the text on the literary level.

By bringing together leading scholars in the field of literary philosophical communication in early China to discuss literary forms of arguments, our intention with this volume is to further awareness of the intricacies of argument-construction in early Chinese written prose. We aim to open up the field of literary philosophical communication in pre-modern China to a broader pub-

---

96 The architecture of text composition in these texts was discussed in detail in Meyer, *Philosophy on Bamboo*.

lic and to connect the questions relevant to our field to wider discourse about strategies of compelling consent in other disciplines.

The realisation of this volume would have been impossible without the engaged, critical and insightful contributions of the conference participants and the excellent papers that we received for this volume. The editors are grateful for the friendly openness of the authors to yield to a new approach, for their receptive and creative responsiveness, as well as for their support and patience throughout the highly labour intensive, yet productive, editing process. We would also like to thank the American Council of Learned Societies in conjunction with the Chiang Ching-kuo Foundation for their generous support of the workshop, the British Inter-university China Centre, as well as The Queen's College, University of Oxford.

References

Ackrill, J.L. *Essays on Plato and Aristotle*. Oxford: Oxford University Press, 1997.

Adler, Jeremy, and Ulrich Ernst. *Text als Figur. Visuelle Poesie von der Antike bis zur Moderne*. Weinheim: VCH Verlagsgesellschaft, 1987.

Allen, R. E., trans. *Plato: The Republic*. New Haven: Yale University Press, 2006.

Baxter, Timothy M.S. *The Cratylus: Plato's Critique of Naming*, Philosophia antiqua 58. Leiden: Brill, 1992.

Behr, Wolfgang, and Joachim Gentz. "Introduction." In *Kunstprosa in klassischen chinesischen Texten*, edited by Wolfgang Behr and Joachim Gentz, *Bochumer Jahrbuch zur Ostasienforschung* 29 (2005): 5–13.

Behr, Wolfgang, and Lisa Indraccolo, eds. *Masters of Disguise? Conceptions and Misconceptions of 'Rhetoric' in Chinese Antiquity*. Berlin: De Gruyter, 2014 (Special Issue of *Asiatische Studien / Études asiatiques* 68.4).

Behr, Wolfgang. "Three Sound-Correlated Text Structuring Devices in Pre-Qin Philosophical Prose." In *Kunstprosa in klassischen chinesischen Texten*, edited by Wolfgang Behr and Joachim Gentz, *Bochumer Jahrbuch zur Ostasienforschung* 29 (2005): 15-34.

Broida, Marian. "Textualizing Divination: The Writing on the Wall in Daniel 5:25." *Vetus Testamentum* 62 (2012): 1–13.

Brooks, Cleanth. *The Well Wrought Urn: Studies in the Structure of Poetry*. London: Methuen, 1968 [1947].

Broschat, Michael R. "Guiguzi: A textual Study and Translation." PhD diss., University of Michigan, 1985.

Brug, John F. "Biblical Acrostics and Their Relationship to Other Ancient Near Eastern Acrostics." In *The Bible in the Light of Cuneiform Literature: Scripture in Context III*, edited by William W. Hallo et al. Lewiston, NY: Mellen, 1990: 305–323.

Carone, Gabriela Roxana. *Plato's Cosmology and Its Ethical Dimensions*. New York: Cambridge University Press, 2005.

Danes, Frantisek. *On Prague School Functionalism in Linguistics*. Trier: Linguistic Agency Univ. of Trier, Series A, paper no. 127, 1984.

Davis, John Francis. "Poeseos sinensis comentarii: On the Poetry of the Chinese." In *Transactions of the Royal Asiatic Society* 2 (1830): 393–461.

De Groot, J.M. "On Chinese Divination by Dissecting Written Characters." *T'oung Pao* 1.3 (1890): 239–247.

De Lubac, Henri. *Exégèse médiévale 2: Les quatre sens de l'écriture*. Paris: Montaigne, 1959; trans. *Medieval Exegesis: The Four Senses of Scripture*, vol. 2, by E.M. Macierowski. Michigan / Edinburgh: T&T Eerdmans and Clark Publishing Co., 2000.

Defoort, Carine, and Nicolas Standaert, eds. "Argument and Persuasion in Ancient Chinese Texts." Special Issue of *Oriens Extremus* 45 (2005).

Dencker, Klaus Peter. *Deutsche Unsinnpoesie*. Stuttgart: Reclam, 1978.

———. *Poetische Sprachspiele. Vom Mittelalter bis zur Gegenwart*. Stuttgart: Reclam, 2003.

Erler, Michael. "To Hear the Right Thing and to miss the Point: Plato's implicit Poetics." In *Plato As Author: The Rhetoric of Philosophy*, edited by Ann N. Michelini. Leiden, Boston: Brill, 2003: 153–173.

Erler, Michael, and Jan Erik Heßler, eds. *Argument und Literarische Form in antiker Philosophie*. Berlin: De Gruyter, 2013.

Ernst, Ulrich. *Carmen figuratum. Geschichte des Figurengedichts von den antiken Ursprüngen bis zum Ausgang des Mittelalters*. Cologne: Böhlau, 1991.

Fingarette, Herbert. *Confucius: The Secular as Sacred*. New York: Harper & Row, 1972.

Gabelentz, Georg von der. "Ein Probestück von chinesischem Parallelismus." *Zeitschrift für Völkerpsychologie und Sprachwissenschaft* 10 (1878): 230–234.

Gallop, David. "The Rhetoric of Philosophy: Socrates' Swan Song." In *Plato As Author: The Rhetoric of Philosophy*, edited by Ann N. Michelini. Leiden, Boston: Brill, 2003: 113–332.

Gentz, Joachim. "Zwischen den Argumenten lesen. Zu zweifach gerichteten Verbindungsstücken zwischen Argumenten in frühen chinesischen Texten." In *Kunstprosa in klassischen chinesischen Texten*, edited by Wolfgang Behr and Joachim Gentz, *Bochumer Jahrbuch zur Ostasienforschung* 29 (2005): 35–56.

———. "Zum Parallelismus in der chinesischen Literatur." In *Parallelismus Membrorum*, edited by Andreas Wagner. Göttingen: Vandenhoeck & Ruprecht / Fribourg: Academic Press, 2007: 241–269.

———. "Rhetoric as the Art of Listening: Concepts of Persuasion in the First Eleven Chapters of the *Guiguzi*." In *Masters of Disguise? Conceptions and Misconceptions of 'Rhetoric' in Chinese Antiquity*, edited by W. Behr and L. Indraccolo. Berlin: De Gruyter, 2014 (Special Issue of *Asiatische Studien / Études asiatiques* 68.4): 1001–1019.

Gilson, Simon A. *Dante and Renaissance Florence*, Cambridge: Cambridge University Press, 2005.

Goldin, Paul R. "Miching Mallecho: The *Zhanguoce* and Classical Rhetoric." *Sino-Platonic Papers* 41 (1993): 1-27; reprint as "Rhetoric and Machination in Stratagems of the Warring States." In *After Confucius: Studies in Early Chinese Philosophy*, by Paul Goldin. Honolulu: University of Hawai'i Press, 2005: 76–89.

Gonzalez, Francisco J. "How to Read a Platonic Prologue: *Lysis* 203a–207d." In *Plato As Author: The Rhetoric of Philosophy*, edited by Ann N. Michelini. Leiden, Boston: Brill, 2003: 15–44.

Gordon, Jill. *Turning Toward Philosophy: Literary Device and Dramatic Structure in Plato's Dialogues*. University Park: Pennsylvania State University Press, 1999.

Graham, Angus C. *Studies in Chinese Philosophy and Philosophical Literature*. Singapore: Institute of East Asian Philosophies, 1986.

———. *Disputers of the Tao: Philosophical Argument in Ancient China*. La Salle, Ill: Open Court, 1989.

———, trans. *Chuang-tzŭ: The Seven Inner Chapters and Other Writings from the Book Chuang-tzŭ*. London: Allen & Unwin, 1981.

Greene, William Chase. "Plato's View of Poetry." *Harvard Studies in Classical Philology* 29 (1918): 1–75.

Griswold, Charles L. "Plato on Rhetoric and Poetry." In *The Stanford Encyclopedia of Philosophy*, edited by Edward N. Zalta (Spring 2012 Edition). http://plato.stanford.edu/archives/spr2012/entries/plato-rhetoric/ (last access 19/02/2014).

Hall, David L., and Roger T. Ames. *Thinking Through Confucius*. Albany, NY: SUNY, 1987.

———. "Chinese Philosophy." In *Routledge Encyclopedia of Philosophy*, edited by E. Craig. London: Routledge, 1998. http://www.rep.routledge.com/article/G001SECT2 (last access 26/10/2014).

Hansen, Chad. "Should the Ancient Masters Valuate Reason?" In *Chinese Texts and Philosophical Contexts*, edited by Henry Rosemont, Jr. Illinois: Open Court, 1991: 179–207.

Harbsmeier, Christoph. *Language and Logic*. Science and Civilisation in China. Vol. 7. Cambridge: Cambridge University Press, 1998.

Heidbüchel, Ursula. "Rhetorik im antiken China: eine Untersuchung der Ausdrucksformen höfischer Rede im Zuo Zhuan, Herzog Zhao." PhD diss., University of Münster, 1993.

Holenstein, Elmar. "Einführung: Von der Poesie und der Plurifunktionalität der Sprache." In *Roman Jakobson: Poetik. Ausgewählte Aufsätze 1921–1971*, edited by E. Holenstein and Tarcisius Schelbert. Frankfurt: Suhrkamp, 1979: 7–60.

Horálek, Karel. "La function de la 'structure des fonctions' de la langue." *Recueil Linguistique de Bratislava* 1 (1948): 39–43; reprint in Josef Vachek, ed. *A Prague School Reader in Linguistics*. Bloomington: Indiana University Press, 1964: 421–425.

Humboldt, Wilhelm von. *Brief an M. Abel-Rémusat über die Natur grammatischer Formen im allgemeinen und über den Geist der chinesischen Sprache im besonderen*, translated by Christoph Harbsmeier. Stuttgart: Frommann-Holzboog, 1970.

Jakobson, Roman. "Two Aspects of Language and Two Types of Aphasic Disturbances." In *Fundamentals of Language*, edited by Roman Jakobson and Morris Halle. The Hague: Mouton, 1956: 115–133; reprint in Roman Jakobson, ed. *On Language*. Cambridge, MA: Harvard University Press, 1990: 115–133.

———. "Linguistics and Poetics." In *Style in Language*, edited by Thomas A. Sebeok. Cambridge, MA: MIT Press, 1960: 350–377.

———. "Grammatical Parallelism and Its Russian Facet." *Language* 42.2 (1966): 399–429; reprint in Roman Jakobson. *Selected Writings III: Poetry of Grammar and Grammar of Poetry*. The Hague 1981: 98–135.

Kablitz, Andreas. *Kunst des Möglichen. Theorie der Literatur*. Freiburg, Berlin, Wien: Rombach Verlag, 2013.

Kern, Martin. "Quotation and the Confucian Canon in Early Chinese Manuscripts: The Case of 'Ziyi' [Black Robes]." *Asiatische Studien / Études asiatiques* 59.1 (2006): 293–332.

———. "The Performance of Writing in Western Zhou China." In *The Poetics of Grammar and the Metaphysics of Sound and Sign*, edited by Sergio La Porta and David Shulman. Leiden: Brill, 2007: 109–174.

Kraus, Manfred. *Name und Sache. Ein Problem im frühgriechischen Denken*. Amsterdam: John Benjamins Publishing Company, 1978.

Langer, Susanne K. *Philosophy in a New Key. A Study in the Symbolism of Reason, Rite, and Art*. Cambridge, MA: Harvard University Press, 1979; orig. 1941.

Leighton, Angela. *On Form: Poetry, Aestheticism, and the Legacy of a Word*. Oxford: Oxford University Press, 2007: 1–29.

———. "About About: On Poetry and Paraphrase." *Midwest Studies in Philosophy*, 33.1 (2009): 167–176.

Levin, Susan B. *The Ancient Quarrel Between Philosophy and Poetry Revisited: Plato and the Greek Literary Tradition*. New York: Oxford University Press, 2001.

Li Ling, "Discussion of the Chu Silk Manuscript and 'Shi-tu'," translated by Jenny F. So. In *New Perspectives on Chu Culture during the Eastern Zhou Period*, edited by Thomas Lawton. Princeton, NJ: Princeton University Press, 1991: 178–183.

Major, John S., Sarah A. Queen, Andrew Seth Meyer, and Harold D. Roth, eds. and trans. *The Huainanzi*. New York: Columbia University Press, 2010.

Lowth, Robert. *De sacra poesi Hebraeorum praelectiones academicae Oxonii habitae*. Oxonii: e tipographeo Clarendoniano, 1753.

Luz, Christine. *Technopaignia, Formspiele in der griechischen Dichtung.* Leiden: Brill, 2010.

Makeham, John. "Names, Actualities, and the Emergence of Essentialist Theories of Naming in Classical Chinese Thought." *Philosophy East & West* 41.3 (1991): 341–363.

———. *Name and Actuality in Early Chinese Thought.* Albany: SUNY Press, 1994.

McCurdy, William James. "Joining the Disputation: Taking Graham Seriously on Taking Chinese Thought Seriously." *Journal of Chinese Philosophy* 19 (1992): 329–355.

Meyer, Dirk. *Philosophy on Bamboo: Text and the Production of Meaning in Early China.* Leiden: Brill, 2012.

———. "Bamboo and the Production of Philosophy: A Hypothesis about a Shift in Writing and Thought in Early China." In *History and Material Culture in Asian Religions*, edited by Benjamin J. Fleming and Richard Mann. London: Routledge, 2014: 21–38.

———. "A Device for Conveying Meaning: The Structure of the Guodian Tomb One Manuscript 'Zhong xin zhi dao'." In *Kunstprosa in klassischen chinesischen Texten*, edited by Wolfgang Behr and Joachim Gentz, *Bochumer Jahrbuch zur Ostasienforschung* 29 (2005): 57–78.

Most, Glen. "What Ancient Quarrel Between Philosophy and Poetry?" In *Plato and the Poets*, edited by Pierre Destrée and Fritz-Gregor Herrmann. Leiden: Brill, 2011: 1–20.

Owen, Stephen. *Readings in Chinese Literary Thought.* Cambridge, MA: Harvard University Press, 1992.

Petraki, Zacharoula A. *The Poetics of Philosophical Language: Plato, Poets and Presocratics in the 'Republic.'* Berlin: Walter De Gruyter, 2011.

Plaks, Andrew. "Where the Lines Meet: Parallelism in Chinese and Western Literatures." *Chinese Literature: essays, articles, reviews* (CLEAR) 10.1–2 (1988): 43–60; reprint in *Poetics Today* 11.3 (1991): 523–546.

———. "Terminology and Central Concepts." In *How to Read the Chinese Novel*, edited by David L. Rolston. Princeton: Princeton University Press, 1990: 75–123.

Pope, Alexander. *An Essay on Man. Moral Essays and Satires.* London, Paris & Melbourne: Cassell, 1891.

Ribeiro, Anna Christina. "Toward a Philosophy of Poetry." *Midwest Studies in Philosophy* 33.1 (2009): 61–77.

Richter, Matthias. "Cognate Texts: Technical Terms as Indicators of Intertextual Relations and Redactional Strategies." *Asiatische Studien / Études asiatiques* 61.3 (2002): 549–572.

———. "Punctuation." In *Reading Early Chinese Manuscripts*, edited by Wolfgang Behr, Martin Kern and Dirk Meyer. Leiden: Brill, forthcoming.

Rosemont, Henry, Jr., ed. *Chinese Texts and Philosophical Contexts: Essays Dedicated to Angus C. Graham.* Illinois: Open Court, 1991.

Schaberg, David. "The Logic of Signs in Early Chinese Rhetoric." In *Early China / Ancient Greece: Thinking through Comparisons*, edited by Steven Shankman and Stephen W. Durrant. Albany: SUNY Press, 2002: 155–186.

———. *A Patterned Past: Form and Thought in Early Chinese Historiography*. Cambridge, MA: Harvard University Asia Center, 2001.

Schefer, Christina. "Rhetoric as Part of an Initiation into the Mysteries: A New Interpretation of the Platonic *Phaedrus*." In *Plato As Author: The Rhetoric of Philosophy*, edited by Ann N. Michelini. Leiden: Brill, 2003: 175–196.

Schlegel, Gustave. *La loi du parallélisme en style chinois: démontrée par la Preface du Si-yü ki*. Brill: Leiden, 1896.

Shorey, Paul. *The Unity of Plato's Thought*. Chicago: The University of Chicago Press, 1903.

Sperber, Dan, and Deirdre Wilson. *Relevance: Communication and Cognition*. Oxford: Blackwell, 1986.

Stausberg, Michael. *Faszination Zarathustra: Zoroaster und die Europäische Religionsgeschichte der frühen Neuzeit*. Berlin: Walter de Gruyter, 1998.

Steiner, Peter. *Russian Formalism—A Metapoetics*. Ithaca: Cornell University Press, 1984.

Strauss, Leo. *Persecution and the Art of Writing*. Glencoe, Ill: Free Press, 1952.

Streif, Christian. *Die Erleuchtung des Nordens: Zum Disput zwischen Sengzhao und Liu Yimin über die Bodhisattva-Idee des Mahayana*. Wiesbaden: Harrassowitz, 2013.

Unger, Ulrich. *Rhetorik des klassischen Chinesisch*. Wiesbaden: Harrassowitz, 1994.

Van Els, Paul, R. Graziani, Y. Pines, and E. Sabattini, eds. *Political Rhetoric in Early China*. Paris: Presses Universitaires de Vincennes, 2012.

Wagner, Rudolf G. "Interlocking Parallel Style: Laozi and Wang Bi." *Asiatische Studien / Études asiatiques* 34.1 (1980): 18–58.

———. "Die Unhandlichkeit des Konfuzius." In *Weisheit: Archäologie der literarischen Kommunikation II*, ed. Aleida and Jan Assmann. Munich: Fink, 1991: 455–464.

———. *The Craft of a Chinese Commentator: Wang Bi on the Laozi*. Albany: SUNY Press, 2000.

———. *Language, Ontology, and Political Philosophy in China*. Albany: SUNY Press, 2003.

Warnock, Robert G., and Roland Folter. "The German Pattern Poem. A Study in Mannerism of the Seventeenth Century." In *Festschrift für Detlev Schumann*, edited by Albert R. Schmitt. Munich: Delp, 1970: 40–73.

Whitehead, Alfred North. *Process and Reality*. New York: Free Press, 1979.

Wu, Joseph S. "Chinese Language and Chinese Thought." *Philosophy East and West* 19.4 (1969): 423–434.

Yang Shuda 楊樹達. *Zhongguo xiucixue* 中國修辭學, Yang Shuda jiang wenyan xiuci 楊樹達講文言修辭. Nanjing: Fenghuang chubanshe, 2009.

Yuan Jinmei, "Analogical Propositions in Moist Texts." *Journal of Chinese Philosophy* 39.3 (2012): 404–423.

Zach, Erwin Ritter von. "Einige Worte zu Prof. Gustav Schlegel's 'La loi du parallélisme en style chinois'." Peking, 1902.

Zhang, Longxi. *The Tao and the Logos: Literary Hermeneutics, East and West*. Durham: Duke University Press, 1992.

Zhou Yuanlong 周淵龍, and Zhou Wei 周為, eds. *Wenzi youxi* 文字遊戲. 2 vols. Beijing: Tuanjie, 1999.

Zuckert, Catherine. "Commentary" to the contributions of Howland, Farness, and Ausland to the volume *Plato As Author: The Rhetoric of Philosophy*, edited by Ann N. Michelini. Leiden: Brill, 2003: 145–151.

CHAPTER 1

A Building Block of Chinese Argumentation: Initial *Fu* 夫 as a Phrase Status Marker

Rudolf G. Wagner

In analytical non-narrative discourse, various rhetorical figures have been used to mark the status of statements as either expressing general rules, exceptions, or side comments. Such status markers might be silent and structural or explicit. Markers of both types exist in classical Chinese, but they are little studied. The consequence is a loss in the precision of the understanding of the arguments proffered.

This is a study of the development of initial *fú* 夫 into a phrase status marker for statements for which a general rather than particular validity is claimed. The methodology used aims at falsifiability. After an outline of the state of the art, the paper offers a qualitative analysis of a randomized sample of phrases in Wang Bi's (AD 226–249) commentaries on the *Zhouyi* and the *Laozi* to develop a plausibilized series of hypotheses. In a second quantitative step, these hypotheses are tested against the entire body of these two texts. The last section sketches the process by which initial *fu* shed its use as a demonstrative and developed into the structuring device for the Chinese rhetoric of argument outlined above.

Introduction

Language uses different markers to signal the status of a statement.[1] A phrase in English that starts with "basically" or "in principle" often indicates that a statement is being made for which general validity is recognized from which, however, in the actual case an exception might have to be made. The phrase "thus I have heard" in the beginning of a Buddhist sutra marks the words that follow as the words of the Buddha with all the accompanying claims to authority this connotes. By contrast, a phrase starting with "let me add" or "by the way" signals a statement that is supplementary to the core argument and will

---

1   Christoph Harbsmeier has been a helpful critic of an earlier version. Wolfgang Behr has kindly helped with bibliographical references. The two editors as well as several readers have shared their critical notes with me. To all of them I am greatly indebted. Needless to say, all mistakes are my own.

not be further elaborated. These are explicit markers, supplemented in the spoken language with sentence intonation, emphasis, and gesture. There are also implicit markers. Examples are the closed grammar often observed in political or propaganda rhetoric[2] or the position of a phrase within an argument, such as a concluding phrase in a prose argument or a non-parallel concluding phrase in Chinese interlocking parallel style constructions.[3] In many cases these markers have been used as the basis for a modern graphic structuring of texts originally written without breaks into phrases, paragraphs, and chapters.[4] Using such structural as well as the explicit markers are economical and effective ways to structure an argument, and this even more so in texts written without visible word, phrase and paragraph separators. A positive knowledge of these markers is crucial for a precise understanding of argumentative procedures in demanding texts from the 'foreign country' of the past, where so much of the context originally shared by authors and readers is lost or as yet unexplored.

Chinese written status markers are treated by specialists under the negative umbrella heading of *xuzi* 虛字, meaning 'empty' characters. This only denotes their *not* referring to a specific subject, action, or quality, but does not give a positive definition. Scholarship has read this as an invitation to disregard them.[5]

In an effort to enhance our understanding of the early Chinese rhetoric of argumentation[6] and, above all, the precision of our grasping the communications intended by the authors, I propose to study one word for which I claim that it became a consistently used phrase status marker in argumentative texts in the classical written language between the Warring States period (475–221 BC) and the third century AD. The word is *fú* in the modern pronunciation (MC bju < OC *[b]a), and it is written with the character 夫. It very often occurs as the first word—very rarely the second word—in a sentence, but also occurs

---

2 See Michael Schoenhals, *Doing Things with Words in Chinese Politics: Five Studies* (China Research Monograph 41, Institute of Chinese Studies, University of California, Berkeley, 1976).

3 See Rudolf Wagner, *The Craft of a Chinese Commentator: Wang Bi on the Laozi* (Albany: SUNY Press, 2000), 53–114, for a detailed study of this type of style.

4 An example: Five of the eight paragraph breaks in Lou Yulie's edition of Wang Bi's 王弼 *Laozi zhilüe* 老子指略 are marked by initial *fú*. Lou Yulie 樓宇烈 ed., *Wang Bi ji jiaoshi* 王弼集校釋 (Beijing: Zhonghua shuju, 1999), 1. 195–99.

5 Examples would be the Thesaurus Linguae Sericae (TLS), accessible online under, http://tls.uni-hd.de/ (accessed November 11, 2014), or dictionaries such as Wang Haifen 王海棻, *Gu Hanyu xuci cidian* 古漢語虛詞詞典 (Beijing: Beijing Daxue chubanshe, 1996).

6 For a general and brilliantly comparative study of early Chinese rhetorical devices see Christoph Harbsmeier, *Chinese Rhetoric in Comparative Perspective*, unpublished manuscript, 2002.

within sentences.⁷ A homoiophonous but probably different word *fú* written with the same character 夫 but a slightly different pronunciation (MC bju < OC *ba) occurs only as the last character in a sentence. It indicates a rhetorical question or a doubt, inviting assent ("is it not so?").⁸ The character 夫 is finally used to represent the word *fū* (MC pju < OC *p(r)a), 'adult male.'⁹ As particles cannot well be graphically represented, the use of 夫 to represent both initial and terminal *fú* must be assumed to be a phonetic loan based on the representation of the similar sounding (homoiophonous) *fū* with the character 夫.¹⁰ The differentiation between the two homoiophonous *fú* 夫, the one initial or within the phrase, the other final, follows unequivocally from their position in the phrase. The differentiation between these two and *fū* 夫, 'adult male,'—a word that in addition hardly ever occurs either at the beginning or the end of a phrase—is context-driven. It seems that these position and context differentiations were unambiguous enough to obviate the need for further graphic differentiation.

The State of the Art

Chinese commentators as well as, in their wake, modern scholars have noted that initial *fu* occurs frequently, and that it often has something to do with structuring text. Their common focus is on Warring States and Former Han (202 BC–9 AD) texts, their assumption being that the bandwidth of functions and meaning to be found then is valid for the entirety of Chinese history. As a consequence none of them traced the history of the word. The tone was set by Liu Xie 劉勰 (~465~522), who defined initial *fu* as "an opening salvo for a start"

---

7   In some rare cases, another word such as *qie* 且 or *ruo* 若 may precede it, often without causing a change of meaning.

8   I follow A.C. Graham in assuming that these two *fu* are two different words and that *fu* 'adult male' is a third one. See his "The Classical Chinese Topic-Marker fu 夫," *Bulletin of the School of Oriental and African Studies* 35.1 (1972): 85–110, 86. On the final particle *fu*, see A.C. Graham, "The Final Particle 'Fwu' 夫," *Bulletin of the School of Oriental and African Studies* 17.1 (1955): 120–132. B. Schindler's assumption that the fact that all these words were written with the character 夫 was an indicator that they originally were one single word that then split up into three seems not well supported. See his "Grammatical Notes II: 夫," *Asia Major*, N.S. III.2 (1953): 162–168.

9   I follow the classification in the on-line supplementary list to William H. Baxter, Laurent Sagart, *Old Chinese: a new reconstruction* (New York: Oxford University Press, 2014), The Baxter-Sagart reconstruction of Old Chinese (Version 1.1, 20 September 2014), http://ocbaxtersagart.lsait.lsa.umich.edu/ accessed March 6, 2015.

10 Particles such as pronouns are as a rule written with loans. I am grateful to Christoph Harbsmeier for pointing this out to me.

(*faduan zhi shouchang* 發端之首唱) and grouped it with other words that start phrases, such as *wei* 惟, *gai* 蓋, and *gu* 故;[11] by Lu Deming 陸德明 (556–627), who marked initial *fu* as a "word used to start [a statement]" (*faduan zhi zi* 發端之字);[12] and by Xing Bing 邢昺 (932–1010), who observed the particular and consistent function of initial *fu* in the *Xiaojing* 孝經 (*Book of filial piety*) and defined it as "a marker for the beginning of a statement" (*fayan zhi duan* 發言之端)[13] and in another passage he says it is "marking the start of a statement, but it is also a demonstrative."[14] In his *Ma shi wentong* 馬氏文通 (1898), Ma Jianzhong 馬建忠 (1845–1900) quotes Xing Bing's statement as a source for earlier definitions, but then developed his own. After grouping initial *fu* with three other words of similar function, he writes: "generally speaking, if *fu* is at the head of a sentence, it always serves to affirmatively link up with the text coming before it (*ding cheng shangwen* 頂承上文) while in addition establishing a new idea (*chongli xinyi* 重立新義) […]. Accordingly, *fu* is still a demonstrative and not just an 'empty word' marking the beginning of a statement."[15] As many chapters in philosophical works and even books of this type actually start with initial *fu*, Ma's claim about the affirmative linkage to earlier text is not well supported. His effort to combine affirmative linkage, 'demonstrative,' and emphatic aspects into a single ahistorical definition has set the framework for most modern Chinese scholars. There are indeed early uses of *fu* both at the beginning and within sentences as demonstratives. An example from the *Zuozhuan* will be given below.

Because the same character was used, scholars felt prompted to offer an explanation covering both functions, even if these efforts remain awkward. In 1959 Zhou Fagao 周法高 classified initial *fu* as either being a noun akin to *bi* 彼, an adjective akin to *na* 那, or a "demonstrative weakening into an initial

---

11 Liu Xie 劉勰, *Wenxin diaolong* 文心雕龍, chapter *zhangju* 章句, quoted in Wang Weifeng 王衛峰, "'Fu' de tongshe lianjie gongneng lun," 夫的統攝連接功能論, *Gu Hanyu yanjiu* 古漢語研究 83 (2009.2): 63–68, 63.

12 Lu Deming 陸德明, *Jingdian shiwen* 經典釋文, quoted in Wang Weifeng, "Fu," 63.

13 And a few lines further down he summarizes: "to make clear that the reasoning from before had its progression further down, therefore it says *fu* to begin it." *Ming qian li er xia you qi qu, gu yan 'fu' yi qi zhi* 明前理而下有其趣故言夫以起之. Xing Bing 邢昺, sub-commentary in *Xiaojing zhushu* 孝經註疏, chapter 7, Ruan Yuan 阮元 ed., *Shisanjing zhushu* 十三經注疏 (Beijing: Zhonghua shuju, 1987), 2558.1 (end). Xing right afterwards also quotes Liu Huan 劉瓛, a philologist active during the Southern Qi, 479–502 AD, with the words: "*Fu* is like *fan* 夫猶凡也."

14 Quoted from Xing Bing's commentary on Guo Pu's 郭璞 (276–324) preface to the *Erya* 爾雅 by Wang Weifeng, "Fu," 63.

15 Ma Jianzhong 馬建忠, *Ma shi wentong jiaozhu* 馬氏文通校注, Zhang Xichen 張錫琛 comm. (Beijing: Zhonghua shuju, 1988), 355.

particle."¹⁶ Inserting a historical dimension, he said that initial *fu* only gradually "transformed into something with the meaning of starting a statement and even an 'empty word' of a purely statement-starting character, although the borders between the two [the demonstrative, and the statement-starting, R.W.] are not clearly marked."¹⁷ This again seems less than convincing. Using mostly quotes from the *Mengzi*, A.C. Graham maintained that initial *fu* was referring only to the noun or nominal phrase directly following it, not to the phrase as a whole, not to mention the pair of phrases following.¹⁸ As we shall see, this effort to link the demonstrative and statement-starting functions fails to account for its very widespread use as a single marker shared by two parallel sentences.

The recent compilations of specialized dictionaries for each of the thirteen classics have not gone beyond claiming that the word "expresses a mood that some summary outline" will follow.¹⁹ In his study of the *Huainanzi*, Hans van

---

16   Zhou Fagao 周法高, *Zhongguo gudai yufa* 中國古代語法, *Chengdai pian* 稱代篇, (1959), repr. (Beijing: Zhonghua shudian, 1990), 177.

17   Ibid., 180, note 1.

18   Graham, "The Classical Chinese Topic-Marker," 92, 93. Strangely, Graham himself notes: "A remarkable feature of *fu*, which has much to do with the impression that it is an initial particle, is that it is not repeated in parallel sentences." Ibid., 94.

19   Many modern Chinese authors have defined, without further linguistic analysis, the functions of initial *fu*. Pei Xuehai followed Ma Jianzhong in claiming an "emphatic function" for it, 有提示作用. Pei Xuehai 裴學海, *Gushu xuzi jishi* 古書虛字集釋 (Beijing: Zhonghua shuju, 1954), 881. Taking the cue from Xing Bing, the *Guoyu da cidian* 國語大辭典 considers it a "speech opener" (*fayu ci* 發語辭). Dongfang shudian 東方書店 comp., *Guoyu da cidian* 國語大辭典 (Taipei: Dongfang shudian, 1972) sub *fu* 夫. See also Song Lian 宋濂 (1310–1381), *Pianhai leibian* 篇海類編 (Shanghai: Shanghai guji chubanshe, 1995–99) *renshilei* 人事類, *fu bu* 夫部. Luo Zhufeng 羅竹風 ed., *Hanyu da cidian* 漢語大詞典 (Shanghai: Shanghai cishu chubanshe, 1986–1994) sub *fu* 夫, similarly makes it into a *faduan zhi zi* 發端之字. Xu Weijian 許偉建 ed., *Shanggu Hanyu cidian* 上古漢語詞典 (Changchun: Jilin wenshi chubanshe, 1998), 98, calls it a character marking the beginning of a paragraph, or a word which conveys a sense of the beginning of a sentence, *jushou yuqici* 句首語氣詞. In the volumes that I have consulted (*Mengzi*, *Lunyu*, *Xiaojing*, and *Chunqiu Guliang*), initial *fu* is uniformly defined—with a formula originally proposed by Yang Bojun 楊伯峻 (1902–1992)—as a term "expressing a mood that some summary outline" will follow 表提挈語. The expression *tiqie* 提挈 is the short form of the *chengyu*: *tigang qieling* 提綱挈領, "give a summary outline." See *Shisan jing cidian* bianzuan weiyuanhui 十三經辭典編纂委員會, *Shisan jing cidian* 十三經辭典 (Xi'an: Shaanxi renmin chubanshe, 2002) *Mengzi juan*, 孟子卷 76, *Lunyu juan*, 論語卷 45, *Xiaojing juan* 孝經卷 13, *Chunqiu Guliang juan* 春秋穀梁卷, 67. Wang Weifeng, "Fu," 63–68 reviews and adds to earlier commentator statements on initial and demonstrative *fu*. His main contribution is on the *fu* within phrases and its function to link elements together. Xu Kuangyi 許匡一 ed., tr., *Huainanzi quanyi* 淮南子全譯 (Guiyang: Guizhou renmin chubanshe,

Ess takes up the claim that the word indicates a phrase that takes up earlier arguments and adds to them, often with the use of metaphor. However, none of the examples given announces itself as a metaphor and there are several cases where the *fu* starts a chapter.[20]

Commentators, as well as modern scholarship, have thus noted that initial *fu* is a marker, but the efforts to define its function remain diffuse and have not been tested with sufficient stringency. As a historian of Chinese philosophy who believes that high accuracy in understanding the argument made in the sources is crucial and who therefore has developed a philological bent, my study is primarily concerned with the rhetorical function(s) which initial *fu* assumes in structuring arguments in texts of interest to the student of Chinese philosophy; the uses to which authors put initial *fu*; and the very practical importance which a more accurate understanding of this word might have for the study of Chinese philosophy. In other words, I am not primarily concerned with mapping the bandwidth of the uses of the character 夫 during the Warring States period, but with its role in a consolidated practice in argumentative texts, if indeed it did develop such a role.

Consolidated Initial *fu*

During my studies of third century AD philosophical texts referred to as belonging to the Xuanxue 玄學 ('Scholarly exploration of the Dark')[21] current, I have noticed a seemingly very special function which they give to initial *fu*, namely to introduce general statements of principle. Two simple examples from Wang Bi's 王弼 (226–249) "*Zhouyi* lüeli" 周易略例 ("The Structure of the *Zhouyi*"):

1995) vol. 1, p.2, note 1, offers a slightly improved variant in his note on the first initial *fu* occurring in the *Huainanzi*, where he writes " 夫 *fu*: "Mood particle for the beginning of a phrase indicating that an argument will be made in the subsequent text." 句首語氣詞，表示下文要發議論.

20 Hans van Ess, "Argument and Persuasion in the First Chapter of *Huainanzi* and its Use of Particles," *Oriens Extremus* 45 (2005/6): 255–270, 258. As to initial *fu* being used for paragraph segmentation, van Ess mostly refers to Western translations. The fine *Huainanzi* edition by Xu Kuangyi quoted in the previous note, while not a critical edition, segments the text. Of the nineteen segments into which Xu divides the first chapter, only eleven start with initial *fu*, but the first chapter alone has 33 initial *fu*.

21 Rudolf Wagner, *Language, Ontology and Political Philosophy in China. Wang Bi's Scholarly Exploration of the Dark (Xuanxue)* (Albany: SUNY Press, 2003).

夫 眾不能治眾 治眾者 至寡者也²²

> *Fu*, the many cannot regulate the many, what regulates the many is that which is the smallest in number.

The phrase explains the principle on which the relationship in many hexagrams between the single dominating line and the remaining five lines is built.

夫陰之所求者 陽也
陽之所求者 陰也²³

> *Fu*, that what the *yin* is striving after is the *yang* and
> that what the *yang* is striving after is the *yin*.

The phrase explains the basic dynamics dominating the relationship between *yin* (broken) and *yang* (unbroken) lines in hexagrams.

In an attempt to solidify these hunches into a falsifiable argument with potentially great practical applications, I will now set up and test the hypothesis whether and under what conditions initial *fu* is used in 3rd century Xuanxue texts as a status marker for argumentative statements claiming a general truth and facticity; whether these statements were always of a specific formal type; and whether the statements tended to be about a certain range of subject matter.

Graham has nicely described the trap of selective examples. "Anybody who insists on the liberty to select his own examples would be in a position to prove any case whatever."²⁴ To avoid this trap I propose to follow a strict discipline of randomization. This will come with a price because randomized examples might need more complex elucidations of context. I will use the Wang Bi commentaries and essays for a first test, because these are key texts in Xuanxue, and I am most familiar with them.

I will proceed in two steps. First I will present the evidence at a stage where the use of initial *fu* has consolidated. This will include the use of quantitative methods and qualitative analysis to test the pervasiveness of a particular use of

---

22 Lou Yulie 樓宇烈 ed., *Wang Bi ji jiaoshi* 王弼集校釋 (Beijing: Zhonghua shuju, 1999), 2.591. I will use this edition of Wang Bi's works on the *Zhouyi*. No critical edition of this text has been made, and this edition is widely available. For Wang Bi's writings on the *Laozi* I will use my own critical edition in Rudolf Wagner, *A Chinese Reading of the Daodejing: Wang Bi's commentary on the Laozi with critical text and translation* (Albany: SUNY Press, 2003).

23 Lou Yulie, *Wang Bi ji jiaoshi*, 2.291.

24 Angus C. Graham, "The final particle fwu 夫," 123.

the word in a given time horizon and the genre or type of statement where this device is most commonly used. Second, I will shortly map the timeline along which this use consolidated.

Two features set this approach apart from existing scholarship. First, it accepts the option of a historical trajectory in word or character use that may include shrinking, diversification, and consolidation of meaning. This differs from one element of the standard approach, namely that of trying to map the totality of the different uses of a word without reference to historical change. Second, it will try to establish a definition of the functions of this word that is based on the analysis of the totality of uses in a given body of works, and a random sample of other texts, and that thus comes with the claim to falsifiability. This differs from another element of the standard approach, namely to disregard quantitative patterns of use.

Fu appears altogether 49 times as the first word in sentences in Wang Bi's *Zhouyi* commentary and 14 times in his systematic elucidation of the structure of the *Zhouyi*, the "*Zhouyi* lüeli." In the latter text, all occurrences are in the first part.[25] In Wang Bi's *Laozi Commentary*, *Laozi zhu* 老子注, initial *fu* appears 24 times, and in his "*Laozi* weizhi lüeli" 老子微指略例 18 times with one occurrence only of *fan* 凡. These are manageable quantities for a first test. As the *Zhouyi* commentary does not set out to systematically introduce the uses of initial *fu*, we may randomize our examples by simply taking the first few items as they occur so as to test the general hypothesis and develop specifications. At this stage the claim for their validity is tested only for the corpus outlined above.

The first occurrence of initial *fu* is in Wang's commentary to the unbroken line in the fifth position of hexagram 1, *qian* 乾. All text in square brackets is mine.

經：九五飛龍在天 利見大人
注：不行不躍而在乎天 非飛而何 故曰飛龍也 龍得[26] 在天則大人之路亨也
夫位以德興
德以位敘
以至德而出盛位 萬物之覩 不亦宜乎

---

[25] In the second part, the "Lüeli xia" 略例下, the term *fu* does not appear at all in this position, but the term *fan* 凡, which by this time had acquired a similar meaning, occurs five times in the initial position otherwise occupied by *fu*. I have as yet been unable to account for this shift in usage.

[26] I read 得 for 德 in accordance with Guo Jing (d. 1127) 郭京, *Zhouyi juzheng* 周易舉正, quoted in Lou Yulie, *Wang Bi ji jiaoshi*, 1.220, n. 18.

The text: Unbroken line in the fifth position: Aflight the dragon rests in the sky: the [others] will have the benefit of seeing the Great Man.
Wang Bi Commentary: "As he [the dragon] does not act and does not jump [anymore as he did on the two previous lines] but 'rests in the sky' how else would this be done but by 'being aflight?' That is why [the text says]: 'Aflight the dragon.' Once the dragon has achieved it to 'be aflight in the sky,' the path of the Great Man will be successful.
Fu,
a position will be brought to full fruition through receipt/capacity; receipt/capacity will provide order by means of a position.[27]
As through supreme receipt/capacity he is residing in the ultimate position, is not the 'observance' [towards him] by the 'ten thousand kinds of entities' [of which the Master in the "Wenyan" commentary speaks] appropriate [=to be expected]?"[28]

I have arrived at my reading of the *Zhouyi* passage from Wang Bi's commentary through extrapolative translation. Wang Bi's commentary starts out with a specific analysis of the *Zhouyi* phrase. He then inserts after *fu* a general comment: "A position will be brought to full fruition through receipt/capacity; receipt/capacity will provide order by means of a position." The two parts of this general comment are parallel. They have the same number of characters, the same grammatical structure, and analogous characters are in the same position. They are dialectically linked and not just juxtaposed separate statements. This leads to a first specification of the hypothesis:

---

27 The term 'position' here refers to the social rank as symbolized by lines two to five in a hexagram. The fifth position, to which this commentary refers, is that of the ruler. 'Receipt/capacity' refers to the double meaning of the word *de* (which is often translated as 'virtue') as being a 'capacity' 德 'received' 得 from the *dao*. It is through this receipt/capacity that the potential given with a royal position will be brought to fruition.

28 Lou Yulie, *Wang Bi ji jiaoshi*, 1.212. The "Wenyan" commentary, to which Wang implicitly refers, runs: "What does 'Aflight the dragon rests in the sky, the [others] will have the benefit of seeing the Great Man' mean? The Master said: 'Corresponding sounds echo each other, similar *qi* attract each other. Water flows towards the moist, fire goes after the dry, clouds follow in the wake of the dragon, wind follows in the wake of the tiger. When the Sage fulfils his function [as ruler] and the ten thousand kinds of entities are in observance, those rooted in heaven will be close to him above while those rooted in earth will be close to those below so that each follows its own kind.'" 字曰同聲相應 同氣相求 水流濕 火就燥 雲從龍 風從虎 聖人作而萬物都 本乎天者親上 本乎地者親下 則各從其類. Ibid., 215. I cannot follow Lou Yulie who suggests to read the *zhi* 之 in 萬物之覩 as *wang* 往 'to go to.' Ibid. 220 n. 20. There is no basis for this in either the *Zhouyi* text or the "Wenyan." Richard Lynn, *I Ching* (New York: Columbia University Press, 1994), 137, does not translate the *fu*.

(1) *Initial* fu *is not simply a speech, or paragraph, opener and does not contain a demonstrative element. It has the function of marking the status of the sentence which it introduces as being of a higher validity than sentences not marked in this manner. Such a sentence might consist of two interlocked parallel segments.*[29]

The *fu* phrase spells out a basic organizing principle of the hexagrams in the *Zhouyi* that has an evident bearing on political life. While lines one and six at the extremes mark the beginning and end of a process, lines 2 to 5 each have a 'position' *wei* 位 with structural links to other positions. Line five, for example, is the position of the ruler. Depending on the hexagram, a particular type of person with a given 'receipt/capacity' (*de* 德) is in such a position. This person is symbolized by a line. The basic classification is into 'weak' and 'strong' receipt/capacity as symbolized by a broken or an unbroken line on the given position. The position of an emperor is elevated, and his actions are considered the root cause both of order and of disorder in society. Wang Bi and others have written much about this. Only if this high position is coupled with *de* 德—and Wang Bi elsewhere defined this as *de* 得, 'get, receive' in the meaning of what is "received from the Dao"—will it unfold its positive effects. Someone with the *de* 德 of a Sage, but without high position, as was the case with Confucius, will not be able to bring order to society. This will be possible only when coupled with a high position as in the ideal of the *sheng wang* 聖王, the sage kings of old.

The *fu* phrase is thus linking the hexagram coding in a highly abstract, general, and philosophical way to a proposition in political philosophy that is shared by a wide array of relevant writings and examples. The claim of the *fu* phrases to validity is further enhanced by the fact that they are often followed by a *gu* 故 'that is why...' as will be documented further down. From this follows a second specification:

(2) *Initial* fu *is a rhetorical marker signalling to the reader the statement of a principle or a rule underlying a body of statements and structures in canonical texts that are supposed to be known to the reader.*

The sentence following *fu* does not tell a story but presents a non-narrative statement of argument. It is articulated in a highly abstract and general way. This gives us a third specification:

---

29 Graham wrongly claimed that initial *fu* only referred to the subsequent noun or nominal phrase.

(3) *Initial* fu *is followed by a non-narrative statement of argument or principle with abstract vocabulary.*

The *fu* sentence does not quote a canonical text but occurs in a commentary to a canonical text. The implicit claim is that without the content spelled out in the *fu* sentence the canonical text remains incomprehensible and that therefore the *fu* phrase spells out as a new abstract philosophical proposition what in an implicit way is contained in the canonical text. It does so, however, in an inter-communicatively rational manner that does not hinge on authority.

The canonical texts derive their authority not from being revealed 'scripture' but from being the bequests of the sages of antiquity. These sages are defined as a small number of human beings with an inborn grasp of the complex workings of the universe, and its fickle brother, human society.[30] Nothing remains of the wealth of examples from which this rule has been distilled. The historical concreteness, and anecdotal specificity, the unending flurry of particular historical circumstances and textual utterances have all been replaced by a sober, rigidly rational rule about the dialectics prevailing between receipt/capacity and position. To extract this rule from the concrete material at hand, and insert it to make people understand the logic of a canonical text is Wang Bi's own contribution, and this is in fact the translation of the *Zhouyi* text altogether from a tool for divination into a philosophically grounded analysis of the political process. The *fu* thus refers to propositions spelling out the principles underlying communications of 'higher validity' such as those addressed in the classics rather than just trivial regularities. Buddhist authors would use this rhetorical device to refer to truths underlying Buddhist texts; the *Huainanzi* will expand its canonical authorities to other persons and to processes in nature.

Rhetorically, the *fu* phrase here states, in a most general way, a rule. Wang Bi inserts his general key for understanding the *Zhouyi* coding for position (*wei* 位) and *de* 德 right into the middle of the argument. The statement comes without further proof, and it has no precedent in the language of the "Wenyan," which, being associated with Confucius, has the stature of a commentary from the hand of a Sage. The *fu* phrase is not accidental to the argument. The logic of the argument actually hinges on the acceptance of the *fu* sentence. At the same time, the insertion of the *fu* sentence establishes the link between the *Zhouyi* language and structure on the one hand and the "Wenyan" interpretation on the other, which is quoted in the succeeding sentence, and is thus proven to be true.

---

30   As I have tried to show elsewhere, Wang Bi does neither accept a proof by authority, nor does he set himself up as a teacher whose word has to be accepted even without proof. Wagner, *Language*, 78.

(4) Initial *fu* alerts the reader to statements claiming to spell out a new insight in an inter-communicatively rational and argumentative way about the general rules or principles underlying texts or reports of higher truth, proving their philosophical viability on the one hand, and affirming the appropriateness of their high status on the other. It is not a marker for a statement claiming the unquestionable authority of the classics as a proof of truth, but comes in a larger context that provides the evidence for the access of the classics to truth.

The analysis of one example netted a fourfold specification of the hypothesis. To verify the plausibility of the hypotheses and the specifications and perhaps add others, I will now go through the next examples as they occur in Wang Bi's commentary.

經；上九 亢龍有悔 用九見群龍 無首 吉
注：九天之德也 能用天德 乃見群龍之義焉
夫 以剛健而居人之首　　則物之所不與也
　　以柔順而為不正之主[31]　**則佞邪之道也**
故 乾吉在無首
　　坤利在永貞 也

Text: Unbroken line in the top position: An overpowering dragon will have cause of regret. [But] when making [proper] use of the unbroken line, he will be showing it to the many dragons. Not being their head [=overpowering leader] is where fortune lies.

Wang's Commentary: "The unbroken (*yang*) line signals the receipt/capacity of heaven. Being able to make [proper] use of this heavenly receipt/capacity has the meaning of 'showing [the right way] to the many dragons.'
Fu,
if [a ruler] makes use of rigour and strength [that is, *qian* 乾], but has his place as the head [=as the overpowering leader] over others, he will be one with whom the others will not associate;
if [a ruler] makes use of softness and obedience [that is, *kun* 坤], but acts as a lord who is not orthodox, this is the way of [bringing about] viciousness and heterodoxy [among those below].
That is why the 'fortunateness' of *qian* is in 'not acting as the head,' and the 'benefit' of *kun* is in being 'perpetually orthodox.'"[32]

---

31 The characters *zhi zhu* 之主 are added on the basis of the Guben 古本 and Zuliben 足利本 manuscript quoted in Ruan Yuan 阮元, *Zhouyi jiaokan ji* 周易校勘記, in Ruan Yuan ed., *Shisan jing zhushu: fu jiaokan ji* 十三經注疏: 附校勘記 (Beijing: Zhonghua shuju, 1987), 1.9b.

32 Lou Yulie, *Wang Bi ji jiaoshi*, 1.212–213. The statement about *kun* here quotes from a phrase about the top line in the *kun* hexagram. It runs: 用六 利永貞, "making use of the broken line will have benefits [for the ruler only] if he is perpetually orthodox." Hexagram *kun* is entirely composed of broken lines. Lou Yulie, *Wang Bi ji jiaoshi*, 1.228.

The *fu* sentence in this example precedes a statement similar to that in the first example. It is followed by two parallel phrases, both of which end this time with the copula *ye* 也. The initial *fu* again cannot be attributed only to the first of the two phrases, but pertains to the statement as a whole. The *fu* phrase is non-narrative and argues a general principle. It exemplifies it with two antonymic cases, the ruler who uses the features of the *qian* hexagram, namely rigour and strength, but then exaggerates this feature by lording it over the others; and the ruler who uses the soft features of the *kun* hexagram, but then exaggerates the 'softness' of these features by being cunning, sly, and 'not correct.' Both deviations end up being counterproductive, the ruler following the first has no officials who will support him to bring order, and the ruler following the second deforms the bureaucracy and society through his model. That is the "cause for regret" of the *Zhouyi* text. The *fu* phrase here brings together parallel statements in both the *qian* and the *kun* hexagrams and tersely shows in rigid parallelism the philosophical principle underlying the canonical narrative, which in itself seems vague.

The philosophical character of the *fu* phrase here is evident from it being counterintuitive. Of course, the ruler who uses "rigour and strength" will be expected to be a strong boss over the others, and the ruler who rules by being "soft and accommodating" will be expected to have cunning ways of getting his will. A highly rational and counterintuitive principle of political philosophy is extracted from statements in two parallel hexagrams which in themselves are rather cryptic. The *fu* sentence shows its function as the philosophical explanation providing the bridge between the first part of the text that is commented upon (*yong jiu jian qunlong* 用九 見群龍) with the second (*wushou ji* 無首 吉) by being continued with a 'that is why' *gu* 故. This *gu* confirms the notion that what was previously stated was a principle or a general rule, as it is now applied to a specific textual passage. What comes after this *gu* is not the new insight, but a recapitulation of the text itself, which is now to be re-read in the new light provided by the preceding *fu* sentence. For this reason *gu* should not be translated as 'therefore' but as 'that is why [the text says].'[33] This means that only by way of the *fu* phrase will the reader be able to understand the underlying reason for the two counterintuitive statements about the *qian* and *kun*

---

33   *Gu* 故 is another literary device to structure an argument that has not been properly analyzed. In the textual environment of Xuanxue, it is followed by something familiar to the reader—often, as in this case, a verbatim quotation from the text Wang Bi comments on. The new argument or principle precedes the *gu* rather than follow it. The reader is expected to revisit a familiar phrase or proposition in the light of the new interpretive framework given before the *gu*. It therefore has an emphatic character: "This [and not what other commentators might have told you] is the reason for ... [the text saying xyz]!" See Wagner, *Craft*, 264–265.

hexagrams. In terms of political philosophy, the argument ties in closely with Wang Bi's arguments in the *Laozi* commentary.

The passage confirms hypothesis 1 by being a rhetorical marker; hypothesis 2 by spelling out the philosophical basis for a canonical text; hypothesis 3 by being non-narrative; and hypothesis 4 by spelling out in a rational way the principle underlying a canonical text. While the resulting political philosophy might be one that is closely associated with Wang Bi, its insertion into the *Zhouyi* as providing the key to the understanding of its cryptic utterances makes at least a claim that this political philosophy is not the predilection of just a school or even a single person, but the underlying thinking of the classics. This twofold status enhancement, of the classic as a philosophically grounded text, and of Wang Bi's philosophy as a key to unlock the teaching of the Sages, has the intended effect of not just appealing to a reader's common sense or previously shared opinions, but of convincing him of the correctness of this philosophy through the fit between the statements in the *fu* phrases and the structural pattern dominating this canonical text. The success of Wang Bi's reading in later Chinese history should be kept in mind in this context.

This might be the moment to suggest a way to make the content of initial *fu* explicit. I suggest going from the non-translation of initial *fu* as an 'empty' character all the way to the opposite end by making very explicit what is implied in the use of this word. The reason for such a radicalism is that for the reader of a translation—and every modern reader, including the scholar with Chinese as his or her native language as well as the Japanese or Western sinologist, is understanding these early Chinese texts through an implicit or explicit translation into a modern vernacular—the particular functions of initial *fu* have to be boldly marked and highlighted to help the reader understand the way the argument is made, to guide an informed reading strategy, and to achieve optimal precision of understanding.

My cumbersome suggestion would be that initial *fu* is a status marker for statements of principle that might appropriately be translated as 'it is a general rule or principle that....' Needless to say, this verbalization of the functions of a rhetorical marker is just an attempt to express its functions in detail. In any given specific situation, other, and shorter, forms might be found to signal the status of the ensuing phrase. For the two examples hitherto studied this would give "*[i]t is a general principle that a position will be brought to full fruition through receipt/capacity, and that receipt/capacity will provide order by means of a position,*" and "*[i]t is a general rule that if [a ruler] makes use of rigour and strength [that is, qian* 乾*], but has his place as the head [=as the boss] over others, he will be one with whom the others will not associate; if [a ruler] makes use of softness and obedience [that is, kun* 坤*], but plays the lord who is not orthodox, this is the way of [bringing about] viciousness and heterodoxy [among those below].*"

The third example explains the first phrase in the *tuan* 彖 statement for the *qian* 乾 hexagram, 大哉乾元 萬物資始 乃統天, "Great indeed is *qian* in its being the origin! The ten thousand kinds of entities draw on it for their beginning and thus it encompasses heaven." The commentary starts:

天　也者 形之名也
乾[34] 也者 用形者也
夫 形　也者 物之累也
有天之形 而能永保無虧
為物之首 統之者
豈非至健哉

Heaven [while being great] is [still] the denomination of a form [insofar as it is restricted to covering all, but not able to support all, which is what earth does]. *Qian* is that which is making use of this form [of heaven]. **It is a general principle that form is that which binds entities [to particularity].** To have the [limited] form of heaven, but still be able to be preserved eternally without decay, and as the head over the entities be that which holds them together, how could this be anything but [as the 'Xici' says] 'the highest strength'?![35]

This *fu* phrase again ends with a *ye* 也. The insertion of this phrase is of crucial importance for explaining the exclamation at the beginning. The first two definitions on heaven and strength also have the definitional 也者 but they stay within the language and particulars of the *Zhouyi*. The *fu* phrase alone articulates a general principle. It defines entities as being bound and limited by form, even entities of the 'great' kind such as heaven. Limited by form also means being subject to the vagaries of time. The inserted phrase does not follow from the immediate context, and is not an echo of a statement somewhere else in the *Zhouyi* or its wings. At the same time, it is a definition that appeals to immediate acceptance. Once the argument is set up that even heaven is the name

---

34 乾 for 健 on the basis of the sub-commentary by Kong Yingda, as first suggested by Guo Jing.

35 Lou Yulie, *Wang Bi jijiaoshi*, 1.213. The last phrase does not seem well transmitted. 為物之首 統之者 does not hold well grammatically. As the text just quoted above made it clear that *wu shou* 無首 "not acting up as the head" brings good fortune, *ji* 吉, it is not clear why here 'being the head' should be extolled. I assume the text might have read in roughly parallel fashion 有天之形而能永保無虧 不為物之首 而統之者 豈非至健哉. "To have the [limited] form of heaven, but still be able to be preserved eternally without decay, not to be acting as the head over the entities, but still be that which holds them together, how could this be anything but the highest strength?!" My reading of the *fu* phrase does not hinge on this conjecture. The 至健 takes up a statement in the "Xici," 夫 乾天下之至健也 "Generally it is true that *qian* is the highest strength under the sky." Lou Yulie, *Wang Bi jijiaoshi*, 2.537.

of something that has a form, the general statement that forms are what limits and binds entities presents no challenge. However, for the subsequent rhetorical question it is only through this insertion that the description of the highest or ultimate strength that is beyond big and small makes sense. The *da zai* 大哉 is then linked to the *zhi jian* 至健 in the "Xici," and both signal something of an absolute order that makes use of forms, but is not bound by them.

Again it should be noted that the theme of name and form, and that of the nameless and formless is a very specific Xuanxue topic that is much explored by Wang Bi. Still, the *fu* phrase cannot be said to make an argument through a backdoor imposition. While there is no hard proof here that *fu* might not be a topical marker referring only to *xing* 形, the main point of the phrase is in the second part, and our hypotheses are all supported by this example.

The fourth example occurs in Wang Bi's comments on the "Wenyan" 文言 commentary to the third unbroken line counting from the bottom.

文言：九三曰 君子終日乾乾 夕惕若厲 無咎 何謂也
子曰
　君子
進德 修業
忠信 所以進德也 修辭立其誠 所以居業也³⁶
知至 至之 可與幾也 知終 終之 可與存義也

注：
處一體之極 是至也 居一卦之盡 是終也
處事之至而不犯咎 知至者也 處終而能令³⁷ 其終 知終者也
　故可與成務矣 [lacuna]
　夫
進物之速者 義不若利 存物之終者 利不及義
　故
靡不有初 鮮克有終
　夫 可與存義者 其唯知終者乎

"Wenyan": "What does it mean that the [text accompanying the] unbroken line in the third position says 'If the gentleman will be active all day and even in the evening he still takes care, he will suffer no blame'?" The master said:

"The gentleman
advances [his] receipt/capacity and cultivates [his] task.
It is honesty and trustworthiness and it is through carefully choosing
through which he advances [his] [his] words and establishing his

---

36　There is a probable transmission mistake here. Either it should be 修業 in both cases or 居業.

37　令 instead of 全 based on one MS quoted in the *Siku quanshu* edition.

receipt/capacity;

Insofar as he understands getting to [the beginning] and brings about this getting to, it is possible for him to join in getting near [to duties being achieved].

truthfulness that he settles [his] task.

understands bringing things to a conclusion, and brings them to this conclusion, it is possible for him to join in preserving righteousness.

Wang Bi Commentary:

[This line], is situated [below] the [lower] extreme of the [upper] trigram, this is what [the text refers to with] "getting to [the beginning]."

is positioned at the end point of the [lower] trigram, this is [what the text refers to with] "conclusion."

Being situated at the starting point of a process and not committing something that will have to be regretted is [what the text means by] "[he] understands getting to [the beginning]."

Being situated at the end [of a process], and being able to keep it fully intact to its end is [what the text means by] "[he] understands bringing things to a conclusion."

That is why [the person occupying this line] is "able to join" in getting assignments done.

Lacuna.[38]

As a general principle it is a fact that
as far as the speed of bringing things forward is concerned, righteousness cannot compare to profit.

as far as keeping things together to their end is concerned, profit does not even get close to righteousness.

That is why [as the "Daya" of the *Book of Songs* says]

"there is nothing that does not have a beginning [but]

few [things] manage to have a proper conclusion."[39]

As a matter of general principle it is a fact that
only the one for whom it "is possible to join in preserving righteousness" is the person who "understands bringing things to their conclusion."[40]

We have two *fu* sentences here. Neither one ends with a *ye* 也. The first is followed by a pair of parallel segments, to both of which it pertains. The first

---

38 There is a lacuna in the text here that parallels 故可與成務矣 of the phrase about 知至. It should run about as follows: 故可與存義矣 or offer a "translation" of 存義. This is confirmed by the parallelism in the "Wenyan" text. I also assume that 處終 should be 處事之終.

39 *Maoshi* 毛詩, no. 245.

40 Lou Yulie, *Wang Bi ji jiaoshi*, 1.214.

segment provides a principle underlying a factual statement in the "Wenyan." For this purpose it takes up one of the terms offered by this text, namely *yi* 義, righteousness, and contrasts it with another term not offered there but 'supplemented' as its regular antonym, namely *li* 利, profit, to arrive at a general philosophical statement concerning the fundaments of effective state management. The antonymic pairing of *li* and *yi* is familiar from many discussions about state management. The sentence confirms all of our four hypotheses. The concluding *fu* sentence drives home the lesson by abandoning the parallel style symmetry, combining in this way two status markers, a structural one that marks the phrase as a general statement pertaining to both of the parallel chains, and a second one through the initial *fu*. It picks up and explains the imbalance between the parallel statements about *zhi* 至 and *zhong* 終 in the "Wenyan," which is signalled by the fact that only *zhong* is adorned with a high register term, namely righteousness, and drives home the point in the form of an abstract principle. Again our hypotheses apply.

We conclude this round with the last two examples from hexagram 1. In the comment to the "Wenyan" about the unbroken line at the top of the first hexagram, Wang Bi writes in a mock dialogue form that patterns itself on the "Wenyan":

乾文言 首不論乾 而先說元 下乃曰乾 何也
夫 乾者 統行四事者也 君子以自強不息行此四者 故首不論乾 而下曰乾元亨利貞

The 'Wenyan' on [hexagram] *qian* initially does not talk about *qian*, but only after having explained *yuan* 元 [and the other three, *heng* 亨, *li* 利 and *zhen* 貞] it speaks about *qian*. Why?

> "*As a matter of general principle*, *qian* is that which overarchingly acts out these four qualities [of *yuan*, *heng*, *li*, and *zhen*]. It is because [as the *xiang* 象 commentary to this hexagram says] 'the gentleman will by way of strengthening himself without rest' practice these four that initially [the "Wenyan"] does not talk about *qian*, but [only] further down says '*qian* is [=encompasses] *yuan*, *heng*, *li*, and *zhen*.'"[41]

The *fu* phrase here offers a definition of *qian* that is well documented and confirms the rational correctness of the "Wenyan" explanation. Again our hypotheses are supported.

The last example again offers a mock question-and-answer sequence.

餘爻 皆說龍 至於九三 獨以君子為目 何也

---

41   Ibid., 1.215.

夫 易者象也 象之所生 生於義也 有斯義然後明之以其物 故以龍叙乾 以馬明坤 隨其事義而取象焉 是故初九九二 龍德皆應其義 故可論龍以明之也 至於九三 '乾乾夕惕' 非龍德也 明以君子當其象矣 統而舉之 乾體皆龍 別而叙之 各隨其義也

The remaining lines [in hexagram *qian*] are all explained [by the line commentaries] with reference to the dragon. When it gets to the unbroken line in the third position [the line commentary] makes an exception and makes the gentleman the topic. Why?

> "*As a matter of general principle it is a fact that* the [*Zhou*]*yi* is [=consists of] images. What generates the images lives from the meaning [intended by the Sages]. Once [they] had a given meaning, they would illustrate it through the appropriate object. That is the reason why they use the dragon to sketch [the meaning of] *qian*, and the horse to illustrate [the meaning of] *kun*, taking images according to the meaning of the matter under consideration. In this sense, for the first and second unbroken lines the receipt/capacity of the dragon corresponded to the meaning—and that is why it was possible to talk about the dragon to explain their [meaning]. Getting to the third unbroken line, the 'active, active, evenings [still] worried' is not [part of] the receipt/capacity of the dragon and illustrating it by way of the gentleman fits this image. Altogether, the substance of *qian* is dragon throughout, but when deviations are detailed, they each correspond to a particular meaning."[42]

This radical definition transforms the *Zhouyi* from an oracle handbook into a philosophical text. As the meaning intended by the Sages defied definitional language, the images serve as a pointer beyond themselves to this meaning. By defining the *Zhouyi* as images, Wang Bi took up much of the structure of the *Zhouyi* itself with its *xiang* commentaries as well as statements in the "Xici" about the way in which the *Zhouyi* had been created by the Sages. At the same time, this definition offered the foundation for Wang Bi's own interpretive strategy, which has come to dominate the Chinese interpretive tradition. Wang Bi further elaborated on this in the "Ming xiang" 名象 (Explaining the images) section of his "*Zhouyi* lüeli" (ZYLL).[43]

In a second step, I will now move to a more quantitative approach to define the types of sentences following after initial *fu*. The data will be the 49 *fu* sentences in Wang Bi's *Zhouyi* commentary[44] and 14 *fu* sentences in his ZYLL.[45] Of the 63 *fu* sentences of the sample, 27 (19/8) are followed by parallel segments

---

42 Lou Yulie, *Wang Bi ji jiaoshi*, 1.215–216.
43 Lou Yulie, *Wang Bi ji jiaoshi*, 2.609.
44 In hexagrams 1(7), 2(2), 3(2), 4(1), 8(5), 9(6), 12(1), 14–16, 26, 27, 32, 34, 42, 44–45, 47, 48 (one each), 49(2), 51(1), 52(1), 54(1), 56(2), 57(1), 62(1), 63(3), 64(1).
45 "Ming tuan" 明彖 (5), "Ming yao" 明爻 (2), "Ming gua" 明卦 (3), "Ming xiang" 明象 (1), "Bian wei" 辯位 (2), "Gua lüe" 卦略 (1).

with the single initial *fu* pertaining to the entire pair.⁴⁶ 28(26/2) make an analytical statement of the kind "**As a matter of general principle it is a fact that** only the one for whom it "is possible to join in preserving righteousness" is the person who "understands bringing things to their conclusion;"⁴⁷ and eight give a definition of the kind "it is a matter of general principle that form is that which binds entities [to particularity]."⁴⁸

Under these circumstances it seems that the traditional notion of initial *fu* as a topical marker is not further helpful for our analysis. Initial *fu* is used here throughout as a status marker for statements and definitions of a general philosophical nature. Understanding its function is in fact crucial to understand the argumentative strategy and result. The phrases throughout confirm the hypothesis and its specifications as outlined above. In the ZYLL, the *fu* phrases are not inserted into a commentarial environment, but offer the underpinnings of Wang Bi's own argument. Within the *Zhouyi Commentary*, they are inserted as key philosophical underpinnings of *Zhouyi* utterances that themselves have no visible philosophical content or connection. Of the 49 *fu* phrases in the *Zhouyi* commentary, 15 are followed by a 'that is why.'⁴⁹ In the ZYLL the 'that is why' normally does not refer to a verbatim formula used in the main text, but rather to a pervasive structure of the main text. Three of the 14 items have such a *gu*.⁵⁰

---

46   In Wang's comments to Hex. 1(3), 2(2), 3(1), 4(1), 8(1), 9(1), 14(1), 27(1), 32(1), 42(1), 43(1), 47(2), 49(1), 56(1), 63(1). In his ZYLL "Ming tuan" (3), "Ming gua" (3), "Ming xiang" (1), "Gua lüe" (1). There is one case in the first section of the ZYLL with two subsequent parallel phrases, each one starting with a *fu*. 夫 眾不能治眾 治眾者至寡者也 夫動不能制動 制天下之動者貞夫一者也. The reason is that the first statement comes with a complete conclusion in a separate sentence, as does the second. This makes it unmanageable to have a single *fu* linking and marking both items.

47   In Wang's comments to Hex. 3(1), 8(4), 9(5), 12(1), 15(1), 16(1), 26(1), 34(1), 44(1), 45(1), 49(1), 51(1), 52(1), 54(1), 57(1), 62(1), 63(2), 64(1). In his ZYLL "Ming tuan" (1), "Ming yao" (1).

48   In Wang's comments to Hex. 1(4) and in his ZYLL "Ming tuan" (1), "Ming yao" (1), "Bian wei" (2). The definitions are better represented in the ZYLL because it gives a systematic analysis of the structure of the *Zhouyi*. There are two items, where *fu* serves to introduce a philosophical definition with a rhetorical question, 夫 象者何也. Even in this case, I would not think it is right to treat *fu* just as a marker of the beginning (although this is the beginning of the entire ZYLL), but would suggest a translation: "What, as a matter of general principle, is a *tuan*?" The second item starts the section "Ming yao tongbian." It refers to two such definitions. 夫 爻者何也 言乎變者也 變者何也 情偽之所為也, "What, as a matter of general principle, is a line statement? It is that which verbalizes a transformation; and what [as a matter of general principle] is a transformation? It is that which brings about the true and the false." Lou Yulie, *Wang Bi ji jiaoshi*, 2.597.

49   In Wang's comments to Hex. 1(3), 9(1), 15(1), 17(1), 32(1), 42(1), 45(1), 49(1), 51(1), 54(1), 57(1), 63(1), 64(1).

50   In Wang's ZYLL two are in the "Ming tuan," and one is in the "Ming yao."

In the entire body of Wang Bi's surviving writings, I have not found a single item that did not fit the analysis given here. We are therefore entitled to reverse the strategy. Instead of proving piece by piece that a given initial *fu* again is used in this manner, we can now assume that all phrases in Wang Bi with initial *fu* must be reckoned as statements of a general [unknown and new] principle or definition. And in a further step—one that is not taken here—this would enable us to locate many if not most of Wang Bi's statements of general principle or philosophical definition by looking for the phrases with initial *fu*. We have analysed initial *fu* as it occurs in a corpus of texts that is narrowly circumscribed in terms of time, genre and content. To situate initial *fu* in the history of Chinese language and argument, I will now trace the history of this feature.

A Sketch of the History of Initial *fu*

Rhetorical devices have their history and particular context. While we may safely say that initial *fu* as defined above is consistently used in Wang Bi's writings, this theoretically could be a stylistic idiosyncrasy. We will therefore go backward through a selection of earlier texts to check this assumption and, if possible, trace the path from a demonstrative use of initial *fu* to becoming the marker of a phrase of general validity. Examples will be given in the notes.

Wang Fu's 王符 (circa 76?–157? AD) *Qianfu lun* 潛夫論 is a well preserved highly argumentative text. It has 127 sentences with initial *fu*, distributed across all thirty-six chapters but numbers 3, 15, and 34. Of these only one occurrence is demonstrative.[51] The proportion of these uses indicates that the use of initial *fu* as a phrase status marker for a statement of general validity had stabilized well before Wang Bi and that demonstrative use was becoming very rare indeed. In their great majority, the initial *fu* sentences in the *Qianfu lun* are at the beginning of an argument. This position, which we also find in Wang Bi's theoretical essays on the *Zhouyi* and the *Laozi* as well as in later non-narrative texts, has led to the assumption that they are simply markers for a paragraph break. Modern editors in turn have based their layout on this assumption.

---

51 Lao, D.C., Chen Fangzheng (Chen Fong Ching) 陳方正 comp., *Qianfu lun zhuzi suoyin* 潛夫論逐字索引, CHANT database (Hong Kong: Commercial Press, 1995). Example for initial *fu* as a phrase status marker: 夫 聖人為天口 賢者為聖譯 是故聖人之言 天之心也 賢者之所說 聖人之意也 (ch. 7) ("As a general principle, the sages act as heaven's mounts and the worthies as the translators of the sages. Therefore the words of the sages are the mind of heaven and what the worthies explain is the meaning of the sages"). The only example for demonstrative use will be found in ch. 35.

Going one step back to a similar type of text, Wang Chong's 王充 (27–97?) *Lunheng* 論衡, we find him using initial *fu* 172 times in the first 20 of his 85 chapters. Of these, 166 occurrences mark sentences of general validity, one is demonstrative,[52] and there are six occurrences of phrases beginning with *fu ru shi* 夫如是, a highly idiosyncratic phrase beginning in Wang Chong that is as rare in other pre-Han and Han texts (one or two occurrences) as it is frequent in the *Lunheng* (44 occurrences). As demonstrative *fu* always refers to specific entities such as persons and never to situations or processes and as all occurrences of 夫如是 here present arguments, I suggest to read them as marking statements of general validity and translate *fu ru shi* as "As a matter of general principle, [things] being like this …." The use of initial *fu* in Wang Chong shows the same high consistency as the later texts already studied.

Liu An's 劉安 (ca. 179–122 BC) *Huainanzi* 淮南子 (mid 2nd cent. BC) has many occurrences of initial *fu* in chapters 1, 2, 6, 7, 9, 11, 12, and 20.[53] All 33 occurrences in chapter 1, one of the two chapters studied by Hans van Ess, conform to the definition. In many cases, the general principle there refers to a principle underlying a process in nature rather than, as in the examples studied hitherto, in society. 14 of these 33 occurrences are followed by a 'that is why,' 故 or 是故, which make the link to a previously stated principle explicit. Random checks in the other chapters confirmed the consistent use.

Jia Yi's 賈誼 (200–168 BC) *Xinshu* 新書 has a use of initial *fu* with eighty occurrences followed by a statement claiming general validity. There is no demonstrative use. To this has to be added his idiosyncratic formula *gu fu* 故夫 with twenty occurrences in these chapters. As these all contain statements of general validity, I suggest translating them as "that is why as a matter of general principle …." Importantly, Jia Yi does not [yet] use initial *fu* regularly at the beginning of an argument to ground it, but mostly at the end to sum it up.

Lü Buwei's 呂不韋 (291–235 BC) *Lüshi chunqiu* 呂氏春秋 (239 BC) already has the same consistent use, as a check through the 38 occurrences of initial *fu* in the first ten chapters shows.[54]

---

52 Example for use as phrase status marker in the *Lunheng*: 夫比不應事 未可謂喻 文不稱實 未可謂是也 (As a general rule, if a comparison does not fit the matter at hand, one cannot call it a metaphor and if a statement does not correspond to reality, one cannot call it truthful). The only example for demonstrative use: 夫秦王者 秦始皇帝也 (THIS [previously mentioned] "King of Qin" is none other than Qin Shi Huangdi).

53 Lao, D.C., Chen Fangzheng (Chen Fong Ching) 陳方正 comp., *Huainanzi zhuzi suoyin* 淮南子逐字索引, CHANT database (Hong Kong: Commercial Press, 2003). Example: 夫 道者 覆天載地 廓四方 柝八極 高不可際 深不可測 包裹天地 稟授無形 (ch. 1) ("As a general principle, the Dao covers heaven and carries earth, extends the four directions, opens up the eight extreme points, [its] height being unlimited, [its] depth unfathomable, it embraces heaven and earth and endows the shapeless").

54 Lao, D.C., Chen Fangzheng (Chen Fong Ching) 陳方正 comp., *Lüshi chunqiu zhuzi suoyin*

The authors preceding Wang Bi, who have been studied here, all also make frequent use of initial *fan* 凡, another phrase status marker that sometimes even occurs in the same paragraph as initial *fu*. This has not been studied here in detail so that a definition of its differences with *fu* has to be left to further research.

I conclude that Wang Bi's use of initial *fu* was not idiosyncratic, but followed a routine firmly established at least since the latter part of the third century BC. Within this now established rhetorical practice, different authors still differed in its particular use. Whether an author would push for philosophical insights that might be radically new and even counterintuitive, restate more generally accepted and perhaps less surprising principles, or would deal with principles underlying natural processes, they were all operating within the same rhetorical convention. As this is a practice and not a law, it cannot be excluded that rare exceptions still persisted.

As may be expected, the use of initial *fu* is much less frequent in narrative texts. Sima Qian's 司馬遷 (circa 140–86 BC) *Shiji* 史記 is a work strong in narrative but without a strong authorial voice stating matters of general principle. In the direct speeches, however, which the *Shiji* amply attributes to or quotes from historical actors, we find altogether about 44 occurrences of initial *fu* marking statements of general principle or definition.[55] Here, we have two phrase status markers, one, initial *fu*, marking the general precedent, and the other, initial *jin* 今, marking the application to the case at hand, as is frequent in legal documents. In his own statements, Sima Qian uses the feature only once, saying "As a matter of general fact, I have no knowledge whatever of the time before Shennong" 夫 神農以前 吾不知已, a sentence that neatly describes the historical time frame for which he could claim to have reliable evidence.[56]

Pushing further back in time, we find that initial *fu* was used in two different functions during the Warring States period, one being the status marker stud-

---

呂氏春秋逐字索引, CHANT database (Hong Kong: Commercial Press, 2003). Example: 夫 以德得民心以立大功名者 上世多有之矣 失民心而立功名者 未之曾有也 (ch. 9.2) ("As a general rule, to reach people's hearts through virtue and thus establish merit and fame was frequent in olden times, but it has never happened that someone failed to win the people's hearts but established merit and fame").

55 Example: 夫 種蠡無一罪 身死亡 今僕有三罪於陛下 而欲求活於世 此伍子胥所以僨於吳也 ("As a matter of principle, that Zhong and Li committed no crime whatever, but [still] went to their death, while I now have committed three crimes before your Majesty and still want to continue to live in this world, this is a case of Wu Zixu failing in Wu"). Sima Qian 司馬遷, *Shiji* 史記 (Beijing: Zhonghua shuju, 1973), 93.2635. Here, we have two phrase status markers, one, initial *fu*, marking the general precedent, and the other, initial *jin* 今, marking the application to the case at hand, as is frequent in legal documents.

56 Ibid., 129.3253.

ied here, the other being that of a demonstrative. For either use no early examples have been found in in the standard sources, namely oracle bones, the *Shijing*, *Shangshu* or Western Zhou bronzes.[57]

An example for the use of initial *fu* as a demonstrative in the beginning of a sentence will be found in the *Zuozhuan*. Reacting to the statement "Although Chu has talents [enough], it is Jin that makes use of them," Zimu is quoted as saying: 子木曰 夫 獨無族姻乎 "Are **they** [Jin] alone in not going by clan and in-laws [in assigning government jobs, R.W.]?"[58] The commentator Du Yu 杜預 (222–284) confirms this demonstrative use with his comment: 夫 謂晉 "*fu* refers to [the state of] Jin." The sentence is part of a narrative dialogue and does not state a principle. Indeed, in all narrative sentences that start with an initial *fu*, its meaning is demonstrative. The dividing line between the two kinds of initial *fu* is neither graphic nor phonetic, but whether the sentence that follows is narrative or states a principle. If the use is demonstrative, this also presupposes that the object has been mentioned previously. The use as a demonstrative was never widespread and ended by the late third century BC. This did not affect the use of *fu* 夫 as a demonstrative pronoun **within** a phrase as in the *Zuozhuan* statement: 日君以夫公孫段為能任其事而賜之州田 "Because the luminous lord considered THIS Gongsun Duan as capable, he entrusted this affair to him and gave him an enfeoffment of Zhoutian."[59] Examples of this kind will be found as late as the Ming and Qing.

The use of initial *fu* as a status marker is much more widespread already in the pre-Qin period. Because of the difficulty of dating pre-Qin texts with any precision, it will be possible to determine that initial *fu* was used as a status marker in argumentative texts of this period, but no clear chronology can be given. Some early texts do make consistent and some even frequent use of the device. They might have been instrumental in establishing the routine. The six cases where it is used in the *Xiaojing* all correspond to this pattern. An example: 子曰 夫 孝 德之本也 教之所由生也 "The Master said: 'As a matter of general principle, filial piety is the basis of receipt/capacity and it is that on the basis of which education comes about.'"[60] The *Sunzi* with its highly sententious offerings of a systematic theoretical treatment of war has ten occurrences, all of them fully consistent with the later pattern.[61] The most

---

57   Wang Weifeng, "Fu," 67.
58   *Zuozhuan*, Duke Xiang 襄公 26th year. In Ruan Yuan 阮元 ed., *Chongkan Song ban Zuozhuan zhushu: fu jiaokan ji* 重栞宋板左傳注疏: 附校勘記 (Shanghai: Jinzhang shuju, 1932), 635.
59   *Zuozhuan*, Duke Zhao 昭公, 7th year, ibid., 763.
60   Ruan Yuan 阮元 ed., *Xiaojing, Chongkan Song ban Xiaojing zhushu: fu jiaokan ji* 重栞宋板孝經注疏: 附校勘記 (Shanghai: Jinzhang shuju, 1932), 10.
61   *Sunzi bingfa* 孫子兵法 (Changsha: Yue Lu shushe, 1993).

extensive use of initial *fu* in pre-Han texts will be found in the *Guanzi* 管子, where I count no less than 242 occurrences that fit the pattern. They are especially frequent in chapters four (13), six (20), nine (45), fifteen (66), seventeen (35), twenty-one (12), and twenty-three (15).[62]

The *Laozi* in the reconstructed Wang Bi edition shows 27 occurrences of initial *fu*, which for such a short text is a large number. Of these nine have the formula *fu wei* 夫唯 (2, 8, 15, 15, 22, 70, 71, 72, 75);[63] in eight cases this formula is followed by a *gu* 故 or *shiyi* 是以 in the beginning of the next segment, giving a meaning "and it is a fact that only because of X the result will be Y," while five more just have *fu* 夫 followed by *gu* 故 or *shiyi* 是以 in the next segment. The remaining occurrences such as *fu hegu* 夫 何故 in *zhang* 50 might be leftovers from the demonstrative use of initial *fu* that predates its consolidation into a standard rhetorical device. The *Laozi* makes use of initial *fu* to stake general claims about counterintuitive dynamics. "It is exactly because he [the Sage] does not install [himself in these particular achievements] that they do not disappear." 夫 唯不居 是以不去.[64] Only in one single case (zhang 38) does it use *fu* for a general definitional statement.

夫 禮者 忠信之薄而亂之首也 前識者 道之華而愚之首也

> It is a general principle [, however,] that ritual is [the result of the] wearing thin of truthfulness and credibility and [thus] the beginning of [social] chaos; while foreknowledge is [the result] of the Way's becoming an [external] ornament and [thus] the beginning of stupidity [=inept tyranny].

The use of initial *fu* is highly consistent within the *Laozi*, even if it differs idiosyncratically from that of other texts. It marks statements of general validity.

The *Lunyu* quotes Confucius several times with initial *fu* phrases, and with one single exception (17.4) they fit the notion of *fu* as a status marker. These uses range from general definitions such as 夫 仁者 …, "As a matter of principle, someone with humaneness is …" (6.30) 夫 達者 …, "As a matter of principle someone with attainment it is …" (12.20) 夫 君子之居喪 …" As a matter of principle the gentleman when in mourning will …" (17.21) to emphatic markers to set off his own practice from that of others as in 夫 我則不暇 … (14.29).[65] With

---

62 Lao, D.C., Chen Fangzheng (Chen Fong Ching) 陳方正 comp., *Guanzi zhuzi suoyin* 管子逐字索引 (Hong Kong: Commercial Press, 2001).
63 The two Mawangdui texts share this feature with one exception (71). The only overlap with the Guodian Laozi is ch. 2, where Guodian A also has the *fu*.
64 *Laozi* 2.5. The formula is in both the Guodian A and the MWD B mss.
65 Yang Bojun 楊伯峻, *Lunyu yi zhu* 論語譯注 (Beijing: Zhonghua shuju, 2006), 72, 146, 212, 175.

altogether ten such occurrences, the *Lunyu* reflects a use of initial *fu* that is fairly consistent. Given the strong elements of spoken language in the *Lunyu*, the use of initial *fu* as a status marker might have its origin in oral communication. While the *Zhouyi* 周易 itself does not have any initial *fu*, two of its philosophical 'wings' do. The "Xici" (6) and "Wenyan" (2) segments both use initial *fu* in a routine manner in the sense outlined here without any deviation, which signals that these terse texts were drawing on an already established routine. The bamboo texts have by and large confirmed this sketch.

In these occurrences, features occur which develop more complex rhetorical patterns. One such pattern is the confrontation of a general principle introduced by *fu* with a particular act deviating from it introduced by *jin* 今;[66] another is the deduction of an 'inevitable' consequence flowing from the principle enunciated earlier, marked by *bi* 必;[67] and a third the application of the principle under consideration to the situation at hand with a *gu* 故, 'that is why ....'

Evidently, this is only a loose sketch made largely possible by the availability of full-text databases (CHANT, Siku quanshu, and Academia Sinica). It does show, however, that patterns can be discovered and that one might even use the innocent initial *fu* to test textual consistency and linkages between different versions of a given text. Initial *fu* fulfills one important feature familiar from authenticity studies in art history, namely that it is not a strong (terminological or argumentative) identifier that would be picked up by someone going for creative text enrichment or homogenization, but is rather a silent and innocuous device. At the same time its function as a phrase status marker offers an altogether different research option.

Conclusions

The study suggests: Initial *fú* is written 夫 in a loan from the homoiophonous *fū* 夫 'adult male.' It is differentiated by context from *fū* 夫 'adult male;' by position in the phrase from a homoiophonous word *fú* 'is it not so?' that is also written 夫 and terminates a phrase; and from demonstrative initial *fú* through the type of sentence it starts, namely a narrative phrase in the case of demonstrative initial *fú*, and an abstract subject with a definitional or argumentative phrase in the case of non-demonstrative initial *fú*.

Scholars have speculated that what I called the status marker might have developed out of the demonstrative, but the evidence seems weak. All uses of

---

66   Examples are *Lunyu* 17.21, *Guanzi* 5.52.30 and 5.53.9.
67   An example is *Guanzi* 4.32.5.

the character 夫 for particles developed during the Warring States period. Already during this period, initial *fu* followed by a statement of principle was used much more frequently than demonstrative initial *fu* with a narrative phrase following. By the late third century BC, the non-demonstrative use was the lone survivor, and words such as *bi* 彼 had replaced demonstrative initial *fu*. Only rare examples have been found for the use of demonstrative initial *fu* even in strongly narrative historical texts. Within sentences, however, *fu* 夫 continued to be used as a demonstrative, as this use was not burdened with ambiguity.

Some Warring States texts already made predominant or exclusive use of the phrase status marker function ("Xici" and "Wenyan" in *Zhouyi*; *Xiaojing*; *Sunzi*; *Laozi*; *Guanzi*). Their status and the presumed link to Confucius in the first three may have been instrumental in popularizing this usage. The development of initial *fu* into a phrase status marker for statements of abstract principle must be read in the context of the shift during the Warring States period to thinking in abstract categories and the need to develop a rhetoric of philosophical argument to express, structure, and hierarchize it.

Departing from the imported prioritization of the 'classics' or the 'classical' period in the study of grammar and rhetoric, the present study first looked at the rhetorical feature of this phrase status marker in its most developed and pervasive form by taking a mid-third century AD philosophical text (Wang Bi's *Zhouyi Commentary* and "Lüeli"). In an effort to avoid the standard mistake of including only examples that fit the argument it presented a randomized sample. Hypotheses were developed through the analysis of individual occurrences, and tested against the random sample.

The result showed a highly consistent use of the rhetorical feature of initial *fu*. It serves the overall function of a sentence status marker for statements of abstract principle. It refers to the entire subsequent sentence, which might consist of two parallel segments. These statements of principle are stated, not argued; their claim to validity is mostly agreement with the insights of the Sages as contained in their written bequests with which the readers are supposed to be familiar. (In Buddhist writings, this would refer to Buddhist "classics").

The proof is often contained in the convincing applicability of the principle stated in the *fu* sentence for deciphering the coding underlying these texts or for understanding real-world dynamics. Such proof is often highlighted by separate sentences that start with an expression such as 'that is why' *gu* 故, or by linked phrases that start with a *ze* 則 'as a consequence' and might contain a *bi* 必 ('by necessity') or a similar word.[68] The claim to validity might be counterintuitive, but it is implied that it should be convincing not just

---

68   This link has been highlighted by Wang Weifeng, "Fu."

in the contexts of the beliefs of a school or a time. The claim is a rational one. Acceptance does not hinge on religious belief or submission to authority. Given these features, *fu* phrases are concentrated in non-narrative argumentative genres.

While I would claim that the more formal features (such as status marker for statement of principle, non-narrative phrase and abstract subject, and concentration in non-narrative genres) are shared by all occurrences, there is some bandwidth in the content definition that needs to be further explored. The uses of this initial *fu* in texts after the third century AD have not been investigated in this study. Anecdotal evidence, which includes Chinese Buddhist writings and commentaries, suggests that the use of initial *fu* as a phrase status marker remained a staple in the rhetorical toolbox of Chinese argumentation until the shift to the modern vernacular.

The study has a philosophical implication by enhancing the precision in the understanding of arguments as it allows us to properly hierarchize different philosophical utterances. Its definition of initial *fu* furthermore can be used for very practical textual diagnosis: namely the location of such statements of principle so as to be able to insert them into a topical map of abstract principles that might be useful for studies of an individual author, of a group, or of broader questions in the history of ideas.

The fact that initial *fu* marks statements for which general validity is claimed does not imply that all such statements start with initial *fu*. It will require further research to ascertain whether statements thus marked share certain features that are not found in other statements with a claim to general validity, or whether use of initial *fu* is discretionary. While this means that no claim is made that all statements of this kind will be located (for the period after the stabilization of this use) by searching for initial *fu*, such a search will still yield substantial results of value for intellectual historians.

Apart from having to be subjected to further randomized tests (and possibly refinements of the analysis), the study suggests further explorations. One evident question would be whether the development of initial *fu* is part of a broader development of rhetorical tools to express abstract arguments. Initial *fan* 凡 is a case in point that has been mentioned. Interlocking parallel style (IPS) developed during the same time horizon as initial *fu* into such a tool. It came with its own status marker for a statement of abstract validity, namely the (normally) non-parallel concluding phrase after a string of interlocked parallel phrases going each through one half each of a totality (heaven/earth; fame/wealth; social standing/personal security; objects/processes, etc.).[69]

---

69   It will be noted that many modern authors writing on the *Laozi* have rightly, yet spontaneously—and without much understanding of the underlying interlocking parallel style pattern—selected these phrases as the mainstay of their analysis.

Even the innocently-looking *gu* 故 or *shiyi* 是以 might offer some surprises and would need more careful study.

Chinese writers of philosophical texts used a wide variety of tools that were in part purely structural and formal and in part explicitly rhetorical, to reduce ambiguity in the presentation of their arguments while staying within the conventions of terse and pointed language. One of their greatest challenges was in reducing ambiguity in their use of abstract concepts. Their standard techniques such as organizing arguments along mutually-defining antonyms have been supplemented by the sophisticated and consistent use of silent (structural) as well as articulated tools to clearly mark and structure statements. Initial *fu* 夫 is one of these tools.

References

Baxter, William H., and Laurent Sagart. *Old Chinese: a new reconstruction*. New York: Oxford University Press, 2014.

———. "The Baxter-Sagart reconstruction of Old Chinese (Version 1.1, 20 September 2014)." http://ocbaxtersagart.lsait.lsa.umich.edu/ (last access 06/03/2015).

Dongfang shudian 東方書店, ed. *Guoyu da cidian* 國語大辭典. Taipei: Dongfang shudian, 1972.

Graham, A. C. "The Final Particle 'Fwu' 夫." *Bulletin of the School of Oriental and African Studies* 17.1 (1955): 120–132.

———. "The Classical Chinese Topic-Marker fu 夫." *Bulletin of the School of Oriental and African Studies* 35.1 (1972): 85–110.

Harbsmeier, Christoph. "Chinese Rhetoric in Comparative Perspective." Unpublished manuscript, 2002.

Harbsmeier, Christoph, et al. "Thesaurus Linguae Sericae (TLS)." http://tls.uni-hd.de/ (last access 20/11/2014).

Lau, D. C., and Chen Fangzheng (Chen Fong Ching) 陳方正, eds. *Guanzi zhuzi suoyin* 管子逐字索引. Hong Kong: Commercial Press, 2001.

———, eds. *Huainanzi zhuzi suoyin* 淮南子逐字索引. Hong Kong: Commercial Press, 2003.

———, eds. *Lüshi chunqiu zhuzi suoyin* 呂氏春秋逐字索引. Hong Kong: Commercial Press, 2003.

———, eds. *Qianfu lun zhuzi suoyin* 潛夫論逐字索引. Hong Kong: Commercial Press, 1995.

Lou Yulie 樓宇烈, ed. *Wang Bi ji jiaoshi* 王弼集校釋. Beijing: Zhonghua shuju, 1999.

Luo Zhufeng 羅竹風, ed. *Hanyu da cidian* 漢語大詞典. Shanghai: Shanghai cishu chubanshe, 1986–1994.

Lynn, Richard. *I Ching*. New York: Columbia University Press, 1994.

Ma Jianzhong 馬建忠. *Ma shi wentong jiaozhu* 馬氏文通校注. Commentated by Zhang Xichen 張錫琛. Beijing: Zhonghua shuju, 1988.

Pei Xuehai 裴學海. *Gushu xuzi jishi* 古書虛字集釋. Beijing: Zhonghua shuju, 1954.

Ruan Yuan 阮元, ed. *Chongkan Song ban Zuozhuan zhushu: fu jiaokan ji* 重栞宋板左傳注疏: 附校勘記. Shanghai: Jinzhang shuju, 1932.

———, ed. *Chongkan Song ban Xiaojing zhushu: fu jiaokan ji* 重栞宋板孝經注疏: 附校勘記. Vol. 11. Shanghai: Jinzhang shuju, 1932.

———, ed. *Zhouyi jiaokan ji* 周易校勘記. In *Shisan jing zhushu: fu jiaokan ji* 十三經注疏: 附校勘記, vol.1, edited by Ruan Yuan. Beijing: Zhonghua shuju, 1987: 5–108.

Schindler, B. "Grammatical Notes II: 夫." *Asia Major*, N.S. III.2 (1953): 162–168.

Schoenhals, Michael. *Doing Things with Words in Chinese Politics: Five Studies*. China Research Monograph 41. Berkeley: Institute of Chinese Studies, University of California, 1976.

Shisan jing cidian bianzuan weiyuanhui 十三經辭典編纂委員會. *Shisan jing cidian* 十三經辭典. Xi'an: Shaanxi renmin chubanshe, 2002.

Sima Qian 司馬遷. *Shiji* 史記. Beijing: Zhonghua shuju, 1973.

Song Lian 宋濂 (1310–1381). *Pianhai leibian* 篇海類編. Shanghai: Shanghai guji chubanshe, 1995–1999.

Sunzi bingfa 孫子兵法. Changsha: Yue Lu shushe, 1993.

Van Ess, Hans. "Argument and Persuasion in the First Chapter of *Huainanzi* and its Use of Particles." *Oriens Extremus* 45 (2005): 255–270.

Wagner, Rudolf. *The Craft of a Chinese Commentator: Wang Bi on the Laozi*. Albany: SUNY Press, 2000.

———. *Language, Ontology and Political Philosophy in China. Wang Bi's Scholarly Exploration of the Dark (Xuanxue)*. Albany: SUNY Press, 2003.

———. *A Chinese Reading of the Daodejing: Wang Bi's commentary on the Laozi with critical text and translation*. Albany: SUNY Press, 2003.

Wang Haifen 王海棻. *Gu Hanyu xuci cidian* 古漢語虛詞詞典. Beijing: Beijing Daxue chubanshe, 1996.

Wang Weifeng 王衛峰. "'Fu' de tongshe lianjie gongneng lun" 夫的統攝連接功能論. *Gu Hanyu yanjiu* 古漢語研究 83.2 (2009): 63–68.

Xing Bing 邢昺. Sub-commentary in *Xiaojing zhushu* 孝經註疏. In Ruan Yuan 阮元 ed., *Shisanjing zhushu* 十三經注疏. Beijing: Zhonghua shuju, 1987: 2539–2561.

Xu Kuangyi 許匡一. *Huainanzi quanyi* 淮南子全譯. Guiyang: Guizhou renmin chubanshe, 1995.

Xu Weijian 許偉建, ed. *Shanggu Hanyu cidian* 上古漢語詞典. Changchun: Jilin wenshi chubanshe, 1998.

Yang Bojun 楊伯峻. *Lunyu yi zhu* 論語譯注. Beijing: Zhonghua shuju, 2006.

Zhou Fagao 周法高. *Zhongguo gudai yufa* 中國古代語法, *Chengdai pian* 稱代篇. Taipei: The Institute of History and Philology, 1959; reprint, Beijing: Zhonghua shudian, 1990.

CHAPTER 2

Beyond Parallelism: A Rethinking of Patterns of Coordination and Subordination in Chinese Expository Prose

Andrew H. Plaks

Among the papers collected in this volume dedicated to logical and rhetorical patterns of composition in Chinese texts, under the broad heading 'literary forms of argument,' a substantial number (those dealing with 'palindromic structures,' 'topological clusters,' 'two and three-step exposition,' 'semiotic webs,' 'tetra-syllabic rhythms' and the like) seem to focus on various techniques of verbal manipulation used to bind separate prose units into more complex discursive structures.[1] Most of these studies appear to take as more or less self-evident the observation that the fundamental grid of classical Chinese expository prose tends to take the form of sets of parallel utterances. Typically, these verbal strings are reeled out in sequences of equal numbers of characters, forming paired units that are to one extent or another isomorphic in their grammatical or syntactic function.[2] Such parallel constructions are most visible—in fact they form the aesthetic core—in *lüshi* ('regulated verse') and other major modes of classical Chinese poetry, but they are by no means absent—albeit in a number of different forms—in most genres of *guwen* ('ancient-style prose') composition. Even in the primarily non-classical mode of traditional fiction, paired lines continue to constitute a very prominent compositional feature, especially conspicuous in the conventional use of parallel couplets as chapter titles, reflecting a loose pairing of the main narrative units comprising a given chapter. When this paradigmatic use of parallel sequences is developed to such a degree that it comes to constitute the primary feature of a part or the whole of a given piece of prose or verse, we are justified in apply-

---

[1] The terms applied to such units vary widely, including such things as 'colon,' 'lemma' and others, depending upon their scale and function in a given analysis.

[2] Quantitative parallelism in Chinese prose was later regularized in various modes and genres, for example in what came to be known as 'four-six prose' (*siliuwen*), and in later periods produced parallel strings of extreme length in the so-called *bagu* ('four-legged') form used in examination essays, and in other genres of prose composition.

ing the Western term 'parallelism,' in which the 'ism' suffix serves to elevate this pattern to the level of an overarching mode of composition.³

In an early essay analysing the workings of this textual phenomenon in a comparative light: "Where the Lines Meet: Parallelism in Chinese and Western Literatures,"⁴ I attempted to lay out those aspects of Chinese parallel composition that set it apart from superficially similar patterns of discourse in other classical literatures. In this piece, I placed particular emphasis on the manner in which certain unique linguistic features of Classical Chinese allow for the rigorous quantitative matching of words in poetic couplets and prose doublets, to an extent unequalled in examples commonly termed 'parallelism' in other cultural contexts—except, that is, for short stretches or in playful exercises. I then proceeded to explore the ways in which Chinese prose masters move in and out of this grid with endless variations on the basic aesthetic pattern, to produce different forms and degrees of full, partial and intermittent parallelism, as well as certain kinds of paired utterances that I called 'pseudo-parallelism,' 'quasi-parallelism,' and 'crypto-parallelism.' Finally, I allowed myself the sweeping claim that these patterns of composition embody one of the greatest cultural achievements of old Chinese civilization, reflecting the tendency of so much of traditional Chinese thought to project a sense of the unity of the cosmos through multiple patterns of dual conceptualization, from the narrow frame of perceptual opposites to the broader coordinates of Chinese correlative thinking writ large.

With the passage of many years of study and teaching, forever struggling to reconcile examples with counter-examples, I have come to reassess the significance of parallelism as the master-mode of traditional Chinese thought and verbal art. On the one hand, I have become more familiar with the wide range of technical variants of parallel composition, including those outlined in such seminal critical writings as *Wenxin diaolong* 文心雕龍 and *Wenjing mifulun* 文鏡秘府論 (better known by the original Japanese title *Bunkyō hifuron*). I have also gained a greater appreciation of the subtle and manifest interplay of

---

3 As is well known, the use of this term in the West is traced to the field of Biblical Studies, where it was first applied by the 18th-century Hebraist Robert Lowth to the poetic form of the Psalms.

4 *Chinese Literature: Essays, Articles, Reviews* 10:1/2 (July 1988): 43-60 (later reprinted in *Poetics Today* 11:3 [1990]: 523–546). See also my other discussions of parallelism in "The Prose of Our Time," in *The Power of Culture*, ed. Willard Peterson (Hong Kong: Chinese University Press, 1994), 206–217, "Means and Means: A Comparative Reading of Aristotle's *Ethics* and the *Zhongyong*," in *Early China/Ancient Greece: Thinking Through Comparisons*, ed. Steven Shankman and Stephen Durrant, (Albany: SUNY, 2002), 187–206, and in my study of the "Lici" chapter of the *Wenxin diaolong*: "Bones of Parallel Rhetoric in the *Wenxin diaolong*," in *A Chinese Literary Mind*, ed. Cai Zongqi (Stanford University Press, 2001), 163–175.

parallelistic and non-parallel rhythms in the greatest Chinese poetic works, this counterpoint seen most tellingly in the structural paradigms of *lüshi* 律詩 versification, but by no means absent in *gushi* 古詩 and in *ci* 詞 and *qu* 曲 song-forms.⁵ In some cases this interplay may take the form of the deliberate withholding of viscerally anticipated parallel rhythms. Conversely, even those *guwen* 古文 masters from Tang (618–807) through Qing (1644–1911) who loudly champion compositional patterns drawn from the models of pristine style found in such revered classics as the *Zuozhuan* 左傳 and the *Shiji* 史記—presumably free of the mannered symmetries of Six Dynasties and later 'parallel prose' (*piantiwen* 駢體文)—frequently slip into parallel *cola* that alternate with what they elevate as the unadorned freshness of 'straight prose.'

What I now wish to present is a more nuanced assessment of the essential yoking of sameness and difference evoked through the conjoining of adjacent verbal structures within Chinese parallel discourse itself. This double sense of what is called 'parallel' may be neatly epitomized in the primary Chinese term for all sorts of parallelistic writing: *dui* 對 (as expanded in different compound expressions: e.g. *duizhang* 對仗, *duiju* 對句, *duishu* 對屬, et cetera), whose essential semantic value suggests two persons or things positioned face to face, whether that be in contrastive opposition (*duili* 對立) or in complementary mutuality (*xiangdui* 相對).

Looking ahead to the primary contention of this essay, I will attempt to demonstrate that, while this sort of antiphony, or polyphony, of varying senses of similarity and difference in matching lines may be considered the 'default mode' of classical Chinese expository prose, still, one finds a significant number of examples in which the assumed governing principle of paratactic coordination of parallel assertions must be qualified—using an analogy to prevailing patterns observed in Indo-European syntax—by a certain concept of *subordination*. By this I mean a concatenation of verbal units whereby the initial impression of matched lines of equal semantic value ranged side-by-side can be shown to mask different types of implied or submerged hypotaxis, in which some of the links in formally similar pairs or chains of utterances do not necessarily stand as separate-but-equal formulations, but may be better construed as subordinate clauses that serve to support a singular primary proposition.⁶

---

5   The best elucidation of the parallel/non-parallel core of *lüshi* poetic structure is still found in the path-breaking study by Kao Yu-kung and Mei Tsu-lin, "Syntax, Diction and Imagery in T'ang Poetry," *Harvard Journal of Asiatic Studies* 31 (1971): 49–133.

6   The distinction between paratactic coordination and hypotactic subordination in basic syntactic and supra-syntactic patterns of composition is clearly seen when one contrasts Classical Chinese sentence patterns with those in comparable examples in Indo-European languages.

Classical Western rhetorical theory is replete with terms and conceptual models employed to describe the manner in which sets of verbal units are strung together to construct larger sequences of argument. From this perspective, many of the vague and overlapping Hellenisms of Western rhetoric can be reduced to different formal mechanisms for describing linked units sharing various kinds and degrees of similarity and difference (for example *anaphora* and *epanaphora*, *antithesis* and *chiasmus*, *parisosis* and *paromoiosis*, *homioteleuton* and the whole alphabet-soup of ill-defined rhetorical terms). At the other end of the scale, many of our looser ways of speaking about rhetorical strategies of argumentation (analogical reasoning, proposition and illustration, syllogisms and other chain arguments, et cetera) might also be characterized as strings of semantically redundant verbal units deployed to convey a common unitary message through more than one mode of presentation. As a general principle, however, the primary thrust in Western rhetorical theory continues to reflect the assumption that in such chains of linked units one portion will always tend to be logically subordinated to the expression of the primary proposition. I will try to demonstrate in the following pages that a similar function can also be observed in certain examples of Chinese parallel argumentation.

It is of course possible to view parallelism in classical Chinese poetry and prose, in many instances, as essentially formal, aesthetic features. Thus, in the various genres of classical verse, one of the most palpable effects of imposing a lexical, grammatical and semantic grid of matching lines is to reinforce the couplet form, in such a way that the filling out of (nearly always) end-stopped lines serves itself as a device of closure—just as the filling-out of longer, numerically-matched strings may also serve as a marker of closure in the periods of Chinese classical prose. In poetry, this compositional feature also functions—along with repeating patterns of rhyme, line-length and balanced tones—to carry forward the rhythmic 'beat' of the lines in a given couplet, in a way not altogether different from the aesthetics of 'quantity' in forms of metrically-defined versification in other classical traditions. With respect to the parallel coordination of periods in expository prose, the aesthetic effect of a litany of well-wrought balanced phrases often lies in raising the rhetorical register to a higher level of abstraction or generality—that is, by directing the reader to contemplate the common ground of meaning expressed in separate lines. Whereas in the paradigmatic structure of 'regulated verse' this function is conventionally reserved for the so-called 'inner couplets,' in which the poet conventionally turns from his personal perspective to expressions of the universal

---

The contrast becomes more complex when comparison is made to Semitic and Altaic syntactic structures.

or the archetypal, in *guwen* prose, by contrast, it is frequently observed in the opening and closing movements of a longer argument, where the pompous symmetries of parallel rhythms evoke the voice of the all-knowing sage pontificating on self-evident truths.[7]

At this point, however, I wish to turn to examples of formally parallelistic style in works of Chinese philosophical argumentation in which the linking of utterances of similar shape and import goes beyond the poetic 'principle of equivalence' as propounded by Roman Jakobson,[8] with the aim of highlighting certain instances of *subordination* (or shall we call it *subjunction*) that may often go unnoticed. To give a very basic initial illustration of the rhetorical function I have in mind, let us consider the use of the word *er* 而, usually taught to Western students of elementary classical Chinese as a conjunctive particle, either accretive or concessive ('and' or 'but'). In many complex usages the signification of this particle may be better explained, I believe, as serving to mark an essentially subordinating, *adverbial* function, that is, identifying one or the other of the conjoined clauses (usually but not always the first in sequence) as setting the conditions for the other, primary predication.[9]

Extrapolating from the explicit function of conjunctive markers to the unmarked use of asyndetic parallel constructions in Chinese expository argumentation, we may now consider certain instances in which tandem patterns of enunciation are harnessed to convey an essentially singular point, for which the interpolation of secondary parallel clauses functions primarily to provide subordinate underpinning or modification for a given proposition. To put this in the most simplistic notation one used to learn in elementary courses on logic, this idea may be expressed, not as P_1 and P_2, but by such formulations as "whereas P_1, therefore P_2," "given P_1, then P_2," or "just as P_1, so too P_2," and the like. In order to illustrate this contention, I have undertaken the exercise of tag-

---

7 Consider, for example, the opening lines in Chapter 5 of the *Hanfeizi* ("The Dao as Guiding Principle" 主道, Chen Qiyou 陳奇猷, *Hanfeizi jishi* 韓非子集釋 [Beijing: Zhonghua shuju, 1974], 67): 道者、萬物之始，是非之紀也。是以明君守始以知萬物之源，治紀以知善敗之端 ("The Dao is the beginning of all things; it is the measuring-cord of right and wrong. For that reason, the enlightened sovereign cleaves to the beginning in order to comprehend the origin of all things; sets in order his frame of reference in order to comprehend the fulcrum success and failure... .").

8 See his seminal article "Closing Statements: Linguistics and Poetics," in *Style in Language*, ed. Thomas A. Sebeok (Cambridge Massachusetts: MIT Press, 1960), 350–377.

9 This function may be compared to the common use of the conjunctive *vav/waw* in classical Hebrew and Arabic syntax (to give a very familiar example: "In the beginning God created ... *and* the spirit of God hovered..."). In analysing such conjunctive and contrastive patterns, one is reminded of the complex calculus of interpenetration of equivalence and non-equivalence in Boolean algebra.

ging and culling from various early Chinese texts examples in which the apparently parallelistic form of dual coordination may mask an underlying logical thrust of singular assertion and subordinated support. For convenience of reference in this preliminary exposition, I have limited myself to some of the most foundational writings: *Lunyu, Mengzi, Daxue, Zhongyong, Xunzi, Daodejing, Zhuangzi, Hanfeizi*, and *Huainanzi*, works whose seminal status in the received tradition allows them to be taken as representative of 'literary argument' in early China, even if they do not necessarily reflect the entire range of rhetorical modes available to writers of the time. Trying to impose a semblance of order on a rather protean file of examples, I will suggest the following tentative division of categories of analysis:

1. sequences of parallel statements culminating in the final assertion of a principal point, one that brings into focus the logical thrust, or sheds new conceptual light, within a given argument;
2. equivalent utterances that function to lead rhetorically up to the presentation of provocative, unconventional or, in certain cases, downright counter-intuitive assertions; and
3. pairs or strings of clauses in which one or another of the units serves to delineate the conditions for the other, thus functioning as a kind of subordinate clause (i.e. what I have termed here an 'adverbial' function).

To be sure, my reading of these examples may often reflect the optical illusion of self-persuasion: the perception of logical thrust, in the final analysis, remains very much in the eyes of the beholder, as we have learned from the inconsistent and overlapping application of Western rhetorical terminology. Despite the essentially subjective nature of this perception, however, a number of more 'objective' stylistic markers may alert us to the possibility of pointed departures from the rhetoric of equivalence. Among these, I would include various devices of 'defamiliarisation' such as: unconventional inversions of word order, insertion of unfamiliar locutions into seemingly predictable parallel sequences, gratuitous use of *variatio*, and deliberate violation of metrical, tonal, and rhyming patterns.

In order to throw into relief those instances in which I perceive a pointed deformation of the apparent logic of parallel syntax, I will first present a number of examples of well-known passages in which true equivalence or simple antithesis seems to be the dominant factor. Let us consider, for example, the following set of passages, in which two or more of the 'members' of a given parallel sequence express complementary aspects of one single point.

1. *Mencius* (孟子) 1A:7[10]
吾力足以舉百鈞，
而不足以舉一羽；
明足以察秋毫之末，
而不見輿薪。
My strength may be sufficient to lift a hundred stone-weights,
but not sufficient to lift a single feather;
my clarity of vision may be sufficient to perceive the tip of an autumn wisp,
but not sufficient to see a cartload of firewood.

2. *Mencius* 4A:2[11]
不以舜之所以事堯事君，不敬其君者也；
不以堯之所以治民治民，　賊其民者也。
For one not to serve one's sovereign in the same manner that Shun served Yao is
 tantamount to a lack of respect for one's sovereign;
For one not to rule the people in the same manner that Yao ruled his people is
 tantamount to robbing the people.

3. *The Highest Order of Cultivation* (大學) 7[12]
身有所忿懥，則不得其正；
有所恐懼，　則不得其正；
有所好樂，　則不得其正；
有所憂患，　則不得其正。
When one's personal relations are governed by animosity and resentment, then
 one is incapable of achieving straightness of mind;
when one is possessed of fear and trepidation, then one is incapable of achieving
 straightness of mind;
when one's consciousness is occupied by feelings of fondness and delight, then
 one is incapable of achieving straightness of mind;
and when one is obsessed with anxiety and grief, then one is incapable of achieving straightness of mind.

4. *The Highest Order of Cultivation* (大學) 8[13]
人之其所親愛而辟焉，
人之其所賤惡而辟焉，
人之其所畏敬而辟焉，
人之其所哀矜而辟焉，
人之其所敖惰而辟焉。

---

10   Yang Bojun 楊伯峻, *Mengzi yizhu* 孟子譯注 (Beijing: Zhonghua shuju, 1988), 15. All
     translations are my own.
11   Yang Bojun, *Mengzi yizhu*, 165.
12   Zhu Bin 朱彬, *Liji xunzuan* 禮記訓纂 (Beijing: Zhonghua shuju, 1996), 871.
13   Zhu Bin, *Liji xunzuan*, 871.

People are drawn to those for whom they feel kinship and affection, and they incline toward them;

their attention is drawn to those for whom they feel disdain and distaste, and they incline away from them;

they are drawn to those whom they hold in awe and respect, and they incline toward them;

they are drawn to those for whom they feel pity and compassion, and they incline toward them;

their attention is drawn to those for whom they regard with arrogance and indifference, and they incline away from them.

5. *Book of the Way and Essential Force* (道德經) 19[14]

絕聖棄智，民利百倍；
絕仁棄義，民復孝慈；
絕巧棄利，盜賊無有。

Exterminate the sages and cast out the wise, and the people will benefit a hundredfold;

exterminate the benevolent and cast out the righteous, and the people will recover the virtues of filial piety and compassion;

exterminate the clever and cast out the sharp-witted; and robbers and bandits will no longer exist.

6. *Book of the Way and Essential Force* (道德經) 45[15]

....
大盈若沖，其用不窮。
大直若屈，...。
大巧若拙，
大辯若訥。

The greatest degree of fullness is akin to vacuity, ...;
the greatest degree of straightness is akin to crookedness, ...;
the greatest degree of cleverness is akin to stupidity;
the greatest degree of rhetorical skill is akin to stammering.

7. *Huainanzi* (淮南子) 1[16]

夫
形者，生之所也；
氣者，生之元也；
神者，生之制也。
...

---

14 Gao Ming 高明, *Boshu Laozi jiaozhu* 帛書老子校注 (Beijing: Zhonghua shuju, 1996), 312.
15 Gao Ming, *Boshu Laozi jiaozhu*, 42–43.
16 He Ning 何寧, *Huainanzi jishi* 淮南子集釋 (Beijing: Zhonghua shuju, 1998), 82, 84 with *suo* 所 instead of *she* 舍 and *yuan* 元 instead of *chong* 充.

```
故夫
形者,非其所安也而處之則廢,
氣,不當其所充　而用之則泄,
神,　非其所宜　而行之則昧。...
```
For the physical form is that in which life is lodged;
the essential breath is that from which life originates;
the spirit is that by which life is regulated.

...

That is why,
when one dwells in one's physical form, but is not at peace with it, then it is destroyed;
when one employs one's essential breath, but does not accommodate its full measure, then it is dissipated;
when one deploys one's spirit, but not in the proper manner, then it is dimmed.

I have allowed myself the pleasure of rehearsing these examples (from among countless others), to demonstrate the paradigmatic functioning of parallel constructions in Chinese expository prose. In the first two passages, I would argue, it is not Mengzi's intent to contrast bodily and visual power (1), or to set Shun's qualities against those of Yao (2), but rather to make more general assertions about human capacity and sagely virtue. Nor does Laozi appear to distinguish between the Confucian values he advocates discarding (5), or between his various illustrations of the notion of strength within apparent weakness (6) in these nearly-proverbial formulations. In each case, he is using multiple parallel statements to make his basic points about the ideal of pristine simplicity, in the one, and the notion of epistemological inadequacy, in the other. Similarly, the initial division among different components of the self in the *Huainanzi* passage cited (7) leads us into a set of nearly interchangeable assertions about these separate topics. By the same token, in the case of the *Daxue* passages given here (3 and 4), the writer consistently hammers away at his unitary point through a series of parallel illustrations.

In many cases, by way of contrast, we may observe the manner in which the intended equivalence of a set of parallel statements may be masked by the contraposition of two or more apparently antithetical phrases. Consider, for example, one very pointed passage in the *Mencius* (7B: 31)[17]:

```
孟子曰：
人皆有所不忍,達之於其所忍,仁也;
人皆有所不為,達之於其所為,義也。
```
Mencius said:

---

17 Yang Bojun, *Mengzi yizhu*, 337.

> For all humans, there is that which they cannot abide. To extend this to that which they can abide: this is true benevolence;
> For all humans, there is that which they are unwilling to do. To extend this to that which they are willing to do: this is true righteousness.

Here our philosopher's initially straight-forward, if somewhat counter-intuitive, point seems driven by a clear contrast between his understanding of the moral force of *ren* and that of *yi*. But on further analysis, I submit, it turns out to be a common aspect of these two values: the notion of 'extending' (*da* 達) from one's visceral aversions to positive modes of moral behaviour, that is being proposed.

When this sort of repetition appears at the end of each occurrence in a chain of apposite statements, we may get the aesthetic effect of an antistrophal refrain. Hanfeizi is particularly fond of this rhetorical device, as we see in the following passage, among many others:

> 愛臣太親，必危其身；
> 人臣太貴，必易主位；
> 主妾無等，必危嫡子；
> 兄弟不服，必危社稷。
> When favoured ministers are granted too much affection, this will inevitably jeopardize one's personal safety;
> when non-royal ministers are granted too much wealth, this will inevitably lead to overthrowing the ruler's position;
> when the ruler and his consorts ignore hierarchical distinctions, this will inevitably jeopardize the legitimate succession;
> when older and younger brothers are not properly deferential, this will inevitably jeopardize the dynastic enterprise.[18]

Clearly, the rhetorical contrasts here between ruler and minister, et cetera, are brought forward to make a single point about the potentially destructive results of improper maintenance of hierarchies.

As I have suggested above with respect to the double sense of the term *dui*, the coordinating function of the typical parallel construction is unaffected when the given assertions are brought forth as a simple antithesis. Consider the following unambiguous illustrations:

---

18   Chapter 4:1 ("Showing Favour to Ministers" 愛臣), Chen Qiyou, *Hanfeizi jishi*, 60. Numerous additional examples in the *Hanfeizi* include Chapter 12 ("Problems of Rhetoric" 說難, Chen Qiyou, *Hanfeizi jishi*, 221 ff.), where the refrain: "He who acts in this way will find himself in danger." (如此者身危) concludes a set of longer parallel propositions.

1. *Book of the Way and Essential Force* (道德經) 3[19]
虛其心,
實其腹,
弱其志,
強其骨。
[The sage] empties his heart,
and fills his belly.
He weakens his will,
and strengthens his bones.

2. *Xunzi* 3 ("Unauthorized Behavior" 不苟)[20]
君子能亦好,不能亦好;
小人能亦醜,不能亦醜 ...
The man of noble character may be viewed favourably, whether he is capable or not;
the man of petty character is regarded with contempt, whether he is capable or not ....

3. *Xunzi* 17 ("On Heaven" 天論)[21]
天行有常,
不為堯存,
不為桀亡。
應之以治則吉,
應之以亂則凶。
The workings of Heaven follow constant patterns:
these do not exist due to sages like Yao;
they do not lapse due to tyrants like Jie.
If one accords with these patterns in implementing orderly rule, then good fortune will result;
if one [claims to] accords with these patterns in justifying disorderly rule, then ill fortune will result.

4. *Hanfeizi* 6 ("Maintaining Proper Measure" 有度)[22]
故,
忠臣危死於非罪,
姦邪之臣安利於無功。
忠臣危死而不以其罪,則良臣伏矣;
姦邪之臣安利不以功,則姦臣進矣.
That is why,

---

19 Gao Ming, *Boshu Laozi jiaozhu*, 237.
20 Wang Xianqian 王先謙, *Xunzi jijie* 荀子集解 (Beijing: Zhonghua shuju, 1988), 40.
21 Wang Xianqian, *Xunzi jijie*, 306–307.
22 Chen Qiyou, *Hanfeizi jishi*, 86.

The loyal minister risks death through no fault of his own,
the deceitful minister indulges in personal benefit with no deeds to his credit.
When loyal ministers risk death through no fault of their own, then good ministers go into hiding;
when deceitful ministers rest in personal benefit with no deeds to their credit, then evil ministers advance in the world.

In my reading of these passages, Xunzi's argument (2) rests on a strict opposition between the *junzi* and the *xiaoren*, and Hanfei (4) is stating a sharp distinction between opposite types of ruler-subject relations. By the same token, Laozi's little rhyming epigram (1) about fullness and strength, or the lack of these, rests on a self-evident contrast between the respective conditions.

In some cases, of course, what at first glance strikes us as an uncomplicated equivalence—whether complementary or contrastive—may, with more profound scrutiny, emerge as a crucial distinction. As an illustration of this sort of rhetorical twist, let us take a closer look at the continuation of the core argument in the opening chapter of the *Zhongyong*[23]:

中也者，天下之大本也；
和也者，天下之達道也。

The 'mean' constitutes the all-inclusive ground of being of the universe as a whole;
whereas the term 'harmony' refers to the unimpeded path of fullest attainment in the realm of human experience.

In my admittedly idiosyncratic reading of this passage, the contraposition of 'equilibrium' (*zhong* 中) and 'harmony' (*he* 和), often felt to be nearly synonymous in common usage, is here brought forward to assert the crucial conceptual division between the phenomenal world (that which has emerged into manifest reality 已發) and the cosmic order (that which remains a latent substrate 未發) that I take to form the logical underpinning of the entire text. In this light, I insist on the disambiguation of *daben* ('the all-inclusive ground of being') and *dadao* ('the unimpeded path of fullest attainment'), as expressing an elusive but far-reaching differentiation of the two separate modes of attainment brought forward in the text: the unchanging balance that characterizes the universal order, and the ceaseless compensatory re-balancing enjoined in the world of men.

I have presented here a brief review of a set of well-known passages in which parallel formulations function primarily to convey a sense of equivalence or

---

23   Zhu Bin, *Liji xunzuan*, 772.

contrast, in order to set off certain counter-examples in which non-coordinate linking of parallel statements seems to me to provide the main rhetorical thrust of a given argument. Let us first examine a few sequences in which formally parallel presentation is applied to a set of propositions expressing a provocative, or even counter-intuitive, conclusion. In my understanding, the rhetorical effect in sequences of this sort lies in creating the aesthetic expectation of simple equivalence or antithesis precisely in order to heighten the force of an unexpected predication, as in passages such as the following:

1. *Lunyu* (論語) 6:23[24]
子曰：
知者樂水，
仁者樂山；
知者動，
仁者靜；
知者樂，
仁者壽。
The Master said:
The wise take delight in flowing waters;
the humane take delight in solid mountains.
The wise seek activity;
the benevolent seek stillness.
The wise strive for happiness;
the benevolent strive for long life.

2. *Lunyu* (論語) 9:19[25]
子曰：
譬如為山，未成一簣，止，吾止也；
譬如平地，雖覆一簣，進，吾往也。
The Master said:
This can be likened to making a great mound: if one ceases one basketful of earth short of completion, then one's project comes to naught;
or it can be likened to levelling a piece of land: if one goes ahead after overturning just one basketful of earth, then one's project moves forward.

3. *On the Practice of the Mean* (中庸) 1[26]
莫見乎隱，
莫顯乎微。
Nothing is more visible than what appears to be hidden;

24　Yang Bojun 楊伯峻, *Lunyu yizhu* 論語譯注 (Beijing: Zhonghua shuju, 1988), 62.
25　Yang Bojun, *Lunyu yizhu*, 93.
26　Zhu Bin, *Liji xunzuan*, 772.

And no things are more manifest than matters of imperceptible subtlety.

4. *On the Practice of the Mean* (中庸) 4[27]
道之不行也，我知之矣：知者過之，　愚者不及也。
道之不明也，我知之矣：賢者過之，不肖者不及也。

The reason why the Way is not practiced is clear to me: it is because men of wisdom tend to overshoot it, while those of lesser intelligence fail to reach the bar;

the reason why the Way is not fully understood is clear to me: it is because men of worth tend to overshoot it, while those of imperfect character fail to reach the bar.

To be sure, each of these examples may be read as rather straight-forward presentations of their respective points. I am convinced, however, that the somewhat opaque assertion of varying preferences of the wise and the good for favoured objects of contemplation in nature, in the first *Lunyu* citation (1), the uncertain meaning of cessation and progress in the second (2), the *Zhongyong*'s Laozi-like play with the paradox of manifest reality (3), and the backhanded equation of "men of wisdom and worth" with "those of lesser intelligence and imperfect character," both being feckless in their different ways (5), all produce a kind of sly ironic touch that subtly transforms the conventional truisms expected in parallel pronouncements such as these. I also see this rhetorical strategy at work in another chain argument in Chapter 17 of the *Xunzi*, in which a set of parallel propositions regarding the workings of Heaven leads up to the interjection of a notion of "knowing Heaven" that may sound rather familiar to Western ears, but strikes one as fairly radical in the context of early Confucian thought, and in that of Xunzi in particular:[28]

天職既立，天功既成，形具而神生，好惡喜怒哀樂臧焉，夫是之謂天情。… 夫是之謂天官。… 夫是之謂天君。… 夫是之謂天養。… 夫是之謂天政。暗其天君，亂其天官，棄其天養，逆其天政，背其天情，以喪天功，夫是之謂大凶。聖人清其天君，正其天官，備其天養，順其天政，養其天情，以全其天功。如是，則知其所為，知其所不為矣 … 夫是之謂知天…

---

27 Zhu Bin, *Liji xunzuan*, 772.
28 Wang Xianqian, *Xunzi jijie*, 309–310. Cf. the introduction of a similar idea of 'knowing Heaven' in the final chapter of the *Mengzi* (7A:1), on the 'fullest realization of the mind' (盡心).

When the hierarchical order of Heaven is in place, and the workings of Heaven are achieved, then the forms of things are all realized and their inner spirit is engendered, so that likes and dislikes, joy, wrath, sorrow and delight are in harmony; this is what is referred to as the true state of Heaven. ... this is what is referred to as the functioning of Heaven. ... this is what is referred to as the sovereignty of Heaven. ... this is what is referred to as the nurturing of Heaven. ... this is what is referred to as the rule of Heaven. ... When the sovereignty of Heaven is eclipsed, the functioning of Heaven is thrown into disorder, the nurturing of Heaven is abandoned, the rule of Heaven is opposed and the true state of Heaven is ignored, so that the workings of Heaven are annulled; this is what is known as "the supreme disaster." The sage brings clarity to the sovereignty of Heaven, correctness to the functioning of Heaven, completeness to the nurturing of Heaven, accord to the rule of Heaven, and healthy nurture to the state of Heaven, so that the workings of Heaven are perfectly maintained. In this way, he fully understands what he is to do and what he is not to do, ... this is what is called "knowing Heaven."

My second category of parallel sequences—those that, to my mind, convey senses other than equivalence or antithesis—includes cases in which a series of formally apposite statements, typically presented in triplets, leads us to a final assertion that markedly alters the direction of the argument. This is how I read such seminal passages as *Lunyu* 1:1[29]:

子曰：
學而時習之，不亦說乎？
有朋自遠方來，不亦樂乎？
人不知而不慍，不亦君子乎？

The Master said:
To have fitting occasions to go over what one has learned: is this not a source of pleasure?
To have like-minded souls come from afar: is this not a source of delight?
To face without rancour the lack of recognition from one's peers: is this not the true mark of the man of noble character?

– where the banality of the first two parallel statements sets the rhetorical stage for a powerful primary assertion about nobility of spirit in a world in which the comforting validation of peer recognition is not always forthcoming. I see the same sort of rhetorical effect in the opening lines of both the *Daxue*[30] and the *Zhongyong*[31]:

---

29 Yang Bojun, *Lunyu yizhu*, 1.
30 Zhu Bin, *Liji xunzuan*, 870. With *xin* 新 instead of *qin* 親.
31 Zhu Bin, *Liji xunzuan*, 772.

大學之道，
在明明德，
在新民，
在止於至善。

The Way of self-cultivation lies in causing the light of one's inner moral force to shine forth;
in bringing the people to a state of renewal;
and in coming to rest in the fullest attainment of the good.

天命之謂性，
率性之謂道，
修道之謂教。

By the term 'nature' we speak of that which is imparted by the ordinance of Heaven;
by the 'Way' we mean that path which is in conformance with the intrinsic nature of man and things;
and by 'moral instruction' we refer to the process of cultivating man's proper way in the world.

In each of these latter passages, I am convinced that the initial sense of equivalence of the three foundational principles projected through parallel formulation demands a revised reading, as we plunge deeper into the texts and discover that the respective notions are not of equal force in the construction of the overall arguments of the two canonic treatises. That is, just as the three key phrases in the opening sections of the *Daxue*: *ming mingde*, *xinmin* (not *qinmin*) and *zhi yu zhishan* prove to be of unequal weight in the construction of the main argument of the work, so, too, the *Zhongyong* opens with highly charged formulas that remain peripheral to the central propositions developed in the text. In both of these treatises, we observe the consistent use of the rhetorical pattern whereby a set of parallel formulations of apparently similar import is followed by a concluding statement that redirects the thrust of the argument. One completely transparent example occurs in Chapter 9 of the *Zhongyong*[32]:

子曰：
天下國家可均也，
爵祿　　可辭也，
白刃　　可蹈也，
中庸不　可能也。
The Master said:

32　Zhu Bin, *Liji xunzuan*, 773.

> It is possible for one to impose uniform rule on a family, on a kingdom, or even on the entire world;
> it is possible for one to renounce official titles and emoluments;
> it is even conceivable for one to tread upon the naked blade of a sword.
> But to put the mean into practice may be beyond the capacity of any individual.

Here the given series of circumstances of profound difficulty presented in parallel fashion clearly serves to undergird the primary assertion about the virtual impossibility of fully attaining the mean. Far less self-evident, however, is the consistent deployment of the rhetorical strategy of redirected parallelism forming the core of many other key passages in this text, as we have seen in the pointed non-equivalence of 'equilibrium' (*zhong*) and 'harmony' (*he*) in the opening section, and more crucially, in the contraposition 'the Way of Heaven' (*tian zhi dao*) and 'the Way of man' (*ren zhi dao*) in Chapter 20.[33]

At the risk of tampering with the conventional reading of one more of our most beloved seminal works, I would like to go one step further and suggest that the same sort of rhetorical analysis may be applied to the opening lines of *The Book of the Way and Essential Force* 1[34]:

> 道可道，非常道。
> 名可名，非常名。
> 無名天地之始；
> 有名萬物之母。
> 故，
> 常無欲，以觀其妙；
> 常有欲，以觀其徼。…
>
> The Way that can be taken as one's guide is not the eternal Way;
> the name that can be denominated is not the eternal Name.
> The state of namelessness: that is the beginning of Heaven and Earth;
> once names exist: that is the mother of all creatures.
> That is why,
> an unchanging lack of desire enables one to perceive the most subtle mysteries;
> and an unchanging state of desire enables one to perceive the most remote contingencies.

Here, too, I am convinced that the initial incontrovertible salvo of metaphysical truth about the Dao in fact represents a rather commonplace proposition,

---

33   See my presentation of the 'integral argument' of the *Zhongyong* in Andrew Plaks, *Ta Hsüeh and Chung Yung: The Highest Order of Cultivation and On the Practice of the Mean* (London: Penguin Books Ltd., 2003), 78–79.

34   Gao Ming, *Boshu Laozi jiaozhu*, 221–224.

whose rhetorical function in this passage lies primarily in leading us to the parallel statement about 'names,' the subject we immediately discover to be the primary topic of the first part of this section of the text. The same may be said of the following passage in Chapter 2 of the *Zhuangzi* ("On the Levelling of All Things" 齊物論),[35] also a favourite among students:

> 有始也者，有未始有始也者，...
> 有有也者，有無也者，有未始有無也者 ...
> 俄而有無矣 ...
> There was a beginning, and there was a time before the inception of this beginning ...
> There is existence, there is non-existence, and there was a time before the inception of non-existence ...
> Suddenly, there is non-existence ...

In my reading, the point of presenting the two examples of infinite regress of existence/non-existence and being/non-being, as evoked by the parallel form of the two initial chain-statements, is to lead us to the moment when this exercise in speculative ontology is abruptly cut short, and we are brought to the speaker's primary point about antinomian epistemology.

Finally, let us take a parting glance at two brief examples that, in my view, demonstrate the use of parallel clauses brought forth neither to corroborate nor to countervail one another, but rather to set one half as the 'adverbial' modifier of the other. In the first of these, we may consider a rather unequivocal analogy drawn in *The Highest Order of Cultivation* (大學) 6[36]:

> 富潤屋，
> 德潤身，
> 心廣體胖，
> Just as wealth lends lustre to a house,
> so does moral force lend lustre to one's personal bearing.
> The heart waxes in breadth
> as the body grows sleek.

Here we experience no difficulty in reading the passage as a simple 'just as ...so too' argument juxtaposing physical and moral well-being. In the second, taken from: *On the Practice of the Mean* (中庸) 26[37]:

---

35   Guo Qingfan 郭慶藩, *Zhuangzi jishi* 莊子集釋 (Beijing: Zhonghua shuju, 1989), 79.
36   Zhu Bin, *Liji xunzuan*, 871.
37   Zhu Bin, *Liji xunzuan*, 777.

誠者自成也，
而道自道也。

The term 'integral wholeness' refers to a process of becoming complete through one's own agency;
just as 'the Way' indicates a path that one sets for oneself.

The initial assertion couched in a philologically dubious etymology of the key term *cheng* is corroborated by the immediately following insertion of a second, rather commonplace definition (a conventional etymology of the term *dao* that is rehearsed in many early texts), in order to set the rhetorical pattern that is here applied to a startlingly original redefinition of the crucial notion of 'integral wholeness' (*cheng*) as a process of self-realization.

I have limited myself here to a small number of passages drawn from the vast corpus of early Chinese prose, in the hope that, by bringing forward a few examples in this exploratory essay, we may at least begin to lay the groundwork for a revised understanding of the significance of parallel discourse in Chinese argumentation. Clearly, a more convincing exposition, even for the 'classical' period alone, would require something approaching a book-length monograph of the subject based on a comprehensive review of the entire spectrum of Warring States through Han prose.

References

Chen Qiyou 陳奇猷. *Hanfeizi jishi* 韓非子集釋. Beijing: Zhonghua shuju, 1974.
Gao Ming 高明. *Boshu Laozi jiaozhu* 帛書老子校注. Beijing: Zhonghua shuju, 1996.
Guo Qingfan 郭慶藩. *Zhuangzi jishi* 莊子集釋. Beijing: Zhonghua shuju, 1989.
He Ning 何寧. *Huainanzi jishi* 淮南子集釋. Beijing: Zhonghua shuju, 1998.
Jakobson, Roman. "Closing Statements: Linguistics and Poetics." In *Style in Language*, edited by Thomas A. Sebeok. Cambridge, MA: MIT Press, 1960: 350–377.
Kao Yu-kung and Mei Tsu-lin. "Syntax, Diction and Imagery in T'ang Poetry." *Harvard Journal of Asiatic Studies* 31 (1971): 49–133.
Plaks, Andrew. "Where the Lines Meet: Parallelism in Chinese and Western Literatures." *Chinese Literature: essays, articles, reviews* (CLEAR) 10.1–2 (1988): 43–60; reprinted in *Poetics Today* 11:3, (1991): 523–546.
———. "The Prose of Our Time." In *The Power of Culture*, edited by Willard Peterson. Hong Kong: Chinese University Press, 1994: 206–217.
———. "Means and Means: A Comparative Reading of Aristotle's *Ethics* and the *Zhongyong*." In *Early China / Ancient Greece: Thinking Through Comparisons*, edited by Steven Shankman and Stephen Durrant. Albany: SUNY Press, 2002: 187–206.

———. "Bones of Parallel Rhetoric in the *Wenxin diaolong*." In *A Chinese Literary Mind*, edited by Zong-Qi Cai. Stanford: Stanford University Press, 2001: 163–175.

———. *Ta Hsüeh and Chung Yung: The Highest Order of Cultivation and On the Practice of the Mean*. London: Penguin Books Ltd., 2003.

Wang Xianqian 王先謙. *Xunzi jijie* 荀子集解. Beijing: Zhonghua shuju, 1988.

Yang Bojun 楊伯峻. *Lunyu yizhu* 論語譯注. Beijing: Zhonghua shuju, 1988.

———. *Mengzi yizhu* 孟子譯注. Beijing: Zhonghua shuju, 1988.

Zhu Bin 朱彬. *Liji xunzuan* 禮記訓纂. Beijing: Zhonghua shuju, 1996.

CHAPTER 3

On the Range and Performance of *Laozi*-Style Tetrasyllables

David Schaberg

It is not entirely without justification that the *Laozi* or *Daodejing*, of all texts transmitted from early times, should for most readers have come to stand for a whole distinct subgenre of philosophical discourse. It is, after all, the single densest concentration of the specific type of gnomic verse that it contains. Among the early texts most commonly read and taught in China and elsewhere, no other relies so heavily on this form, and few others adhere so strictly to the generic conventions that inform much of the *Laozi*. But to regard the forms of the *Laozi* as entirely *sui generis*, or to find parallels only in such 'Daoist' texts as the *Zhuangzi*, would be to ignore an important and broadly influential development in the history of Chinese philosophical argumentation. Read in their larger context, the *Laozi* tetrasyllables appear to have resulted from a refinement of existing conventions for didactic verse. This refinement produced a verse that was markedly limited in its lexicon and in its repertoire of syntactical patterns and figures of speech, that depended heavily upon a set of standard dichotomies, and that focused on a small set of themes. The copious amount of verse of this kind preserved in Western Han texts suggests not only that the verse form was itself especially popular during that period, but also that the people who were capable of composing it were themselves valued: they were sought out and supported as clients and, one suspects, as advisors, and their mastery of this verse form was key to their authority. In the courts of certain Western Han princes and lesser patrons, the practitioners of this subgenre were in a position to present themselves as sages and their words as verbal models of the *dao*. Although there can be no doubt that verse of this kind had its uses in private meditation, then, it also cannot be denied that it had its interpersonal, quasi-oratorical uses, and that composition and live performance in courts and private establishments would have helped to perpetuate the form and to extend its influence in later literary and intellectual history.

For an example of what I mean by *Laozi*-style tetrasyllables, consider the second chapter of the *Laozi*:

故		This is why
有無相生，	A	Being and non-being give birth to each other,
難易相成，	A	Hard and easy complete each other,
長短相形，	A	Long and short give each other form,
高下相傾，	A	High and low set each other off,
音聲相和，	B	Tones and sounds harmonize with each other,
前後相隨。	B	And van and rear put each other in line.[1]

The term 'tetrasyllabic' is potentially misleading in that neither the *Laozi* nor the other texts I identify as belonging to the same subgenre confine themselves slavishly to tetrasyllabic lines.[2] Nevertheless, tetrasyllables predominate, both in *Laozi* and in the texts that contain *Laozi*-like material. Other features that make the genre recognizable include the avoidance of narrative and more generally of historical references; use of binomes in descriptions of cosmic and natural phenomena and the character of accomplished individuals; foregrounding of dichotomies, as in *Laozi* 2; gestures of questioning and exclamation; and employment of a somewhat restricted vocabulary, especially in rhyme positions.[3] Cousins of the *Laozi* subgenre within the larger genre of didactic prosimetric writing may share one feature or another, while obviously serving some very different intellectual purpose. They may, for instance, depart from typical *Laozi* style by mentioning historical events, or they may address themes well outside the descriptive and prescriptive territory the *Laozi* and its successors favoured.

In gathering texts for consideration here, I have excluded *Shijing* and songs and, generally speaking, most texts that are rhymed throughout; it seems to be definitive of the tetrasyllabic form I am examining that it is typically juxtaposed with unrhymed material, and that it serves as an introduction to, or interruption of, or conclusion to, prose passages.[4] One exception to this

---

1 For rhymes, see Jiang Yougao 江有誥, *Yinxue shishu* 音學十書 (Beijing: Zhonghua, 1993), 162.
2 Bernhard Karlgren, *The Poetical Parts in Lao-tsï*, (Göteborgs Högskolas Årsskrift 38.3, Göteborg: Elanders boktryckeri aktiebolag, 1932), 4. The genre was perhaps prosimetric to begin with, building into discourse the alternation between relatively unpatterned prose and patterned, metered rhyme.
3 William Baxter enumerates rhetorical tendencies of *Laozi* in "Situating the Language of the *Lao-tzu*," reprinted in *Lao-tzu and the Tao-te-ching*, eds. Livia Kohn and Michael Lafargue (Albany: State University of New York Press, 1998), 240–243. Harold D. Roth offers some refinements of Baxter's observations in his analysis of the "Nei ye" chapter of *Guanzi*. See *Original Tao: Inward Training (Nei-yeh) and the Foundations of Taoist Mysticism* (New York: Columbia University Press, 1999), 15–17.
4 In his consideration of the genre of the *Laozi*, William Baxter notes straightforwardly that "both rhyme and semantic patterning are used as poetic devices" and that "passages containing either device should be considered verse, not just those in which there is rhyme." See

general exclusion of song-like material is my inclusion of *Chuci* passages with clear resemblances to *Laozi*. To repeat, the *Laozi* tetrasyllable as practiced before and during the Han appears to have developed as a refinement within a broader genre of didactic prosimetrum, a form that it ultimately came to overshadow.

Didactic Tetrasyllables Beyond the Laozi

Tetrasyllabic rhyming in China is not quite as old as the oldest rhymed texts or the oldest song texts. Early rhymed bronze inscriptions do not show a persistent preference for tetrasyllabic syntactical patterns, while a number of early tetrasyllabic texts, including examples in the "Zhou song" 周頌, did not have to be rhymed. Of course, certain of the "Zhou song" were densely rhymed and strictly tetrasyllabic.[5] By the late Spring and Autumn period, bell inscriptions were showing a coincidence of rhyming and tetrasyllabic tendencies in inscriptions that sought to capture and control the harmonious sociality of bell music.[6] Meanwhile, sacrificial prayers, blessings, oaths and curses, wedding songs and marching songs, and many of the other occasional songs useful in the social interactions of the period were being sung in rhymed tetrasyllables. For the specialists and ordinary people who used these songs, as for latecomers who learned the *Shijing* as a collection of classical texts, the language of ritual authority was tetrasyllabic.

The *Zuozhuan*'s depictions of noblemen reciting (*fu* 賦) *Shijing* songs for one another during the feasts following important diplomatic occasions have long been recognized as evidence for the pedagogical importance of the *Shijing*. Among the elite, at least among members of the elite who hoped to be qualified to participate in the most important interstate occasions, extensive memorization of the songs was *de rigueur*. Oddly, however, in the speeches attributed to those same noblemen and their kind, rhymed tetrasyllables are rare in the extreme. They did not speak that way in their own time, or the people who supplied their speech during the later composition of the *Zuozhuan* did not remember their speech that way. To judge from the *Zuozhuan*, noblemen might adopt any degree of rhetorical intricacy in the arrangement of the words

---

"Situating the Language of the *Lao-tzu*," 237. I focus on rhyme merely as a distinctive intensifying feature very commonly, though not inevitably, found in examples of this genre.

5 E.g., "Zhi jing" 執競 (Mao 274), "You gu" 有瞽 (Mao 280), "Yong" 雝 (Mao 282), "Zai jian" 載見 (Mao 283).

6 See, for example, the "Xuzi 許子 zhong," in Shirakawa Shizuka 白川靜, *Kinbun tsûshaku* 金文通釋, *Hakutsuru bijutsukan shi* 1–56 (1962–1984), 37:314–317.

of their speech, but speaking in rhyme was beneath them. Except in citation and recitation, rhyming was the province of employed specialists, diviners and physicians in particular, and with them it retained close connections with song, being introduced as a distinct rhythmic form framed by and separate from ordinary speech.[7]

It is in texts dating from the late fourth century BC and after that rhymed tetrasyllables appear alongside and often interspersed with unrhymed prose, in passages of straight instruction or argumentation, to form a distinct genre of didactic prosimetrum. A fine example for dating the form and perhaps for capturing it in a moment of transition is the recovered text "Min zhi fumu" 民之父母, one of a large number of texts on bamboo purchased in 1994 by the Shanghai Museum. The text has close parallels in received literature, namely in the "Kongzi xianju" 孔子閑居 chapter of the *Liji* and in the "Lun li" 論禮 chapter of *Kongzi jiayu* 孔子家語, but without this earliest manuscript exemplar, thought to date to around 300 BC, it would have been difficult to know how early rhymed tetrasyllables were being used in the midst of prose and far outside the characteristic habits of the *Laozi*. In a discussion of the *Shijing* line "Father and mother to the people," Confucius explains to Zixia 子夏 the 'five perfections' (*wu zhi* 五至) and the 'three withouts' (*san wu* 三無), further illustrating the latter with *Shijing* tags. In the closing lines of the piece, Confucius follows these 'three withouts' through a series of transformations:

亡聲之樂，		In music without sound,
氣志不違；	A	the *qi* and ambition are not crossed;
亡體之禮，		In ritual without the body,
威儀遲遲；	A	awesome dignity is at ease;
亡服之喪，		In mourning without mourning clothes,
內恕洵悲。	A	the inner compassion is expansively melancholy.[8]
亡聲之樂，		Music without sound
塞于四方；	B	fills up the four quarters;
亡體之禮，		Ritual without the body
日逑月相；	B	matches up day by day and assists every month;
亡服之喪，		In mourning without mourning clothes,

---

7 Jiang Yougao *Yinxue shishu* records all the instances of non-*Shijing* rhyming in the *Zuozhuan* in a mere three pages, 124–126. For a physician's rhyme, see *Chunqiu Zuozhuan zhu* 春秋左傳注, ann. Yang Bojun 楊伯峻, rev. ed. (Beijing: Zhonghua shuju, 1990), 4:1221 (Zhao 1.12e). For a diviner's rhyme, see Xi 15.4g (Yang, 363–365). The well-born Zifu Huibo of Lu does use rhymes in a *Zhouyi*-based prognostication at Zhao 12.10b (Yang, 1337).

8 For this identification of the graph transcribed *xun* 洵 with *jie* 皆, see Huang Xiquan 黃錫全, "Notes on reading Volume 2 of *Warring States Chu Bamboo Writings Collected by the Shanghai Museum* (1)" 讀上博楚簡二札記壹, http://www.bamboosilk.org/Wssf/2003/huangxiquan01.htm. (November 2014)

純德同明。	B	purity and virtue shine together.
亡聲之樂，		Music without sound
施及孫子；	C	extends to the descendants;
亡體之禮，		Ritual without the body
塞于四海；	C	fills up the four seas;
亡服之喪，		In mourning without mourning clothes,
為民父母；	C	one becomes father and mother to the people.
亡聲之樂，		In music without sound,
氣志既得；	C	the *qi* and ambition are already attained;
亡體之禮，		In ritual without the body,
威儀翼翼；	C	awesome dignity is careful;
亡服之喪，		In mourning without mourning clothes,
施及四國。	C	these extend to the neighbouring states on four sides.
亡聲之樂，		In music without sound,
氣志既從；	D	the *qi* and ambition are already compliant;
亡體之禮，		In ritual without the body,
上下和同；	D	superiors and inferiors are in harmony and in unison;
亡服之喪，		In mourning without mourning clothes,
以畜萬邦。	D	one fosters the myriad states.[9]

That the conversation revolves at first around a *Shijing* line, touches on several others, and then echoes the *Shijing* again in this closing passage is significant for what it suggests about the history of speech among students of the classics. Knowing the *Shijing* as well as the *Zuozhuan* noblemen were supposed to know it—and taking delight in his student's questions about the relevance of the text—Confucius is here made to do what *Zuozhuan* speech-makers did not do, that is, to engage in rhyming himself. His peroration has a foot in both worlds: on the one side, in the fanciest rhetoric of the *Zuozhuan*, with its repetitions and structured permutations and classical citations, and on the other side, in the thematics of 'not-having' (*wu* 無), with its complementarity with 'having' (*you* 有) and, perhaps, a whole implied science of the meaning and uses of nothingness.[10] Further, as Matthias Richter has argued in his extended

---

[9] I follow the text of Matthias L. Richter in *The Embodied Text: Establishing Textual Identity in Early Chinese Manuscripts* (Leiden: Brill, 2013), 161. See also Ma Chengyuan 馬承源 et al., ed., *Shanghai bowuguan cang Zhanguo Chu zhushu* 上海博物館藏戰國楚竹書, Vol. 2 (Shanghai: Shanghai guji, 2002), 151–180. Wording and order differ somewhat in the received counterparts to the text. Rhymes for the *Liji* version of the text are in Jiang Yougao, *Yinxue shishu*, 123.

[10] Other texts that juxtapose *Shijing* quotations with newly made rhymes suggest some continuity between classical learning and rhyme-prose composition. See, e.g., *Xunzi jijie* 荀子集解, ann. Wang Xianqian 王先謙, 2 vols. (Beijing: Zhonghua shuju, 1988), 1: 6–10 (Jiang Yougao, *Yinxue shishu*, 211), where the content is quite traditional but the rhetorical character of the rhymed passages is similar in some ways to *Laozi*-verse.

analysis of "Min zhi fumu," the character of the text tends to confirm that it required explanations from a teacher and was thus embedded in a world of oral usage informed by the needs of a "specific social group of its users."[11] The engagement with rhyme would have made a model of the teacher who can speak both the older language of citation and the newer language of tetrasyllables.

A pair of passages from the *Chuci* merit mention here, even though the pieces they come from, which rhyme throughout, have been understood as poetry or song rather than as essays. The cosmogonic opening lines of the tetrasyllabic "Tian wen" 天問, with their binomes and their references to 'limits' (*ji* 極), to *yin* and *yang*, and to 'transformation' (*hua* 化), share many characteristics with *Laozi*-verse.[12] The bulk of the "Tian wen" differs from *Laozi*-verse in its abundant references to legendary and historical events. There are enough other passages of Warring States tetrasyllable revolving around historical legends that one suspects singing or chanting about such legends was a widespread practice,[13] but the "Tian wen" juxtaposition of the usually separate modes, cosmogonic and historical, is suggestive; perhaps this piece preserves a moment in the development of the former mode or subgenre within the larger genre of rhyming.

The "Yuan you" 遠遊 is likewise suggestive. A passage set apart by *yue* 曰, 'it is said,' in the middle of the poem shifts away from the prevailing 3 + 2 rhythm of the surrounding material, adopting instead a more strictly tetrasyllabic rhythm, and at the same time a more didactic tone focused on a description of the *dao*.[14] For the purposes of the singers of these *Chuci* pieces, the *Laozi* style was a distinct option within their larger practice, and was distinguished not only by its metrical features, but also by its eschewal of historical references (as

---

11   Richter, *The Embodied Text*, 190.

12   *Chuci buzhu* 楚辭補注, ann. Hong Xingzu 洪興祖 (Beijing: Zhonghua shuju, 1983), 85–87.

13   See the rhymes attributed to the sage Yao 堯 at *Analects* 20.1 (*Lunyu jishi* 論語集釋, ann. Cheng Shude 程樹德, 4 vols. [Beijing: Zhonghua shuju, 1990], 4: 1345); the extraordinary "Zhou zhu" 周祝 chapter of *Yi Zhou shu* 逸周書, possibly a reflection on the beginnings of the Zhou, but with hints of the dichotomous logic of the *Laozi* (*Yi Zhou shu huijiao jizhu* 逸周書彙校集注, ann. Huang Huaixin 黃懷信 et al., 2 vols. [Shanghai: Shanghai guji chubanshe, 1995], 2: 1120–1147); King Wu's reflections on the fall of the Shang in the "Xian shi" 先識 chapter of *Lüshi chunqiu* (*Lüshi chunqiu jiaoshi* 呂氏春秋校釋, ann. Chen Qiyou 陳奇猷, 2 vols. [Shanghai: Xuelin chubanshe, 1984], 2: 945–946); the comment on secret communication between the Duke of Zhou and Sheng Shu in the "Jing yu" 精諭 chapter of the same work (*Lüshi chunqiu jiaoshi*, 2: 1167); and the rhymes attributed to Zihuazi 子華子 in the "Zhi du" 知度 chapter (*Lüshi chunqiu jiaoshi*, 2:1092).

14   *Chuci buzhu*, 167.

in "Tian wen") and of references to ecstatic travel (as in "Yuan you"). *Laozi*-style verse would also rigorously avoid reference to the emotional state of the speaker, whether desirous or melancholy or otherwise passionate, as in so many *Chuci* pieces. The self-references found in *Chuci* songs, as well as the depictions of tetrasyllable-users found in some of the anecdotes discussed below, suggest that the people who used rhyme in their teachings were seen as somewhat extraordinary individuals. But in the *Laozi* and in pieces that resemble it generically, there is no place in the verse for references to the performer.

Essays on a wide range of subjects adopt tetrasyllabic rhyming, apparently borrowing the *gravitas* that the form carried with it. Examples are worth considering as foils to the more restricted *Laozi*-style form that was developing at around the same time. Certain rhymed texts were didactic in the sense that they were clearly directed to students. The "Dizi zhi" 弟子職 (Duties of a disciple) chapter of the *Guanzi*, for example, is rhymed throughout. It begins:

先生施教，		As the master bestows his teachings,
弟子是則。	A	the disciple makes these his principle.
溫恭自虛，		Warm, respectful, making himself empty,
所受是極。	A	he pursues to its limit what he has received.
見善從之，		Seeing the good, he follows it;
聞義則服。	A	Hearing of the right he submits to it.
溫柔孝悌，		Warm, gentle, filial, brotherly,
毋驕恃力。	A	He never arrogantly falls back on physical strength.
志毋虛邪，		In his aims there is nothing false or perverse,
行必正直。	A	And in his conduct he is sure to be just and straight.
游居有常，		Whether he travels or resides, there is a constant to it;
必就有德。	A	He is sure to take to the virtuous.
顏色整齊，		His countenance is well ordered,
中心必式。	A	And his heart within takes standards as a necessity.
夙興夜寐，		At dawn he rises, at night he sleeps,
衣帶必飭。	A	And his robes and belt are sure to be adjusted.
朝益暮習，		By day he gains new material, by evening he reviews,
小心翼翼。	A	Being careful and cautious.
一此不解，		Doing this alone and never letting up:
是謂學則。	A	This is known as the principle of study.[15]

A single, highly regular rhyme (in the *zhi* 職 category) ties the whole passage together.[16] Slightly archaic syntax (such as the use of *shi* 是 in the second and

---

15　*Guanzi jiaozhu* 管子校注, ann. Li Xiangfeng 黎翔鳳, 3 vols. (Beijing: Zhonghua, 2004), 3:1144–1164.
16　Jiang Yougao, *Yinxue shishu*, 176.

fourth lines), as well as the *Shijing* line "Being careful and cautious,"[17] give the passage a feel of tradition. Meanwhile, the choice of rhyme words—especially *ji* 極, but also *de* 德 and *li* 力—introduces the highly stereotyped vocabulary of rhymes that operates in strictly *Laozi*-style verse, where 'the limit' (*ji* 極) and the other words appear very frequently at line-ends. Thematically the passage has little to do with *Laozi* tetrasyllabes. Formally and lexically, however, there is a clear kinship.[18]

Rhymed tetrasyllables carry other sorts of teachings as well. The "Ren di" 任地 chapter of the *Lüshi chunqiu* offers, in rhymes placed between prose passages, abstracted advice on the "Great Recipe for All Cases of Plowing" 凡耕之大方 as well as a series of questions attributed to the patron saint of all ploughmen, Lord Millet himself. The passage on plowing is interesting for the rhymed adversative figures that precede a more practical prose passage on land-types and plows. The rhymed passage reads:

力者欲柔，		The strong want softness,
柔者欲力。	A	the soft want strength.
息者欲勞，		The rested want exertion,
勞者欲息。	A	the exerted want rest.
棘者欲肥，		The leached want fertilizing,
肥者欲棘。	A	the fertilized want leaching.
急者欲緩，		The quick want moderation,
緩者欲急。	B	the moderate want quickness.[19]
溼者欲燥，		The moist want dryness,
燥者欲溼。	B	the dry want moisture.[20]

The conviction that opposites complement each other and that proper action corrects one extreme by moving toward the other was also basic to the thought behind the *Laozi*-tetrasyllables.

The Lord Millet passage is remarkable for its unusual attribution and for its use of insistent questioning, a figure likewise found in *Laozi*:

---

17 Found in *Shijing*, "Da ming" 大明 (Mao 236) and "Zheng min" 蒸民 (Mao 260).

18 Other texts that are didactic in a strict sense and employ rhymed tetrasyllables are *Guiguzi* 鬼谷子 (rhymes in Jiang, 240–241) and the Guodian text "Yucong si" 語叢四, for which see 顧史考 (Scott Cook), "Cong *Chuci* yunli kan Guodian Chujian 'Yucong si'" 從楚辭韻例看郭店楚簡語叢四, *Xian-Qin Liang-Han xueshu* 5 (2006): 187–216.

19 According to Xia Weiying 夏緯瑛, cited in *Lüshi chunqiu jiaoshi* 呂氏春秋校釋, ann. Chen Qiyou 陳奇猷, 2 vols. (Shanghai: Xuelin chubanshe, 1984), 2:1737–1738, the "quick" and the "moderate" refer to moist and dry soil respectively, while "strong" and "soft" above refer to the quality of the soil itself.

20 *Lüshi chunqiu jiaoshi*, 2:1731. Rhymes in Jiang Yougao, *Yinxue shishu*, 226.

后稷曰：		Lord Millet said:
子能以窐為突乎？		Can you make a hollow a hump?
子能藏其惡而揖之以陰乎？		Can you hide the dry soil and gather it with moisture?
子能使吾土靖而甽浴土乎？	A	Can you make our soil pure and rinse it with channels?
子能使保溼安地而處乎？	A	Can you make it keep its moisture and remain at peace in the land?
子能使雚夷毋淫乎？	B	Can you keep the *huan* and *ti* weeds from sprouting?
子能使子之野盡為冷風乎？	B	Can you make your fields all open to the light breezes?
子能使槁數節而莖堅乎？	C	Can you make the stalks many-jointed and the stems sturdy?
子能使穗大而堅、均乎？	C	Can you make the tassels large, sturdy, and even?
子能使粟圜而薄糠乎？	D	Can you make the kernels round and the bran thin?
子能使米多沃而食之彊乎？	D	Can you make the grains many and fat and fortifying to eat?[21]

In its detailed references to agricultural problems and plant anatomy, the passage recalls such *Shijing* pieces as "Qi yue" 七月 (Mao 154), with its verse calendar of farming duties, and "Sheng min" 生民 (Mao 245), with Hou Ji's own story. Instead of using strict tetrasyllables, each line frames two phrases of three or four characters in a standard questioning form, disrupting the song-like quality the rhymes might otherwise have had. If the repeated questions resemble *Laozi*-rhymes, the content here, in contrast to the rhymed passage above, shows no likeness at all to the *Laozi*. This is conceivably farmers' verse, useful for teaching new generations the aims of plowing, or something more elevated, like the georgic verses of Hesiod or Vergil.[22]

Advice on medicine, on statecraft, and on economic management could, like other didactic material, take the form of rhymed tetrasyllables. The *Huangdi neijing Su wen* 黃帝內經素問 and *Lingshu* 靈樞, for example, include quite a bit of rhyme, which seems only at one point to adopt a full complement of *Laozi*-style features:

---

21 *Lüshi chunqiu jiaoshi*, 2:1731. I have emended the lines following suggestions given in *Lüshi chunqiu jiaoshi*, 2:1733–1737. Rhymes in Jiang Yougao, *Yinxue shishu*, 226.

22 Also to be considered as agricultural tetrasyllables are passages in *Guanzi*, "Du di" 度地 and "Qingzhong ji" 輕重己; see *Guanzi jiaozhu*, 3:1050–1070, 1540, Jiang Yougao, *Yinxue shishu*, 175, 177.

黃帝曰：嗚呼遠哉！		The Yellow Emperor said: Alas! How far it is!
閔閔乎若視深淵，	A	I am as anxious as if I were gazing into a deep abyss,
若迎浮雲，	A	or facing an oncoming fog.
視深淵尚可測，	B	Gazing into a deep abyss one may yet fathom it,
迎浮雲莫知其際，	B	But facing an oncoming fog no one knows its edges.
聖人之術，		The technique of the sage
為萬民式，	B	is to be a model for the myriad people.
論裁志意，		To discourse and determine aims and intents,
必有法則，	B	he must have his rules and norms.
循經守數，		He follows the classics and keeps to the specifications,
按循醫事，	B	following according to the affairs of the physician,
為萬民副。	B	And becomes an aid to the myriad people.
故事有五過四德，	B	Thus in his affairs there are five mistakes and four virtues.
汝知之乎？		Do you know them?
雷公避席再拜曰：		Lord Lei stepped away from the mat, bowed twice, and said:
臣年幼小，		Young in years I am,
蒙愚以惑，	B	and befuddled by stupidity and confusion.
不聞五過與四德，	B	I have not heard of the five mistakes and four virtues.
比類形名，	C	As I put together categories and forms and names
虛引其經，	C	and vainly draw upon the classics,
心無所對。		there is nothing in my mind for an answer.[23]

As in certain passages of tetrasyllabic verse that will be examined below, here both speakers are made to speak in rhyme. Lord Lei's rhymed humble response is unusual, but the exclamatory metaphors for the techniques of the sage, with their images of depth and unfathomable vastness, fit well with descriptions of the *dao* in *Laozi*-style verse.

Among all early texts, the *Guanzi* especially uses rhymed tetrasyllables in conjunction with unrhymed prose to express notions of statecraft that are, apart from their unusual mode of expression, entirely traditional.[24] Two of these statecraft passages are notable for their inclusion of elements that recall the *Laozi*'s themes and rhetoric. The "Si shi" 四時, for example, opens and closes with rhymes, which serve to introduce and summarize the longer prose

---

23 *Huangdi neijing Su wen Ling shu* 黃帝內經素問靈樞, ann. Wang Bing 王冰 (Tainan: Dafu shuju, 1992), 23.12b; the passage may also be found in "Liu wei zhilun" 六微旨論. Jiang Yougao *Yinxue shishu*, 233.

24 See Jiang Yougao's treatment in *Yinxue shishu*, 168–177, of "Mu min" 牧民; "Ban fa" 版法; "Si cheng" 四稱; "Qi chen qi zhu" 七臣七主; "Ban fa jie" 版法解.

discussion. The first few lines treat the subject as a matter of mysterious wisdom:

令有時，		Commands have their proper timing,
無時，	A	and if they do not,
則必視順		then one must look to and follow
天之所以來，	A	the path Heaven takes,
五漫漫，		The five are vast,
六惛惛，		the six dim:25
庸知之哉？	A	how can one know them?
唯聖人知四時。	A	Only the sage knows the four times,
不知四時，	A	And whoever does not know the four times,
乃失國之基。	A	Will lose the foundation of his state.26

Although the passage has a strong prosaic quality in the opening sentences, moving toward a tetrasyllabic order only in the closing rhymes, the binomes and the exclamatory question, as well as the advertisement of a sagely way that starts from heaven's own order, mark the contact with *Laozi*'s verse, while the otherwise workaday and traditional elements of statecraft advice point to older antecedents. Worth mentioning here as well is a rhymed passage in the "Qin shi" 親士 chapter of the *Mozi*, the only rhymes in that text to show any resemblance to *Laozi*. Here the deaths of loyal officers are understood in terms of the inevitable and natural workings of the world:

今有五錐，		If now we have five awls,
此其銛，		and this one among them is the sharpest,
銛者必先挫，	A	then this sharpest one is sure to be the first to be broken.
有五刀，		If we have five blades,
此其錯，		and this one is the filigreed one,
錯者必先靡。	A	then this filigreed one is sure to be the first to be whetted.
是以甘井近竭，	B	Therefore a well that is sweet brings its own exhaustion,
招木近伐，	B	The tree that grows broad draws near to the woodcutters,
靈龜近灼，	C	The turtleshell that is sacred brings burning upon itself,
神蛇近暴。	C	And the magical snake invites attacks.27

---

25 The "five" are five policies for agricultural management, detailed in the prose section of the chapter. The "six" are *yin*, *yang*, and the four directions.

26 *Guanzi jiaozhu*, 837. Rhymes in Jiang Yougao, *Yinxue shishu*, 172.

27 *Mozi jiaozhu* 墨子校注, ann. Wu Yujiang 吳毓江, 2 vols. (Beijing: Zhonghua, 1993), 1:2. Rhymes in Jiang Yougao, *Yinxue shishu*, 197.

The chapter's emphasis on employing good men and its résumé of martyred heroes are commonplace, but its assimilation of these to a natural mechanics of destruction is something new and quite foreign to the ways of thought exemplified in the core chapters of the *Mozi*.[28]

Given the contacts between early economic thought and some of the key concepts of the *Laozi* and *Zhuangzi*—especially apparent in the *Shiji* biography of Fan Li 范蠡 in his later life as Lord Zhu of Tao 陶朱公[29]—it is predictable that some rhymed tetrasyllables on economic policy would show similarities to *Laozi*-verse. The "Chi mi" 侈靡 chapter of the *Guanzi* advises the ruler on handling the challenges to his power that come from the wealthiest men of the domain:

用其臣者，		In using his ministers,
予而奪之，	A	by giving he takes away,
使而輟之，	A	By employing them he stops them,
徒以而富之，	B	By giving idly he enriches them,
父繫而伏之，	B	By implicating them in their father's crimes he brings them down,
予虛爵而驕之。	C	By granting them empty titles he makes them arrogant,
收其春秋之時		By collecting their seasonal stocks
而消之，	C	he reduces them,
有集禮我而居之。	D	By gathering them for rituals and ceremonies he keeps them in their places,
時舉其強者以譽之。	D	And from time to time he raises an exceptional one among them and sings his praises.[30]

The opening lines' reference to "giving and taking away" and the penultimate line's apparent reference to limiting travel recall *Laozi* passages (chapters 36 and 80 respectively). But given the text's other features, these lines are clearly neither allusions to nor necessarily influenced by the *Laozi*, even if they were composed after some version of that text was already in circulation. Both the language and the notion of manipulation belong to a habit of rhyme composition rather than to a particular thinker or way of thought.[31]

---

28 Another unusual rhymed passage relating to statecraft is Su Qin's extended and rhetorically beautiful warning against the dangers of rhetorical beauty, delivered to the Qin king at *Zhanguo ce* 戰國策 (Shanghai: Shanghai guji, 1978), 1: 81. Rhymes in Jiang Yougao, *Yinxue shishu*, 196–197. The passage does not in any way echo *Laozi* tetrasyllables.

29 *Shiji* (Beijing: Zhonghua, 1959), 41:1753–1755.

30 *Guanzi jiaozhu*, 653. Rhymes in Jiang Yougao, *Yinxue shishu*, 170.

31 Another rhymed passage relating to economic matters is the fascinating reflection on tax collection in the "Shan mu" 山木 chapter of the *Zhuangzi*. The verse relates to the mysti-

Verbal Models of the Dao in Performance

Baxter has already conjectured, on the basis of rhetorical and phonological analysis of the *Laozi* and a small set of comparison texts—including several *Guanzi* chapters and the writings associated with *Laozi* B in the Mawangdui finds—that "the *Lao-tzu* and similar texts emerged from a distinctive tradition of philosophical verse with strong oral elements and little concept of individual authorship," and that the *Laozi* itself dated to the beginning or middle of the fourth century BC.[32] The examples of tetrasyllable raised in the previous section demonstrate that, as might be predicted on the basis of Baxter's view, the genre was represented in many texts besides the ones he considered. They show further that the genre was surrounded by verse that, though in one or another way formally similar, had different didactic aims. *Laozi*-style verse and this larger field of verse seem to have coexisted for some centuries.

If the extant written record is representative, then while the genre of didactic tetrasyllables merely endured, it was the subgenre of *Laozi*-style verse that flourished. As the *Huainanzi* (middle second century BC) and the *Wenzi* 文子 (buried 55 BC) attest, huge amounts of this verse were being composed and committed to writing during the Western Han. Before we consider the context in which this verse was solicited and performed, what can we say about the characteristics of the verse itself? What literary and rhetorical peculiarities might account for its lasting popularity?

Two writers in particular have examined the rhetorical characteristics of *Laozi* verse. Baxter, in his article on the language of the *Laozi*, noted that rhyme was used in conjunction with semantic patterning in individual passages in the text, and that together these made up its characteristic "verse." He remarked also on patterns of repetition, both a "chain repetition pattern" and plain repetition of words in the same positions in successive lines. Finally he noted a use of "paradoxical statements" and an absence of narration.[33] Rudolf Wagner, refuting the notion that individual paragraphs in the *Laozi* are unstructured congeries of sayings, showed numerous examples of an 'interlocking parallel style': a pervading use of *chiasmus* or 'crossing,' by which two or more topics are treated in order two or more times. As Wagner writes, "interlocking parallel style presupposes an argument where there can be parallel

---

cal perfection of the tax-collector rather than to the collecting itself, but nonetheless suggests a use for *Laozi*-style verse and *Laozi*-style actors in the practical money matters of the domain. *Zhuangzi jishi* 莊子集釋, ann. Guo Qingfan 郭慶藩 (Beijing: Zhonghua, 1961), 676–679. Rhymes in Jiang Yougao, *Yinxue shishu*, 184.

32 Baxter, "Situating the Language of the *Lao-tzu*," 249.
33 Baxter, "Situating the Language of the *Lao-tzu*," 234–240.

talk on two opposite subjects, together forming a whole." Beyond these two opposite subjects, philosophical texts point to an encompassing whole that has none of the subjects' own characteristics and therefore cannot be described in language.[34]

A feature of *Laozi*-verse even more fundamental than its verbal patterns is the strangely limited material from which it creates these patterns. As a result of the exclusion of narration noted by Baxter, the tense of the discourse is almost always a generalized present, except in occasional passages of cosmogony. Particulars of most kinds—names of historical or imaginary individuals, or names of places—are absent. Everything takes place somewhere above the ordinary world of instants and things in which we live, and ordinary objects are introduced into consideration only through metaphors. More notable still is the great narrowing of the vocabulary in comparison to that of other didactic verse and philosophical discourse. A word frequency count for all examples of the subgenre would show that a small collection of keywords are disproportionately represented, that even the descriptive binomes that are sometimes used are highly stereotyped, and that overall the language is unnaturally reduced. Charitably speaking, it is a purified language. Less charitably, it is dull.

There was in early China another example of a purified philosophical language. The Neo-Mohists of the later Warring States period (475–221 BC) had undertaken a deliberate effort to create an artificial language that was internally coherent and grounded in rigorous definition of every term. The whole project of the 'canons' (*jing* 經) is to construct this language and to use it in the defense of new propositions that are consistent with the older core of Mohist thought, the Ten Fundamental Doctrines.[35] No doubt the processes that led to the constraints on *Laozi* language were very different from the highly self-conscious work the Mohists did. Composers of *Laozi*-verse worked within a set of generic expectations that they had inherited rather than made. Yet the example of a special language for thought, or even the existence of a group of thinkers who recognized the advantages of an artificially limited language, could have inspired the many composers who isolated the subgenre of *Laozi*-verse from its larger generic context and gave it its mature form. Whether in writing or in live delivery, the constrained language of the form, combined with its metrical features, its semantic patterning, and its repetitions, would have lent

---

34 Rudolf Wagner, "Interlocking Parallel Style: Laozi and Wang Bi," *Asiatische Studien* 34.1 (1980): 18–56, 57; *The Craft of a Chinese Commentator: Wang Bi on the* Laozi (Albany: State University of New York Press, 2000), 53–113.

35 A.C. Graham, *Later Mohist Logic, Ethics, and Science* (Hong Kong: Chinese University Press, 1978).

it philosophical weight. This lexicon and this set of rhetorical features were the tools specifically adapted for this sort of investigation.

Like the lexicon, this investigation itself was remarkably constrained. A diagram of the frequency of various themes in *Laozi*-verse would be at least as top heavy as the word-frequency count. *Laozi*-verse is overwhelmingly devoted to descriptions of the *dao* and the sage, to illustrations of the *dao*'s workings in nature and in human life, and to prescriptions for the ruler who would become a sage user of the *dao*. For the consumers of the form, be they students or rulers or readers, reflections on these themes were what the form was expected to deliver.

It may, however, be misleading to call these reflections on themes. With the example of the Neo-Mohist language in the background, and with the observations of Baxter and Wagner on internal patterning in mind, it is possible to think of exercises in *Laozi*-verse not as external to their subject (reflections on, analyses of), but as attempts to create a verbal model of the subject, a microcosmic version of it that illustrates some of its functions by putting them in play in the words themselves. Since this would not be analysis, nothing like deduction would be necessary or even desirable. The satisfactions of patterning that come with the interlocking parallel style, the repetitions and successive modulations, would not be about the *dao*, but would be the *dao* in a miniature, experimental version.

The interaction of rhymed and unrhymed passages in such verbal models would on the one hand serve to intensify certain aspects of the model, perhaps by implying older sources and authorities behind it, and on the other hand would encourage in the listener a particular openness and attentiveness to patterning of all kinds. Rhyming passages are often introduced by *gu yue* 故曰, 'thus it is said,' a phrase that is used elsewhere to introduce corroboratory material from outside a text. Rhyming passages can come at the end of unrhymed passages, creating a concluding climactic effect. They can introduce or frame unrhymed passages, which then come to look like the more accessible parts of the discourse. The person who delivered such rhymes aloud would command a specific sort of attention, since by his ability to introduce rhyme in the midst of unrhymed speech he would liken himself to physicians and religious specialists and others who were required to use rhyming in their work.

The notion of verbal models of the *dao* and specialists competent to deliver them begs the question of speech and occasion. Baxter mentions but does not stress the orality of the tradition that produced the *Laozi*. It is clear enough from his attention to rhyme, and especially to *Shijing* rhyme distinctions preserved in *Laozi* and lost in later texts, that he regards this text and the others like it as efforts to represent speakable material accurately. But this is to beg a question: speakable by whom, then, and to whom, and in what settings?

Numerous texts depict the live delivery of tetrasyllables in the course of teaching or persuasion. We have already seen one above, in the "Min zhi fumu." The "Peng zu" 彭祖, among the Shanghai Museum texts, contains some rhymes in this subgenre.[36] The "Ai gong" 哀公 chapter of the *Xunzi* attributes a perfect bit of *Laozi*-style tetrasyllable to Confucius in conversation with Lord Ai of Lu.[37] In the "Zhi yi" 執一 chapter of *Lüshi chunqiu* a certain Tian Pian 田駢 delivers another to the king of Qi.[38] A fascinating set of examples is found in the "Yue yu" 越語 chapter of the *Guoyu*, where Fan Li guides King Goujian of Yue toward revenge with a series of speeches that include *Laozi*-style tetrasyllables.[39] At least in historical memory, even of events dating to the end of the Spring and Autumn period (770–476 BC), some transmitters of anecdotes regarded it as possible that a minister would instruct a ruler using this form. To repeat, however, representations in *Zuozhuan* never include *Laozi*-style tetrasyllables, and generally do not attribute rhyming to ministerial speakers except where they are citing rhymed material such as *Shijing*. It may well be that during the late Warring States period there was a shift in how rhyming instruction was regarded.

The richest source of anecdotes featuring performance of *Laozi*-style tetrasyllables is of course the *Zhuangzi*. In "Renjian shi" 人間事, Yan He 顏闔, setting off on the dangerous assignment of acting as tutor for the Wei heir apparent, receives instruction from Qu Boyu 蘧伯玉 in the form of tetrasyllables.[40] In "Ying diwang" 應帝王, Lao Dan 老聃 teaches Yang Ziju 陽子居 about "the governance of the clear-eyed king" (*mingwang zhi zhi* 明王之治) in tetrasyllables.[41] In "Zai you" 在宥, Lao Dan offers Cui Qu 崔瞿 a vision of the long decline of culture, describing the situation partly in tetrasyllables.[42] In the same chapter, Cloud General (*yun jiang* 雲將) asks tetrasyllabic questions of Vast Covering (*hong meng* 鴻蒙) about putting the world in order, and receives tetrasyllabic answers from him.[43] In "Tian di" 天地, a recluse uses tetrasyllables

---

36 Ma Chengyuan 馬承源 et al., ed., *Shanghai bowuguan cang Zhanguo Chu zhushu* 上海博物館藏戰國楚竹書, vol. 3 (Shanghai: Shanghai guji, 2003), 119–128, 301–308.
37 *Xunzi jijie*, 2:541–542.
38 *Lüshi chunqiu jiaoshi*, 2:1133.
39 *Guoyu jijie* 國語集解, ann. Xu Yuangao 徐元誥 (Beijing: Zhonghua shuju, 2002), 575–579.
40 *Zhuangzi jishi*, 164–169.
41 *Zhuangzi jishi*, 295–297.
42 *Zhuangzi jishi*, 371–377.
43 *Zhuangzi jishi*, 385–392.

to teach the sage king Yao.⁴⁴ Zhunmang 諄芒 uses them as he finishes answering a series of questions from Yuanfeng 苑風.⁴⁵ The Yellow Emperor uses them in describing the Xianchi 咸池 music to Beimen Cheng 北門成.⁴⁶ The North Sea uses them in his teachings to the River Earl.⁴⁷ Guan Yin 關尹 uses them in describing the sage to Liezi 列子.⁴⁸ The cicada-catcher uses them as he speaks of his technique to Confucius.⁴⁹ Zhuang Zhou uses them in an explanation to his disciples.⁵⁰

It is surely significant that when the performance of tetrasyllables is staged in *Zhuangzi*—that is, when some narrative frame is given, and tetrasyllabic verse is attributed to one or more speakers within the narrative—the scene is invariably one of instruction, and typically one in which the versifier is positioned, partly through the attribution of tetrasyllables and partly by other means, as more advanced in wisdom than his interlocutor. Given the stereotypical content of the *Laozi*-style material conveyed in rhyme, it is as if these narratives are designed to dramatize the superior speaker's access to the bland, impersonal, sometimes paradoxical truths of the *dao*. The moment the idiosyncratic prose of speech gives way to the familiar regularities of the *Laozi* style, the pedagogical demonstration is complete: any questioner's doubts, his political or personal aporias, his questions about nature and the cosmos, are resolved in the comfort of vague and rhyming truisms.

The question is whether these anecdotes, most of which feature mythical or plainly allegorical characters speaking outside any particular historical frame, capture anything at all of real scenes of teaching. Assuming that there were indeed specialists in the oral delivery of *Laozi*-style tetrasyllables, and that the broad diffusion of their form of verse in texts of the late first millennium BC bespeaks the existence of a large group, even a class, of such practitioners, then in what venues and on what sorts of occasions were their services regarded as valuable? What supported them and promoted the continued modelling and production of this genre of verse?

To judge from the character of the verse itself and from the scenes that dramatize its use, these specialists most likely presented themselves as healers of a particular kind: experts in addressing the connection between the health of

---

44 *Zhuangzi jishi*, 420–423.
45 *Zhuangzi jishi*, 439–443.
46 *Zhuangzi jishi*, 401–410.
47 *Zhuangzi jishi*, 584–585.
48 *Zhuangzi jishi*, 633–638.
49 *Zhuangzi jishi*, 639–641.
50 *Zhuangzi jishi*, 667–668.

the collective and the personal physical, moral, and spiritual health of the person charged with governing that collective. *Laozi*-style tetrasyllables take as given the nexus laboriously constructed in the sorites of the "Great Learning" ("Da xue" 大學), which ties the governing of the state (*zhi guo* 治國) to more restricted forms of familial and personal cultivation. The connection is so fundamental to the *Laozi* itself that modern readers can sometimes entirely neglect the statecraft advice that is central to the text, regarding it as a metaphorical extension of directives on self-cultivation that are somehow more basic. In truth, however, the call to self-reform that is found in that text and in the larger corpus of tetrasyllables always makes the health of the ruler and of the collective (family, state, world) interdependent, and the cure for the latter always proceeds from the cure for the former.

In private use among specialists, tetrasyllables of the kind we have been examining would no doubt have belonged, as Harold Roth has shown they must have, to the "body of oral and written texts that grew up surrounding inner cultivation practice as it originated and evolved." In this context, rhyme and regularity would have been useful for purposes of memorization.[51] The affiliations of tetrasyllables in texts such as *Laozi* and "Nei ye" with tetrasyllables used in other sorts of texts may have something to tell us about where the users of tetrasyllables saw themselves in relation to their societies and their patrons and followers, including rulers. To speculate beyond the range of direct evidence, one might suppose that the tetrasyllabists saw themselves as linked historically or socially with physicians, who were both masters of certain forms of mythological and magical knowledge and users of tetrasyllabic incantations.[52] In this role, or in some version of this role, they would perhaps have enjoyed a special access to the patron or ruler. In contrast to roving persuaders, who presented themselves first in the assembly hall or court and spoke in the presence of gathered officials or retainers, seeking ultimately to win their way into a persuasive intimacy with the decision-maker, the verse-users may have traded on their status as healers or healer-like figures to move directly to private interviews with the head man.[53] Certainly in depictions of tetrasyllables in action

---

51 Roth, *Original Tao*, 168.
52 Donald Harper, *Early Chinese Medical Literature: The Mawangdui Medical Manuscripts* (London: Kegan Paul International, 1998), 234, 291–292.
53 In several texts on rhetorical practice, intimacy with the ruler is held up as the ultimate aim of the persuader, since a personal relationship offers the most efficient form of influence. See, for example, *Han Feizi jishi* 韓非子集釋, ann. Chen Qiyou 陳奇猷 (Shanghai: Shanghai Renmin, 1974), 222; the opening anecdote of the *Zhuangzi* chapter "Renjian shi" 人間世 likewise ends with a vision of closeness between persuader and ruler; see *Zhuangzi jishi*, 148.

the norm is not the address in open court, but the one-on-one encounter between wise visitor and perplexed ruler.

In examples like the following, again from *Zhuangzi*, cultivation of the self trumps statecraft both as an area of effort for the ruler and as an area of expertise for the teacher, but as the personal (*zhi shen* 治身) supplants the political (*zhi guo* 治國) it is nonetheless clear that the basic truths for both forms of control (*zhi* 治) are derived from natural regularities and are naturally captured in tetrasyllables. After nineteen years in power, the Yellow Emperor learns that Guangchengzi 廣成子 (whose name means something like 'Master Broad Completion') is at Mount Kongtong 空同 'Empty, Hollow,' perhaps in reclusion, and goes to ask him, as one accomplished in the perfected way (*zhidao* 至道), how he can rule in such a way as to grasp the essence of Heaven and earth, promote the growth of the five grains, and foster the people; he wishes to master *yin* and *yang* in order to bring all livelihood to its fruition. Predictably—and despite the emperor's interest in fundamentals of nature—the master turns him away, claiming that what he is addressing in his governing of the world (*zhi tianxia* 治天下) is no more than the substance and the dregs of material reality. He adds a personal insult, calling the emperor a narrow-minded prattler (*ningren zhi xin jianjian zhe* 佞人之心翦翦者) and hardly worth talking with about such a thing as the perfected way. In a move entirely predictable to readers of *Zhuangzi* anecdotes, the emperor abdicates and resides in an isolated hut for three months before again approaching Guangchengzi, this time creeping up from downwind on his knees and bowing before asking a slightly different question: "I have heard that you, sir, have attained the perfected way. I presume to ask how I can govern myself (*zhi shen* 治身) so that I may last long." And now that the question is posed with suitable humility and starts not from nature or the ruled world but from the questioner's own self, Guangchengzi consents to answer, beginning with a masterly move reminiscent of Confucius and proceeding quickly to tetrasyllables: "A question well asked! Come, I will speak to you of the perfected way" 善哉問乎！來, 吾語女至道:

至道之精,	A	The essence of the perfected way
窈窈冥冥；	A	Is obscure and dark.
至道之極,	B	The far limit of the perfected way
昏昏默默。	B	Is clouded and silent.
無視無聽,	A	Look not, listen not,
抱神以靜,	A	But clasp your spirit to you and be tranquil,
形將自正。	A	And then your form will of itself become regulated.
必靜必清,	A	You must be tranquil, you must be clear,
無勞女形,	A	Never overworking your form,

無搖女精，	A	Never agitating your essence,
乃可以長生。	A	And then you can live long.
目無所見，		When there is nothing your eyes see,
耳無所聞，		When there is nothing your ears hear,
心無所知，		When there is nothing your mind knows,
女神將守形，	A	Then your spirit will keep to your form,
形乃長生。	A	And your form will live long.
慎女內，		Take care for what is within you,
閉女外，	B	And close yourself off to what is outside of you:
多知為敗。	B	An abundance of knowledge makes for failure.

Here he returns to prose, and although he would not have spoken if the emperor had not abandoned his ambition to rule the world, it immediately becomes clear that—from the perspective of the anecdote-makers at least—the connection has not been forgotten.

> For you I have ventured to the heights of the great brightness, reaching the source of perfect *yang*; for you I have entered within the gates of obscurity and darkness, reaching the source of perfect *yin*.

天地有官，		Heaven and earth have their offices,
陰陽有藏。	C	and *yin* and *yang* have their hidden treasures.
慎守女身，		Take care and preserve your body,
物將自壯。	C	And things will flourish of themselves.
我守其一，		I have kept to this oneness
以處其和。		In such a way as to reside in its harmony.

> Therefore I have for one thousand two hundred years cultivated myself, and my form has never yet wasted away.

The emperor bows and declares that what Guangchengzi is speaking of is the heavenly itself. Guangchengzi concludes by completing the political element of the lesson and reasserting his own detachment. "Come, I will speak of it to you:

彼其物無窮，	D	Though things themselves are without end,
而人皆以為有終；	D	Everyone imagines they have an end;
彼其物無測，	B	Though things are without measure,
而人皆以為有極。	B	Everyone imagines they have a limit.

> Whoever learns my way will be an august ruler under the best circumstances, a king under the worst; whoever fails in my way will under the best circumstances see the light and under the worst become earth.

今夫百昌皆生於土	E	Now every flourishing thing is born from the earth
而反於土。	E	and returns to the earth.
故余將去女,	E	So I will leave you
入無窮之門,		And enter the gate of the inexhaustible
以遊無極之野。	E	So as to roam in the wilds of the limitless.
吾與日月參光,	C	I will share the light of sun and moon,
吾與天地為常。	C	And I will be as constant as Heaven and earth.
當我, 緡乎!	F	To those who cling to me I am indistinct;
遠我, 昏乎!	F	To those who stay far from me I am clouded.
人其盡死,		Men will die, every last one of them,
而我獨存乎!」	F	But I alone live on.[54]

Taken as a whole, the piece has more resonances in literature than in anything we know of historical realities. The verse belongs to the larger corpus of *Laozi*-style tetrasyllables. The interview of the self-abasing ruler with the reclusive and dismissive sage and its embedding of verse within narrative and discursive prose recall numerous other anecdotal passages in *Zhuangzi* and in associated works such as *Wenzi*, *Liezi*, and *Huainanzi*. The reference to flight recalls the *Chuci* piece "Far Traveling" ("Yuan you" 遠遊) and of course looks forward to early Han *fu* like Sima Xiangru's 司馬相如 "Great Man" ("Daren fu" 大人賦) and the enduring subgenre of travel *fu*. But none of this need necessarily point beyond the world of fiction: despite the demands of rhyme to be pronounced aloud, scenes of instruction of this kind were conceivably confined entirely to the world of imagination and reading. Even under such constraints they might of course have had far-reaching effects on their audiences. But there is some reason to think that such scenes really did take place, though they are almost never represented in historical works.

Conclusion: Historical Occasions for Tetrasyllable Performance

One reason available accounts of tetrasyllables in performance would tend to be presented as overtly fictional rather than as historical or quasi-historical is that speech of this sort was designed not for open court but for the private audience. To judge from the traits of the genre of tetrasyllables, prescriptions for the patron's spiritual and political malaise would clearly have depended upon the hearer's willingness to undertake some individual process of self-transformation. The practitioner, claiming a secretive expertise, rather like a physician, would aim to treat the ruler-patient in private, one on one. Given

---

54 *Zhuangzi jishi*, 379–384.

the power that the prescribed transformations were purported to bring, it is easy to understand why our texts have little to tell us of historical individuals' experiences.

Nonetheless, there is a strong possibility that there were, on the scene of the late Warring States and Han, speakers—some of them perhaps the tellers of just such anecdotes as we have examined in the last few pages—who specialized in the performance of *Laozi*-style tetrasyllables in a fashion resembling Guangchengzi's, that is to say, in a therapeutic way addressed to the ruler's personal and political governance (*zhi* 治). Certainly the final years of Qin Shihuang's life suggest a receptivity to *Laozi*-style talk. That by the end of the third century the Qin ruling philosophy had assimilated certain principles from *Laozi* is clear from the *Han Feizi*, whose "Jie Lao" 解老 and "Yu Lao" 喻老 chapters cite *Laozi* tags with the words *gu yue* 故曰 "Thus it is said"... . And Qin Shihuang appears to have adopted the role prescribed for the ruler in the *Han Feizi*'s elaborations of *Laozi*. As part of his general quest for immortality and for contact with spiritually advanced beings, he is said to have sought to attract a "True Man" (*zhenren* 真人), and for this purpose, on the advice of one Master Lu 盧生, reconstructed his palace as a vast interconnected labyrinth in which he could travel untraced, thus becoming the invisible and unknowable figure of the *Han Feizi*'s prescriptions.[55] The oft-noted popularity of Huang-Lao 黃老 thought during the first seven decades of the Han dynasty, especially given the presence of *Laozi*-style tetrasyllables in the texts associated with that branch of thought, hints at a continued fascination with talk of this kind.[56] Huang-Lao was reportedly suppressed—along with Forms and Names (*xingming* 形名) thought and other strains of thought—after the death of its most highly placed proponent, the Empress Dowager Dou, in 135 BC. That Liu An, Prince of Huainan, was able to produce, with the help of gathered scholars and clients, a text so thoroughly informed by *Laozi*-style rhymes certainly suggests that the practice of 'Huang-Lao speech' (*Huang Lao zhi yan* 黃老之言) still enjoyed strong currency by the time the text was presented to Wudi in 139 BC.[57] And that the same man was known for his understanding of

---

55 *Shiji*, 6.257.
56 *Shiji*, 104.2775 (before 200 BC); 54.2029 (194 BC); 102.2756 (ca. 156 BC); 120.3112 (before 140 BC); 12.452 (140 BC) (cf. 28.1384, 107.2843, 121.3117); 120.3105 (before 135 BC); 101.2748 (ca. 135 BC). For the link between Huang-Lao and the thought of Shen Buhai and Han Fei, see *Shiji*, 63.2146. *Laozi*-style rhymes are abundant in the Mawangdui texts thought to represent early Han Huang-Lao thought; see Leo S. Chang and Yu Feng, *The Four Political Treatises of the Yellow Emperor*, Monographs of the Society for Asian and Comparative Philosophy, no. 15 (Honolulu: University of Hawai'i Press, 1998).
57 Ban Gu 班固, *Hanshu* 漢書, 12 vols. (Beijing: Zhonghua, 1962), 44.2145.

Chuci pieces and his facility with the *fu* form, and according to Martin Kern may even have presented the *Huainanzi* to court with a *fu* delivered aloud (the "Yao lüe" 要略 that concludes the work), reinforces the sense of a deep connection between two distinct literary practices, the *fu* and the *Laozi*-style tetrasyllables.[58] Indeed, one notable tie between the larger genre of *fu* and the tetrasyllables would be the psycho-physiological curative function attributed in some cases to both. A tetrasyllabic piece like the "Inward Training" ("Nei ye" 內業) chapter of the *Guanzi* has in common with the "Seven Stimuli" ("Qi fa" 七發) of Mei Sheng, and with any of a number of *fu* on stilling the passions (*ding qing* 定情), and with a much broader range of literarily patterned pieces performed in early China, the assumption that words can cure.[59]

To bring together the various parts of this demonstration, then, it is clear first that the type of verse exemplified in the *Laozi* and submitted to formal analysis by Wagner and others belonged to a much larger corpus of rhyming tetrasyllabic material, some of it sharing the *Laozi*'s distinctive lexical, figural, and thematic features, the rest of it perhaps reflecting the matrix of tetrasyllabic rhyming practices within which the *Laozi* style grew up. Examples suggest that tetrasyllabic verses were useful especially in didactic and curative contexts. While the *Laozi* verses come to us entirely without narrative frame, the many anecdotes in which verses in the same style are attributed to speakers in conversation show certain common traits: the user of such verses presents himself as a teacher or healer, whatever the status of his pupil-patient; their encounter normally takes place in private; and the treatment or cure, while directed primarily to the hearer's regulation of his personal physical and spiritual health (*zhi shen* 治身), also promises to have resonance in larger efforts at governance (*zhi guo* 治國). Although these anecdotes present themselves unapologetically as fictions, these common elements in their narratives open the way to a plausible account of the way *Laozi*-style tetrasyllables were actually being used in the courts of the patrons and rulers of the Warring States

---

58 Martin Kern, "Creating a Book and Performing It: The 'Yaolüe' Chapter of *Huainanzi* as a Western Han *Fu*," in *The* Huainanzi *and Textual Production in Early China*, eds. Michael Puett and Sarah A. Queen (Leiden: Brill, 2014), 124–150. Some pieces acknowledged to belong to the genre of *fu* are in fact *Laozi*-style tetrasyllabic compositions. See the "Owl *fu*" ("Funiao fu" 服鳥賦) attributed to Jia Yi 賈誼, *Shiji*, 84.2496–500.

59 On the function of language in "Neiye," see Roth *Original Tao*, 129–133. On Mei Sheng, see David R. Knechtges and Jerry Swanson, "Seven Stimuli for the Prince: The *Ch'i-fa* of Mei Ch'eng," *Monumenta Serica* 29 (1970–71): 99–116. A fine recent overview of the *dingqing* genre of *fu* is to be found in Lawrence C.H. Yim, "Between Self-Indulgence and Self-Restraint—Tao Qian's 'Quieting the Passions'," *Zhongguo wenzhe yanjiu jikan* 中國文哲研究集刊 22 (2003): 35–64.

and Han. Similar to the roving persuaders (*youshui zhi ke* 遊說之客), a class of experts in *Laozi*-style tetrasyllables would appear to have made their living as clients of the powerful, promising with their verses both personal health and political power, and operating largely in private. That texts of the late Warring States and especially of the first century of the Han are so rich in examples of their peculiar form of verbal art would be a sign both of the prestige these experts enjoyed and of writers' interest in recreating for their readers some of the curative effects of speakers' rhymes.

References

Ban Gu 班固. *Hanshu* 漢書. 12 vols. Beijing: Zhonghua shuju, 1962.

Baxter, William. "Situating the Language of the *Lao-tzu*." In *Lao-tzu and the Tao-te-ching*, edited by Livia Kohn and Michael Lafargue. Albany: SUNY Press, 1998: 231–253.

Chang, Leo S. and Yu Feng. *The Four Political Treatises of the Yellow Emperor*, Monographs of the Society for Asian and Comparative Philosophy, no. 15. Honolulu: University of Hawai'i Press, 1998.

Chuci buzhu 楚辭補注. Annotated by Hong Xingzu 洪興祖. Beijing: Zhonghua shuju, 1983.

Chunqiu Zuozhuan zhu 春秋左傳注. Annotated, revised and edited by Yang Bojun 楊伯峻. Beijing: Zhonghua shuju, 1990.

Graham, A.C. *Later Mohist Logic, Ethics, and Science*. Hong Kong: Chinese University Press, 1978.

Gu Shikao 顧史考 (Scott Cook). "Cong *Chuci* yunli kan Guodian Chujian 'Yucong si'" 從楚辭韻例看郭店楚簡語叢四. *Xian-Qin Liang-Han xueshu* 先秦兩漢學術 5 (2006): 187–216.

Guanzi jiaozhu 管子校注. Annotated by Li Xiangfeng 黎翔鳳. 3 vols. Beijing: Zhonghua shuju, 2004.

Guoyu jijie 國語集解. Annotated by Xu Yuangao 徐元誥. Beijing: Zhonghua shuju, 2002.

Han Feizi jishi 韓非子集釋. Annotated by Chen Qiyou 陳奇猷. Shanghai: Shanghai Renmin, 1974.

Harper, Donald. *Early Chinese Medical Literature: The Mawangdui Medical Manuscripts*. London: Kegan Paul International, 1998.

Huang Xiquan 黄锡全. "Notes on reading Volume 2 of *Warring States Chu Bamboo Writings Collected by the Shanghai Museum* (1)" 讀上博楚簡二札記壹 (Feb 2003). http://www.bamboosilk.org/Wssf/2003/huangxiquan01.htm (last access 11/2014).

Huangdi neijing Su wen Ling shu 黃帝內經素問靈枢. Annotated by Wang Bing 王冰. Tainan: Dafu shuju, 1992.

Jiang Yougao 江有誥. *Yinxue shishu* 音學十書. Beijing: Zhonghua shuju, 1993.

Karlgren, Bernhard. *The Poetical Parts in Lao-tsï*, Göteborgs Högskolas Årsskrift 38.3. Göteborg: Elanders boktryckeri aktiebolag, 1932.

Kern, Martin. "Creating a Book and Performing It: The 'Yaolüe' Chapter of *Huainanzi* as a Western Han *Fu*." In *The* Huainanzi *and Textual Production in Early China*, edited by Michael Puett and Sarah A. Queen. Leiden: Brill, 2014: 124–150.

Knechtges, David R., and Jerry Swanson. "Seven Stimuli for the Prince: The *Ch'i-fa* of Mei Ch'eng." *Monumenta Serica* 29 (1970–71): 99–116.

Lunyu jishi 論語集釋. Annotated by Cheng Shude 程樹德. 4 vols. Beijing: Zhonghua shuju, 1990.

Lüshi chunqiu jiaoshi 呂氏春秋校釋. Annotated by Chen Qiyou 陳奇猷. 2 vols. Shanghai: Xuelin chubanshe, 1984.

Ma Chengyuan 馬承源 et al., eds. *Shanghai bowuguan cang Zhanguo Chu zhushu* 上海博物館藏戰國楚竹書, vol. 2. Shanghai: Shanghai guji, 2002.

———. *Shanghai bowuguan cang Zhanguo Chu zhushu* 上海博物館藏戰國楚竹書, vol. 3. Shanghai: Shanghai guji, 2003.

Mozi jiaozhu 墨子校注. Annotated by Wu Yujiang 吳毓江. 2 vols. Beijing: Zhonghua shuju, 1993.

Richter, Matthias L. *The Embodied Text: Establishing Textual Identity in Early Chinese Manuscripts*. Leiden: Brill, 2013.

Roth, Harold D. *Original Tao: Inward Training (Nei-yeh) and the Foundations of Taoist Mysticism*. New York: Columbia University Press, 1999.

Shirakawa Shizuka 白川靜. *Kinbun tsûshaku* 金文通釈. 56 vols. *Hakutsuru bijutsukan shi* 白鶴美術館誌. Kobe, 1962–1984.

Sima Qian 司馬遷. *Shiji* 史記. Beijing: Zhonghua shuju, 1959.

Wagner, Rudolf. "Interlocking Parallel Style: Laozi and Wang Bi." *Asiatische Studien / Études asiatiques* 34.1 (1980): 18–58.

———. *The Craft of a Chinese Commentator: Wang Bi on the* Laozi. Albany: SUNY Press, 2000.

Xunzi jijie 荀子集解. Annotated by Wang Xianqian 王先謙. 2 vols. Beijing: Zhonghua shuju, 1988.

Yi Zhou shu huijiao jizhu 逸周書彙校集注. Annotated by Huang Huaixin 黃懷信 et al. 2 vols. Shanghai: Shanghai guji chubanshe, 1995.

Yim, Lawrence C.H. "Between Self-Indulgence and Self-Restraint—Tao Qian's 'Quieting the Passions'." *Zhongguo wenzhe yanjiu jikan* 中國文哲研究集刊 22 (2003): 35–64.

Zhanguo ce 戰國策. Shanghai: Shanghai guji, 1978.

Zhuangzi jishi 莊子集釋. Annotated by Guo Qingfan 郭慶藩. Beijing: Zhonghua shuju, 1961.

CHAPTER 4

Defining Boundaries and Relations of Textual Units: Examples from the Literary Tool-Kit of Early Chinese Argumentation

Joachim Gentz

Introduction

At the beginning of his major work *Ten Thousand Things*, Lothar Ledderose describes a Chinese jigsaw puzzle, which he was given as a child, to introduce his ideas about the modular nature of Chinese culture in general. This puzzle had pieces without curved edges or interlocking shapes, all simple rectangles, with no fixed position for each piece. It was a puzzle that could be put together in a variety of ways: "The mountains could go into the middle of the landscape or to the right; the tower would as easily fit between the peaks as on the plain, and the rider could be placed heading toward the hills or returning. A coherent panorama invariably emerged. The trick to completing this puzzle was that, on every single piece, the horizon crossed the left and right edges exactly at midpoint. The pieces could thus be put together in ever new combinations, thousands of them, yet the continuous horizon always guaranteed an intelligible composition."[1]

Brian Moloughney has suggested that Chinese texts resemble this kind of Chinese jigsaw puzzle.[2] Accordingly, the trick of making sense of an early Chinese text (the units of which had already been identified) would lie in something analogous to the horizontal line that provides a sign of connection between the pieces.

This paper will argue that similar lines of connections are drawn between units of early Chinese texts. They are constructed by internal references that are neither built on external sources nor on an internal logical unity of syllogistic forms but rather on a range of signifiers that gain their specific meaning in the textual argument through their placement in relation to, and affiliation

---

1 Lothar Ledderose, *Ten Thousand Things: Module and Mass Production in Chinese Art* (Princeton, NJ: Princeton University Press, 2000), vi.
2 Brian Moloughney, "Derivation, Intertextuality and Authority: Narrative and the Problem of Historical Coherence," *East Asian History* 23 (2002): 129–148, 129–130.

with, other signifiers of the same argumentative line. Such lines of arguments are typically produced by linking textual parts, regardless of whether these parts are distinguishable formal elements from other sources or not. These lines are mostly arranged in parallels or oppositional chains. They are moulded into literary forms of parallelisms, repetitive referential signifiers, rhythmical metre, rhyme connotations, binary chains, correlative classifications, and other symmetric or regular figures that generate textual patterns. Such literary forms on the one hand structure the text into separate parts and on the other indicate the relationship of these parts to each other, thus generating meaning. I will argue that this literary arrangement of a text is an integral part of its argumentation. In many cases the argumentative line of a text can only be reconstructed in an unambiguous way through the reconstruction of its literary arrangements, which embody and encode the argument as a whole. In early Chinese texts literary forms are often used as means of providing the necessary links that classify what appear as separated units in a text as belonging to lines of arguments which run through the whole text. Reading such literary forms as arguments requires first of all an identification of the textual parts and their respective connections within an open net of possible relations.

This understanding of Chinese texts builds on my earlier idea about Chinese canonical texts consisting of single textual units.[3] It focuses on the way these units are, first, constructed literally: how they are formally framed and, without fixed and systematic inner-textual markers of paragraphing or inter-

---

3 J. Gentz, *Das* Gongyang zhuan. *Auslegung und Kanonisierung der* Frühlings- und Herbstannalen (Chunqiu) (PhD 1998, Wiesbaden: Harrassowitz, 2001), 2. In 1999, Rudolf G. Wagner has formulated his idea of "The Guodian MSS and the 'Units of Thought' in Early Chinese Philosophy" (unpublished conference Paper, presented at the Guodian Conference, Wuhan, October 15-18, 1999). Meyer called them "components" (Dirk Meyer, "The Power of the Component and the Establishment of the Guodian Tomb One Bamboo-slip Manuscript 'Zhōng xìn zhī dào' as a Text," MA Dissertation, Leiden University, 2002; also same author, "A device for conveying meaning: The structure of the Guodian Tomb One manuscript 'Zhōng xìn zhī dào'," *BJOAF* 29 [2005]: 57–78); Boltz prefers to talk about "building blocks" (William G. Boltz, "The Composite Nature of Early Chinese Texts," in *Text and Ritual in Early China*, ed. Martin Kern [Seattle: University of Washington Press, 2005], 50–78), which Richter breaks down to "literarische Kleinstformen" including such small units of expressions as proverbs, sayings, four character phrases (Matthias Richter, "Der Alte und das Wasser: Lesarten von *Laozi* 8 im überlieferten Text und in den Manuskripten von Mawangdui," in *Han-Zeit: Festschrift für Hans Stumpfeldt aus Anlaß seines 65. Geburtstages,* ed. M. Friedrich, R. Emmerich, H. van Ess, 253–273 [Wiesbaden: Harrassowitz, 2006], 254). Broschat calls them "constituents" or "paragraphs" (Michael R. Broschat, "Guiguzi: A textual Study and Translation" [Doctoral dissertation, University of Michigan 1985], 87–127).

punctuation,⁴ become identifiable as demarcated units. And, secondly, made into arguments by formally establishing specific relationships of identity, opposition or aspectuality between them.

Intertextuality,⁵ collage,⁶ allusion and quotation⁷ have been identified as typical features of early Chinese textual compositions, based on a "logic of signs," which refers to sources that lie outside the text.⁸ Indeed, most early texts consist of what Matthias Richter calls "formal elements," which appear also in other texts as well and carry specific literary forms into a text,⁹ William Boltz even holds that all pre-imperial Chinese texts are composite in nature.¹⁰

To make textual parts and their arrangements explicit, Chinese texts were written down spatially in early China,¹¹ and diagrammatic representations

---

4   For punctuation in early Chinese manuscripts see Matthias Richter, *The Embodied Text—Establishing Textual Identity in Early Chinese Manuscripts* (Leiden: Brill, 2013). Id., chapter "Punctuation" in: *Reading Early Chinese Manuscripts: Texts, Contexts, Methods*, ed. Wolfgang Behr, Martin Kern, Dirk Meyer (Handbook of Oriental Studies, Leiden: Brill, forthcoming).

5   Paul Fischer, "Intertextuality in Early Chinese Masters-Texts: Shared Narratives in *Shi Zi*," *Asia Major* 22.2 (2009): 1–34.

6   Christian Schwermann, "Collage-Technik als Kompositionsprinzip klassischer chinesischer Prosa: Der Aufbau des Kapitels 'Tang wen' (Die Fragen des Tang) im *Lie zi*," *Bochumer Jahrbuch zur Ostasienforschung* 29 (2005): 125–157.

7   See the contributions to issue 17 (1995) of *Extrême-Orient, Extrême-Occident*: "Le travail de la citation en Chine et au Japon": François Martin, "Le *Shijing*, de la citation à l'allusion: La disponibilité du sens," 5–39; Jean Levi, "Quelques examples de détournement subversif de la citation dans la littérature classique chinoise," 41–65; Michael Lackner, "Citation et éveil. Quelques remarques à propos de l'emploi de la citation chez Zhang Zai," 111–130. See also the two studies discussing the quotations in the *Ziyi*: Joachim Gentz, "Composition as grammar of a topological semantic flow. A comparison of the two 'Tzu-i'-versions from Kuo-tien and the Li-chi," EACS Conference Papers, Turin, 2000 (CD-ROM-Publication, 2002), and Martin Kern, "Quotation and the Confucian Canon in Early Chinese Manuscripts: The Case of 'Zi yi' (Black Robes)," *Asiatische Studien* 59.1 (2005): 293–332.

8   David Schaberg, "The Logic of Signs in Early Chinese Rhetoric," in *Thinking Through Comparison: Ancient China and Greece*, eds. Stephen Durrant and Steven Shankman (New York: SUNY, 2002), 155–186.

9   Matthias Richter, "Self-Cultivation or Evaluation of Others?: A Form Critical Approach to Zengzi li shi," *Asiatische Studien / Études asiatiques* LVI, 4 (2002): 879–917.

10 William Boltz, "The Composite Nature of Early Chinese Texts." Dirk Meyer has rightly pointed out "that we should not conclude from this that the feature of the building block results in a 'composite nature' of these texts that opposes 'integral, structurally homogeneous texts' (see Boltz 2005, 70–71)." See Dirk Meyer, *Philosophy on Bamboo: Text and the Production of Meaning in Early China* (Leiden: Brill, 2011), 177, n 1.

11 Vera Dorofeeva-Lichtmann, "Spatial Composition of Ancient Chinese Texts," in *History of Science, History of Text*, ed. Karine Chemla (Dordrecht: Springer, 2005), 3–47. And id.,

were developed as didactic means especially since Song times (960–1279) to visualise their parts and the relationship between them.¹² The paper will argue that early Chinese texts provide signifiers that allow a similar mapping of textual parts and their relation necessary for constructing the text's meaning in the process of reading. As the lexical meanings of singular characters are quite under-determined and differ in different textual contexts, even within one text, literary forms of composition provide harder indications of the meaning of a text than lexical semantics. The function of a term within a literary form can have its common lexical meaning overruled by its literary placement. The literary form therefore has to be taken much more seriously in our reconstruction of early Chinese arguments than we are used to in text interpretations that are still mainly based on European philological methodologies.¹³

The paper will present three such literary forms (double-directed parallelism, enumerative catalogues and referential signifiers) to finally conclude with an example that combines all these forms. While the first three examples are taken to discuss one particular literary form of argument, the last example is taken to demonstrate that such literary forms are, probably, in most cases

---

"Spatiality of the Media for Writing in Ancient China and Spatial Organization of Ancient Chinese Texts," *Göttinger Beiträge zur Asienforschung* 1 (2001): 87–135.

12 Michael Lackner, "Die Verplanung des Denkens am Beispiel der *tu*," in *Lebenswelt und Weltanschauung im frühneuzeitlichen China*, ed. Helwig Schmidt-Glintzer (Stuttgart: Steiner, 1990), 133–156; id., "Argumentation par diagrammes. Une architecture à base de mots. Le *Ximing* (*l'Inscription Occidentale*) depuis Zhang Zai jusqu'au *Yanjitu*," *Extrême Orient-Extrême Occident* 14 (1992): 131–168; id., "La position d'une expression dans le texte: explorations diagrammatiques de la signification," *Extrême Orient-Extrême Occident* (1996): 35–51; id., "Was Millionen Wörter nicht sagen können: Diagramme zur Visualisierung klassischer Texte im China des 13. bis 14. Jahrhunderts," *Zeitschrift für Semiotik* 22.2 (2000): 209–237; id., "Diagrams as an Architecture by Means of Words: the *Yanji tu*," in *Graphics and Text in the Production of Technical Knowledge in China: The Warp and the Weft*, ed. Francesca Bray et al. (Leiden: Brill, 2007), 341–381. Joachim Gentz, "Hermeneutics of Multiple Senses: Wang Jie's 'Explanations and Commentary with Diagrams to the *Qingjing jing*'," *Journal of Chinese Philosophy* 37.3 (2010): 346–365.

13 For a similar point see Michael Broschat, who for his text analysis uses what he calls "constituent analysis" as "an analytic process in which significant constituent parts are identified, their relations to other parts are identified and specified, and the general effect of these constituents and their structural inter-relations on the meaning of the whole text is considered," in id., "Guiguzi," 87–127 with this quote on pp. 88–89. See also his quote on p. 104 of Seymour Chatman: "One function of [rhyme] ... is to fix or cement the meaning in a more unified and aesthetically satisfactory way than by mere juxtaposition. But in its lexical function, rhyme, like metaphor or epithet, limits meaning by asking us to consider suddenly the connection of two things whose sound shapes happen to be resemblant" ("Comparing Metrical Styles," in *Style in Language*, ed. T. Sebeok [Cambridge: M.I.T., 1960], 149–172, 153).

combined and interwoven in argumentative texts. Specific literary forms of arguments are sometimes preferred by certain authors, but they do not correspond to particular genres of texts. They are devices of argumentation that can be, and are in most early Chinese texts, combined in many possible ways.

Double-directed Parallelism

The literary form of argument I want to start with is a parallelism with a very specific function. I call it 'double-directed parallelism' because it is a parallelism of which the first sentence concludes the first part of the text and the second introduces the second part.[14] The literary form of the parallelism suggests a connection between the two textual parts and has therefore to be regarded as an argumentative device.[15]

Text examples
Shijing "Xia wu" 下武 (Mao 243)

The "Xia wu" 下武 Ode from the *Shijing* (Mao 243) is the earliest text in which I have found this literary form so far.[16] By looking at both the structure and content of the poem, Shaughnessy has pointed out that the poem is split into two halves. In terms of structure, the poem uses the literary figure of anadiplosis, repeating the last line of a stanza by using it again as the first line of the next stanza (indicated by symbols ↓ and ↑), a figure identified as *chanlian ge* 蟬聯格 by Yu Xingwu in his comment to the "Wen wang 文王" Ode (Mao 235). Yu

---

14 A literary form with a similar function has been identified and named by Chinese commentators of classical literature (first by Kong Yingda 孔穎達, 574–648): *chengshang qixia* 乘上啟下. "In the language of classical prose and poetry criticism, the fixed terms 'introduction' (*ch'i*) and 'development' (*ch'eng*) are modified to describe the manner in which a given textual unit may both take up a point introduced earlier and simultaneously lead in a new direction (*ch'eng-shang ch'i-hsia* 乘上啟下), that is, in terms of the function of interconnecting contiguous narrative units." Andrew Plaks, "Terminology and Central Concepts," in *How to Read the Chinese Novel*, ed. D.L. Rolston (Princeton: Princeton UP, 1990), 75–123, 95. The form has survived as a feature of a good essay style which Chinese children nowadays are taught in school as *guodu ju* 過渡句, transitional sentences, defined as sentences which summarise the above text and introduce into the text below (總結上文, 引出下文, also 乘上啟下).

15 See my "Zwischen den Argumenten lesen. Doppelt gerichtete Parallelismen zwischen Argumenten als zentrale Thesen in frühen chinesischen Texten," in *Komposition und Konnotation—Figuren der Kunstprosa im Alten China*, eds. W. Behr and J. Gentz, special issue of *Bochumer Jahrbuch für Ostasiatische Forschung* 29 (2005): 35–56.

16 I am indebted to my PhD student Jörn Grundmann who pointed this out to me.

argues that this literary form reflects a further step of development from Middle Western Zhou rhyming Bronze inscriptions and accordingly dates the "Wen wang" poem to Late Western Zhou.[17] The second line of stanza three and the first line of stanza four are an exception to this pattern (indicated by symbols O) and mark a clear break in the middle of the poem. This break is further supported by parallelisms of identical members (or lines) in stanzas one and two (世), two and three (永言), four and five (茲), and five and six (於萬斯年), which bind these stanzas together.[18] Shaughnessy takes this break to support a change of content in the poem which he thinks follows a binary composition model found in a number of bronze inscriptions such as the "Shi Qiang" *pan* 史牆盤 and the "Qiu" *pan* 逑盤 which juxtapose praises of the Zhou kings and the ancestors of another family.[19] However, two figures of literary form have also been chosen to emphasise the relationship between the two parts as being interconnected, a parallelism of identical lines, not a repetition of the last line of stanza three and the first of stanza four as in all the other stanzas, but a parallelism of the third lines of stanzas three and four (永言孝思), and the rhyme (職) of stanzas three and four,[20] the only stanzas that rhyme.[21]

---

[17] Yu Xingwu 于省吾, *Zeluoju* Shijing *xinzheng, Zeluoju* Chuci *xinzheng* 澤螺居詩經新証、澤螺居楚辭新証, (Beijing: Zhonghua, 2009), 142, again, I am grateful to Jörn Grundmann for pointing this commentary out to me.

[18] I define a "parallelism of identical members" as a literary form in which one or several identical graphs take a parallel position in two adjacent lines or stanzas. A "parallelism of identical lines" accordingly is a literary form in which two identical lines take a parallel position in successive stanzas (not couplets!). William Baxter has described the same phenomenon of a "semantic parallelism or antithesis with corresponding words in adjacent lines" in his "Situating the Language of the *Lao-tzu*," in *Lao-tzu and the Tao-te-ching*, eds. Livia Kohn and Michael LaFargue (Albany: SUNY, 1998), 231–253, 236. My definition is restricted to *identical* words or lines and does not include corresponding words or lines that are not identical.

[19] Edward Shaughnessy, "Writing and Rewriting the Poetry," 8–14, Paper for the "International Symposium on Excavated Manuscripts and the Interpretation of the *Book of Odes*," The University of Chicago, 12 September 2009. URL: http://cccp.uchicago.edu/archive/2009BookOfOdesSymposium/2009_BookOfOdesSymposium_EdShaughnessy.pdf (24.10.2014).

[20] Haun Saussy has pointed out how in the *Shijing* in general "rhyme is a bond, a semantic glue." "Rhyme belongs among the manners, the devices, of composition." See his "Repetition, Rhyme, and Exchange in The Book of Odes," *Harvard Journal of Asiatic Studies* 57.2 (1997): 519–542, 532, 542.

[21] Phonetic reconstruction according to William H. Baxter, Laurent Sagart, *Old Chinese: a new reconstruction* (New York: Oxford University Press, 2014).

下武 (Mao 243)[22]

	下武維周、世有哲王。*ɢʷaŋ (陽)	三后在天、王配于京。*kraŋ (陽) ⏋
⏋	王配于京、世德作求。*gu (幽)	永言配命、成王之孚。*pu (幽) ⏋
⏋	成王之孚、下土之式。*lək (職)	永言孝思、孝思維則。*tsˤək (職) O

O	媚茲一人、應侯順德。*tˤək (職)	永言孝思、昭哉嗣服。*bək (職) ⏋
⏋	昭茲來許、繩其祖武。*maʔ (魚)	於萬斯年、受天之祜。*gˤaʔ (魚) ⏋
⏋	受天之祜、四方來賀。*gˤaj (歌)	於萬斯年、不遐有佐。*tsˤarʔ-s (歌)

Three types of literary forms are thus used to mark inner-textual relationships in this ode: parallelisms of identical members/lines, repetitions, and rhyme. The parallelisms are equally distributed over the whole poem and connect all lines (1-2: 世, 2-3: 永言, 3-4: 永言孝思, 4-5: 茲, and 5-6: 於萬斯年) to demonstrate the unity of the text. The repetitions of the last lines of the stanzas as first lines of the following stanzas mark a break in the middle of the text, and the rhyme connects the two middle stanzas. Although a textual break is clearly indicated by one kind of literary form (repetition of lines) and defines two greater units within the text, the connection of the two parts is indicated by another (rhyme) and thus signalises the unity of the text as a twofold entity. In regard to content, the literary forms emphasise the parallel between the virtues of the Zhou kings and the ancestors of the Ying family and, probably, make a claim of similarity, analogy, or even identity by means of the textual form.

Laozi 66

The *Laozi* is another early text that makes use of the literary form of a double-directed parallelism. The fortunate circumstances that the tomb libraries excavated in the last decades include different early editions of this text allow us even to analyse the historical development of this literary form, in chapter 66 for example (Guodian A2).

---

22 Links to all Chinese texts of this article with coloured graphs can be found on my website following the bibliographical data of this article under "publications" (http://www.ed.ac.uk/schools-departments/literatures-languages-cultures/asian-studies/staff/joachim-gentz/publications). Its purpose is to allow readers to follow my analysis of the textual structures more easily.

Guodian "Laozi" A2

Text presentation according to bamboo slips, excavated 1993 from tomb no. 1 in Guodian, in Jingmen, Hubei Province, dated ca 300 BC:[23]

江海所以為百谷王。　　以其能為百谷下。　是以能為百谷王。

聖人之

　其

　其

　其

在民前也，以身後之。
　　　↕
在民上也，以言下之。
　　　↕
在民上也，民弗厚也。
　　　↕
在民前也，民弗害也。

天下樂進而弗厭。　　以其不爭也。　　故天下莫能與之爭。

That by which rivers and seas are kings over the many mountain streams is their ability to be below the many mountain streams. For this reason they are able to act as kings over the many mountain streams.

1a The sage	*stands in front of the people,*	b <u>because he puts</u> himself behind them.
2a **He**	**stands on top of the people,**	b <u>because he puts</u> his speech below them.
3a **He**	**stands on top of the people,**	b <u>but the people don't</u> admire him.
4a He	*stands in front of the people,*	b <u>but the people don't</u> harm him.

All under Heaven enjoys bringing him forward without getting tired of it. Because he is someone who does not compete. This is why in all under Heaven nobody is able to compete with him.

The verse consists of two parts, each expressing a particular idea. The first part is about the idea that to put yourself behind and below puts you on top and in front. This rule is taken over from the realm of nature into the realm of human social order. The second part argues that nobody adores or harms the ruler despite his being on top or in front of the people but that people rather wish to support him. It is only in the last sentence that the connection between these two thoughts is formulated. Formally the two parts are clearly marked through the parallels of the second lines 1b and 2b as well as 3b and 4b. The connection between sentences 1–2 and 3–4 is only formally indicated through the striking identity of the lines 2a and 3a which through the exact repetition bridges the dividing line between the two parts of the verse that runs between sentences 2

---

23 I follow the transcription of the edition of Jingmenshi Bowuguan 荊門市博物館 (ed.), *Guodian Chu mu zhujian* 郭店楚墓竹簡, (Beijing: Wenwu chubanshe, 1998), 11.

and 3. The almost identical form of the lines 1a and 4a forms a further brace which makes the parallel identity of the first lines (a) appear to be composed in a mirror structure along an axis of symmetry according to the pattern ABBA. The second lines (b) of the sentences, however, are composed in an AABB pattern.

The parallelism of the lines 2a and 3a has the function of a double-directed parallelism which binds two unrelated parts of an argument together merely through the parallelism of their form.

Beida "Laozi"

If we compare the Guodian text with the *Laozi* version of the Beida slips (chap. 30), which in its arrangement (not its exact wording) is identical to chapter 66 of the transmitted Wang Bi (226–249) version,[24] we find a slightly different arrangement of the same verse.

```
        江海之所以能為百谷王者，   以其善下之也。 故能為百谷王。
是以
    1a 聖人之         欲高民也，b 必以其言下之。
    2a 其            欲先民也，b 必以其身後之。
是以
    3a               居上       b 而民弗重。
    4a               居前       b 而民弗害也。
是以
        天下樂推而弗厭也。        不以其無爭邪？ 故天下莫能與之爭。
```

As to that by which rivers and seas are able to be kings over the many mountain streams: it is because they are good at putting themselves below them. This is why they can be kings over the many mountain streams.
    For this reason:
If a sage wants to overtop the people, he must with his speech   put himself below them.
If he wants to precede the people,   he must with his own person put himself behind them.
    For this reason:
He resides above   but the people do not consider him grave.
Resides in front   but the people do not harm him.
    For this reason:

---

24   See Beijing Daxue chutu wenxian yanjiusuo 北京大學出土文獻研究所 (ed.), *Beijing Daxue cang Xihan zhushu* 北京大學藏西漢竹書 (Shanghai: Shanghai guji chubanshe, 2012), vol. 2, 137. For a comparative overview over eight versions of this chapter see pp. 185–186.

All under Heaven enjoy pushing him forward without getting tired of it. Isn't this because he has no fights? This is why in all under Heaven nobody can fight against him.

Apart from many interesting differences in wordings which I will not deal with here, we find that the identity of the parallel lines 1a:4a and 2a:3a of the Guodian version is abandoned in the composition of the Beida version, and the ABBA identical parallelism of the first parts (a) of the Guodian sentences is replaced by a syntactical AABB (欲x民也–欲x民也–居x–居x, also supported by the second lines [b] of the sentences) and a thematic ABAB (高–先–上–前) structure of non-identical parallelisms (AA*, BB* and AB, A*B*). In the Beida version, the logical relationship between part one and part two is not expressed through the literary form of a parallelism between sentences 2a and 3a, which in the Guodian version connects part one and part two on a formal level. Instead, the relationship of these two sentences in the Beida version is made explicit on the semantic level, through the illative conjunction "*shiyi*" 是以. The same logical connection through the insertion of the conjunction *shiyi* is also established between the two framing sentences (the parallelism of which is strengthened through the double usage of *gu* 故 instead of one *gu* and one *shiyi* as we find it in the Guodian version) and the argumentative inner part (sentences 1–4).

This verse in its two variants therefore serves as a wonderful illustration of how in the course of history the argumentative function of the literary form was reformed into a linguistic form of a semantically explicit logical conjunction. The "*shiyi*" 是以 translates the connective literary form of a parallelism into a logical connector on the linguistic level.

The two *Laozi* versions excavated in 1973 from tomb no. 3 in Mawangdui (MWD) represent a transitory stage. They both are closer to the Beida/Wang Bi texts than to the Guodian version. In both Mawangdui versions, like in Beida/Wang Bi, the *shang* 上 is put first in the first lines (a). In the first lines (a) of the sentences in the "Laozi A" version, however, we find the same ABBA parallelism that we also find in the Guodian text (although in reverse sequence: 上→先→前→上). In "Laozi B" we find the same ABAB structure as in Beida/Wang Bi. Nevertheless in both versions the illative conjunction "*gu*" 故 (therefore) is inserted between sentences 2 and 3.[25] The translation of literary forms of arguments into explicit linguistic forms of arguments had thus already started in the early second century BC.

---

25 Gao Ming 高明 (ed.), *Boshu Laozi jiaozhu* 帛書老子校注, 145–149.

Laozi 41

Like the *Shijing* ode "Xia wu," chapter 41 of the *Laozi* operates with diverse kinds of literary forms that fulfil different functions and create a contradictory tension between two literary forms that has not only a rhetorical[26] but also an *argumentative* function. Rudolf Wagner, trying to reconstruct the chapter in the literary form of an 'Interlocking Parallel Style' (IPS) could not solve the structural problem of this verse and has, as he asserts, "left the puzzle in place."[27] Although the *Laozi* is full of IPS, this literary form is not used in chapter 41. Five other literary forms are used instead: "parallelisms of identical members,"[28] tetrasyllabic metre, rhymes, the semantic markers of textual units *gu* 故 and *fu* 夫, and Michael Broschat has pointed out another instance of what I call a 'double-directed parallelism.' This double-directed parallelism occurs in the rhymed tetrasyllabic part of *Laozi* 41,[29] and it is constructed through a combination of the two formal signifiers: "parallelism of identical members" and rhyme.

The chapter consists of two parts. The first unit of lines 1–3 is clearly marked by the strong parallelisms of their first lines and the self-contained trinity of 'superior' (*shang* 上), 'middling' (*zhong* 中), and 'inferior' (*xia* 下) which introduces these lines.

1 上士聞道，勤而行之；
2 中士聞道，若存若亡；
3 下士聞道，大笑。不笑，不足以爲道。

These lines are always translated in the following sense:

> If superior men hear about the Way, they diligently put it into practice.
> If middling men hear about the Way, they sometimes retain it, and sometimes lose it.
> If inferior men hear about the Way, they laugh out loud. If they didn't laugh, it would not be worth being considered as the Way.

---

[26] Baxter describes these textual features in the *Laozi* as rhetorical features of the text, see his "Situating the Language of the *Lao-tzu*," 237.

[27] Rudolf Wagner, *Language, Ontology and Political Philosophy in China. Wang Bi's Scholarly Exploration of the Dark (Xuanxue)* (Albany: SUNY Press, 2003), 263–264.

[28] See my definition in footnote 18 above.

[29] The Mawangdui (B3, text corrupt in A), Guodian (B5) and Beida (4) versions follow the same scheme as the transmitted Wang Bi text.

DEFINING BOUNDARIES AND RELATIONS OF TEXTUAL UNITS

As I will demonstrate below, the literary form forces us to rethink this commonly accepted translation.

The second part is marked as a second distinct unit by four different literary forms: the two semantic markers of textual units *gu* 故 and *fu* 夫 that frame it, and the tetrasyllabic metre and rhyme, which give the unit a coherent shape.

4 故建言有之：	This is why an established saying goes:	
5 明道若昧，	The *dao* when bright	is as if it were dark,
6 進道若退，	the *dao* when advancing	is as if it were retreating,
7 夷道若纇，	the *dao* when level	is as if it were uneven,
8 上德若谷，	the moral power when great	is as if it were a glen,
9 大白若辱，	a Great white	is as if it were grimy,
10 廣德若不足，	the moral power when ample	is as if it were insufficient,
11 建德若偷，	the moral power when erected	is as if it were low,
12 質真若渝，	plain truth	is as if it were changing,
13 大方無隅，	a Great square	has no corners,
14 大器晚成，	a Great vessel	can hardly be completed,
15 大音希聲，	a Great tone	has a soft sound,
16 大象無形，	a Great image	has no form,
17 道隱無名。	the *dao*	has no name.

18 夫唯道，善貸且成。 Actually, the *dao* alone bestows and accomplishes.

The unit is structured by a rhyme scheme that divides it into four parts, and by five different "parallelisms of identical members" that include three, five, or eight identical members.

The first three identical members of these parallelisms are the graphs *dao ruo* 道若, which thereby mark lines 5–7 as a tripartite unit.

The second parallelism of identical members is an expansion of the first parallelism and consists of the eight *ruo* 若 all in the same position in lines 5–12 which is thereby marked as a widened unit. Rudolf Wagner split this widened unit of lines 5–12 into two halves of four lines, which he thought had to be parallel (with the oppositions of lines 5:9, 6:10, 7:11, and 8:12). The links, however, were too weak to be convincing and, as he himself ascertains, "not evident from the text."[30]

---

30 Wagner, *Language*, 263–264.

The parallelism of the identical members *de* 德 in lines 8, 10, and 11 supports the division of the widened unit 5–12 into the two subunits of lines 5–7 (*dao* 道) and 8–12 (*de* 德).

A next unit of lines 13–16 is marked by the parallelism of the initial *da* 大. The *da* 大 in line 9 might function as a kind of 'prelude' that announces unit 13–16. In combination with *ruo* 若 it is reminiscent of chapter 45.

The following parallelism of the identical members *wu* 無 in lines 13, 16, and 17 seems to be connected to the parallelism of the initial *da* 大 as both are combined in lines 13 and 16. Moreover, the meaning of the graphs *wan* 晚 and *xi* 希 that take the positions of *wu* 無 in lines 14 and 15 is very close to that of *wu* 無 in the lines 13, 16, and 17 and should be interpreted as semantic parallels to *wu* 無. The *da* 大 in turn refers to the *dao* 道, the initial *dao* 道 in line 17 could therefore also be taken as a parallel to *da* 大. These parallels suggest that unit 13-16 should be widened to include line 17, and we will see that the rhyme supports this interpretation.

Based on these five parallelisms of identical members (道若, 若, 德, 大, 無) we thus arrive at a basic twofold structure of the proverbial (*jian yan* 建言) passage consisting of units 5–12 and 13–17 of which unit 5–12 can be further divided into subunits 5–7 and 8–12.

Turning to the rhymes in this passage as a further literary device of structuring the text we find, like in the *Shijing* example above, a structure which runs counter to the structure of the parallelisms and challenges the neat division into two (or three) units.

The rhyme divides the passage into four parts and thereby turns line 13 into a double-directed parallelism:

4	故建言有之：	OC rhymes[31]	
5	明道若昧，	*$m^ˤut$-s	(微)
6	進道若退，	*$ŋ^ˤəp$-s	(微)
7	夷道若纇，	*rut-s	(微)
8	上德若谷，	*$C.q^ˤok$	(屋)
9	大白若辱，	*nok	(屋)
10	廣德若不足，	*$tsok$	(屋)
11	建德若偷，	*$l̥^ˤo$	(侯)
12	質真若渝，	*lo	(侯)

---

31 According to Baxter and Sagart, *Old Chinese: A New Reconstruction*, 2014.

13	大方無隅，	*ŋo	(侯)
14	大器晚成，	*m-deŋ	(耕)
15	大音希聲，	*l̥eŋ	(耕)
16	大象無形，	*ɢˤeŋ	(耕)
17	道隱無名。	*C.meŋ	(耕)
18	夫唯道，善貸且成。	*m-deŋ	(耕)

Broschat was the first to observe that line 13 "performs an interesting transition to the next section."[32] As a matter of fact, line 13 performs the typical janus-faced function of a double-directed parallelism. It is syntactically linked to lines 14–17 (and possibly 18) by its initial *da* 大 in combination with the *wu* 無, and phonetically linked to lines 11–12 by its rhyme. As a hybrid, line 13 bridges the two basic parts of this textual passage (5–12 and 13–18) and suggests, like all the other double-directed parallelisms, a connection between these two parts. As rhyme is a strong device to mark belonging, its syntactical belonging to unit 14–17 is strengthened by holding both members of the parallelisms: *da* 大 at the first and *wu* 無 at the third position. The only other line which holds both of them is line 16 which thereby, in a similar double-directed alignment, connects back to line 15 and forth to line 17.[33]

Although lines 5–12 are syntactically parallel, with *ruo* 若 always at the third position, this *ruo*-group is divided into three distinct rhyme groups (5–7: ut-s/əp-s;[34] 8–10: ok; 11–13: o), each consisting of three rhymes, of which the first group (5–7) is further marked as a proper subunit of the *ruo*-group by the parallelism of the *dao* 道 at the second position as we have pointed out above. The second subunit of the *ruo*-group (8–12, loosely marked by the occurrence of the *de* 德 at the second position), however, is split by the strict threefold rhythm of the rhyme.

Yet, the basic twofold structure established by the parallelisms of the two dominant identical members *ruo* 若 (5–12) and *da* 大 (13–16/17) is confirmed by the

---

32 Michael Broschat, "Guiguzi," 105.
33 Mawangdui, Guodian and Beida versions have *tian* 天 instead of *da* 大 in line 16.
34 Baxter discusses the phonetic shift from *-ps to *-ts at length under A.1 in the appendix of his *Handbook of Old Chinese Phonology* (Berlin: Mouton de Gruyter, 1992), 565–566. This shift must have occurred rather early as we find the integration of *-ps and *-ts rhymes in *Shijing* odes already. Baxter & Sagart reconstruct a stage of Old Chinese that precedes the *Laozi*. At the time of the *Laozi* 退 already rhymed with 昧 and 類. For an analysis of *Laozi* rhymes and languages see also Baxter's "Situating the Language of the *Lao-tzu*." I wish to thank Wolfgang Behr for all these references.

double-directed parallelism of line 13 which serves to bridge exactly these two parts and, together with the other parallelisms (of rhyme and *wu* 無 at the third position), redefines the basic two parts of this unit as consisting of lines 5–13 and 13–17, with 13 as an overlapping, bridging line.

Let us now turn back to the first lines, 1–3:

1 上士聞道，勤而行之；
2 中士聞道，若存若亡；
3 下士聞道，大笑。不笑，不足以爲道。

The strong presence of the *ruo* 若 in line 2 is striking and suggests an association with the first part of the proverbial passage (lines 5–12), which was also marked by a dominant *ruo* 若. Even more surprising appears the *da* 大 in line 3 as it might suggest a connection of this line to lines 13–16 (13–18). Strictly following this formal interpretation of inner-textual references, the *da xiao* 大笑 thereby gains a new connotation in line with the other expressions of the *dao*: 大方, 大器, 大音, and 大象. The 'inferior man' all of a sudden, and quite unexpectedly, appears as the sage (compare chapter 66 above where the one in front and above puts himself behind and below) who laughs loudly, and it is this laughter that decides whether something is worth being considered as the Way. The 'superior man' in turn appears as representative of the busy Ru class, acting (*wei* 為) diligently to put the *dao* into practice, yet without success. The middling sometimes grasps the *dao* (lines 3–5) and sometimes loses it and only realises *de* (lines 8–12) which is not worth (不足 line 10) being considered as the Way.

The rhyme scheme of these first lines supports this interpretation as it sets the third line apart from the other two. *Xing* 行 (*gˤraŋ-s) and *wang* 亡 (*maŋ) rhyme (both belong to the same rhyme group *yang* 陽) and thus belong to one group (of those who do not grasp the *dao*). *Xiao* 笑 (*s-law-s) and *dao* 道 (*lˤuʔ-s) rhyme as well.[35] They are thus identified. The laughter is like the *dao*. The third line is different, independent and self-sufficient, like the *dao*, which only refers to itself. It only rhymes with itself.

---

35 They belong to the rhyme groups *xiao* 宵 and *you* 幽 which are considered as "impure rhymes" (*heyun* 合韵) but according to Jiang Yougao rhyme [*tongyun* 通韵] here. See Jiang Yougao 江有誥, *Jiangshi yinxue shishu* 江氏音學十書 (1812, repr. Shanghai: Shanghai Zhongguo shudian 1928), vol. 6, *Laozi* part, 10. Based on an analysis of excavated texts, Hua Xuecheng and Xie Rong'e argue that these two rhyme groups rhymed in the Chu dialect (which would include the *Laozi*). See Hua Xuecheng 華學誠 and Xie Rong'e 謝榮娥, "Qin Han Chu fangyanqu wenxian zhong de youbu yu xiaobu" 秦漢楚方言區文獻中的幽部與宵部, *Yuwen yanjiu* 語文研究 (2009.1): 1–4.

A number of questions have to remain open. Why does the rhyme separate lines 8-10 from lines 11-12 while the *ruo* 若 and the *de* 德 hold them together? To keep the tripartite structure intact? How do we interpret the parallel *bu zu* 不足 in lines 2 and 10 which appears exactly at the point where the rhyme also breaks lines 10 and 11? I have to leave another piece of the puzzle in place as my interpretation does not suffice (不足) to solve it completely.

Conclusion

These examples show first of all how old the literary form of the double-directed parallelism is. The second example of *Laozi* 66 suggests, secondly, that in later versions of texts this literary form—possibly because of new priorities in argumentative strategies—was sometimes abandoned and the logic of the argument was expressed through logical terms rather than formal compositions or literary forms. This has to be taken as a preliminary hypothesis, which needs to be proven systematically in the light of more comparative examples of excavated and transmitted texts. The fact that the arrangement of the Guodian "Ziyi" is generally regarded as more regular and better structured than that of the transmitted *Liji* "Ziyi" seems to point in a similar direction.[36] Thirdly, the first (*Shijing*) and third (*Laozi* 41) examples show that double-directed parallelisms exist in different forms, as syntactical parallelisms or as phonetic parallelisms of rhyme. They also show that these forms can be combined. In the *Laozi* 41 case, one line combines a phonetic parallelism backward and a syntactical parallelism forward and thereby bridges the two parts of a text.

As can be shown by looking at other examples of this literary form of an argument,[37] the literary form of the double-directed parallelism generally suggests a connection between the two sentences that constitute the parallelism. It thereby connects two textual parts: the first of which is concluded by the first and the second of which is introduced by the second sentence of these kinds of parallelisms. These two parts often have an aspectual relationship that in our modern languages would normally be expressed by means of metalinguistic formulations such as: 'first ... second ...' or: 'another aspect connected to this ...' or: 'further ... ,' 'moreover ...' etc.

---

36 The editors of the first edition claim the order of the sections in the Guodian text to be 'more reasonable' (*heli* 合理). See Jingmenshi bowuguan 荊門市博物館 (ed.), *Guodian Chumu Chujian* 郭店楚墓楚簡, (Beijing: Wenwu, 1998), 129. Cf. also Martin Kern, "Quotation and the Confucian Canon," 308.

37 For further examples from Lu Jia's *Xinyu* and the *Chunqiu fanlu*, chap. "Chu Zhuang wang" 楚莊王, see my "Zwischen den Argumenten lesen."

The literary form of the double-directed parallelism claims a connection between first and second sentences. *This claim has to be taken as a central hypothesis of the text.* In any interpretation of the double-directed parallelism we have to keep in mind that these two sentences have to be taken in most cases as two different aspects of one and the same topic and have to be related to each another. It is the task of the reader to find out the exact relationship between the two parts connected by the double-directed parallelism.

Defining the Argumentative Field: Enumerative Catalogues as Signs of Encyclopaedic Completeness: *Sunzi* "Shi ji" 始計

Argumentative texts often include catalogues of virtues, social relations or social strata, cultural, agricultural, ritual or political activities, emotional or bodily functions, cosmological powers etc. Their manifold cultural functions include amplifications, summaries, and probative functions, they serve as mnemonic and recording devices and their formal consistency often covers up the incoherence of the various items.[38] In early Chinese texts the function of these catalogues (which can be regarded as a form of parallelism) in an argument is the definition of groups of key analytical terms that create the particular conceptual field the argument deals with. This field is defined and structured (in hierarchical or binary orders) by determining a numerical set of constituents (which in turn may consist of further sub-constituents) claiming to fully represent the field. These constituents not only show how far the argument extends and what exactly it includes in its discourse, they further demand additional information about how the discursive field made up of these constituents is structured by ascribing to them specific functions or tasks in a greater political, social, military or ethical programme. They thus act as operators. Like organs, they regulate the discursive field, which is then accordingly divided into sub-discourses. Enumerative catalogues, however, serve to claim completeness (sometimes according to an established numerological pattern of two, three, five, nine or ten) and unity behind these sub-discourses, coherency and

---

38 See for a highly nuanced discussion of (up to 21!) different functions of catalogues in the ancient Greek context John T. Fitzgerald, "The Catalogue in Ancient Greek Literature," in *The Rhetorical Analysis of Scripture: Essays from the 1995 London Conference*, ed. Stanley E. Porter and Thomas H. Olbricht (Sheffield: Academic Press, 1997), 275–293, 288–289, n. 5. I am indebted to one of our anonymous reviewers for pointing out this valuable reference.

potential efficacy of the constituents.³⁹ Positive consequences of such catalogues are described as resulting from an application of these constituents in their proper functions in social or political practice. The central assumption and claim behind these numerical sets is that these, not others, not more or less, are the necessary constituents to achieve the positive consequences outlined at the end of the texts. If only the constituents a, b and c are known or applied then the consequences x, y and z will necessarily follow. The constituents appear like ingredients of a special recipe with which the particular field can be brought to order or be 'healed' (*zhi* 治).

Catalogues can be combined into catalogues of catalogues. The *Yi Zhoushu* contains many chapters in which several catalogues are first listed in the form of closed numerical sets (such as, for example, "the four emotional expressions" 四徵, "the six extremes" 六極, "the eight governing social roles" 八政, and the nine virtues" 九德)⁴⁰ to be then consecutively explained, one after the other.⁴¹

We should note that catalogues of a specific number can be associated with other catalogues of the same number belonging to another field which does, however, follow the same basic principles of order. A certain number of social or political functionaries can, for example, be associated with the same number of virtues, each embodying one of these virtues: positions of family members can become associated with positions of officials etc.

The *Sunzi* makes particularly frequent use of this literary form of argumentation. It thereby gains a character somewhere between an expert handbook which has to consider all aspects of war to give responsible guidance on rather

---

39 See for a similar character of ancient Mesopotamian lists, Amar Annus, who refers to these lists as "knowledge texts" that reflect an "encyclopaedic curiosity" ("On the Beginning and Continuities of Omen Sciences in the Ancient World," in *Divination and Interpretation of Signs in the Ancient World*, ed. A. Annus [Chicago: The Oriental Institute of the University of Chicago, 2010], 1–18, 2, referring to Jean Bottéro, *Mesopotamia: Writing, Reasoning, and the Gods* [Chicago: University of Chicago Press, 1992], 127).

40 See chapter 3: "Changxun jie" 常訓解 in Huang Huaixin 黃懷信 et al. *Yi Zhoushu huijiao jizhu* 逸周書彙校集注 (Shanghai: Shanghai guji chubanshe, 1995), 53–56.

41 See chapters 3: "Changxun jie" 常訓解, 4: "Wenzhuo jie" 文酌解, 8: "Da wu jie" 大武解, 9: "Da mingwu jie" 大明武解, 21: "Fengbao jie" 鄷保解, 22: "Da kai jie" 大開解, 27: "Da kaiwu jie" 大開武解, 28: "Xiao kaiwu jie" 小開武解, 29: "Baodian jie" 寶典解, 30. "Fengmou jie" 鄷謀解, 33: "Wumu jie" 武穆解, 38: "Wenzheng jie" 文政解, 47: "Cheng kai jie" 成開解, and 58: "Guanren jie" 官人解 and 69: "Quanfa jie" 銓法解 in a slightly different manner. Chapters such as 4: "Wenzhuo jie" 文酌解, 38: "Wenzheng jie" 文政解, 69: "Quanfa jie" 銓法解 etc. even consist of nothing but listings of catalogues. Huang Huaixin 黃懷信 1995.

existential matters and an encyclopaedia with the aspiration of giving a comprehensive overview on the diverse fields of warfare (supported by the frequent use of the term *fan* 凡). Its insights are formulated, like well ordered troops but certainly also for mnemonic reasons, in catalogue form and appear as "orally transmitted aphorisms" or "bundled maxims" which secure the maximum momentum of the textual configuration.[42] The illatives *gu* 故 or *shigu* 是故 are used in high frequency throughout the text, often without strong logical implications and rather as "false illative conjunctions" which artificially link up the sections as Mair observes.[43] The following first chapter of the *Sunzi bingfa* provides a good example of enumerative catalogues that claim completeness. At the same time it combines a number of different methods of marking and relating textual units by means of literary forms.

孫子兵法 《始計》	Sunzi, *The Art of War*, First chapter: "Initial Assessments"
孫子曰：	"Master Sun said,
1 兵者， 國之大事。	1 Warfare is a great affair of the state.
死生之地，	The field of life and death,
存亡之道，	The way of preservation and extinction.
不可不察也。	It cannot be left unexamined.
故	This is why,
A 經之以五事，	A Measure it in terms of five factors,
B 校之以計，而索其情，	B Weigh it by means of seven assessments, and seek out its circumstances.
A1	A1
一曰道，	The first factor is the Way,
二曰天，	The second is Heaven,
三曰地，	The third is Earth,
四曰將，	The fourth is Generalship,

---

42 Victor Mair, *The Art of War: Sun Zi's Military Methods* (New York: Columbia University Press, 2009), 31, quoting Mark Lewis, "Writings on Warfare Found in Ancient Chinese Tombs," *Sino-Platonic Papers* 158 (2005): 1–15, 6.

43 Victor Mair, *The Art of War*, 33. In his sub-commentary to the "Quli shang" 曲禮上 chapter of the *Liji* 禮記, Kong Yingda 孔穎達 (574–648) notes that "*gu* [is a word] that continues the (text) above and initiates the (text) below" (故，乘上啟下之辭).

五曰法。

The fifth is Method.

A1.1
道者，令民與上同意，可與之死，可與之生，而不畏危也。

A1.1
The Way is that which causes the people to be of the same mind with their superior.
They are commited to die with him,
They are commited to live with him,
And not fear danger.

天者，陰陽，寒暑，時制也。

Heaven comprises yin and yang, cold and heat, the ordering of time.

地者，遠近，險易，廣狹，死生也。

Earth comprises distant or near, precipitous or gentle, broad or narrow, positions conductive to death or life.

將者，智，信，仁，勇，嚴也。

Generalship comprises knowledge, trustworthiness, humaneness, bravery, and sternness.

法者，曲制，官道，主用也。

Method comprises organization of units, official channels, and control of matériel.

凡此五者，將莫不聞，知之者勝，不知者不勝。

The general must be informed about all five of these factors, but only he who truly understands them will be victorious, while those who fail to understand them will be defeated.

故

This is why,

B
校之以計，而索其情。曰：

B
when weighing warfare by means of seven assessments and seeking out its circumstances, one should ask:

B1
主孰有道，
將孰有能，
天地孰得，

法令孰行，

兵眾孰強，

B1
Which side's ruler possesses the Way?
Which side's general is more capable?
Which side possesses the advantages of Heaven and Earth?
Which side exercises the rules and methods more rigorously?
Which side has the stronger army?

士卒孰練，

賞罰孰明，

吾以此知勝負矣。

將聽吾計，　用之必勝，留之；

將不聽吾計，用之必敗，去之。

計利以聽，乃為之勢，以佐其外；

勢者，因利而制權也。

2
兵者，詭道也。

故

2.1
能而示之不能，

用而示之不用；

近而示之遠，

遠而示之近。

故

2.2
利而誘之，

亂而取之，

Which side has officers and troops that are more highly trained?
Which side is more transparent in dispensing rewards and punishments?
Through these considerations, I can foretell victory or defeat.

If you will heed my assessments and act on them, you will certainly be victorious, and I shall remain here; if you will not heed my assessments and act on them, you will certainly be defeated, and I shall leave.

When an advantageous assessment has been heeded, one must create for it a favourable configuration to assist the war effort externally. A favourable configuration is one that signifies the creation of power in accordance with advantage.

2
Warfare is a way of deception.

This is why,

2.1
When one is capable, give the appearance of being incapable.
When one is active, give the appearance of being inactive.
When one is far, give the appearance of being near.
When one is near, give the appearance of being far.

This is why,

2.2
When one's opponents are greedy for advantage, tempt them.
When one's opponents are in chaos, seize them.

實而備之， When one's opponents are secure, prepare for them.

強而避之， When one's opponents are strong, evade them

怒而橈之； When one's opponents are angry, aggravate them.

卑而驕之， When one's opponents are humble, make them arrogant.

佚而勞之， When one's opponents are at ease, make them weary.

親而離之； When one's opponents are friendly to each other, divide them.

2.3
攻其無備，
出其不意。

此兵家之勝，不可先傳也。

2.3
Attack them when they are unprepared;
Come forth when they are not expecting you to do so.

Herein lies the victoriousness of the strategist, which cannot be divulged beforehand.

3
夫
未戰而廟算勝者，　得算多也；
未戰而廟算不勝者，　得算少也。
多算勝，
少算敗，
況無算乎！

3
Now, he who is victorious in the temple computations before battle is the one who receives more counting rods. He who is not victorious in the temple computations before battle is the one who receives fewer counting rods. The one with more counting rods wins, and the one with fewer counting rods loses. How much less chance of winning is there for someone who receives no counting rods at all!

吾以此觀之，勝負見矣。

Through our observation of these calculations, victory and defeat are apparent."[44]

The composition of the chapter gives us the following relationship of units:

---

[44] Transl. Victor Mair with slight modifications, *The Art of War*, 76–79.

1
    A
    B
        A1
            A1.1
    B
        B1
2
    2.1
    2.2
    2.3
3

The textual units are clearly marked through the choice of differing literary forms. They are further distinguished by the insertion of conjunctions, by repetitions of programmatic clauses that indicate the beginning of a new unit and by conclusive clauses that mark the end of a unit. We find six different ways of relating the thus differentiated textual units:

First, the conjunction *gu* 故 is used four times to link textual units, the conjunction *fu* 夫 is used once. In the light of the articulate literary forms all five conjunctions are unnecessary to mark the textual units. Only the first *gu* makes sense as a deductive connector. The others are either "false illative conjunctions" or they indicate the subordination of the following unit. The lack of a *gu* between 2.2 and 2.3 however indicates that these two despite their difference in literary form are regarded as belonging together to a common unit.

Second, two enumerative catalogues, one of five factors and one of seven assessments, form the two main bodies of part one of this chapter. Both are linked to one of the two sentences which introduce them (經之以五事 and 校之以計，而索其情).

Third, the repetition of the second of these introductory sentences clearly marks the beginning of a new unit within part one and creates a parallel structure between the two parts 1A and 1B.

Fourth, the repetition of the definition of the central term *bing* (兵者…) clearly introduces a second part on the same level as the first.

Fifth, the second part (2) is divided into two subunits (2.1 and 2.2/3) not only by the conjunction between 2.1 and 2.2 but even more by the literary form of strict parallelisms.

Sixth, the usage of *ci* 此 as a term referring back to and summarising the subunits closes a unit in four cases with a conclusive statement about victory or defeat thereby referring back to the opening paragraph. We thus see a chapter clearly divided into units by means of a range of different literary forms.

Many of the relationships between the units are subordinations. Thus from statement 1 about warfare two basic methods follow. The first (A) is further defined in A1, which in turn is further explained in A1.1. The second (B) is repeated verbatim to indicate the beginning of the second part and then further explained in B1. Part 2 lists eleven illustrations of the principle of deception in three sets of parallel clauses.

The basic structure of the chapter is threefold with the first part introducing the topic from its correct and virtuous side. It gives definitions that can be used as principal guiding lines, that can be learnt and known in advance. They are part of the battle preparations. The first part is also the most sophisticated in terms of content and argumentation. It is divided into two subunits.

Subunit 1A comes first: it is more elaborated and lays out the five most important concepts of warfare in a sequence of conceptual hierarchy. Absolute criteria are then listed according to which these factors can be measured in a standardised way (*jing* 經).

Subunit 1B is more about the practice of conducting war. It includes the five concepts from 1A (道,將,天,地,法) in the first four assessments, yet the sequence follows the importance of the role these factors play in a battle. Therefore the general is placed before the conditions of heaven and earth. In the last three assessments more concepts of lower status (soldiers, troops) are added. The first three assessments are connected with the last three through the concept of rules and methods (*fa ling* 法令) which represents the central point where high and low status meet. This subunit 1B similarly lists criteria of strength but deals with the strategic assessment of the real conditions through comparison (*jiao* 校) with the enemy.

Subunit 1B takes a middle position between 1A and 2 and has thus a double-directed bridging function. Like 1A it lists basic factors (half of them identical with the ones listed in 1A) in its first half, and like 2 it instructs the reader to take action according to the given circumstances in its second half. The last sentence of 1B even parallels the first sentence of part 2 by providing a definition of the form 'a 者,b 也.'

The second part deals with the reverse side of the same coin. Warfare is not only about knowledge of a range of circumstances that have to be measured and assessed, but also about deception. This depends on the situation and has to be decided in situ. Part two entirely deals with how (in a deceptive way) one should react to diverse situations in case-by-case scenarios. Although it starts formally, like part one, with a parallel definition of the central term *bing* (warfare) and seems to reveal a second and similar important aspect of warfare, the much plainer argumentation in its repetitive literary form makes this part appear inferior in status.

In the change of literary form between 2.1 and 2.2, a rupture is emphasised by the insertion of the conjunction *gu* 故, which marks a shift of perspective from the army's own conditions to the situation of the enemy. As 2.3 continues the perspective of 2.2 the change of literary form only indicates the shift from quite specific instructions to a more general statement. Therefore no *gu* is inserted indicating that it is the particular perspective which determines the division of part two into two main subunits 2.1 and 2.2/3 with the second unit being further subdivided by the change of literary form into 2.2 and 2.3. Yet again, the literary form of 2.2 suggests this unit being a double-directed unit which bridges 2.1 and 2.3 by following the form of 2.1 (a 而 b 之) yet introducing the perspective of 2.3. For a reader sensitive to interpreting literary forms of argumentation no insertion of a *gu* would have been necessary to provide an unambiguous interpretation of the relationships between the three units of part two.

The third part is introduced by the particle *fu* 夫 and thus is not a subordinate unit of part two. It would otherwise, as in the other cases of subordinate units, be introduced by *gu*. The *fu* rather suggests that this part has to be read as a statement of abstract principle.[45] It is a general reflection on the importance of properly preparing for war with a new argument, which continues and concludes the discussion. At the same time it serves as further proof of the concluding sentence of the first paragraph, that this cannot be left unexplored (*bu ke bu cha ye* 不可不察也) of which this whole chapter was an example.

The catalogues used in this chapter purport to cover all the important aspects of warfare. In the first part they introduce and give an overview over all the basic factors involved in warfare and the main criteria that have to be assessed strategically prior to waging war. These factors and criteria can be learned and known (through a book like the *Sunzi bingfa* which lists them in catalogues, complete as in an encyclopaedia and of practical relevance like in a handbook). If properly known (*zhi* 知) and applied (*yong* 用) the consequences of victory (*sheng* 勝) and defeat (*fu* 負 or *bai* 敗) will necessarily (*bi* 必) follow. The catalogues in the second part work differently. They are meant to cover the basic possible situations in which deception can be used to gain victory. They serve as examples, which can help to make spontaneous decisions about deceptive strategic moves. They are not as obvious as the factors in part one and decisions related to them should remain hidden.

---

45   See Wagner's article on *fu* in this volume.

Repetition as identity markers of position: *Xunzi* "Xing e" 性惡

Argumentative texts often develop particular positions through constructing oppositional pairs of positions that clearly define both positions by means of contrasts. The beginning of the "Xing e" 性惡 chapter of the *Xunzi* is a fine example, entirely constructed through parallelisms and oppositional pairs.[46] The argumentation in this chapter does not, as in the previous examples, lie in the composition of the text as a whole and the way its units are constructed and related. It rather proceeds step by step, building up two opposite chains of terms that progressively illuminate two contrasting positions. I will therefore proceed differently in my interpretation and translate and comment each unit of the text to re-enact the way the textual argument is set up through literary forms.[47]

1
人之性惡，其善者偽也。
Human nature is bad, what is good in it is artificially acquired.

The first sentence constructs an opposition between a: bad nature 性惡 and b: artificially acquired goodness 善偽.

2
今人之性，
Now, as to human nature,

    Elaboration of position "a":
    a) 生而有好利焉，
    順是，故爭奪生　而辭讓　　亡焉；
    b) 生而有疾惡焉，
    順是，故殘賊生　而忠信　　亡焉；
    c) 生而有耳目之欲，有好聲色焉，
    順是，故淫亂生　而禮義文理亡焉。

---

[46] Translations of this chapter have been published by Burton Watson, *Hsün Tzu: Basic Writings* (New York: Columbia University Press, 1964), Hermann Köster, *Hsün-Tzu* (St. Augustin: Steyler, 1967) and John Knoblock, *Xunzi: A Translation and Study of the Complete Works*, vol. 3 (Stanford: Stanford University Press 1994), 150–151.

[47] I follow the text edition by Wang Xianqian 王先謙, *Xunzi jijie* 荀子集解 (Beijing: Zhonghua 1988), 434–435.

> *Born, humans enjoy profit.*
> *If they comply with this [propensity] then fighting and stealing occur and self-restraint and yielding disappear.*
> *Born, humans have feelings of envy and hatred.*
> *If they comply with this [propensity] then cruelty and crime occur and loyalty and trustworthiness disappear.*
> *Born, humans have sensual desires and love music and beauty.*
> *If they comply with this [propensity] then exorbitance and chaos occur and ritual, righteousness, refinedness and order disappear.*

This unit defines three basic human dispositions a), b), c) as three aspects of human nature and their consequences (*shun shi* 順是) in regard to the two positions "a" and "b."

The three consequences are then summarised as follows:

> 然則
> a) 從人之性，
> b) 順人之情，
> 必出於爭奪，合於犯分亂理，而歸於暴。

> *So following the nature of human beings and complying with their circumstances, this will necessarily start out with fighting and stealing, join in with transgressing social ranks and disturbing good order and end up in violence.*

The new "a" term *qing* 情 (circumstances) is introduced by using the established term *shun* 順 (complying with) and setting the new term in a parallel position with *xing* 性 (nature). The summary of the above three "a" consequences takes over the compound *zhengduo* 爭奪 (fighting and stealing), the following compound *luanli* 亂理 (disorder) combines the two earlier terms chaos (*luan*) and order (*li*). With *bao* 暴 (violence) another new "a" element is introduced. By means of a summary a number of new terms is introduced and embedded within established terms so that their meaning as belonging to the "a" position is unambiguous.

> ***Elaboration of position "b":***
> 故必將有
> a) 師法之化，
> b) 禮義之道，
> 然後出於辭讓，合於文理，而歸於治。

> *This is why it is necessary to have*
> *a) the transformation by teachers and models and*
> *b) the way of rites and righteousness*

so that this then will start out in self-restraint and yielding, join in with refinedness and order and end up in regularity.

In parallel fashion to the preceding unit this unit elaborates position "b" as an imperative. Again a mixture of established and new terms as well as parallels secure the unambiguous introduction of new elements. The usage of the compound rites and righteousness (*liyi* 禮義) link this unit to the unit above and provides a parallel for the introduction of the new compound teacher-and-model (*shifa* 師法). The parallel usage of the same three elements that indicated the three consequences above: 'to start out with' (*chuyu* 出於), 'join in with' (*heyu* 合於), and 'end up in' (*guiyu* 歸於) indicates that this is the summary of the opposite part of the above elaboration of consequences (*shun shi* 順是). The identical first element *cirang* 辭讓 indicates exactly what this refers back to; the second element repeats the third one above, like the *li* 理 before but now with the whole compound *wenli* 文理; and the third element *zhi* 治 (regularity) is introduced as a new "b" element.

Conclusion
用此觀之，人之性惡明矣，其善者偽也。

Using this [argumentation] and looking at it, it has become clear that human nature is bad. Its goodness is artificially acquired.

The conclusion is formulated as a repetition of the above hypothesis with which it forms a frame of the first argument. It marks the end of the first argumentative unit.

3
故
a) 枸木必將待檃栝、烝矯　　然後直；
b) 鈍金必將待礱厲　　　　　然後利；

This is why
a) crooked wood necessarily has to be treated with bevel and steam force to become straight;
b) blunt metal necessarily has to be treated with a grindstone to become sharp.

The opposition of positions "a" and "b" is translated in an analogy of the artisanal production that takes place in craftsmanship.

今人之性惡，
a) 必將待　　師法　　然後正，
b) 得　　　　禮義　　然後治，

Now, [in the same way], given that human nature is bad
a) it has to be treated with teachers and models to become rectified,
b) it has to receive ritual and righteousness to become regulated.

The parallels *bi jiang... er hou* 必將 … 然後 (has to be treated with... to) suggest a continuation of the craftsmanship argument in favour of position "b." The repetition of the two concepts *shifa* 師法 (teachers and models) and *liyi* 禮義 (ritual and righteousness) further confirms this connection. Making use of these identical earlier "b" elements from the text above one new "b" element, *zheng* 正 (rectified/rectification), is introduced and set in parallel position to *zhi* 治 (regulated/regularity), which is the new third element that was introduced earlier on the "b" side.

今人
a) 無師法，則偏險而不正；
b) 無禮義，則悖亂而不治，

Now, if humans
a) have no teachers and models　　then there is partial narrowness and no
*　　　　　　　　　　　　　　　　　　rectification,*
b) have no ritual and righteousness　then there is rebellious disorder and no
*　　　　　　　　　　　　　　　　　　regularity.*

Turning the four thus established "b" elements negative, two further "a" elements are introduced as clear "a" oppositions: *pianxian* 偏險 (partial narrowness) and *beiluan* 悖亂 (rebellious disorder) with *luan* 亂 (disorder) being familiar as part of two other compounds belonging to position "a".

古者聖王以人性惡，以為
a) 偏險而不正，
b) 悖亂而不治，
是以為之
b) 起禮義，
a) 制法度，

As human nature is bad, the sage kings of antiquity considered humans to be
a) partial, narrow and no rectified,
b) rebellious, disordered and not regulated
Because of this for the sake of humans they

b) raised ritual and righteousness and
a) institutionalised models and measures

This is the same argument in reverse form, starting with *pianxian* 偏險 ('partial narrowness') and *beiluan* 悖亂 ('rebellious disorder') and ending with *liyi* 禮義 ('ritual and righteousness') and *fadu* 法度 ('models and measures') (also in the reverse order from above where it was first *shifa* 師法, 'teachers and models', and then *liyi* 禮義, 'ritual and righteousness'). The terminology is almost a pure repetition of known elements with one new element, *du* 度 ('measures') in the compound *fadu* 法度 ('models and measures') which replaces the compound *shifa* 師法 ('teachers and models'), a slight move which reflects the new political context of *zhi* 制 ('institutionalisation') versus the educative *hua* 化 ('transformation') above. The sage kings of antiquity act like craftsmen and invent tools for the rectification and regulation of the crooked and blunt human nature.

a) 以矯飾人之情性而正之，
b) 以擾化人之情性而導之也，

a) in order to forcefully adorn human nature and rectify it,
b) in order to train and transform human nature and guide it with the Way.

Four "b" elements that have been introduced in different passages above (*jiao* 矯, *zheng* 正, *hua* 化 and *dao* 導 replacing *dao* 道) are combined to formulate a coherently deduced new complex "b" position against the two basic "a" elements which are now combined in the compound *qingxing* 情性 ('human circumstances and nature').

始皆出於治，合於道者也。

So that for the first time all started out with regularity and joined in with the way (dao).

Using two of the familiar deductive elements, 'to start out with' (*chuyu* 出於) and 'to join in with' (*heyu* 合於), which indicate an identical deduction as seen in the case above, a new parallel is created from the above established arsenal of "b" terms, 治 and 道. Through this parallelism the historical case as an exemplum of concrete action further reinforces the argument which was developed above as an abstract argument only.

今人之
a) 化師法，積文學，　道禮義者為君子；

b) 縱性情，安恣孳，而違禮義者為小人。

Now, humans
a) being transformed by teachers and models, accumulating refinedness and learning and realizing the way of rituals and righteousness can be considered as gentlemen;
b) indulging their nature, at ease with abandon and abundance and offending ritual and righteousness can be considered as petty men.

This last conclusion is in its first part a) like an equation that adds established "b" elements with the final sum being a gentleman (*junzi* 君子). The second part b) however introduces a number of new elements and affirms their belonging to the opposite "a" chain first by using *zong xingqing* 縱性情 ('indulging their nature') as a variant of the above formulation *cong ren zhi xing, shun ren zhi qing* 從人之性，順人之情 ('following human nature and complying with human circumstances'), by constructing a clear antagonism through the oppositional parallelism 'realising the way of rituals and righteousness' (道禮義 *dao liyi*) versus 'offending ritual and righteousness' (*wei liyi* 違禮義), and, finally, by making use of the established opposition of 'gentleman' (*junzi* 君子) and 'petty men' 小人 (*xiaoren*).

用此觀之，人之性惡明矣，其善者偽也。

Using this [argumentation] and looking at it, it has become clear that human nature is bad. Its goodness is artificially acquired.

The conclusion of this second argumentative unit is an exact repetition of the above conclusion of the first argumentative unit and thus also as signifier of the end of this second unit.

Having marked in colour (see fn 22) all repetitive elements that clearly signify one of the two positions we notice how economical and dense the argument is. Apart from the three basic human dispositions at the beginning and the analogy with practices of craftsmanship there are hardly any words in black that carry any argumentative weight. This technique of making consecutive use of identical terms and incrementally linking them with further terms in order to define greater groups of terms that define a particular (and progressively more complex) position or perspective in a binary constructed argument is a formulaic way to mark specific positions in a text. At the same time the text employs arguments by means of literary forms claiming that the propositions that make use of the same terms and formulations have to be related to one another and by suggesting the belonging of terms to a position by means of parallel style.⁴⁸ The argumentative technique of always embedding a new element within a group of established elements to secure its belonging within this group can also be found in earlier texts such as the "Zhongxin zhi dao" from Guodian.⁴⁹ This technique is reminiscent of the principle of three-point suspension in dangerous rock climbing (the principle of moving only one hand or foot at a time, leaving the other three appendages to secure the body on the rock for balance, as in a tripod). It is a very careful and defensive technique which proceeds slowly because great attention is paid to secure the position from which the argument moves on further and great effort is spent in double and triple affirming the belonging of concepts and terms to one of the two contrasting sides by means of literary repetitions of terms. Smaller textual units are marked by parallelisms, greater units by the repetition of clauses. Linguistic markers such as *gu* 故, *jin* 今 or *ran ze* 然則 are also used to mark textual divisions. The relationship between textual units is either one of identity or of opposition. The sharp contrasts based on a strict oppositional terminology allow the reader to identify these relations quite easily.

Starting with an argumentation that is bound to strict parallel formulations and ending with a much more playful and free style, the architecture of the argument resembles very much the *Xunzi*'s idea of accumulation (*ji* 積) in the process of learning that eventually frees one from the rigid rules of ritual which define the framework for appropriate behaviour. As he says in his first chapter on learning:⁵⁰

積土成山，風雨興焉；
積水成淵，蛟龍生焉；
積善成德，而神明自得，聖心備焉。
If you accumulate earth to form a hill, wind and rain will arise at it;
If you accumulate water to form a pool, flood dragons will be born in it;

---

48 In Daoist and Buddhist philosophical texts from the 3rd century AD on this technique is used very successfully to clearly differentiate oppositional positions and perspectives. An example from the 14th century demonstrates that this technique is also used in later texts. It shows that not only two but also three different positions can be marked by using identical terms repeatedly. Written in the 1370s by Ming Taizu the *Sanjiao lun* 三教論 is an essay that, to quote Judith Berling, "is quite obscure and does not lend itself to coherent translation" (*The Syncretic Religion of Lin Chao-en*, [NY: Columbia UP, 1980], 275 n. 40). The essay is an impressive example of a text which can only be properly understood and correctly translated if its compositional structure and the literary forms of argument employed by the first emperor of the Ming are understood. See my "Zum 'Synkretismus' Ming Taizus. Die *Abhandlung zu den Drei Religionen (Sanjiao lun* 三教論)," unpubl. manuscript.

49 See Dirk Meyer, *Philosophy on Bamboo*, 40, n. 19.

50 Wang Xianqian, *Xunzi jijie*, 7.

If you accumulate goodness to form moral power, divine brightness will be acquired of itself and a sage heart-and-mind will be accomplished.

And on ritual:[51]

凡禮,始乎梲,成乎文,終乎悅校。
Generally speaking, rites start off from the basic pillars, are accomplished in cultivated forms and end in pleasure and beauty.

Combination of 1–3: *Da Dai Liji* "*Zhu yan*" 主言

The last example is representative of a broad range of early Chinese texts, which combine a variety of literary forms to formulate their arguments. We will find all three literary forms introduced in the earlier parts of the paper (double-directed parallelism, enumerative catalogues and referential signifiers) combined in this last text example. The "Zhu yan" 主言 (Words concerning Rulers) chapter no 39 from the *Da Dai Liji* is the first transmitted chapter of this book. As with a number of other chapters from the *Da Dai Liji* a version of this chapter is also transmitted in the *Kongzi jiayu* (chapter three, "Wang yan jie" 王言解, Words concerning Kings Explained).[52]

The chapter is divided into three main parts: a frame narrative that sets the scene of the dialogue between Confucius and Zengzi defines the topic and gives it significance and grandeur. A core statement in the form of an introductory speech forms the second part. The third part consists of further elaborations on this introductory core statement in three sub-parts, each in turn divided into two. The introductory narrative runs as follows

Part I
孔子閒居,曾子侍。
孔子曰:
「參,今之君子,惟士與大夫之言之聞也,其至於君子之言者甚希矣。於乎!吾主言其不出而死乎?哀哉!」

---

51 Wang Xianqian, *Xunzi jijie*, 355.
52 No translation of this text into English exists. Richard Wilhelm translated it into German as chapter 14 (*Herrscherworte*) of his *Li Gi. Das Buch der Riten, Sitten und Gebräuche* (Jena: Diederichs, 1930, 2nd ed. Düsseldorf, Köln: Diederichs, 1981), 217–223. Benedykt Grynpas translated it into French in his *Les écrits de Tai l'ancien et le petit calendrier des Hia. Textes Confucéens Taoïsants* (Paris: Librairie d'Amérique et d'Orient Adrien Maisonneuve, 1972), 29–36. R.P. Kramers translated the *Kongzi jiayu* variant of the chapter ("Royal Words Explained") in his *K'ung-tzu chia-yü: Family Sayings of Confucius* (Leiden: Brill, 1950), 207–212.

曾子起曰：
「敢問：何謂『主言』？」

孔子不應。[53]
曾子懼，肅然攝衣下席曰：
「弟子知其不孫也，得夫子之閒也難，是以敢問也。」
孔子不應。
曾子懼，退負序而立。
孔子曰：
「參！女可語明主之道與？」
曾子曰：
「不敢以為足也，得夫子之閒也難，是以敢問。」

Kongzi was dwelling in leisure, Zengzi was attending.
Kongzi said: "Shen,[54] today's gentlemen are idle only with talk concerning petty and great officials. Those who measure up to the words of gentlemen have been very few. Alas! Will my words concerning rulers never be uttered before I die? This is so desolate!"
Zengzi said: "May I venture to ask, what do you mean by 'words concerning rulers'?"
Kongzi didn't respond.
Zengzi was frightened. Reverently he lifted his dress, left his mat and said: "Your disciple knows that he is not prudent. It is so difficult to get the opportunity of meeting the master in leisure. This is the reason why I dared to ask."
Kongzi didn't respond.
Zengzi was frightened. He backed away and stood turned against the wall.
Kongzi said: "Shen, can you talk about the way of the enlightened rulers?"
Zengzi said: "I do not venture to consider myself as sufficing. It is so difficult to get the opportunity of meeting the master in leisure. This is the reason why I dared to ask."

This introductory frame narrative introduces the topic as something of existential meaning for Confucius, something he would not easily talk about and he would not easily find someone to discuss with. It sets up a contrast between 'words concerning petty and great officials' (*shi yu dafu zhi yan* 士與大夫之言), 'words of gentlemen' (*junzi zhi yan* 君子之言), and the equations: 'words concerning rulers' (*zhuyan* 主言) and 'the way of enlightened rulers' (*mingzhu zhi dao* 明主之道). This setting of the text opens the stage for the master's expository performance. The reader knows that the following is appropriate for the ears of enlightened rulers only, that Kongzi is reluctant to speak about it even

---

[53] This reaction of Confucius is also reported in an episode in which Baigong asks Kongzi about subtle words (白公問孔子曰：「人可與微言乎？」孔子不應), transmitted in the *Lüshi chunqiu*, *Huainanzi* and *Liezi*, texts more closely associated with what is called a "Daoist" position.

[54] Shen is Zengzi's name.

to his close disciple and it is fortunate that indeed Zengzi made him speak about this principal matter at all. The following part represents the core of the overall text. It opens with the basic binary division into *dao* 道 and *de* 德 and proceeds in classic interlocking parallel style (IPS):[55]

Part II:
孔子曰：
「吾語女：
unit II.1

1.1 道者, 所以明德也	德者, 所以尊道也
是故	1.2 非德不尊
非道不明	
1.3 雖有國焉, 不教不服, 不可以取千里。	
	雖有博地眾民, 不以其地治之, 不可以霸主

Kongzi said: "Let me tell you:
1.1 The Way is that by which moral power is illuminated.

                  Moral power is that by which the Way is revered.

        Therefore

                  1.2 Without moral power it is not revered.

Without the Way it is not illuminated.

1.3 Even though one has a state, if one does not instruct and people do not obey one cannot gain a territory one thousand miles away.

                  Even though one has a vast territory and numerous people, if one does not govern them according to their local needs one cannot rule as hegemon.

---

55   For an introduction to IPS see Rudolf G. Wagner, "Interlocking Parallel Style: Laozi and Wang Bi," *Asiatische Studien / Études asiatiques* 34.1 (1980): 18–58 and id., *The Craft of a Chinese Commentator: Wang Bi on the* Laozi (Albany: SUNY, 2000), 53–113.

In the first unit of this core speech the main topic is in a first step (1.1) split up into the two basic concepts of the Way (*dao*) and moral power (*de*), a conceptual tension, which we also find in other early Chinese texts. Here, the argument points to an interesting circle: The Way illuminates what in turn serves to revere it, there is a self-referential momentum in this construction as moral power appears as a means of self-reference for the Way. In a second step (1.2a) the statement is repeated in negative form using the same terms and thus formulating a parallelism in the negative mode, mirrored also in the reverted textual arrangement as *de* comes first and then *dao*. Logically, this reversion to the negative claims that these and only these are the causes for their illumination and reverence: there are no other possible factors that fulfil the same function. This parallelism in the negative mode appears as a logical deduction. At the same time it also serves as preparation for the following pair of sentences (1.3) which are added without the insertion of a *shigu* 是故 which clearly demarcated the negative parallelism as a second subunit (1.2) from the first subunit (1.1). The case is thus very similar to what we have seen in the *Sunzi* above where subunit 2.2 was demarcated from the formally highly similar subunit 2.1 by a *gu* 故 but not from the following subunit 2.3 which was similar in content but not in form. Subunit 1.2 seems to operate in a similar way as a double-directed unit which bridges 1.1 and 1.3 by formally solely turning 1.1 negative (in an elliptic form) yet introducing the perspective of 1.3 and embedding the new material into the established binary structure of the abstract statements on *dao* and *de* which in turn are illustrated by the new material.

是故昔者明主

unit II.2a	unit II.2b
內脩七教 七教脩焉,可以守 七教不脩,雖守不固	外行三至 三至行焉,可以征 三至不行,雖征不服
是	故
明主之守也,必折衝乎千里之外;	其征也,衽席之上還師。

Such being the case, the enlightened rulers in antiquity, inwardly cultivated the Seven Teachings and

        outwardly practised the Three Perfections.

Once the Seven Teachings had been cultivated they could by this means protect [the state]

        Once the Three Perfections were practised, they could by this means conduct punitive attacks.

When the Seven Teachings were not cultivated then even when the state was protected it was not secure.

When the Three Perfections were not practised then even if punitive attacks were conducted there was no obedience.

Such being the case,

the way the enlightened rulers protected their states was that they always destroyed the enemy outside their territory of thousand miles.

The way they conducted punitive attacks was that they were comfortably on their mat when returning with their troops.

The interlocking parallel style is continued into the medium of the historical narrative introduced by the severing marker *shigu* and the typical reference to historical precedents. The binary contrast set up in the first part is further developed with inner cultivation on the *dao* side and outer practice on the *de* side. Each is connected to a catalogue consisting of an apparently established closed numerical set very much reminiscent to the examples from the *Yi Zhoushu* referred to above.[56] They appear as historically approved political programmes claiming completeness. In the following we see the same strategy of adding further terms to both sides extending the arsenal of positioned signifiers through the introduction of new pairs of terms thereby generating two chains of terms which in this case express complementary (not oppositional) positions: 'protection' (*shou*) and 'punitive attack' (*zheng*). The two catalogues are presented as conditions for the success of the political tasks of protection on the inner *dao* side and attack on the outer *de* side. The following sentences start as parallelisms that have been turned negative (七教不脩 and 三至不行), yet the second part is not a mere repetition in the negative mode but introduces a new idea. Its function is to make a new point, not to lead over to the following sentence. It therefore does not function as a double-directed element as seen in the cases above. The *shigu* is therefore also not inserted before but comes after and clearly demarcates the two following conclusive sentences as independent statements from the earlier part of the unit. Further elabo-

---

56   See footnote 41.

rating on the two newly established terms 'protection' and 'punitive expedition,' these conclusions demonstrate again (as in the *Xunzi*) the real consequences of the earlier more abstract statements in the concrete action of the sage kings.

In the third great part of the overall text this second unit of the second part is discussed in regard to its unlocked components 2a and 2b respectively. All the concepts of this unit serve as referential markers throughout this later explanative discussion in the text.

是故

unit II.3a	unit II.3b
內脩七教而上不勞，	外行三至而財不費，

此之謂明主之道也。」

Such being the case,

When inwardly the Seven Teachings are
cultivated then the superiors will not be exhausted.

        When outwardly the Three
        Perfections are practised then the
        resources are not wasted.

This is what is meant by 'the Way of the enlightened rulers.'"

Another *shigu* demarcates this last unit of the core part from the second unit. The significance of this demarcation is not evident from the text itself. This last sentence could very well have served as a further conclusive statement, which emphasises the economic effect of both catalogues (superiors are not exhausted and resources are not wasted). Yet, in the continuation of the following part of the overall text, this last short unit of the core part is the first to be discussed as an independent topic. New pairs of terms are introduced as further referential signifiers: *shang* 上 and *lao* 勞 on the one side and *cai* 財 and *fei* 費 on the other. The unit is closed with the typical final clause *ci zhi wei x ye* 此之謂 x 也 with x repeating Kongzi's initial question to Zengzi about the Way of the enlightened rulers. This end of the core part is further confirmed through the end of Kongzi's speech in the dialogue and the question from Zengzi which follows it.

The following third part consists of a further explanatory expansion of the topics laid out in this core part. As a translation and interpretation of this part would not substantially add to my analysis of the way literary forms are employed to construct arguments, I will simply focus on the role played by signifiers of textual repetition towards an understanding of the structure of the argument. The third part is basically structured in three main subunits the beginning of which is marked by three main questions posed by Zengzi:

May I venture to ask, can "not wasting" and "not being exhausted" be regarded as [the main outcomes of] being enlightened?

敢問：不費、不勞，可以為明乎？

May I venture to ask, what is meant by the Seven Teachings?

敢問：何謂七教？

May I venture to ask, what is meant by the Three Perfections?

敢問，何謂三至？

Zengzi thus starts to ask about the last unit of the core piece II.3a and II.3b. He then asks about unit II.2a and then about unit II.2b. Unit II.1 of the core piece is not further discussed.

The end of each unit is marked as well by literary forms. In the same manner as the end of the textual unit of the core speech (part II) is marked by the repetition of the introductory topic (此之謂明主之道也) so is the end of each unit of the following part III also marked by the repetition of central signifiers of the units from part II to which they relate. Unit III.1.1 ends with reference to its central topic of being exhausted (明主奚為其勞也？), unit III.1.2 with reference to its topic of waste (明主焉取其費也？), and units III.2 and III.3 with explicit references to the concluding sentences of the related units II.2a: 此之謂『明主之守也, 必折衝乎千里之外 』 此之謂也。and II.2b: 此之謂『衽席之上還師』。

Each of the three subunits of part III is further subdivided into two parts. Unit III.1 into subunits III.1.1 explaining exhaustion (*lao* 勞) and III.1.2 explaining waste (*fei* 費), each with reference to authoritative historical narratives about governance practices of sage kings in antiquity. Subunits III.2 and III.3 are each divided by a further question of Zengzi which seeks further clarification ("Your disciple does obviously not suffice. The Way is indeed so supreme!" 弟子則不足，道則至矣。and: "May I venture to ask, what does this mean?" 敢問：何謂也？) and thus allows the text to expand upon the topics beyond the listings of seven respective three principles and their seven respective three ways of putting these principles into practice in the seven respective three social strata that are given as basic explanations for 七教 and 三至 in the first half of these parts.

These expansions in the second halves are in turn divided into two subunits. The first subunits (III.2.2.1 and III.3.2.1) add further listings in numbers of seven respective three. They conclude with two similar sentences: "if these seven are cultivated then there will be no punishments of people within the Four Seas" 此七者脩，則四海之內無刑民矣 and "if a ruler who possesses land cultivates these three then everybody within the Four Seas will bow to him and follow him" 有土之君脩此三者，則四海之內拱而俟. The second subunits (III.2.2.2 and III.3.2.2) provide further listings (in different numbers) and adduce analogies with the natural order (如四時春秋冬夏 and 猶時雨也) before in a final conclusion they formulate two parallel sentences that, like a closing reminder, give examples of the two principles of 'not being exhausted' (*bu lao* 不勞) and 'not wasting' (*bu fei* 不費) to finally end with the quotes of the concluding sentences of the respective units of part II introduced by *ci zhi wei* 此之謂 (this is what is meant by…).

The basic structure of the third part can thus be determined by a skeleton of signifiers, which looks like the following:

Part III:
III.1. Discussion on the conclusive sentence II.3a/b (內脩七教而上不勞, 外行三至而財不費, 此之謂明主之道也) introduced by Zengzi's question: 敢問：不費,不勞,可以為明乎？
  III.1.1 Discussion of topic: 勞, ending with: 明主奚為其勞也？
  III.1.2 Discussion of topic: 費, ending with: 明主焉取其費也？
  III.2.1 七教 basic catalogues introduced by Zengzi's question: 敢問：何謂七教？
  III.2.2 七教 further explanations introduced by Zengzi's question: 弟子則不足，道則至矣。
    III.2.2.1 七教 further explanations ending with 此七者脩，則四海之內
    III.2.2.2 七教 further explanations using natural analogies: 如四時春秋冬夏 and ending with the conclusive sentence from II.2a: 此之謂『明主之守也, 必折衝乎千里之外』此之謂也。
  III.3.1 三至 basic catalogues introduced by Zengzi's question: 敢問，何謂三至？
  III.3.2 三至 further explanations introduced by Zengzi's question: 敢問：何謂也？
    III.3.2.1 三至 further explanations ending with 脩此三者，則四海之內
    III.3.2.2 三至 further explanations using natural analogies: 猶時雨也 and ending with the conclusive sentence from II.2b: 此之謂『衽席之上還師』。

What, after this analysis and according to this skeleton, appears as a rigorously symmetrical organisation of the explanatory parts and a strict parallelism between parts III.2 and III.3 is in the textual reality blurred by the formal diversity of the inserted material and its manifold contents.[57] The greater discursive units, which on the sublevel are further separated by a great variety of

---

[57] A link to the full Chinese text of the "Zhu yan" chapter in an analytical presentation together with a translation can be found on my website following the bibliographical data of this article under "publications" (http://www.ed.ac.uk/schools-departments/literatures-languages-cultures/asian-studies/staff/joachim-gentz/publications). Its purpose is to allow readers to relate my analysis of the structural skeleton of its third part to the entire text. The repetitive signifiers that I have analysed are marked in colour so that the formal features of the text can easily be grasped by the readers.

diverging literary forms as well as (false or real) illatives *shiyi, gu, shigu* etc. would be hardly recognisable without the repetitive signifiers which clearly mark the beginning, the end, and the relation of these units to other units. The chapter thus appears to consist of diverse material arranged in a framework that is made up of a set of signifiers, which are composed in a strictly symmetric fashion. These signifiers are not just devices of literary composition. Foremost they function as landmarks in an otherwise quite disconnectedly arranged collage of material. They serve as orientation aids, which are conditional for a correct reconstruction of the main arguments. Any systematic interpretation of such a text must therefore necessarily start from an identification of these signifiers and relate the rest of the material framed by them to the topics connected to them.

This last example represents what is probably the most common way in which literary forms are used in argumentative texts to construct arguments. Most texts combine different literary forms of argumentation. The interweaving of different literary forms, which at the same time carry argumentative functions, complicates the identification of these forms which, as isolated signifiers, are sometimes hidden in the messiness of an oscillating text that is full of allusions and saturated with intertextuality.

A text very similar in form to this "Zhu yan" chapter is the "Min zhi fumu" 民之父母 from the Shanghai Museum collection of manuscript texts.[58] It is also written in dialogical form, with Zixia asking Kongzi and using the same interrogative formula as Zengzi: "*gan wen he wei x*" 敢問何謂 x? Kongzi responds in a similar way by referring to the Five Perfections (*wuzhi* 五至) and the Three Withouts (*sanwu* 三無) and it is interesting that it is not the Five Perfections but the Three Withouts that are similar to the Three Perfections (*sanzhi* 三至) of the "Zhu yan 主言" text analysed above. The Three Withouts in the "Min zhi fumu" are: music without tones, ritual without embodiment and mourning without (mourning) garments (無聲之樂，無體之禮，無服之喪). The Three Perfections from the "Zhu yan" text were: perfect ritual does not yield and yet 'all under Heaven' is regulated, perfect rewards are not lavish and yet the *shi* officers in All under Heaven enjoy them, perfect music is without tones and yet in all under Heaven the people are harmonious. (至禮不讓而天下治，至賞不費而天下之士說，至樂無聲而天下之民和)

---

58 For an analysis of this text see Richter, *Embodied Text*, 127–187.

Conclusion

In this paper I have focused on literary forms of Chinese texts which on the one hand structure the text into separate parts and on the other indicate the relationship of these parts to each other. I have argued that this literary arrangement of a text is an integral part of its argumentation. Analysing several examples of texts and literary forms of arguments it can be seen that during the second century BC this particular argumentative function of literary forms might have been increasingly supported by linguistic expressions, which made the extent of textual units as well as their mutual relationships explicit. These linguistic markers may have been inserted as structural markers in texts because the structuring and argumentative function of their literary forms were no longer understood by a growing readership. Reading marks, which we find in excavated texts, might have served a similar purpose. How exactly the utilisation or abandoning of punctuation markers relate to this process of making textual units and their relationships explicit remains to be investigated.

Looking further at the invention, utilisation and development of literary forms of arguments from a historical point of view, a number of factors might have contributed to changes in argumentative styles. The compilation projects of late Zhanguo and Early Han times undertaken by influential text specialists might have fostered the use of collage techniques which in turn necessitated new ways of marking inner-textual relationships in order to formulate new arguments with the available old materials. The technique of labelling textual units by means of repetitive signifiers of belonging that we have seen so masterly executed in the "Xing e" chapter of the *Xunzi* might have occurred as the result of a new understanding of the function of texts as mere instruments of argumentative operation. The composition of texts into a core piece and following explanative parts required new methods of inner-textual referencing. Inner-textual commentaries had to be identifiable through techniques of textual subordination. The increasing role of disciples in the process of recording and disseminating texts might have led to the preference of presenting arguments in a dialogical form. The growth of specialised discourses combined with the development of correlative systematics could have encouraged authors to enrich their arguments with analogous aspects from diverse discourses to prove the validity of their arguments.

As the analysis of the literary forms of arguments in early China is still at an elementary stage historical developments of these forms are difficult to grasp. This paper attempts to present and discuss some of these literary forms. Beyond parallelisms of different kinds, double-directed elements, enumerative catalogues, and repetitive markers of relation, we have yet to explore more of the vast array of the diverse literary forms of argument in order to be able to fully appreciate the multidimensionality and complexity of early Chinese argumentation, all the while taking the risk that in the end they may not convince us.

References

Annus, Amar. "On the Beginning and Continuities of Omen Sciences in the Ancient World." In *Divination and Interpretation of Signs in the Ancient World*, edited by A. Annus. Chicago: The Oriental Institute of the University of Chicago, 2010: 1–18.

Baxter, William H. *Handbook of Old Chinese Phonology*. Berlin: Mouton de Gruyter, 1992.

——. "Situating the Language of the *Lao-tzu*." In *Lao-tzu and the Tao-te-ching*, edited by Livia Kohn and Michael LaFargue. Albany: SUNY Press, 1998: 231–253.

Baxter, William H., and Laurent Sagart. *Old Chinese: a new reconstruction*. New York: Oxford University Press, 2014.

Beijing Daxue chutu wenxian yanjiusuo 北京大學出土文獻研究所, ed. *Beijing Daxue cang Xihan zhushu* 北京大學藏西漢竹書. Vol. 2. Shanghai: Shanghai guji chubanshe, 2012.

Berling, Judith. *The Syncretic Religion of Lin Chao-en*. New York: Columbia University Press, 1980.

Boltz, William G. "The Composite Nature of Early Chinese Texts." In *Text and Ritual in Early China*, edited by Martin Kern. Seattle: University of Washington Press, 2005: 50–78.

Bottéro, Jean. *Mesopotamia: Writing, Reasoning, and the Gods*. Chicago: University of Chicago Press, 1992.

Broschat, Michael R. "Guiguzi: A textual Study and Translation." PhD diss., University of Michigan, 1985.

Chatman, Seymour. "Comparing Metrical Styles." In *Style in Language*, edited by Thomas A. Sebeok. Cambridge: M.I.T., 1960: 149–172.

Dorofeeva-Lichtmann, Vera. "Spatial Composition of Ancient Chinese Texts." In *History of Science, History of Text*, edited by Karine Chemla. Dordrecht: Springer, 2005: 3–47.

——. "Spatiality of the Media for Writing in Ancient China and Spatial Organization of Ancient Chinese Texts." *Göttinger Beiträge zur Asienforschung* 1 (2001): 87–135.

Fischer, Paul. "Intertextuality in Early Chinese Masters-Texts: Shared Narratives in *Shi Zi*." *Asia Major* 22.2 (2009): 1–34.

Fitzgerald, John T. "The Catalogue in Ancient Greek Literature." In *The Rhetorical Analysis of Scripture: Essays from the 1995 London Conference*, edited by Stanley E. Porter and Thomas H. Olbricht. Sheffield: Academic Press, 1997: 275–293.

Gao Ming 高明, ed. *Boshu Laozi jiaozhu* 帛書老子校注. Beijing: Zhonghua shuju, 1996.

Gentz, Joachim. *Das Gongyang zhuan. Auslegung und Kanonisierung der* Frühlings- und Herbstannalen (Chunqiu). Wiesbaden: Harrassowitz, 2001.

———. "Composition as grammar of a topological semantic flow. A comparison of the two 'Tzu-i'-versions from Kuo-tien and the *Li-chi*." Paper presented at the EACS Conference, Turin, August 30–September 2, 2000 (CD-ROM-Publication, 2002).

———. "Zum 'Synkretismus' Ming Taizus. Die *Abhandlung zu den Drei Religionen* (*Sanjiao lun* 三教論)." Unpublished manuscript, 2003.

———. "Zwischen den Argumenten lesen. Doppelt gerichtete Parallelismen zwischen Argumenten als zentrale Thesen in frühen chinesischen Texten." In *Komposition und Konnotation—Figuren der Kunstprosa im Alten China*, edited by Wolfgang Behr and Joachim Gentz, *Bochumer Jahrbuch zur Ostasienforschung* 29 (2005): 35–56.

———. "Hermeneutics of Multiple Senses: Wang Jie's 'Explanations and Commentary with Diagrams to the *Qingjing jing*'." *Journal of Chinese Philosophy* 37.3 (2010): 346–365.

Grynpas, Benedykt. *Les écrits de Tai l'ancien et le petit calendrier des Hia. Textes Confucéens Taoïsants*. Paris: Librairie d'Amérique et d'Orient Adrien Maisonneuve, 1972.

Hua Xuecheng 華學誠, and Xie Rong'e 謝榮娥. "Qin Han Chu fangyanqu wenxian zhong de youbu yu xiaobu" 秦漢楚方言區文獻中的幽部與宵部. *Yuwen yanjiu* 語文研究 (2009.1): 1–4.

Huang Huaixin 黃懷信 et al. *Yi Zhoushu huijiao jizhu* 逸周書彙校集注. Shanghai: Shanghai guji chubanshe, 1995.

Jiang Yougao 江有誥. *Jiangshi yinxue shishu* 江氏音學十書. 1812; reprint, Shanghai: Shanghai Zhongguo shudian, 1928.

Jingmenshi Bowuguan 荊門市博物館, ed. *Guodian Chu mu zhujian* 郭店楚墓竹簡. Beijing: Wenwu chubanshe, 1998.

Kern, Martin. "Quotation and the Confucian Canon in Early Chinese Manuscripts: The Case of 'Zi yi' (Black Robes)." *Asiatische Studien / Études asiatiques* 59.1 (2005): 293–332.

Knoblock, John. *Xunzi: A Translation and Study of the Complete Works*. Vol. 3. Stanford: Stanford University Press, 1994.

Köster, Hermann. *Hsün-Tzu*. St. Augustin: Steyler, 1967.

Kramers, R.P. *K'ung-tzu chia-yü: Family Sayings of Confucius*. Leiden: Brill, 1950.

Lackner, Michael. "Die Verplanung des Denkens am Beispiel der *tu*." In *Lebenswelt und Weltanschauung im frühneuzeitlichen China*, edited by Helwig Schmidt-Glintzer. Stuttgart: Steiner, 1990: 133–156.

———. "Citation et éveil. Quelques remarques à propos de l'emploi de la citation chez Zhang Zai." *Extrême Orient-Extrême Occident* 17 (1995): 111–130.

———. "Argumentation par diagrammes. Une architecture à base de mots. Le *Ximing* (l'*Inscription Occidentale*) depuis Zhang Zai jusqu'au *Yanjitu*." *Extrême Orient-Extrême Occident* 14 (1992): 131–168.

———. "La position d'une expression dans le texte: explorations diagrammatiques de la signification." *Extrême Orient-Extrême Occident* (1996): 35–51.

———. "Was Millionen Wörter nicht sagen können: Diagramme zur Visualisierung klassischer Texte im China des 13. bis 14. Jahrhunderts." *Zeitschrift für Semiotik* 22.2 (2000): 209–237.

———. "Diagrams as an Architecture by Means of Words: the *Yanji tu*." In *Graphics and Text in the Production of Technical Knowledge in China: The Warp and the Weft*, edited by Francesca Bray et al. Leiden: Brill, 2007: 341–381.

Ledderose, Lothar. *Ten Thousand Things: Module and Mass Production in Chinese Art*. Princeton, NJ: Princeton University Press, 2000.

Levi, Jean. "Quelques examples de détournement subversif de la citation dans la littérature classique chinoise." *Extrême Orient-Extrême Occident* 17 (1995): 41–65.

Lewis, Mark Edward. "Writings on Warfare Found in Ancient Chinese Tombs." *Sino-Platonic Papers* 158 (2005): 1–15.

Mair, Victor. *The Art of War: Sun Zi's Military Methods*. New York: Columbia University Press, 2009.

Martin, François. "Le *Shijing*, de la citation à l'allusion: La disponibilité du sens." *Extrême Orient-Extrême Occident* 17 (1995): 5–39.

Meyer, Dirk. "The Power of the Component and the Establishment of the Guodian Tomb One Bamboo-slip Manuscript 'Zhōng xìn zhī dào' as a Text," MA diss., Leiden University, 2002.

———. "A device for conveying meaning: The structure of the Guodian Tomb One manuscript 'Zhōng xìn zhī dào'." In *Komposition und Konnotation—Figuren der Kunstprosa im Alten China*, edited by Wolfgang Behr and Joachim Gentz, *Bochumer Jahrbuch zur Ostasienforschung* 29 (2005): 57–78.

———. *Philosophy on Bamboo: Text and the Production of Meaning in Early China*. Leiden: Brill, 2011.

Moloughney, Brian. "Derivation, Intertextuality and Authority: Narrative and the Problem of Historical Coherence." *East Asian History* 23 (2002): 129–148.

Plaks, Andrew. "Terminology and Central Concepts." In *How to Read the Chinese Novel*, edited by D.L. Rolston. Princeton: Princeton University Press, 1990: 75–123.

Richter, Matthias. "Self-Cultivation or Evaluation of Others?: A Form Critical Approach to Zengzi li shi." *Asiatische Studien / Études asiatiques* LVI, 4 (2002): 879–917.

———. "Der Alte und das Wasser: Lesarten von *Laozi* 8 im überlieferten Text und in den Manuskripten von Mawangdui." In *Han-Zeit: Festschrift für Hans Stumpfeldt aus Anlaß seines 65. Geburtstages*, edited by M. Friedrich, R. Emmerich, H. van Ess. Wiesbaden: Harrassowitz, 2006: 253–273.

———. *The Embodied Text—Establishing Textual Identity in Early Chinese Manuscripts*. Leiden: Brill, 2013.

———. "Punctuation." In *Reading Early Chinese Manuscripts: Texts, Contexts, Methods*, edited by Wolfgang Behr, Martin Kern, Dirk Meyer, *Handbook of Oriental Studies*. Leiden: Brill, forthcoming.

Saussy, Haun. "Repetition, Rhyme, and Exchange in The Book of Odes." *Harvard Journal of Asiatic Studies* 57.2 (1997): 519–542.

Schaberg, David. "The Logic of Signs in Early Chinese Rhetoric." In *Thinking Through Comparison: Ancient China and Greece*, edited by Stephen Durrant and Steven Shankman. New York: SUNY Press, 2002: 155–186.

Schwermann, Christian. "Collage-Technik als Kompositionsprinzip klassischer chinesischer Prosa: Der Aufbau des Kapitels 'Tang wen' (Die Fragen des Tang) im *Lie zi*." In *Komposition und Konnotation—Figuren der Kunstprosa im Alten China*, edited by Wolfgang Behr and Joachim Gentz, *Bochumer Jahrbuch zur Ostasienforschung* 29 (2005): 125–157.

Shaughnessy, Edward L. "Writing and Rewriting the Poetry." Paper presented at the "International Symposium on Excavated Manuscripts and the Interpretation of the *Book of Odes*," University of Chicago, September 12, 2009. http://cccp.uchicago.edu/archive/2009BookOfOdesSymposium/2009_BookOfOdesSymposium_EdShaughnessy.pdf (last access 24/09/2014).

Wagner, Rudolf G. "Interlocking Parallel Style: Laozi and Wang Bi." *Asiatische Studien / Études asiatiques* 34.1 (1980): 18–58

———. "The Guodian MSS and the 'Units of Thought' in Early Chinese Philosophy." Unpublished conference Paper, presented at the Guodian Conference, Wuhan, October 15–18, 1999.

———. *Language, Ontology and Political Philosophy in China. Wang Bi's Scholarly Exploration of the Dark (Xuanxue)*. Albany: SUNY Press, 2003.

———. *The Craft of a Chinese Commentator: Wang Bi on the* Laozi. Albany: SUNY Press, 2000.

Wang Xianqian 王先謙, ed. *Xunzi jijie* 荀子集解. Beijing: Zhonghua shuju, 1988.

Watson, Burton. *Hsün Tzu: Basic Writings*. New York: Columbia University Press, 1964.

Wilhelm, Richard. *Li Gi. Das Buch der Riten, Sitten und Gebräuche*. Jena: Diederichs, 1930; reprint, Düsseldorf, Köln: Diederichs, 1981.

Yu Xingwu 于省吾. *Zeluoju* Shijing *xinzheng, Zeluoju* Chuci *xinzheng* 澤螺居詩經新証、澤螺居楚辭新証. Beijing: Zhonghua shuju, 2009.

CHAPTER 5

The Philosophy of the Analytic *Aperçu*

Christoph Harbsmeier

Surveying the superabundant Chinese literature excavated, edited and annotated during the last few decades one cannot help but admire the judicious care with which Liu Xiang 劉向 (c. 77–6 BC) and Liu Xin 劉歆 (c. 50 BC–AD 23) chose and edited so many of our ancient books. If they were working from anything like those excavated versions of traditionally transmitted texts that we have this shows the immense task Liu Xin and Liu Xiang must have been facing as editors. The classical case study on the process of compilation by which this sort of editing was done still remains Piet van der Loon, "On the transmission of the Kuan-tzu."[1]

Writing is always 'writing as.' Correspondingly, reading has always had to be 'reading as.' Writing is never just the writing of text. It is the writing of a certain type of text from a certain culturally pre-defined repertoire of 'canonised' possible types of text, the repertoire of written genres. The philosophy of literary genres is a necessary precondition for any possible analytic history of literature. For China, it seems to me, this precondition is still very far from having been met.

The genres of Chinese literature were many. The *logia* and *apophthegms* in the Confucian *Analects* were examples of one such early genre; one hose history has been studied by Donald Holzman.[2] The genre style of the *Analects* comports a philosophical message: the intellectual message of the book was not conceived as an art of successful one-way communication and of precise argumentation. The message was all about illustrating through live *dicta* and *apophthegms* in context, the living sagehood or higher wisdom of certain individuals as it operates differently in its varying contexts. In particular this was so of the sayings and dialogues involving Confucius and his disciples. The *Analects* give both Confucius and several of his disciples a distinct voice all of their own. That vulnerable and often playful reflexive Master's 'voice' in the *Analects* matters at least as much as whatever true opinions they were maintaining—more or less successfully and clearly.

---

1 *T'oung Pao* 41.1 (1952): 357–393.
2 "The Conversational Tradition in Chinese Philosophy," *Philosophy East and West* 6.3 (1956): 223–230.

The more extensive dialogues typical of the *Mencius* are another, problematising variety. Here again, the genre style comports an overall 'structural' message. The intellectual message of the book was conceived as a kind of propositional wisdom that is presented as winning out in dialogue and in disputation, and by and large not just in one-way philosophical or moral pontification. The figure of Mencius presented in this anonymous compilation is given no interesting 'voice' in the book. To the extent he is engagingly funny, it is unwittingly and in spite of himself. What counts here is the superiority of his arguments, and his superior analyses of important issues.

The very chapter headings of the *Xunzi* 荀子 gives away the genre style as well as the intellectual aspirations of this work. The intellectual ambition is not only to argue for certain theses, but to treat coherently, argumentatively, and precisely of certain general issues such as those of ritual, government, nomenclature, study method and so on. Even this compilation does mention Xunzi by name, in the third person, but somehow the author comes out as much more 'professorial' in the sense of Michel Foucault's lectures at the Collège de France. The style of the non-poetic parts of this book comports and 'oozes' a kind of classroom message atmosphere. It begins to smell of a classroom in ways that the book *Mencius* does not, because in the *Mencius* the discourse on intellectual issues is not yet disconnected from the painfully concrete social and political reality of the author, and the school that was to develop into an ivory tower had not yet emerged. (One is tempted to say that Xunzi's didactic style with its repetitious parallelisms as well as the more pedestrian repetitiveness in *Mozi* 墨子 mark a move towards a 'classroom' style academic prose. For the emergence of such a classroom mentality in Europe see Jacques LeGoff, *Intellectuals in the Middle Ages*).[3]

The rhyming wisdom poetry of the *Laozi* by itself comports again an intellectual programme: this is the self-doubting, vulnerable, ephemeral and situational discourse that provides the intellectual meat in the *Analects*. Here the genre style of ponderous and deliberate, polished and spiritual epigrammatic apophthegm comports a message in itself. The form of the rhymed mystifying provocative epigram excludes anything other than celebrating with rhythmic and rhyming pomp its own spiritual superiority, and mysteriously all-important wisdom.

Within what today is one long ancient book, separate literary genres are often represented, as indeed one might in the "collected works" of any famous writer. Thus the *Guanzi* 管子 contains dialogue sections that need to be read as moralising contextualised dialogue in the spirit of the *Mencius* on the one

---

3 Oxford: Blackwell/Wiley, 1993.

hand, mystical *fang shu* 方術 treatises of edifying self-cultivation, thematic argumentative sections in the spirit of the *Xunzi* on the other, and then a crucial third professionalist almost practical text sort represented in the extensive *Qing zhong* 輕重 "economic chapters" that needs to be read as an administrative handbook.

Moving closer to my subject at hand, the dialogue sections of the book *Mozi* must be 'read as' belonging to a very different text sort from what today is commonly referred to as the *Mo jing* 墨經, the Mohist Dialectical Chapters. Within these Dialectical Chapters, the often enigmatically short and unrevealing *jing* 經 'canons,' need to be read and interpreted as very different text sorts from the *shuo* 說 'explanations.' A.C. Graham has shown how within these *jing* 'canons' again, two profoundly different text sorts have to be distinguished: one part has to be read as definitions and the other as propositions. Understanding the Mohist *Dialectical Chapters* involves acquiring a systematic ability for each subtext to 'read it as' the text sort it is written as and thus intended to be. And there again, the scheme of text sorts in the *Dialectical Chapters* in itself comports something like an intellectual framework. It delineates, as it were, an overall topology of the intellectual space in which definitions of conceptual schemes are treated radically differently from propositions about the details within this conceptual space thus defined.

The present paper wishes to argue in some detail that an excavated text like the so-called "Yucong" 語叢 1 excavated at Guodian 郭店 presents another case in point, in some profound ways like the *Mo jing*: "Yucong" 1 needs to be very much 'read as' a variety of a text in the tradition of the *Dialectical Chapters*, except that these were not Mohist, and more importantly, the parts are in no way intended to be construable as forming a systemic whole. I am tempted to call them 'intellectually pointilistic.'

The "Yucong" 1 is identified entirely on the basis of physical characteristics of the bamboo stationery used to write it on. We are told that the content was not taken into account when identifying the individual bamboo slips that had to go into this pile of slips. Now this "Yucong" 1 does not simply inscribe itself into the genre mould of the *Dialectical Chapters* at all. It constitutes a philosophically significant genre of its own. Let me try to outline some of the components of this "Yucong" 1 text sort.

The genre style of this text is well-defined: it can be read as consisting of two kinds of material:

A. Short sequences of sometimes loosely interconnected short provocative analytic statements.

B. Isolated short provocative analytic statements.

The genre style of this text comports one crucial feature of its intellectual message:

There is no humble self-doubting reflexiveness *à la* Confucius to be expected in a book of this stylistic form,

There is no socially connected argumentative interface *à la Mencius*,

There is no coherently overall discursive elucidation *à la Xunzi*,

There is no narrative celebration of the moral excellence of an author *à la Yanzi Chunqiu* 晏子春秋.

There is no morally proselytising, educational or missionary overtone in any of the "Yucong" 1 pieces that would invite the reader to *shu yu dai* 書於帶 "write it down on his sash" as a moral motto of any kind whatever.

There is none of the intellectually self-righteous pomposity imposed by extensive rhyme *à la Laozi*.

There is no witty, free-wheeling self-humour as cultivated occasionally in the outrageously free genre style *à la Zhuangzi*.

There is no egg-headed, provocative and systematically intellectualist narrative, *à la Hanfeizi* 韓非子.

There is also no attempt at organised coherent and systematic analytic theorising *à la Mojing*.

The "Yucong" 1 turns out analytically pointilistic and quite predominantly provocative through a particular genre style, namely that of the programmatically enigmatic, pithy, and un-argued for analytic *jing* 經 'propositions, statements, or theorems' which often are badly in need of a *shuo* 說 'elaborating explanation.' I would like to show that as in the proverbially obscure *dicta* of Heraclitus ("The way up and the way down are one and the same")[4] in the aphorisms of "Yucong" 1 one learns to expect to be surprised.

Only very occasionally do its theorems get organised into sequences of equally enigmatic and provocative theorems.

This paper then will present some of these theorems in English by way of illustration of the mainly stylistic and rhetorical points above. In an earlier publication I have provided an elaborated explanation which tries to bring out explicitly their provocative analytic edge.[5]

There will probably come a point when it will appear that my attempt fails. I shall happily leave it to the reader to decide where exactly this begins to be the case.

4　Fragment 69.

5　Christoph Harbsmeier, "A Reading of the Guodian 郭店 Manuscript *Yucong* 語叢 1 as a Masterpiece of Early Chinese Analytic Philosophy and Conceptual Analysis," *Studies in Logic* 4.3 (2011): 3–56.

Let me begin with the title:

凡物由亡生。

One can indeed read this, as modern Chinese and all Western commentators I have heard of seem to read it, as repeating a cosmological proposition inspired by *Laozi*: "All things arise from nothing."

One thing is that this represents a misreading of the word *fan* 凡 which never means 'all' but is a modal particle meaning something like 'as a matter of principle.'[6] The point that interests us in this context is that this interpretation feels free to read this title according to what another text says and without any reference to what is in the present text itself. Now the present text itself has nothing whatsoever to do with cosmology or the origins of the universe and all the things in it.

But if we are not to read this along the lines of the parallel in *Laozi*, then how are we to understand it in the context of the present material? We need to find a reading that relates to conceptual analysis. We need a reading that does not tell a story about how things arise, but a reading which presents a conceptual analysis of a key concept. And also: the analysis has to have something unexpected or witty.

Now the concept of a thing is not intelligibly analysed in terms of it arising from nothing. On the other hand, the concept of 'arising' itself, which is a dominant theme throughout "Yucong" 1 is exquisitely analysed in terms of the fact that if you want to arise somewhere, you had better not already be wherever it is you want to arise. In other words, arising is something that has to happen where whatever arises was not. That is exactly what this very appropriate header, which is repeated in the body of the text, does indeed say.

The question now arises how exactly to arrange the excavated material under the heading we must hope we have correctly interpreted. Since in general the arrangement of the material remains completely uncertain one had better begin with some pieces that clearly do go together in the order we are reconstructing for them:

人亡能為.

Here again, current philological wisdom suggests that the text must be read differently. It must be emended to read: 仁亡能為 "Kind-heartedness one can in no way go about deliberately." This is indeed what would fit together very well with 義亡能為也 "Rectitude one can in no way go about deliberately." Such an emended reading creates coherence in a text that looks incom-

---

6 See Christoph Harbsmeier, *Aspects of Classical Chinese Syntax* (London/Malmö: Curzon Press, 1981), ch. 6 "The so-called adjectival quantifier *fan* 凡." See also Wagner's contribution to the volume.

prehensible. For, surely, any man can act! The text, at first, makes no sense. Emendation is necessary. Moreover this new reading is phonetically not only plausible. We do have a perfect fit: the two words are exact homophones. What more can one ask for as an argument to defend the reading?

One might ask for another example where the character 人 is also clearly a scribal mistake for 仁, which of course, in much of the early excavated literature, is written with an entirely different character, with the heart radical under 身. For in these matters one isolated reading without support from other similar cases carries little plausibility and has a touch of the arbitrary.

But there is a much more powerful argument against this reading and indeed for interpreting the text as it stands. That is that the text as it is makes excellent sense in context. The translation we have seen provides exactly that kind of paradoxical sophistication that we shall observe in so many other statements. To come back to Heraclitus: our text makes a statement embarrassingly close in kind to Heraclitus' when he says: "Into the same river we enter and we do not enter. We are, and we are not."[7]

In one sense we can "be ourselves." We can't even help being ourselves, in fact! Not we! (As Heraclitus puts it: "We are.") But then there is this other aspect under which "Yucong" 1 considers the matter, the aspect of what man can go about doing, decide to do, do deliberately and so on. Among these things that he can set about doing, "being oneself" is not one of them.

The structural crux is this: the isolated statements in "Yucong" are not merely cumulative, like for example the "Tancong" 談叢 chapter of the *Shuoyuan* 說苑. Like La Rochefoucauld's (1613–1680) aphorisms they cohere. They add up to an overall vision that is intimately linked to the aphoristic form itself. This overall vision, which does not add up to any reasoned system, is articulated through a series of analytic *aperçus*. Some of these do fall into natural groups or unordered sets. It is important to realise that in these groups the individual members, though interrelated, always retain their semantic and rhetorical independence. They also share important stylistic features: none are narrative. None are moralising or moralistic. None of them contain injunctions of any kind. Those that are related to ethics will be shown to focus not on ethics as such but on the conceptual framework used to describe moral or ethical phenomena. None of them are cosmological in focus: those that appear to be related to cosmology will be shown to focus not on cosmology itself but on the conceptual framework used to describe cosmological or physical phenomena. None argue from scriptural authority. None contain arguments *ex auctoritate*. None of them contain any other references of any sort to named individuals.

---

7 Fragment 41.

None of them display any dogmatic adherence to any school of thought. None are descriptive in any detail, or are in any way poetic in diction or style. None are explicitly discursive, involving complex arguments. None of them involve synonym compounds like *pengyou* 朋友. Extraordinarily, many are provocative, deliberately paradoxical. Nearly all of them are—in a broad sense—analytic. All of them are maximally concise—cut to the analytic bone.

Much of Chinese philosophical literature tends to be fond of historical narrative references and narrative illustration of philosophical points. This is even true of the Confucian *Analects*, and also of the introduction to the book *Gongsunlongzi* 公孫龍子 which is primarily concerned with logical analysis. "Yucong," like the *Laozi*, eschews all narrative or historical context. I shall try to show that its focus is squarely conceptual.

Much of Chinese philosophical literature involves different forms of advice: it analyses moral and prudential questions in order to arrive at prudential rules, moral advice, and valid ethical principles. From the *Analects* and the *Laozi* onwards, and for the prudential part—in such books as the *Hanfeizi* and the *Guanzi*—this has been the dominant mode of the *zhuzi* 諸子 literature. Significantly, the "Yucong" rhetorical style eschews all of this, focussing on conceptual analysis instead.

From the *Laozi* and the *Zhuangzi* onwards, Chinese *zhuzi* literature has paid intermittent attention to questions of cosmology and particularly the origin of the universe.[8] Much cosmological speculation is indeed represented in the excavated literature such as that from *Guodian* 郭店 and from *Yinque* 銀雀. Here again the "Yucong" style imposes a different conceptual perspective on cosmology. There is not one cosmological statement in "Yucong" 1.

From the *Analects* onwards, the appeal to authoritative and unquestionably valid written sources of wisdom has been ubiquitous. There are exceptions to this rule, such as the *Laozi*, the *Wenzi* 文子, and a whole range of the excavated literature. But even when there is no overt quotation, there is in most of our extant texts, including the *Laozi*, that notoriously traditionalist but often enigmatic phrase *gu yue* 故曰 "That is why it is said: ... ." It is deeply significant that in *Yucong gu yue* occurs nowhere. To the writers of this text it does not matter what is "being said" by this authority or that—or even by themselves elsewhere. Their concern is directly with the subject matter at hand.

Scriptural reference is often to anonymous documents. But in addition to this there is the very common appeal to what Laozi 老子 said, what Zi Mozi 子墨子 said, or what Kongzi 孔子 said, or indeed what *fuzi* 夫子 '(our) Master'

---

[8] John Henderson, *The Development and Decline of Chinese Cosmology* (New York: Columbia UP, 1984).

said and so on, where the idea is that the person referred to is incontrovertibly right. (Although it is to be noted that at least in the *Analects* the Master's voice is not at all treated as infallible.) Intellectual insight, in Late Warring States China as in many places elsewhere, tends to want to strengthen its case by an appeal to the personal authority of men of incontrovertible wisdom. The refusal to make any such appeal in a book like the *Laozi* is a stylistic feature of that text. But at the same time that stylistic feature comports a fundamental point about the message in the *Laozi*: this message has, and is, its own authority. It is, as it were, intellectually autonomous, although it does show certain features of intertextuality the detail of which need not concern us here. What does concern us is the fact that "Yucong" refuses to make such appeals to any authoritative person because it speaks in its own intellectual right, and is beholden to no authority past or present.[9]

Most of Chinese philosophical literature—again from the *Analects*, which mention many dozens of individuals, onwards—makes frequent reference to the cases of certain individuals of various kinds. These texts have a strong tendency to the sort of anthropocentrism that links points of view in direct or indirect ways to the fates, experiences, strengths, or weaknesses of certain individuals. Han Fei refers to hundreds of individuals in his highly philosophical and highly analytic book and many excavated texts contain such personal references. The stylistic constraints in "Yucong" are such that references of this sort are excluded. The focus is not on historical or personal embedding of the propositions proposed. It is ahistorical in a provocatively 'un-Chinese' manner. Its defiant focus is on conceptual analysis alone.

Much of Chinese philosophical literature takes part and indeed takes sides in the broad on-going conversation between what Arthur Waley memorably called "ways of thought in ancient China."[10] For example, the *Mencius* sees itself embattled against the Mohists and against what it thinks of as the 'Yangists' as well as the 'Agriculturalists' (A.C. Graham), and in the process it sees no alternative but to stoop so low as to engage in 'disputation': *bu de yi* 不得已 "he saw no alternative." Other texts like the *Hanfeizi* aim to reconcile or

---

9   See for a distinction between references to external authorities and internal argumentative evidence Rudolf G. Wagner, "Der Vergessene Hinweis: Wang Pi über den Lao-tzu," in *Text und Kommentar: Archäologie der literarischen Kommunikation IV*, eds. Jan Assmann and Burkhard Gladigow (Munich: Fink, 1995), 257–278, 272; id. *The Craft of the Chinese Commentator. Wang Bi on the Laozi* (Albany: SUNY, 2000), 251–252; Joachim Gentz, *Das Gongyang zhuan* (Wiesbaden: Harrassowitz, 2001), 70, and Dirk Meyer who distinguishes argument-based and context-dependent texts, *Philosophy on Bamboo* (Leiden: Brill, 2012), 1, 227–233.

10 See Arthur Waley, *Three Ways of Thought in Ancient China* (London: Routledge, 1939).

accommodate perceived ideologies in the *Laozi* with statist ideologies attributed to the (entirely pragmatic and not ideological) Lord of Shang. Some texts, like the *Lüshi chunqiu* juxtapose different ways of thought in some unmediated kind of encyclopaedic eclecticism. But by and large most transmitted texts we have, relate in one way or another to these 'schools of thought.' Strikingly, we find less of this positioning in relation to current ways of thought in the excavated literature written for specialists. "Yucong" cannot be called a Confucian text just because it mentions virtues like *ti* 悌 'brotherly love' and filial piety. Nor can it possibly be taken to advocate the teachings of *Laozi* just because it does make advanced use of concepts of *wu wei* 無為 'non-assertive action.' "Yucong" 1 discusses concepts as such, quite independently of their appurtenance to this way of thought or that. Its rhetorical constraint signifies an intellectual and analytic focus.

Vivid description and characterisation of persons and things is a hallmark of Chinese prose literature from the *Analects* onwards. Descriptive *ekphrasis* as in the description of the 'myriad holes' in *Zhuangzi*, ch. 2 is much rarer in Chinese literature than it is in Greek literature. But still, the descriptive mode is not absent in the Chinese tradition, whereas it is clinically absent in "Yucong" 1. The rhetorical constraint on vivid description is again the result of an intellectual discipline of analysis.

One might have thought that the notion of 'that is why' (*gu* 故) is absolutely indispensable in philosophical discourse. Indeed, the word marks the pivotal moment where an author passes from his premises to his conclusion. There are forty-three chapters of the fairly non-argumentative book *Laozi* in which the word *gu* figures and often establishes a fairly vague semantic link between what precedes and what follows. Sometimes one is even tempted to see this *gu* between different parts of a chapter as no more than a mark of a compiler's bad conscience. Nonetheless, all this awkwardness only serves to put our point into even clearer perspective: The *Laozi* was compiled by people who, increasingly as time went on,[11] imposed on themselves an intellectual *régime* involving the idea that the chapters needed to show an argumentative systematicity rather than a mere general coherence. Now the systematic rhetorical avoidance or at least absence of *gu* in all of "Yucong" 1 acquires a striking meaning. It signals a style of thought that I have called pointilistic, intuitively analytic, almost aphoristic, and averse to logically concatenated argumentative discourse.

Now I wish I could garnish my survey of what is not to be found in "Yucong" 1 with examples. But it is in the nature of things that what does not exist cannot

---

11 See the analysis of the *Laozi* 66 versions by Gentz in this volume.

THE PHILOSOPHY OF THE ANALYTIC APERÇU 167

be 'shown' or exemplified as not existing. Thus, instead of illustrating what I have just summarised I shall proceed to give one example of what comes closest to refuting my basic thesis. This is the case of a sequence of statements that do in fact 'go together,' although there are no discourse particles to mark this fact. They go together in the sense that they constitute so much of a tight and strictly coherent logical argument that it would seem to be doing violence to the strips to read them separately, as isolated propositions. Strips can 'go together' for plain grammatical reasons when an unfinished sentence seems very clearly to continue on to a new strip. Strips can also go together for perhaps less plain, logical reasons when an unfinished argument on one strip seems very clearly to continue on another strip. Of course, both in the judgement of cases of grammatical coherence and in the judgement of cases of logical coherence there will often remain an inescapable element of subjectivity. Given the limited evidence we have from ancient China, our interpretation of the coherence of these texts can rarely be more than tentative.

1. **On the impossibility of managing to do what one makes a point of doing**
   為孝，此非孝也。
   為悌，/此非悌也。
   不可為也，/而不可不為也。
   為之，/此非也。
   弗為，此非也。
   義亡能為也。■
   If one makes a point of showing filial piety, then that is not filial piety;
   if one makes a point of showing brotherly love, [slip 55] then that is not brotherly love.
   These things one cannot make a deliberate point of practising (they must be spontaneous), [slip 56] and yet they must not be left unpractised.
   If one deliberately makes a point of practising them, [slip 57] this is not right;
   and if one refuses to practise them, that is (also) not right. ... [slip 58]
   Rectitude one can in no way deliberately make a point of acting out. [slip 53]

2. **On the possibility of investigating the good and the impossibility to set out to be good (because one would only be pretending to be good)**
   有察善，亡為善。■
   There is the possibility of probing goodness/excellence (in others), but there is no way of going deliberately about practising goodness. [slip 84]

In this proposition, the generalisation is consummated: the issue, in all the propositions about the virtues, has been all along that of what is moral

3. On the impossibility of setting out to be the person one is
人亡能為。■

"The person one is" one can in no way deliberately make a point of being/becoming? [slip 83]

Here comes the thunderous corollary, which would be even more stunning, if we did not have the similarly stunning and similarly aphoristic Heraclitus: "The same river we enter and we enter not. We are, and we are not." "Yucong," like Heraclitus, manages to problematise what it is to be the one one is. But "Yucong" does this in a civilisation, which is such that even after more than two thousand years of intellectual development it is still not ready to understand him. In their desperation about this proposition 1.4 it has been suggested that 人 should be read as 仁. This sounds plausible because it would make the text comfortably repetitive and nicely predictable. But, of course, "Yucong" 1 is not generally nicely repetitive and comfortably predictable in the first place. It is a manifestly provocative text at many points. It is true enough that the reading 仁 for the character 人 is unattested anywhere else in the hundred thousand bamboo slips that have been carefully sifted in Bai Yulan's 白於藍 *Jiandu boshu tongjiazi zidian* 簡牘帛書通假字字典.[12] However, since we know of no difference in the ancient pronunciation of these two characters it is quite easy to imagine that one character was carelessly miswritten for the other. Thus when a text with 人 'man' cannot be interpreted as it stands but makes excellent sense when one reads 人 as intended to represent the word 仁 'humaneness' then one might well need to understand 人 as if it were 仁 in order to make sense of the text. However, this does not mean that one is entitled to read 人 as 仁 anywhere, at will, *sine necessitate* (without being forced to by the context), as medieval logicians would have put it. In my interpretation I take the liberty of assuming that our scribe had good reason for choosing the character 人

---

12   Xiamen: Fujian renmin chubanshe, 2008. See now Bai Yulan 白於藍, *Zhanguo Qin Han jianbo gushu tongjiazi huizuan* 戰國秦漢簡帛古書通假字彙纂 (Xiamen: Fujian renmin chubanshe, 2012), which lists a number of instances where 人 is interpreted as 仁. 人 occurs tens of thousands of times in the corpus of excavated literature. The fact that in some cases philologists have found it necessary to read this common character as 仁 certainly does not justify a philological method according to which all instances of 人 are taken to invite the natural reading 仁.

here, and not the character 仁. And I have been led to do so by what I reconstruct as the overall internal logic of "Yucong" 1.

4. On things and the criteria of their identity as the things they are and on naming and names as the criterion of the names naming the things they name

有物有容，有稱有名。■

There being things, there are outlines> 'physiognomies' (of these things), there being calling, there is a name (for the thing called by that name). [slip 13]

For a thing to be the thing it is there must be a criterion of identification of that thing as the thing that it is, and that is its *rong* 容 'physiognomy.'

5. On two apparently contradictory types of investigation

察所知，察所不知。

One investigates what one understands, and one investigates what one does not understand. ... [slip 85]

6. On existence being a function of having a name

有生乎名。■

Existence arises from having a name. [slip 96]

7. On the nature of punitive coercion

刑非嚴也。■

Physical punishment is not a matter of showing severity. [slip 64]

8. On ontological self-determination

亡物不物，皆至焉，而/亡非己取之者。■

There is no (category of) creature/thing that fails to act as the thing it is,
and they all get to this point (of being themselves),
and [slip 71] none are such that they have not themselves determined themselves.
[slip 72]

The proposition that "no thing fails to thing," in all its defiant and entirely original departure from ordinary grammar, makes a point of ontology which in fact involves the dramatisation of ontology: the notion of choice, in this instance, involves a certain level of personification. It involves a kind of abstract personification that is not common in early Chinese literature.

9. On the completeness condition for being called a sage
盈聖之謂聖。■

When one fills out (>completely fulfils the criteria for) being a sage one is called a sage. [slip 100]

This literal transcription, if correct, would attribute to this text a statement puzzlingly close to the statement "Snow is white is true if snow is white."

10. On the consummate conceptual essence of sagehood
備之謂聖。■

Providing completely the (relevant) criteria (scil.: for sagehood) is called sagehood. [slip 94]

11. On a logical entailment of sagehood
有聖有善。■

There being sagehood there is excellence. [slip 17]

12. On the ontogenesis of human-heartedness
喪，仁之端也。■

Being in mourning is the starting-point of humanheartedness. [slip 98]

13. On the genealogy of precedence
兄弟，識先後也。■

From (the case of) elder and younger brothers
one becomes aware of who takes precedence. [slip 70]

14. On the genealogy of social hierarchy
父子，識上下也。■

From (the cases/concepts of) 'father' and 'son' one becomes aware of the relation between superior and inferior. [slip 69]

15. On two subtypes of elective relations: the hierarchical versus the horizontal
君臣、朋友，其擇者也。■

Relations between ruler and minister, and between friends, are the sort that are elective. [slip 87]

16. On the fundamental distinction between kinship relations versus elective relations
(孝敬？？)父，有親有尊。/

長悌，親道也。
友、君臣，/無親也。■
(In the case of X-ing the) father
there is blood relation and reverence. [slip 78]
Treating with fraternal respect
is a Way involving blood-bonds.
Among friends, and between ruler and minister [slip 80] there is no blood relation. [slip 81]

17. On affection-generating versus respect-generating virtues

[厚於仁，薄]於義，親而/不尊。
厚於義，薄於仁，/尊而不親。■
[If one emphasises humanheartedness
and one deemphasises] rectitude,
then one will be affectionate, but [slip 77] not reverent;
If one emphasises rectitude and one deemphasises humanheartedness, [slip 82]
then one will be reverent but not affectionate. [slip 79]

18. On the double origin of man's superior status in the world

天生百物，人為貴。
人/之道也，或/由中出，或由外入。■
When Heaven originated all kinds of creatures
man counted as the noblest of these.
As for the Way [slip 18] of man, in some cases [slip 19] it emerges from the inside/is endogenic, in other cases it enters from the outside/is exogenic. [slip 20]

19. On endogenic versus exogenic virtues, humanheartedness and rectitude

仁生於人，義生於道。/
或生於內，或生於外。/
Humanheartedness arises from (within) a person, rectitude arises (outside) from the Way. [slip 22]
The one arises from within, the other arises from without. ... [slip 23]

Humanheartedness, being endogenic, and a subjective virtue, has its origin within the person, rectitude, being exogenic, and an objective virtue has its origin within the Way.

The second proposition does NOT say the obvious, namely that 仁生於內，義生於外. ("Humanheartedness arises from within; rectitude arises from without"). It lifts the discourse onto a more abstract, analytic level. Some virtues/values have their origin outside, others inside.

20. On the endogenic versus the exogenic virtues

由中出者：
仁忠信。
由【外入者：
禮樂刑。■】

As for those that emerge from the inside/the endogenic ones:
these are humanheartedness, devoted effort, and good faith.
As for those [which enter from the outside
these are ritual propriety, music, and punishments] [slip 21]

21. On the epistemic conditions for mass education

察天道以化民氣。■

One investigates the Way of Heaven in order to transform the vital spirits of the people. [slip 68]

22. On epistemic antecedence I

知天所為，知人所為，/然後知道。■
知道然後知命。■

Only when one understands how Heaven works, and when one understands how man works, [slip 29] does one understand the Way; and only when one understands the Way does one understand ordained fate. [slip 30]

23. On epistemic antecendence II

知己而後知人，
知人而後／知禮，
知禮而後知行。■

Only when one understands oneself does one understand others,
only when one understands others does one [slip 26] understand ritual propriety,
only when one does ritual propriety does one understand (proper) conduct. [slip 27]

Conclusion

Surveying the pithy precision of these *dicta* in "Yucong" one is struck by their logical independence on the one hand, and by the stylistically manifested intellectual coherence of their approach on the other. As one feels that one is getting under the skin of some of these propositions, one feels invited to go on constructing new ones, thinking along these lines of critical analysis. It is a little bit like reading Wittgenstein. Not like reading the *Tractatus*—which does avoid quotation and the like, yet which organises its propositions on a structured tree of subordination—but more like reading *On Certainty*. One feels invited to listen in on an intense intellectual effort that manifests itself not through a chain of well-rehearsed argumentation but through a jumpy and knotty sequence of highly polished analytic *aperçus*. To a Western reader these *aperçus* seem to hold a vague promise that they may constitute insights that constitute conditions for the possibility of any future account of the scheme of Chinese conceptual schemes, much in the spirit of Immanuel Kant. And the curious thing is this: these propositions are written as if they are intended very much that way. And it is not a coincidence that we find the punctuation marks in this pretty well exactly where we would have hoped to see them anyway. The text works indeed as a pointilistic attempt at conceptual clarification that is a perceived prerequisite for any future intellectual transparency. The Mohist logicians felt that way. It now appears that the Mohist milieu was not the only one in which this historically jejune, non-pragmatic and non-moralistic, ethereal analytic intellectualism was cultivated to an almost professionalistic, dry, and caustic perfection.

The social pendant to this analytic independence of mind, I like to think, was a cultural independence vis-à-vis any particular 'school of thought' or indeed 'way of thought' that the authors of these propositions may have been adherents of. These propositions do not give off the scent of polite submissions to a ruler. Defiantly they leave the prevalent hierarchical structures of communication in Late Warring States China. There is no advice here to a ruler. There is no intended audience of disgruntled courtiers either. The status of the authors is entirely irrelevant. It is their implicit argumentation that counts. And the argument matters only to those who happen to have that 'philosophical' taste for abstract de-contextualised conceptual analysis. The discourse is not *ad personam,* directed at this or that intended individual. The discourse is intertextual, but it poses as being abstractly self-contained. These propositions set out to establish an apolitical, independent, autonomous realm of what one might indeed call 'academic' discourse. They apply cold-blooded and iconoclastic logical analysis to what were the holiest of virtues in their time. The exciting thing is that these propositions seem to pose as philosophically non-partisan, unattached to any one particular philosophical school rather than another. And unlike Zhuang Zhou 莊周, the authors of these propositions avoid all manner of dogmatic social, ideological or moral conclusions, even of any narrative sceptic relativism, Montaigne style. Our text poses as curiously cool and abstract, analytically above all philosophical or social factionalism.

References

Bai Yulan 白於藍. *Jiandu boshu tongjiazi zidian* 簡牘帛書通假字字典. Xiamen: Fujian renmin chubanshe, 2008.

———. *Zhanguo Qin Han jianbo gushu tongjiazi huizuan* 戰國秦漢簡帛古書通假字彙纂. Xiamen: Fujian renmin chubanshe, 2012.

Gentz, Joachim. *Das Gongyang zhuan. Auslegung und Kanonisierung der Frühlings- und Herbstannalen (Chunqiu)*. Wiesbaden: Harrassowitz, 2001.

Harbsmeier, Christoph. "A Reading of the Guodian 郭店 Manuscript *Yucong* 語叢 1 as a Masterpiece of Early Chinese Analytic Philosophy and Conceptual Analysis." *Studies in Logic* 4.3 (2011): 3–56.

———. *Aspects of Classical Chinese Syntax*. London: Curzon Press, 1981.

Henderson, John. *The Development and Decline of Chinese Cosmology*. New York: Columbia University Press, 1984.

Holzman, Donald. "The Conversational Tradition in Chinese Philosophy." *Philosophy East and West* 6.3 (1956): 223–230.

LeGoff, Jacques. *Intellectuals in the Middle Ages*. Oxford: Blackwell/Wiley, 1993.

Meyer, Dirk. *Philosophy on Bamboo: Text and the Production of Meaning in Early China*. Leiden: Brill, 2012.

Van der Loon, Piet. "On the transmission of the Kuan-tzu." *T'oung Pao* 41.1 (1952): 357–393.

Wagner, Rudolf G. "Der Vergessene Hinweis: Wang Pi über den Lao-tzu." In *Text und Kommentar: Archäologie der literarischen Kommunikation IV*, edited by Jan Assmann and Burkhard Gladigow. Munich: Fink, 1995: 257–278.

———. *The Craft of the Chinese Commentator. Wang Bi on the Laozi*. Albany: SUNY Press, 2000.

Waley, Arthur. *Three Ways of Thought in Ancient China*. London: Routledge, 1939.

CHAPTER 6

Speaking of Poetry: Pattern and Argument in the "Kongzi Shilun"

Martin Kern

The "Kongzi shilun" 孔子詩論 (Confucius' Discussion of the *Poetry*) is by far the most prominent text among the Shanghai Museum corpus of bamboo manuscripts dated to roughly 300 BC. Since its publication in December 2001,[1] it has attracted hundreds of articles and several book-length studies. In the months immediately following the initial publication, a vigorous online debate arose[2] during which at least six different sequential arrangements of the altogether twenty-nine bamboo slips were proposed. Moreover, Li Xueqin 李學勤 has argued that the text by no means reflects "Confucius' Discussion of the *Poetry*" but rather a 'discussion' that invokes Confucius; his proposed shorter title "Shilun" 詩論 (Discussion of the *Poetry*) is by now widely accepted[3] and for this reason alone—and against better judgment (see below)—will be used in the present study. Aside from detailed palaeographic analysis and vigorous discussions of interpretation and textual arrangement,[4] much research has been devoted to two questions: the authorship of the anonymous manuscript text[5] and, often related to the question of authorship, the text's position vis-à-vis the received *Mao Shi* 毛詩 where it has been compared to both the "Great

---

1 Ma Chengyuan 馬承源, ed., *Shanghai bowuguan cang Zhanguo Chu zhushu* (*yi*) 上海博物館藏戰國楚竹書（一）(Shanghai: Shanghai guji chubanshe, 2001), 13–41, 121–168.
2 On http://www.jianbao.org, the principal online forum for academic discussions of early Chinese manuscripts.
3 For a convenient survey of these discussions, see Xing Wen, "Guest Editor's Introduction," *Contemporary Chinese Thought* 39.4 (2008): 3–17.
4 The three most important books, all reflecting the extensive discussion in the field, have been Huang Huaixin 黃懷信, *Shanghai bowuguan cang Zhanguo Chu zhushu* "Shilun" *jieyi* 上海博物館藏戰國楚竹書《詩論》解義 (Beijing: Shehui kexue wenxian chubanshe, 2004); Liu Xinfang 劉信芳, *Kongzi shilun shuxue* 孔子詩論述學 (Hefei: Anhui daxue chubanshe, 2002); and Chen Tongsheng 陳桐生, *Kongzi shilun yanjiu* 《孔子詩論》研究 (Beijing: Zhonghua shuju, 2004). Chen, 315–341, provides a survey of the large number of publications on the manuscript that appeared just between December 2001 and March 2004. Recently, long after the present essay was completed, a massive new study has appeared: Zhao Fulin 晁福林, *Shangbo jian 'Shilun' yanjiu* 上博簡《詩論》研究 (Beijing: Shangwu yinshuguan, 2013).
5 At stake, of course, is not the identity of the writer, or copyist, of the recovered manuscript but of the text that is contained in this particular manuscript and that, so it is presumed, existed also in other manuscripts.

Preface" ("Daxu" 大序) and the "minor prefaces" (*xiaoxu* 小序) that accompany the individual poems in the transmitted anthology.⁶

To my mind, some of this scholarship operates on unwarranted assumptions derived from tradition. This is evident in fantasies that attribute the text to some hazy figure such as Confucius' disciple Zixia 子夏 (or some other, even more obscure persona);⁷ and it further appears in the way the text has been titled: with or without inserting Confucius into the title, the use of the term *lun* 論 (discussion) is not only an anachronistic designation of a literary genre that cannot be traced back into pre-imperial times. It also suggests that the "Shilun" is some sort of reasoned exposition on the *Classic of Poetry*, originally composed in writing (another unproven and most likely anachronistic assumption) by a single authorial figure (yet another such assumption) and addressed to some unspecified general audience. Through all this, the text is elevated to participate in the type of philosophical discourse that the tradition, beginning in the early empire, has constructed and systematized into its grand narrative of ancient Chinese thought, complete with a range of rivalling schools represented by an impressive line-up of 'masters' (*zi* 子) and their faithful disciples. It is undoubtedly—if perhaps unconsciously—in order to place the text at these lofty heights of discourse that the "Shilun" has been assigned a known author valorized by tradition.

I consider this approach to the text misguided and misleading. It imbues the text with qualities it does not have while suppressing some properties that a closer reading may be able to reveal. I am not arguing for the "Shilun" to be read exclusively on its own terms (or in those of *New Criticism*); but I do oppose the false historicization that forces newly discovered texts into the traditional (and thoroughly retrospective) framework of tradition. This anachronistic histori-

---

6   See, e.g., Ma Yinqin 馬銀琴, "Shangbo jian 'Shilun' yu 'Shixu' shishuo yitong bijiao: jianlun 'Shixu' yu 'Shilun' de yuanyuan guanxi" 上博簡《詩論》與《詩序》詩說異同比較—兼論《詩序》與《詩論》的淵源關係, *Jianbo yanjiu* 簡帛研究 2002–2003: 98–105.

7   E.g., in arguing for Zixia's authorship of the "Shilun," Li Xueqin 李學勤 and others base themselves on (a) Confucius' praise for Zixia's understanding of the *Poetry* in *Lunyu* "Bayi" 八佾 (3.8) and (b) three brief statements on Zixia's teaching of the *Poetry* in texts that range from the *Hanshu* 漢書 "Monograph on Arts and Letters" ("Yiwen zhi" 藝文志, first century AD) to Lu Deming's 陸德明 (556–627) *Jingdian shiwen* 經典釋文 preface—that is, sources postdating Confucius (or Zixia) by five hundred to one thousand years. As Chen Tongsheng 陳桐生 has noted, the later the source, the more emphatically and extensively it speaks of Zixia as an expert on the *Poetry*. Yet on the basis of just these sources, Xing Wen, "Guest Editor's Introduction," 6, has stated: "According to the transmitted textual evidence available to us, Zixia is very likely the author of the bamboo 'Shilun'." For the more clear-headed view that we cannot identify the anonymous author, see Chen Tongsheng 陳桐生, "*Kongzi shilun*" *yanjiu*《孔子詩論》研究 (Beijing: Zhonghua shuju, 2004), 85–88.

cization is ideological not so much because it views the "Shilun" as 'Confucian' but because it defines the nature and purpose of the text exclusively within the retrospectively applied parameters of early Chinese textuality. By all accounts, these parameters did not exist before the grand project of ordering the textual heritage according to the needs of the early imperial state, most notably in successive waves of canonization and censorship from the Qin (221–207 BC) through the Western Han (202 BC–AD 9), culminating in the collection and catalogue of the imperial library at the end of the first century BC[8] and solidified by the subsequent Eastern Han (9–220 AD) commentarial canonization of a newly emerging 'book culture.' I believe that the shift from a ritual- to a text-centred culture,[9] or what one might call a shift from mythographic to historiographic authority, has not only blinded us to the purposes and properties of received pre-Qin texts but now blinds us further to those of newly discovered manuscripts. The search for the author of the "Shilun" is not merely a futile exercise; far more consequential, it is the subjugation of the text under a specific and anachronistic ideology of textual production. Before the empire, vast amounts of text were authorless—not because they were missing something, but because the very absence of authorship was a function of traditional authority.[10] In the mythographic mindset, that which "is said" was transmitted, believed, and true precisely because it was not individually authored, and precisely because it was not tied to a historical moment;[11] by contrast, the historiographic mindset of the early empire required the figure of the author in order to arrange the textual heritage into meaningful teleological and genealogical contexts of early Chinese thought. Thus, the absence of the author function[12] in the "Shilun," far from being a defect to be emended by modern research, is a

---

8   See Martin Kern, *The Stele Inscriptions of Ch'in Shih-huang* (New Haven: American Oriental Society, 2000), 183–196.
9   See Michael Nylan, "Toward an Archaeology of Writing: Text, Ritual, and the Culture of Public Display in the Classical Period (475 BCE–220 CE)," in *Text and Ritual in Early China*, ed. Martin Kern (Seattle: University of Washington Press, 2005), 3–49; Martin Kern, "Ritual, Text, and the Formation of the Canon: Historical Transitions of *wen* in Early China," *T'oung Pao* 87 (2001): 43–91.
10 Note that not a single one of all recently found early Chinese manuscripts contains an identification of its author. For a discussion of the entire problem, see Yu Jiaxi 余嘉錫, *Gushu tongli* 古書通例 (Shanghai: Shanghai guji chubanshe, 1985), 15–49.
11 As argued by Paul Veyne, *Did the Greeks Believe in Their Myths? An Essay on the Constitute Imagination* (Chicago: The University of Chicago Press, 1988), 23, 64.
12 To use Michel Foucault's term; see Foucault, "What is an Author?" in *Textual Strategies: Perspectives in Post-Structuralist Criticism*, ed. Josué V. Harari (Ithaca: Cornell University Press, 1979), 141–160. (Orig., "Qu'est-ce qu'un auteur?" 1969).

rhetorical feature of the text that underlies much of its discursive force. To consider the "Shilun" a general 'discussion' and to identify Zixia or any other traditional icon as its author are two ideological constructions that necessitate one another; together, they pre-empt the analysis of the "Shilun" as a truly original text that does not fit the traditional narrative of elevated 'masters' literature.

While no consensus has been reached on either the authorship of the manuscript text or its relation to Han dynasty (202 BC–AD 220) readings of the *Shijing*,[13] the text comes to us without historical context—not only because it was looted from its original site and then sold on the Hong Kong antique market, a process that erased all traces of specific provenance; but also because the *manuscript* was almost certainly taken from a tomb, which, in turn, was most likely not the *text's* original environment.[14] As a result, the "Shilun" has a certain disembodied quality to it: we have the (fragmentary) text, but we do not know why we have it—whether it was put into a tomb, and if so, what its purpose proper was prior to, and outside of, that particular material context.

In this situation, a gap has opened between specific palaeographic study and detailed interpretation on the one hand, and general historical contextualization on the other. This gap concerns the literary form as well as the pragmatic function of the "Shilun"—two core aspects of the text critical to any interpretation or contextualization. In my view, it is the particular literary form of the "Shilun" that marks it as a specific type of text, which in turn is defined by its particular function. Moreover, in the absence of any external information on the actual uses of the "Shilun"—its *Sitz im Leben*—there is little choice but to turn directly to a rhetorical analysis of its literary pattern and argumentation and try to see what the text does and how it does what it does. What does the text itself, through its particular aesthetic features, reveal about its own historical situation—its uses, its audience, its functions, and its purposes? If it was indeed part of an exegetical or teaching tradition of the *Poetry*, what

---

13 These issues are at the heart of Chen Tongsheng, *"Kongzi shilun" yanjiu*; on the debate over authorship alone, see 36–96. After reviewing the different proposals of a particular author for the text, Chen wisely concludes that we cannot identify the author of the manuscript beyond the general observation that he was a Warring States man, learned in the *Poetry* and influenced by the discussions on self-cultivation that were current at the time and that have appeared, for example, in the "Xingqing lun" 性情論 and "Xing zi ming chu" 性自命出 manuscripts found among the Guodian 郭店 and Shanghai Museum collections (and are often associated with the elusive figure of Zisizi 子思子).

14 Although this particular physical manuscript may have been produced just for the tomb, there is no reason to assume that the text it contains was composed for that purpose.

can we learn from the "Shilun" about the ways, or at least one way, in which such exegesis or teaching worked?

The received textual tradition has not prepared us for a text like the "Shilun": nothing like it has been transmitted, although one might suspect that it represents the raw material of a type of text that in the received literature—had it survived—would be more polished, generalized, and philosophized. From its diction, it appears that the text served more immediate concerns, in more immediate contexts, than, say, the "Great Preface" that, in a scholastic exercise geared toward an anonymous readership, pulled together statements on poetry and music from various earlier sources and as such established itself within an already existing tradition.[15] Perhaps this difference is brought out best by Socrates' statement on writing in the *Phaedrus*:

> You know, Phaedrus, writing shares a strange feature with painting. The offsprings of painting stand there as if they are alive, but if anyone asks them anything, they remain most solemnly silent. The same is true of written words. You'd think they were speaking as if they had some understanding, but if you question anything that has been said because you want to learn more, it continues to signify just that very same thing forever. When it has once been written down, every discourse roams about everywhere, reaching indiscriminately those with understanding no less than those who have no business with it, and it doesn't know to whom it should speak and to whom it should not. And when it is faulted and attacked unfairly, it always needs its father's support; alone, it can neither defend itself nor come to its own support.[16]

---

15   As is well-known, the initial sections of the "Great Preface" are adapted from an earlier discourse on music found in the "Yueji" 樂記 chapter of the *Liji* 禮記 as well as in the "Yueshu" 樂書 chapter of the *Shiji* 史記. In turn, these discussions are influenced by the earlier discourse on music in the *Xunzi* 荀子 chapter "Yuelun" 樂論, the music chapters in the *Lüshi chunqiu* 呂氏春秋, and other sources. Likewise, the core formula *shi zhe zhi zhi suo zhi ye* 詩者志之所之也 ("poetry is where the intent goes") has antecedents in a range of early sources, including the "Yaodian" 堯典 chapter of the *Shangshu* 尚書, the *Lüshi chunqiu*, and the *Zuo zhuan* 左傳. See Steven Van Zoeren, *Poetry and Personality: Reading, Exegesis, and Hermeneutics in Traditional China* (Stanford: Stanford University Press, 1991); Kurihara Keisuke 栗原圭介, *Chūgoku kodai gakuron no kenkyū* 中國古代樂論の研究 (Tokyo: Daitō bunka daigaku tōyō kenkyūjō, 1978).

16   *Phaedrus* 275d–e; translation from Alexander Nehamas and Paul Woodruff, *Plato, Phaedrus* (Indianapolis: Hackett Publishing, 1995), 80–81. Matthias Richter, in his monograph *The Embodied Text: Establishing Textual Identity in Early Chinese Manuscripts* (Leiden: Brill, 2013), 190, has likewise invoked this passage from the *Phaedrus* to argue—in my view correctly—that early manuscripts in general were much more bound to specific situational contexts than our reading habits of the transmitted literature have prepared us to recognize.

Socrates' scepticism about the written artifact that goes into a world of infinite and unknown audiences describes our problems with the "Shilun" quite well: with us, it surely reaches "those who have no business with it," nor can it "defend itself" or "come to its own support." The texts of the received tradition have overcome these problems because they are either—as in the case of the "Great Preface" or the 'masters' texts—generalized (and hence appearing philosophical), or they are connected to a larger framework of historical anecdotes, or they are "defended" and "supported" by thick layers of commentary. Nothing of this is true for the "Shilun." It is a text that does need its "father's support" in order to speak to us "who have no business with it." It makes little effort to explain itself, nor is it supported by additional layers of explication that would have accrued around a text preserved by tradition. The fact that within months of its original publication by the Shanghai Museum, a series of different arrangements of the bamboo slips were proposed bespeaks its somewhat disjointed overall structure. This is not merely due to the fact that the manuscript is fragmentary to the extent that we do not even know how much of it is missing; the problems of arranging and interpreting the text are also, and perhaps even more, due to its lack of linear organization. While scholars like Li Xueqin and Huang Huaixin have succeeded to group clusters of bamboo slips according to the parallel structures within the text, the connections between these clusters remain tentative.

At the same time, the hitherto unknown format of the "Shilun" makes it a valuable source for what it might tell us about the actual teaching of the *Poetry* in the fourth century BC. It appears not as a general treatise about the *Poetry* but as a specific school text—a pedagogical device—to teach how to interpret and how to apply the ancient poems. As such, it should not be called "Shilun" or, equally problematically, "Shixu" 詩序 (Preface to the *Poetry*),[17] because it is not at all an overall "discussion" of, or overall introduction to, the *Poetry*. What is more, as genre designations, both *lun* or *xu* are anachronistic and misleading for the Warring States period (475–221 BC). The shift toward an autonomous discourse on literature that happened in Greece in the fifth and fourth centuries BC, freeing the discussion of literary texts from immediate ethical, social,

---

17   As proposed by Jiang Guanghui 姜廣輝, "Guanyu gu "Shixu" de bianlian, shidu yu dingwei zhu wenti yanjiu" 關於古《詩序》的編連、釋讀與定位諸問題研究, *Zhongguo zhexue* 中國哲學 24 (2002): 165–168; translated as "Problems Concerning the Rearrangement, Interpretation, and Orientation of the Ancient Preface to the Poetry (Shixu)," *Contemporary Chinese Thought* 39.4 (2008): 43–45.

and religious concerns and leading to the discovery of both genres and authors,[18] did not occur in pre-imperial China but only began to develop in Han times.

Rhetorical Patterns in the "Shilun"

The "Shilun" is a brief, fragmentary text of little over a thousand characters that does not proceed in a single expository style.[19] It is a patchwork of various rhetorical patterns, including quotations attributed to Confucius, on disconnected and mostly broken bamboo slips. There is no consensus on the sequence of the individual sections and, hence, on the actual overall argument—if there is any—of the text. For the purposes of the present paper, I will use the sequence proposed by Huang Huaixin, which improves further the one suggested by Li Xueqin.[20] In this reading, the entire text of twenty-nine slips is divided into thirteen sections. On the level of individual graphs and the words they are presumably writing, scholars disagree in a considerable number of cases, often with equally plausible reasoning—first on the transcription of the graph and then on the interpretation of the word it is writing. In my presentation of the text that follows, I have chosen the readings that I find most convincing; readers interested in the often complex and technical discussions behind these choices will find them easily available elsewhere.[21] For the same reason, I also refrain from printing any direct transcriptions of the original characters; instead, I use the modern characters that reflect those interpretations of the characters in the manuscript that I find most convincing. In a number of cases,

---

18   See Andrew Ford, *The Origins of Criticism: Literary Culture and Poetic Theory in Classical Greece* (Princeton: Princeton University Press, 2002).

19   Selected passages from the following analysis are also included in Martin Kern, "Lost in Tradition: The *Classic of Poetry* We Did not Know," in *Hsiang Lectures on Chinese Poetry* 5, ed. Grace S. Fong (Montreal: Centre for East Asian Research, McGill University, 2010), 29–56. The present essay contains a number of corrections of my earlier analysis.

20   Huang Huaixin 黃懷信, *Shanghai bowuguan cang Zhanguo Chu zhushu "Shilun" jieyi* 上海博物館藏戰國楚竹書《詩論》解義 (Beijing: Shehui kexue wenxian chubanshe, 2004), 1–22. Huang's well-argued and compelling arrangement of the slips has been almost exactly reproduced by Thies Staack, "Reconstructing the *Kongzi Shilun*: From the Arrangement of the Bamboo Slips to a Tentative Translation," *Asiatische Studien/Études Asiatiques* 64 (2010): 857–906. Staack only places a single slip (#17) in a slightly (and inconsequentially) different position.

21   Excellent sources for these debates are the books by Chen Tongsheng, Huang Huaixin, and especially Liu Xinfang mentioned above.

these choices are still contested, but I will not enter these discussions because they do not affect my rhetorical analysis.

The first section in Huang Huaixin's reconstruction of the text comprises slips 10, 14, 12, 13, 15, 11, and 16 from the original arrangement by Ma Chengyuan 馬承源 and his fellow Shanghai Museum editors.[22] It displays some of the core rhetorical characteristics of the entire text. I distinguish three paragraphs in this section:

> (§ 1) The transformation of "Guanju," the timeliness of "Jiumu," the wisdom of "Hanguang," the marriage in "Quechao," the protection in "Gantang," the longing in "Lüyi," the emotion in "Yanyan"—what of these?

> (§ 2) It is said: "As they are set in motion/move the audience, [these poems] all surpass what they put forth initially."[23] "Guanju" uses [the expression of] sexual allure to illustrate ritual propriety [...] the pairing (?), its fourth stanza is illustration. It uses the pleasures [one derives] from the zithers as a comparison to lustful desire. It uses the delight [one derives] from the bells and drums as {a comparison to}[24] the liking of [...] As it guides back toward ritual propriety, is this not indeed transformation? In "Jiumu," good fortune is with the gentleman. Is this not {indeed timeliness? "Hanguang" teaches not to pursue what cannot} be achieved, not to tackle what cannot be accomplished. Is this not indeed knowing the constant way? In "Quechao," [the young woman] departs with a hundred carriages. Is this not indeed still leaving [her family behind]? That in "Gantang," {one longs} for the man and cherishes his tree is because [the Duke of Shao's] protection [of the people] was magnanimous. The cherishing of the "Gantang" tree is {because} of the Duke of Shao [...] emotion, is love.

> (§ 3) The transformation of "Guanju" is about [the man's] longing being excessive. The timeliness of "Jiumu" is about [the man's] good fortune. The wisdom of "Hanguang" is about knowing what cannot be obtained. The marriage of "Quechao" is about [the woman's] departure being [...] {The protection of "Gantang" is about the longing for} the Duke of Shao. The sorrow of "Lüyi" is about

---

22   Hereafter, all slip numbers are according to the original arrangement by the Shanghai Museum editors.

23   As an alternative, the word *dong* 動 here might be understood as "as they move [the listener]." Furthermore, some scholars have suggested to read the character in question as *zhong* 終 ('in the end' or 'as they end'), which is a possible but phonologically inferior choice.

24   Throughout this essay, I am using { } parentheses for tentative suggestions of missing words in the text. In many cases, I am following the perspicacious proposals offered by Huang Huaixin, *Shanghai bowuguan cang Zhanguo Chu zhushu*.

longing for the ancients. The emotion of "Yanyan" is about [the man's sentimental] uniqueness.

(§ 1) 《關雎》之改，《樛木》之時，《漢廣》之智，《鵲巢》之歸，《甘棠》之報，《綠衣》之思，《燕燕》之情，曷？

(§ 2) 曰：動而皆賢于其初者也。《關雎》以色喻于禮【。。。】兩矣。其四章則喻矣。以琴瑟之悅擬好色之願，以鐘鼓之樂{擬}【。。。】好。反納于禮，不亦能改乎？《樛木》福斯在君子，不{亦有時乎？《漢廣》不求不}可得，不攻不可能，不亦知恆乎？《鵲巢》出以百兩，不亦有離乎？《甘{棠思}及其人，敬愛其樹，其保厚矣。《甘棠》之愛以召公{之固也。}【。。。】情，愛也。

(§ 3)《關雎》之改，則其思益矣。《樛木》之時，則以其祿也。《漢廣》之智，則知不可得也。《鵲巢》之歸，則離者【。。。】{《甘棠》之保，思}召公也。《綠衣》之憂，思古人也。《燕燕》之情，以其獨也。[25]

While the lacunae in paragraphs 2 and 3 leave us with some uncertainty, the overall formulaic and repetitive nature of the passage—which displays only very minor syntactic variation—suggests a tightly coherent passage and supports Li Xueqin and Huang Huaixin's re-arrangement of the order of the slips. Most likely, the lacuna in paragraph 2 that follows the discussion of "Gantang" and ends before "emotion, is love" (情，愛也) contained discussions of both "Lüyi" and "Yanyan," with the remark on "emotion" being the concluding comment on the latter. What can be glanced from this short section?

First, and this is true for the entire "Shilun," nothing in the text advances the kind of historical and political interpretation we know from the *Mao Poetry*. There is no historical reference except for one poem that mentions the Duke of Shao. This is in complete contradiction to the Mao reading which historicizes the poems based on information, or assumptions, from outside the poems themselves. The reference to the Duke of Shao, by contrast, is already within the poem and therefore not an external historicization brought to it from another source. Nothing suggests that the author of the "Shilun" was integrating the poems into a historical context, nor did he refer to any other text to explain them.

This should not be surprising. The historicizing impulses of early imperial readers and commentators are part and parcel of the broader shift in textual

---

25 Huang Huaixin, *Shanghai bowuguan cang Zhanguo Chu zhushu*, 23–50.

culture that began with the Han[26] where the poetry from the past was reframed in several ways. Within the overall organization of pre-imperial history into a meaningful, ethical and political narrative, poetry served as a privileged voice not about but *from within* the historical account, attributed to the historical actors themselves.[27] At the same time, poetry became tied to specific meaningful moments in the progress of a teleological history that led into, and explained the historical evolution of, the early empire; in this function, specific poems attained new meanings as markers of specific historical events. In the fusion of poetry and history,[28] the ancient poetry was thus embedded into a new framework of meaning that transcended any specific, locally confined interpretation and instruction toward a rapidly expanding, anonymous audience of court-affiliated scholars and statesmen; it became part of the literary canon that furnished knowledge about the past, available to any potential student. The passage quoted above offers nothing to lend itself to this overall historical approach.

A second conspicuous feature of the passage is its initial paragraph of single-word characterizations of seven poems that are then followed by the interrogative particle *he* 曷 ('what of these?'). The question then prompts an elaboration—in paragraphs 2 and 3—on these single-word characterizations in two separate and cumulative ways. But where do these apodictic, unexplained, single-word characterizations come from? They appear to be taken for granted and hence are one of two things: either they are based on an existing, agreed-upon understanding of the poems, or they rhetorically claim (and impose) such an understanding in order to respond to a prevailing indeterminacy in the interpretation of the *Poetry*. As such, they do not serve the purpose of explaining the poems, and far less are they suited for a general treatise on the *Poetry*.

---

26 See Nylan, "Toward an Archaeology of Writing"; and Kern, "Ritual, Text, and the Formation of the Canon."

27 On this practice in Han historiography, see Martin Kern, "The Poetry of Han Historiography," *Early Medieval China* 10–11.1 (2004): 23–65. This phenomenon can already be found in the *Zuo zhuan*, though in a different way: here, new poems are impromptu compositions and performances mostly by anonymous folk (while members of the recognized elite give performances of already existing poems from the *Poetry*); see David Schaberg, "Song and the Historical Imagination in Early China," *Harvard Journal of Asiatic Studies* 59 (1999): 305–361.

28 As noted by Jeffrey Riegel, "Eros, Introversion, and the Beginnings of *Shijing* Commentary," *Harvard Journal of Asiatic Studies* 57.1 (1997): 143–177, 171, the Han exegetical lineages known from the received tradition treat the *Poetry* as "history told in verse."

The interrogative particle *he*, moreover, rhetorically introduces a teaching situation; as such, the text resembles the catechistic structure of, for example, the *Gongyang* 公羊 interpretation of the *Chunqiu* 春秋. This situation is further emphasized by the single word that introduces the following paragraph: 'it is said' (*yue* 曰) or, perhaps, some unspecified master "has said" or "would say." How are we to understand *yue*? To my mind, it cannot refer to a specific subject in the sense of "I say" but points in exactly the opposite direction. Widely used in early Chinese expository prose, *yue* is a marker of authoritative speech that derives its authority precisely from the fact that it is *not* tied to any individual or authorial voice.[29] Instead, *yue* marks the following utterance as a commonly accepted 'saying' sanctioned and perpetuated by tradition.[30] In other words, the rhetorical use of *yue* is a conventional stylistic pattern that further emphasizes the absence of a specific authorial voice—and hence confirms the observations above on the absence of authorship in the "Shilun": this absence is not a deficiency but a positive quality, marking the text as an expression of traditional authority.

The catechistic, authoritative nature of the text is further apparent from its rigorously formulaic nature. The "Shilun" never argues in any explicit way; instead, it issues pronouncements. Such a style is, of course, another form of argument: an implicit claim for tradition and authority that does not require explicit reasoning or explanation to be compelling. Complementary to Foucault's notion of the "author function,"[31] a text like the "Shilun" involves the notion of the authorless voice—a function just as powerful as that of the author, and typical of authoritative texts in traditional societies.[32]

In my understanding, 'it is said'—answering to the question "what of these?"—only refers to a single sentence, namely "As they are set in motion/move the audience, [these poems] all surpass what they put forth initially" (*dong er jie xian yu qi chu zhe ye* 動而皆賢于其初者也). This is the central hermeneutical statement of the text. Marked as a proverbial piece of

---

29   On the rhetorical use of such markers of direct speech, see Martin Kern, "Style and Poetic Diction in the *Xunzi*," in *Dao Companion to Xunzi*, ed. Eric L. Hutton (New York: Springer, forthcoming).

30   The often non-individualized, non-authorial voice in early Chinese expository prose involves even the explicit use of the first-person pronoun which frequently does not mean "I" but, on the contrary, the impersonal "one"; see See Christoph Harbsmeier, "Xunzi and the Problem of Impersonal First Person Pronouns," *Early China* 22 (1997): 181–220.

31   Foucault, "What Is an Author?" 141–160.

32   See Veyne, *Did the Greeks Believe in Their Myths*, 59–70, for the example of ancient Greece.

unquestioned common wisdom, it sets the stage for the following two-fold elaboration on each poem, asserting that poetry is not merely what it seems to be, and opening a space to expand the shorthand one-word characterizations. "What they put forth initially" is the surface meaning of the poems, yet it does not exhaust the textual meaning; the texts mean always more than what they say. To advance to this deeper meaning requires a hermeneutical procedure.

With the following pattern of elaboration, the text reverts to the didactic voice of a teacher who makes emphatic use of rhetorical questions in the pattern of "不亦...乎" that is familiar from the first entry in the *Lunyu* 論語.[33] "Is this not indeed transformation?" "Is this not indeed knowing the constant way?" and so on are not explanations; they merely affirm the single-word characterizations presented at the outset. In doing so, they gesture once again at precedent and experience. "Is this not," like the earlier "it is said," appeals to the recognition of what is already established.

Already with its initial paragraphs (if this is what they are), the "Shilun" aims at a high level of generalization both in its pronouncements on particular poems and in its use of hermeneutic tools. In addition to the statement that the poems mean more than their initial appearance might suggest, the first section introduces two technical terms of poetic rhetoric: *yu* 喻 'illustration' and *ni* 擬 'comparison.' *Yu*, which also appears elsewhere in the "Shilun," is of particular importance and comes close to 'analogy.' As such, it appears in the Mawangdui "Wuxing" 五行 manuscript where it is explained through the example of "Guanju."[34] In the "Shilun," *yu* and *ni* are not explained but their understanding is presumed; they are applied to a particular poem or stanza much in the way the later imperial discussion would identify certain passages in the poems as *xing* 興 'stimulus.' In its high level of generality, the "Shilun" abstains from specific discussions of words, phrases, or lines; any reader not already familiar with a poem had virtually nothing from which to imagine its actual content or diction. In other words, the "Shilun" does not supply what is needed to understand the poems it mentions; the missing parts would have to come from elsewhere. But for which purpose?

The likeliest context of the "Shilun" was some sort of textual community where the text played a specific, and limited, role in the instruction on how to interpret and how to apply the *Poetry*. It is also in such a context where the

---

33 子曰：學而時習之，不亦說乎？有朋自遠方來，不亦樂乎？人不知而不慍，不亦君子乎？

34 See Ikeda Tomohisa 池田知久, *Maōtai Kanbo hakusho gogyōhen kenkyū* 馬王堆漢墓帛書五行篇研究 (Tokyo: Kyūko Shoin, 1993), 533–545; Riegel, "Eros, Introversion, and the Beginnings of *Shijing* Commentary," 176–177.

introduction of hermeneutical tools like *yu* and *ni* had their place. Like *xing*, both are categories of interpretation, not of composition, that helped to identify particular features of the *Poetry* as something different from, and more than, what their surface might suggest. What the "Shilun" offers here is not a discussion of the *Poetry* but an approach to it. It guides, but it does not debate.

The general core meaning of each poem, the "Shilun" suggests, could be applied to various specific situations without being tied to any one in particular. To this end, the disinterest of the "Shilun" in matters of authorship or compositional circumstances is programmatic. An interpretation of the poems that emphasizes their possible application to new situations is fundamentally reception-centred and amounts to an erasure of original authorship; in the way they are presented in the "Shilun," no original author had ever owned the poems, and hence no poem could be discredited by finding fault with its author. Likewise, following Foucault's insight that true authorship implies accountability and potential punishment for the text, no author could be blamed for the poem. This positions the "Shilun" in diametrical opposition to the transmitted Han readings of the *Poetry*, and first and foremost to the "minor prefaces" of the Mao tradition. Furthermore, the "Shilun" shows no interest in any aesthetic considerations of poetic style; strikingly, no early Chinese discussion of the *Poetry* is concerned with beauty. When according to the *Zuo zhuan* 左傳, Prince Ji Zha 季札 of Wu 吳 visits Lu 魯 in 544 BC and is treated to an extensive song and dance performance of the *Poetry*, his repeated exclamations of appreciation refer not to poetic beauty but to the excellent performance that lends itself to a perceptive moral and political appraisal.[35] For both Ji Zha and the "Shilun," poetic beauty—or rather, appropriateness—is a given that needs no further discussion.

"As they are set in motion/move the audience, [these poems] all surpass what they put forth initially," teaches a fundamental principle in the *understanding* of the poems but not the second step of *applying* them. In the three-step process of mastering the *Poetry*—grasping a poem's literal surface, understanding its implied core meaning, and on this basis applying it to various situations—the "Shilun" is concerned with the second step. It is not the most basic introduction to the *Poetry* because it already presupposes a definite, agreed-upon understanding of the literal surface that requires no further discussion. Thus, the elaborations in paragraphs 2 and 3 do not amount to extensive and detailed commentary; as their terse form reveals, they speak to

---

35   Yang Bojun 楊伯峻, *Chunqiu Zuo zhuan zhu* 春秋左傳注 (Beijing: Zhonghua, 1993), Xiang 29, 1161–1165; David Schaberg, *A Patterned Past: Form and Thought in Early Chinese Historiography* (Cambridge: Harvard University Asia Center, 2001), 86–95.

readers who already know the poems. In other words, it is this formal quality of the "Shilun" that reveals much about its own situational use. The way it is composed, the "Shilun" cannot function as a general discussion of the *Poetry*. It is only within a didactic framework that already relies on the audience's familiarity with the poems that the "Shilun," by way of a catechistic procedure, provides prompts and brief elaborations while leaving a fuller, more detailed interpretation to be accomplished elsewhere—most likely, in actual scenes of instruction. The "Shilun" is then best understood as either one of two things, or perhaps even both: as the tool that triggers a more comprehensive discussion of the poems, perhaps even for mnemonic purposes, or as the somewhat abstracted summary of such discussion.

Either way, the "Shilun" appears as a school text of a particular intellectual lineage of *Poetry* interpretation where the initial format of question and answer opens an ideal scene of dialogical instruction. Instead of trying to determine, and hence limit, the meaning of specific expressions, it assigns a repertoire of broad semantic categories to the poems. Through this instruction in the *Poetry*, the poems could easily be mentally arranged and remembered under the columns of their respective characterizations and then be called upon in social intercourse as we know, for example, from the diplomatic encounters in the *Zuo zhuan*.[36] In this, the "Shilun" appears to answer Confucius' challenge in *Lunyu* 13.5 ("Zilu" 子路), namely, that knowing the poems by heart is useless without being able to apply them under specific circumstances.[37]

---

36 Among many other studies on the topic, a comprehensive account of *Poetry* citations in the *Zuo zhuan* is given in Zeng Qinliang 曾勤良, *Zuo zhuan yinshi fushi zhi shijiao yanjiu* 左傳引詩賦詩之詩教研究 (Tapei: Wenjin chubanshe, 1993); in addition, see Mark Edward Lewis, *Writing and Authority in Early China* (Albany: SUNY, 1999), 147–176, and David Schaberg, *A Patterned Past*, 72–78, 234–242, passim. For examples of the flexible interpretation of the *Poetry* see the excellent study by O Man-jong 吳萬鍾, *Cong shi dao jing: Lun Maoshi jieshi de yuanyuan ji qi tese* 從詩到經：論毛詩詩解釋的遠遠及其特色 (Beijing: Zhonghua shuju, 2001), 16–43.

37 With this, I do not mean to suggest that the *Lunyu*, in part or as a whole, predates the *Zuo zhuan*. I do not subscribe to the idea that the *Analects* can be stratified into different chronological layers, with some of them dating to the time of Confucius' own disciples. Instead, I accept the competing view that the text was compiled in the Western Han out of a multiplicity of statements attributed to, and anecdotes involving, Confucius; see John Makeham, "The Formation of *Lunyu* as a Book," *Monumenta Serica* 44 (1996): 1–24; Zhu Weizheng 朱維錚, "Lunyu jieji cuoshuo" 論語結集脞說, *Kongzi yanjiu* 孔子研究 1 (1986): 40–52; and Mark Csikszentmihalyi, "Confucius and the *Analects* in the Han," in *Confucius and the Analects: New Essays*, ed. Bryan Van Norden (Oxford: Oxford University Press, 2002), 134–162. This view of the *Analects* is strongly substantiated by Michael Hunter, "Sayings of Confucius, Deselected" (Ph.D. diss. Princeton University, 2012).

The "Shilun" thus offers guidance for the poem's use in the present and future, not instruction in the poetic past.

As noted above, the "Shilun" is a text that draws on existing authority. In addition to the anonymous hermeneutic tradition expressed in the "it is said" statement, the one named figure of authority is Confucius. His statements are drawn upon through the introductory formula 'Confucius said' (*Kongzi yue* 孔子曰)[38] no less than six times throughout the "Shilun" fragments. In these quotations, Confucius speaks in an emphatically personal voice.

A passage that Li Xueqin and Huang Huaixin consider to follow directly upon the initial section quoted above begins with a long quotation by Confucius. In it, Confucius uses a repetitive, fixed rhetorical pattern to issue brief statements on a series of four poems (although the original text may have extended to additional pieces). For each poem, Confucius begins his discussion with the pattern ("From [this poem], I obtain [such and such a meaning]") that is then followed by some further elaboration. In other words, Confucius is given a highly stylized voice here: on the one hand intensely personal; on the other hand extremely formulaic. Together, these characteristics exude complementary aspects of authority and as such a form of argument: the personal Confucius is the true sage, speaking from the heart; the formulaic one, given to rhythmic repetition, expresses himself in a ritualized, institutional idiom.

The pattern "From [this poem,] I obtain ...," albeit without the subsequent elaboration, has a direct parallel in how a different series of poems from the *Poetry* are discussed in the "Jiyi" 記義 chapter of the *Kongcongzi* 孔叢子, a text traditionally dated into the late third century BC but most likely composed only in Eastern Han times, even if including earlier material.[39] The fact that the rhetorical pattern resurfaces almost verbatim in the *Kongcongzi* indicates that it had a place in the Confucius lore of assembled sayings that can be found across a wider range of texts. In fact, as Chen Tongsheng has shown,[40] Confucius is quoted yet again with the same rhetorical pattern elsewhere: first, discussing the *Poetry* in *Kongzi jiayu* 孔子家語 and *Yantie lun* 鹽鐵論 and second, discussing the *Documents* (*Shangshu* 尚書) in *Shangshu dazhuan* 尚書大傳 and also *Kongcongzi*. Of the four poems discussed in this section of the "Shilun,"

---

38   I am wondering whether "Kongzi yue" indeed means 'Confucius said.' Another, perhaps more intriguing possibility is 'Confucius would have said,' which avoids the simple attribution while making the figure of Confucius, and his sayings, far more interesting as well as trustworthy.

39   For an extensive discussion of the *Kongcongzi* passage, see Huang Huaixin, *Shanghai bowuguan cang Zhanguo Chu zhushu*, 282–315.

40   Chen Tongsheng, *"Kongzi shilun" yanjiu*, 62–63.

only "Mugua" 木瓜 is also commented upon in the *Kongcongzi*. Yet while the two statements on "Mugua" in the "Shilun" and the *Kongcongzi* can be interpreted as advancing similar ideas, their actual texts are completely different.

> Confucius said: From "Getan," I obtain the poetic expression of respecting origins. This is the nature of the common folk: when one sees the beauty of something, one invariably wants to trace it to its root. Thus, *ge* (kudzu) is sung about because of its luxuriant leaves.[41] That Lord Millet is esteemed is because of the virtue of Kings Wen and Wu.[42] From "Gantan," I obtain the respect for the ancestral temple. This is the nature of the common folk: if one deeply cherishes the person, one invariable respects his position.[43] If one delights in the person, one invariably is fond of his deeds; and if one detests the person, it is again like this. {From "Mugua," I obtain} that (the ritual presentation of) money and silk cannot be abandoned. This is the nature of the common folk: as one's intent is hidden inside, there must be a way of giving expression to it. [The poem] says that there first has to be something to be delivered and only then does one receive something in return, or that one first presents something and later enters into the exchange; people cannot oppose this. From "Didu," I obtain that noble rank [...]

> 孔子曰：吾以《葛覃》得氏初之詩。民性固然。見其美必欲反其本。夫葛之見歌也則以【。。。】萋葉。后稷之見貴也，則以文武之德也。吾以《甘棠》得宗廟之敬。民性固然。甚貴其人必敬其位。悅其人必好其所爲。惡其人者亦然。{吾以《木瓜》得}幣帛之不可去也。民性固然。其隱志必有以俞也。其言有所載而後納，或前之而後交，人不可干也。吾以《杕杜》得爵【。。。】[44]

As in the preceding section, this invocation of the purported words by Confucius presumes complete familiarity with the text of the poems; the brief comments do not introduce the poems but only relay what Confucius—the sage who uses the first-personal pronoun *wu* 吾 in rhythmic repetition—"obtains" from them. Yet Confucius does even more here: following his perceptive understanding of each poem, he generalizes about "the nature of the common folk," connecting his own subjectivity to the larger human and social truth that is grounded in the inborn nature of the people. Furthermore, he reasons why a

---

41 That is, kudzu is the root of the beautiful clothes that are made out of its leaves.
42 That is, the latter manifestations of the virtue of Zhou that originated with Lord Millet.
43 A more substantial analysis of the ancient discussion of "Gantang" is Michael Hunter, "Contextualizing the Kongzi of the 'Kongzi Shilun' 孔子詩論," paper presented at the "International Symposium on Excavated Manuscripts and the Interpretation of the *Book of Odes*," University of Chicago, September 12, 2009.
44 Huang Huaixin, *Shanghai bowuguan cang Zhanguo Chu zhushu*, 51–61.

particular poem is composed the way it is: because its method of indirect expression resonates with "the nature of the common folk." Once again, this reasoning is driven by reference not to compositional circumstance but to the poem's reception by the common folk—and it is the perceptive mind exemplified in Confucius that is able to discern this true nature of poetic expression. In other words, the "Shilun" invites its reader to emulate the model of the sage to comprehend at once both the *Poetry* and human disposition, and to recognize the former as a *natural* representation of the latter: for example, as humans like to trace the origins of virtue and beauty, "Getan" can praise the kudzu plant because its fibres are the origin of beautiful clothes. Here, the "Shilun" comes close to developing an explicit argument on the nature and ideal perception of the *Poetry*, buttressed by the authority of Confucius. Furthermore, a comparison of the "Shilun" with the *Kongcongzi* suggests that Confucius' comments in the former include two distinct layers: while both sources share the initial "From [this poem], I obtain …" pattern, only the "Shilun" contains the larger, generalizing claim as to how the *Poetry* matches "the nature of the common folk."

The personal voice of Confucius is even more pronounced in another passage. Here, the master responds to the poems not with a discussion but with a mere personal judgment—a judgment that is implicitly authoritative because it comes from the sage who, once again, emphatically uses the first-person pronoun in every phrase:

> Confucius said: "Wanqiu" I find excellent. "Yijie" I find delightful. "Shijiu" I find trustworthy. "Wen Wang" I praise. "Qing {miao} I revere. "Liewen" I enjoy. "Haotian you chengming I} […]
>
> 孔子曰：《宛丘》吾善之。《猗嗟》吾喜之。《鳲鳩》吾信之。《文王》吾美之。《清{廟吾敬之。《烈文》吾悅之。《昊天有成命》吾}【。。。】之。[45]

These single-word expressions of emotional response are then briefly expanded: for each poem, two lines (a couplet or two separate lines) are quoted, followed again by the same statements of "I find excellent," "I find delightful," "I find trustworthy" et cetera that were given to the poem as a whole. In doing so, the discussion narrows the perspective on each poem by identifying its key lines that are considered "excellent," "delightful," "trustworthy" and so on. To a

---

45 Slips 21 and 22 of the original arrangement. Huang Huaixin, *Shanghai bowuguan cang Zhanguo Chu zhushu*, 200–220.

certain extent, the selection of the poetic lines intimate how Confucius understands each poem, even though the actual interpretation is left to the reader of his comments. In fact, the combination of two selected lines with Confucius' extremely general statement says nothing specific about the text; instead, it prompts the reader to respond with his or her own hermeneutical process in order to understand what exactly it is that Confucius finds "excellent," "delightful," and "trustworthy" et cetera in these lines, and how the lines then come to stand for the entire poem. In short, this part of the "Shilun" engages the reader with both Confucius' exemplary judgment and, by way of it, the poems of the *Poetry*.

Yet the brief formulaic section intimates something else in addition. The master's personal comments are not about the poems; they are about Confucius' reaction as the person who truly understands the *Poetry*. His structurally repetitive remarks thus stand as a model of profound insight—an insight now to be grasped, and thereby repeated, by the reader. As the text inspires the reader to pursue the sage's model of perception and appreciation, it becomes an exercise in self-cultivation. It is not a closed text to take home and read; it is an open text that demands and then also guides a response from its audience. Most importantly, it offers a statement on how to approach, and how to speak of, the *Poetry*. Needless to say, the Confucius of the "Shilun," as in the section discussed before, is nothing but a chiffre: his highly stylized and pithy statements are a rhetorical artifice, and so is his 'personal' engagement with the *Poetry*.

The remaining sections of the text continue to show a variety of rhetorical patterns. To some extent, the voices of the author and of Confucius seem to merge, as both are equally elliptic. A passage that is difficult to parse—it is not clear where it ends—but that begins with "Confucius said" reads:

> Confucius said: "Xishuai" is about understanding difficulty. "Zhongshi" is about the gentleman. "Beifeng" does not cut off the anger of the people.

孔子曰：《蟋蟀》知難。《仲氏》君子。《北風》不絕人之怨。[46]

Compare this to the following section, which apparently is in the "Shilun" textual voice:

> "Dongfang weiming" contains incisive phrases. Of the words in "Qiang zhong," one must be afraid of. In "Yang zhi shui," the love of the wife is strong. In "Caige,"

---

46 Slip 27; see Huang Huaixin, *Shanghai bowuguan cang Zhanguo Chu zhushu*, 69–80.

the love of the wife is [...] "{Junzi} yangyang" is about a petty man. "You tu" is about not meeting one's time. The final stanza of "Datian" shows knowing how to speak and to conduct oneself according to ritual. "Xiaoming" is about not [...][47] being loyal. "Bozhou" in the "Airs of Bei" is about depression. "Gufeng" is about grief. "Liao'e" is about having a filial mind. In "Xi you changchu," one has obtained [a family] but regrets it [...][48] speaks of detesting without pity. "Qiang you ci" is about guarded secrets that cannot be told. "Qingying" is about knowing [...] "Juan'er" is about not recognizing people.[49] "Shezhen" is about the cutting off. "Zhu'er" is about a serviceman. "Jiaozhen" is about a wife. "Heshui" is about understanding [...]

《東方未明》有利詞。《將仲》之言，不可不畏也。《揚之水》其愛婦烈。《采葛》之愛婦【。。。】《{君子}陽陽》小人。〈有兔〉不逢時。《大田》之卒章知言而禮。《小明》不【。。。】忠。《邶柏舟》悶。《鼓風》悲。《蓼莪》有孝志。《隰有萇楚》得而悔之也。【。。。】言惡而不憫。《墻有茨》慎密而不知言。《青蠅》知【。。。】《卷而》不知人。《涉溱》其絕。《著而》士。《角枕》婦。《河水》知。[50]

Comparing this passage to the one attributed to Confucius, it seems impossible to discern what distinguishes one from the other. Both passages give extremely brief characterizations of the poems, often reduced to a single word. No particular order is noticeable in their sequence, nor is there any progression of analysis in the discussion of the poems.[51] The text could go on

---

47 Based on the parallel passage in *Kongcongzi*, the lacuna here includes another song, "Jie nan shan" 節南山; see Huang Huaixin, *Shanghai bowuguan cang Zhanguo Chu zhushu*, 111–115.

48 Huang Huaixin assumes that the comment following the missing characters refers to "Xiang shu" 相鼠; see *Shanghai bowuguan cang Zhanguo Chu zhushu*, 127–129.

49 My understanding of *zhi ren* 知人 as 'recognizing people' is based on Matthias Richter's discussion of the term in "From *shi* 士 Status Anxiety to Ru 儒 Ethics," paper presented at the conference "Ideology of Power and Power of Ideology in Early China," Institute for Advanced Studies, The Hebrew University of Jerusalem, May 1–6, 2012; see also Richter, *Guan ren: Texte der altchinesischen Literatur zur Charakterkunde und Beamtenrekrutierung* (Bern: Peter Lang, 2005).

50 Slips 17, 25, 26, 28, and 29 of the Shanghai Museum's arrangment; see Huang Huaixin, *Shanghai bowuguan cang Zhanguo Chu zhushu*, 94–153. Here, slip 29 breaks off. It is not clear to me whether or not the section continues onto slip 23, as Huang Huaixin assumes.

51 Most pieces can be identified with counterparts in the received *Poetry*, although in some cases, it contains more than one song of the same title. Listed with their Mao numbers, the poems in this passage are of the following sequence: Mao 76, 68, 72, 67, 70, 212, 207, 191, 26, 35, 148, 202, 52, 46, 219, and 3, followed by four pieces that do not appear under the

forever until all the pieces from the *Poetry* are covered—or maybe not. The brief comment on one poem does not illuminate the one on another. But what does this mean? Are we to assume that the author of the "Shilun" just randomly listed a range of diverse titles regardless of their place in the anthology? That the received anthological order did not yet exist, or was not known to him? That the poems listed here were just the ones he knew? That they were in some sense representative? Whatever the case, I would hesitate to presume that the "Shilun" text *just did not make sense*. Both the terse characterizations and the seemingly haphazard order in which they appear seem to confirm once again that this manuscript text was not a self-contained written artifact, open and available to whoever encountered it. Consider again what Socrates had to say about the written text that, as an artifact of writing, leaves behind its original context of face-to-face communication: it "roams about everywhere" and "doesn't know to whom it should speak"; it will be faulted and attacked while being unable to defend itself. Could it be that the barely comprehensible comments, delivered in a seemingly arbitrary sequence, mark the fact that, first and foremost, they are not to be read in isolation—that is, in the way we encounter them today? Whatever the underlying argument of the passage above might be, it is not open to us. This situation, one can argue, is not a deficiency of the text; it merely alerts us to the fact that we are the wrong audience because we do not have access to the scene of instruction in which such a passage may once comfortably played its role.

Yet to be sure, some passages in the "Shilun" seem to rise to the level of philosophical generality familiar from transmitted sources such as the "Great Preface." In the "Shilun," the most famous of these is the one the Shanghai editors have placed at the very beginning of the text, while Li Xueqin has placed it right at the end. Either position signals its exceptional nature:

> Confucius said: The *Poetry* does not hide the intent, its music does not hide the emotion, and its formal patterns do not hide its words.[52]

---

same titles in the received *Poetry*. For these, Chinese scholars have advanced a number of different proposals regarding their identity with transmitted pieces known under different titles; for a discussion of the different suggestions see Huang Huaixin, *Shanghai bowuguan cang Zhanguo Chu zhushu*, 135–147. However, despite some partial clustering—Mao 68, 72, 67, and 70 are all from the "Wang feng" 王風 section—it seems impossible to discern a particular meaning in their sequence in the "Shilun."

52 Most scholars understand *wen* 文 here as "written characters." I consider this reading anachronistic and wrong; see Kern, "Ritual, Text, and the Formation of the Canon."

孔子曰：詩亡隱志，樂亡隱情，文亡隱言。[53]

Here again, the text appeals to the sagely authority of Confucius, but in a rather different fashion. The Confucius of this statement is still formulaic, but no longer personal; what he announces is not his own sagely judgment but a general, apodictic truth on the fundamental relationship between poetry, music, and language on the one hand to human intent and emotion on the other. Considering how isolated this statement appears from the rest of the "Shilun," it carries the distinct flavor of having been incorporated either from some other discourse on the *Poetry* or as a commonplace saying. Indeed, it reads precisely like the kind of generalizing statement that could have survived in the received tradition.

• • •

Given the fragmentary nature of the "Shilun," broader claims about the text can only remain tentative. However, some of its features of content and style suggest that the text represents a particular type of discourse that has not survived in the received tradition. The analysis above has identified a series of patterns of literary rhetoric; by way of conclusion, I would now like to consider to which extent these patterns contribute to an actual argument.

Evidently, the "Shilun" cannot be read as a discursive treatise written for a larger, anonymous readership; other than being concerned with the *Poetry*, it does not seem to have a particular topic (and no title), nor does it stake out a particular philosophical position. It also does not furnish a general introduction to the *Poetry*, nor does it discuss the anthology as a whole or explain any of its poems in detail. In fact, no uninitiated reader not already familiar with the poems would be able to reconstruct any one of them on the basis of how it is dealt within the "Shilun." Thus, as the text presupposes an intimate and perhaps even comprehensive knowledge of the *Poetry*, it does not stand on its own; it only makes sense to those who have learned the poems before. On this basis, the "Shilun" suggests a higher mastery of the *Poetry*: to penetrate the textual surface toward the core meaning of each of the poems.

From this perspective, the first argument of the "Shilun," however implicit, is that the different poems do have specific, different, and discernable meanings, that each poem can indeed be reduced to one particular meaning and that, in their sum, the poems represent an entire catalogue of meanings conducive to an ethical way of life. While the "Shilun" has nothing to say about the

---

53   See Huang Huaixin, *Shanghai bowuguan cang Zhanguo Chu zhushu*, 267–271.

aesthetic qualities of the *Poetry*, its pronouncements on particular poems—whether in the voice of the anonymous author or attributed to Confucius—are concerned with moral and social values: ritual propriety, the good fortune of the gentleman, timeliness in action, knowledge of the constant way, marriage, longing for the ancients, meeting one's time, recognizing people, the virtue of the sage kings, or respect for the ancestral temple, to name just some of the topics raised in the quoted passages above. This catalogue of sanctioned practices and attitudes marks the second, again implicit, argument of the "Shilun": poetry serves as a tool of moral edification, and the "Shilun" itself serves as a tool to discern the specifically moral meaning within each poem. Here again, the "Shilun" does not stand on its own: its system of moral and social ideals is a given, and it would be impossible to understand the *Poetry* without recourse to these established ideals.

The very emphasis on moral edification is an argument in itself, as it implies a hierarchy of values in poetry. Here, moral edification and aesthetic delight operate in opposition to one another, as can be seen with those poetic genres in Chinese literature that have been taken to emphasize the latter over the former—for example, the Western Han *fu* 賦[54] and or late Six Dynasties poetry.[55] As noted by Andrew Ford, the shift from moral to aesthetic concerns is the fundamental point of Aristotle's *Poetics*: for both poetry and poetic criticism to become an autonomous intellectual and technical enterprise, "the *Poetics* inaugurates literary criticism as a technical appreciation of poetry that was distinct from the abundant moral, social, and religious critiques" of the archaic period and hence established "explanatory principles ... independent of those in any other domain of inquiry."[56] This is the step that the "Shilun"—or any other early Chinese poetic discourse—never takes; it begins and ends with the unquestioned assumption that poetry serves moral purposes, and indeed *only* these.

This assumption is grounded in tradition, the reference to which constitutes another argument. Whether in the formula 'it is said,' the use of rhythmic and repetitive (and hence highly ritualized) language, in the attribution of such language to Confucius, in the emphatic representation of Confucius' personal voice, or with the final apodictic statement on poetry and music, the "Shilun" is organized around implicit and explicit claims for traditional authority.

---

54 See Martin Kern, "Western Han Aesthetics and the Genesis of the *Fu*," *Harvard Journal of Asiatic Studies* 63 (2003): 383–437.

55 See Xiaofei Tian, *Beacon Fire and Shooting Star: The Literary Culture of the Liang (502–557)* (Cambridge: Harvard University Asia Center, 2007).

56 Ford, *The Origins of Criticism*, 269.

Confucius' pronouncements may be pithy, but they are authoritative because of the a priori presumed authority of their charismatic speaker; and what "is said" may come without further reasoning, but it must be accepted because it comes from received wisdom. Therefore, strictly speaking, the "Shilun" does not pretend to offer a new or unique approach to the *Poetry*. To the contrary—or so the text suggests—its claims regarding the meaning of particular poems are only restating what is already established.

Such restating does not require the text to explain itself by way of reasoning; it may content itself with terse pronouncements that by their very nature need not and cannot be debated. These pronouncements are not merely elliptic but apodictic—or, more precisely, culminating in single-word definitions of entire poems: they are elliptic to the point where they can only be accepted as apodictic. As such, the very form of expression *is* already (in McLuhan's sense) the message.[57] It is the absence of any overt reasoning or arguing that constitutes the text's most forceful claim for truth.

This also explains the most conspicuous way in which the "Shilun" differs from early imperial approaches to the *Poetry*: it abstains from historicizing the individual poems. It does not categorize them according to the "praise and blame" (*baobian* 襃貶) paradigm of eulogistic versus satirical verse, it does not reference how the poems had been used before, it offers nothing in terms of a philological commentary, and it disregards questions of authorship or scenes of composition. As a result, its terse judgments and characterizations operate on a level of abstraction and generality where challenges by way of historical reference do not reach. At the same time, the "Shilun" affirms the semantic openness and wide-ranging applicability of the poems that are on display in pre-imperial sources such as the *Zuo zhuan*.

It is this openness, then, where the "Shilun" situates its own purpose, function, and quality. Not hermeneutically confined by historical contextualization, the pithy statements shared by Confucius and the textual voice advance claims not of historical knowledge but of superior poetic perception of the self-cultivated mind. In this, the "Shilun" presents an argument on its own behalf: if Confucius is the established yet bygone authority of the *Poetry*, the "Shilun," modeled on his example, takes his place in the present. While Confucius expresses himself with emphatic emotion, the unauthored "Shilun" speaks with the force of traditional wisdom. At the same time, the text also responds to the issues of the day—chief among them the discourse on self-cultivation—known from other contemporaneous manuscripts such as the "Wuxing" or the

---

57 Marshall McLuhan, *Understanding Media: The Extensions of Man* (New York: McGraw-Hill, 1964).

"Xing zi ming chu" 性自命出/"Xing qing lun" 性情論 from the Guodian 郭店 and the Shanghai Museum corpora.

The central quality the "Shilun" discerns in the *Poetry* is that its pieces speak properly and compellingly of matters of the human mind and the human condition: as noted above, poetry is the way to express social and moral norms. Yet as the *Poetry* is interpreted as such, the "Shilun" reveals the cultivated mind of the interpreter. This is particularly obvious in the intensely personal, charismatic voice given to Confucius, but also in the rhetorical questions and occasional exclamations by the textual voice of the "Shilun." In this way, the "Shilun," if it indeed was an actual pedagogical tool, also serves as the ideal representation of such a tool. Early on, it offers the key to its own raison d'être: "As they are set in motion/move the audience, [these poems] all surpass what they put forth initially." In other words, the "Shilun" argues that the *Poetry* requires a hermeneutic procedure to unlock them—and the following statements on individual poems then prove the capacity of the "Shilun" itself to perform this very procedure. In this logic, the "Shilun" does just as much for the *Poetry* as the *Poetry* does for the "Shilun." If Li Xueqin and Huang Huaixin are correct with their arrangement of the bamboo slips, the text is triumphantly capped by stating the accomplishment of its own task, a feat already prefigured and celebrated by Confucius, the sagely interpreter: "The *Poetry* does not hide the intent, its music does not hide the emotion, and its formal patterns do not hide its words." The unauthored poems have found their second master in the unauthored text.

References

Chen Tongsheng 陳桐生. *"Kongzi shilun" yanjiu* 《孔子詩論》研究. Beijing: Zhonghua shuju, 2004.

Csikszentmihalyi, Mark. "Confucius and the *Analects* in the Han." In *Confucius and the Analects: New Essays*, edited by Bryan Van Norden. Oxford: Oxford University Press, 2002: 134–162.

Ford, Andrew. *The Origins of Criticism: Literary Culture and Poetic Theory in Classical Greece*. Princeton: Princeton University Press, 2002.

Foucault, Michel. "What is an Author?" In *Textual Strategies: Perspectives in Post-Structuralist Criticism*, edited by Josué V. Harari. Ithaca: Cornell University Press, 1979: 141–160; orig. "Qu'est-ce qu'un auteur?" 1969.

Harbsmeier, Christoph. "Xunzi and the Problem of Impersonal First Person Pronouns." *Early China* 22 (1997): 181–220.

Huang Huaixin 黃懷信. *Shanghai bowuguan cang Zhanguo Chu zhushu "Shilun" jieyi* 上海博物館藏戰國楚竹書《詩論》解義. Beijing: Shehui kexue wenxian chubanshe, 2004.

Hunter, Michael. "Contextualizing the Kongzi of the 'Kongzi Shilun' 孔子詩論." Paper presented at the "International Symposium on Excavated Manuscripts and the Interpretation of the *Book of Odes*," University of Chicago, September 12, 2009.

———. "Sayings of Confucius, Deselected." PhD diss., Princeton University, 2012.

Ikeda Tomohisa 池田知久. *Maōtai Kanbo hakusho gogyōhen kenkyū* 馬王堆漢墓帛書五行篇研究. Tokyo: Kyūko Shoin, 1993.

Jiang Guanghui 姜廣輝. "Guanyu gu 'Shixu' de bianlian, shidu yu dingwei zhu wenti yanjiu" 關於古《詩序》的編連、釋讀與定位諸問題研究. *Zhongguo zhexue* 中國哲學 24 (2002): 165–168; translated as "Problems Concerning the Rearrangement, Interpretation, and Orientation of the Ancient *Preface to the* Poetry (Shixu)." *Contemporary Chinese Thought* 39.4 (2008): 43–45.

Kern, Martin. *The Stele Inscriptions of Ch'in Shih-huang. Text and Ritual in Early Chinese Imperial Representation*. New Haven: American Oriental Society, 2000.

———. "Ritual, Text, and the Formation of the Canon: Historical Transitions of *wen* in Early China." *T'oung Pao* 87 (2001): 43–91.

———. "Western Han Aesthetics and the Genesis of the *Fu*." *Harvard Journal of Asiatic Studies* 63 (2003): 383–437.

———. "The Poetry of Han Historiography." *Early Medieval China* 10–11.1 (2004): 23–65.

———. "Lost in Tradition: The *Classic of Poetry* We Did not Know." In *Hsiang Lectures on Chinese Poetry* 5, edited by Grace S. Fong. Montreal: Centre for East Asian Research, McGill University, 2010: 29–56.

———. "Style and Poetic Diction in the *Xunzi*." In *Dao Companion to Xunzi*, edited by Eric L. Hutton. New York: Springer, forthcoming.

Kurihara Keisuke 栗原圭介. *Chūgoku kodai gakuron no kenkyū* 中國古代樂論の研究. Tokyo: Daitō bunka daigaku tōyō kenkyūjō, 1978.

Lewis, Mark Edward. *Writing and Authority in Early China*. Albany: SUNY, 1999.

Liu Xinfang 劉信芳. *Kongzi shilun shuxue* 孔子詩論述學. Hefei: Anhui daxue chubanshe, 2002.

Ma Chengyuan 馬承源, ed. *Shanghai bowuguan cang Zhanguo Chu zhushu (yi)* 上海博物管藏戰國楚竹書（一）. Shanghai: Shanghai guji chubanshe, 2001.

Ma Yinqin 馬銀琴. "Shangbo jian 'Shilun' yu 'Shixu' shishuo yitong bijiao: jianlun 'Shixu' yu 'Shilun' de yuanyuan guanxi" 上博簡《詩論》與《詩序》詩說異同比較—兼論《詩序》與《詩論》的淵源關係. *Jianbo yanjiu* 簡帛研究 (2002–2003): 98–105.

Makeham, John. "The Formation of *Lunyu* as a Book." *Monumenta Serica* 44 (1996): 1–24.

McLuhan, Marshall. *Understanding Media: The Extensions of Man*. New York: McGraw-Hill, 1964.

Nehamas, Alexander, and Paul Woodruff, transl. *Plato, Phaedrus*. Indianapolis: Hackett Publishing, 1995.

Nylan, Michael. "Toward an Archaeology of Writing: Text, Ritual, and the Culture of Public Display in the Classical Period (475 BCE–220 CE)." In *Text and Ritual in Early China*, edited by Martin Kern. Seattle: University of Washington Press, 2005: 3–49.

O Man-jong 吳萬鍾. *Cong shi dao jing: Lun Maoshi jieshi de yuanyuan ji qi tese* 從詩到經：論毛詩解釋的遠遠及其特色. Beijing: Zhonghua shuju, 2001.

Richter, Matthias. *Guan ren: Texte der altchinesischen Literatur zur Charakterkunde und Beamtenrekrutierung*. Bern: Peter Lang, 2005.

———. "From *shi* 士 Status Anxiety to Ru 儒 Ethics." Paper presented at the conference "Ideology of Power and Power of Ideology in Early China," Institute for Advanced Studies, The Hebrew University of Jerusalem, May 1–6, 2012.

———. *The Embodied Text: Establishing Textual Identity in Early Chinese Manuscripts*. Leiden: Brill, 2013.

Riegel, Jeffrey. "Eros, Introversion, and the Beginnings of *Shijing* Commentary." *Harvard Journal of Asiatic Studies* 57.1 (1997): 143–177.

Schaberg, David. "Song and the Historical Imagination in Early China." *Harvard Journal of Asiatic Studies* 59 (1999): 305–361.

———. *A Patterned Past: Form and Thought in Early Chinese Historiography*. Cambridge: Harvard University Asia Center, 2001.

Staack, Thies. "Reconstructing the *Kongzi Shilun*: From the Arrangement of the Bamboo Slips to a Tentative Translation." *Asiatische Studien / Études asiatiques* 64 (2010): 857–906.

Tian, Xiaofei. *Beacon Fire and Shooting Star: The Literary Culture of the Liang (502–557)*. Cambridge, MA: Harvard University Asia Center, 2007.

Van Zoeren, Steven. *Poetry and Personality: Reading, Exegesis, and Hermeneutics in Traditional China*. Stanford: Stanford University Press, 1991.

Veyne, Paul. *Did the Greeks Believe in Their Myths? An Essay on the Constitute Imagination*. Chicago: The University of Chicago Press, 1988.

Xing Wen. "Guest Editor's Introduction." *Contemporary Chinese Thought* 39.4 (2008): 3–17.

Yang Bojun 楊伯峻. *Chunqiu Zuo zhuan zhu* 春秋左傳注. Beijing: Zhonghua shuju, 1993.

Yu Jiaxi 余嘉錫. *Gushu tongli* 古書通例. Shanghai: Shanghai guji chubanshe, 1985.

Zeng Qinliang 曾勤良. *Zuo zhuan yinshi fushi zhi shijiao yanjiu* 左傳引詩賦詩之詩教研究. Tapei: Wenjin chubanshe, 1993.

Zhao Fulin 晁福林. *Shangbo jian 'Shilun' yanjiu* 上博簡《詩論》研究. Beijing: Shangwu yinshuguan, 2013.

Zhu Weizheng 朱維錚. "Lunyu jieji cuoshuo" 論語結集脞說. *Kongzi yanjiu* 孔子研究 1 (1986): 40–52.

CHAPTER 7

Structure and Anti-Structure, Convention and Counter-Convention: Clues to the *Exemplary Figure's* (*Fayan*) Construction of Yang Xiong as Classical Master

Michael Nylan

With the vast majority of the texts dating from the Zhanguo (475–221 BC) through Han (206 BC–AD 220) periods, finding the structure of the text goes a long way toward helping the reader establish the meaning within the text. Well organized ventures, in the received literature and the newly excavated texts, generally reflect a profound knowledge of earlier and contemporaneous traditions, and an unexpectedly forthright approach to probing the kinds of knowledge they have seen or heard through intertextual conversations—intent as they are to analyse a particular subset of the questions remaining in the universe of meaning that they have inherited. These texts demand a leap of faith so familiar to modern readers that they routinely fail to discern the outlandish premise that underlies all examples of this dominant textual form: that meaning can be formulated and articulated via language,[1] and, more narrowly, the establishment of precise terminology manipulated within a few preferred grammatical constructions. Think, for example, of the rhetoric favoured by the *Xunzi* 荀子 or the *Han Feizi* 韓非子 when laying out propositions about social engineering, or the Guodian and Mawangdui manuscripts' descriptions of the complex relations binding body, heart, and soul, in this life and the next.

However, a very few texts composed by philosophical masters during the classical era consciously challenge the confident assertions about meaning and form that the usual class of texts encourage. They do this, I would argue, by obscuring and scrambling the very structures of meaning on which the usual

---

1 This premise the "Xici zhuan" 繫辭傳 [Appended Phrases] undercuts, as does Yang in *Fayan* 5/13. All refs. are to the numbers employed in Han Jing 韓敬, *Fayan zhu* 法言注 [Fayan Commentary] (Beijing: Zhonghua shuju, 1992), which agree with those found in Wang Rongbao 汪榮寶, *Fayan yishu* 法言義疏 [Fayan, Interpretations] (Beijing: Zhonghua shuju, 1987; c. 1933; comp. 1899, with more complete notes in 1911), 2 vols. Readers should consult *Exemplary Figures: a complete translation of Yang Xiong's Fayan*, trans. Michael Nylan (Seattle: University of Washington Press, 2013).

type depends. For pat question-and-answer, they substitute infinite regressions and *reductio ad absurdum*. They replace the patterned essay with constellations of fragmented ideas that fail to cohere or build to a satisfying conclusion. They are by no means averse to reminding readers how contingent and context-driven is each and every act of linguistic transmission deemed a rousing success. It is into this second and more rarefied class of texts that there falls the *Zhuangzi* 莊子 and Yang Xiong's 楊雄 (53 BC–AD 18) *Fayan* 法言. That the *Zhuangzi* is a special sort of text most readers would readily concede, but few, if any readers, if the extant corpus is any guide, have regarded Yang Xiong's *Fayan* as anything but a moralistic tract—a tract more sophisticated and well-wrought than most, perhaps, but a humourless, didactic tract nonetheless. Readers before me have read into the format of the *Fayan*—where dialogues are interspersed at seemingly random intervals with pronouncements rendered in more archaizing language—a concerted attempt merely to imitate the *Lunyu* 論語, and undoubtedly that characterization suffices to elicit some superficial resemblances in the first round of reading. (Some have gone so far as to treat the *Fayan* as the first commentary on the *Analects*.)[2] But that comparison falls short of the whole truth, or so it seems to me. The *Fayan* is hardly a coded text whose message can be 'unlocked' by reference to the *Analects* it mimics, for it is chockfull of puzzles that the *Analects* ignores and the *Analects* analogues cannot elucidate.

In the end, I will suggest, the *Fayan* works primarily by forcing its readers to toss out structure altogether. To advance in understanding the *Fayan*, readers must begin by asking themselves two related questions: (1) What calculations may have prompted Yang to devise this odd mixture of formats in the *Fayan* to promote his particular set of teachings?[3] and (2) Why does Yang adopt this peculiar format, where his "dialogues" with unnamed interlocutors are often so manifestly monologic, his carefully constructed persona as classical master so autocratic? Why not, for example, employ the formal essay form, avoiding the first-person altogether, when condemning others or advancing new ideas, given the prior employment of the essay form to these very ends by previous Confucian masters such as Mencius and Xunzi—models Yang himself celebrates?[4] Alternatively, why not choose to compile a chronicle, since that type of

---

2 See Matsukawa Kenji 松川健二, *Rongo no shisōshi* 論語の思想史 [History of Thinking about the Analects] (Tokyo: Kyūko Shoin, 1994), which has been translated into Chinese by Lin Qingzhang 林慶彰 (Taipei: Wanjuan lou tushu, 2006.)

3 NB: The *Analects* also includes such maxims, in addition to the dialogues for which it is better known.

4 See *Fayan* 2/19, 12.5.

composition was expressly associated with the "praise and blame" (*baobian* 褒貶) fashioned by Kongzi himself, if his chief goal was merely to follow the earlier Master? Answers to these quite basic questions are anything but self-evident, but a host of other questions soon occur to diligent readers of the *Fayan*, three of particular interest when it comes to assessments of Yang Xiong as author: What did Yang Xiong hope to achieve by parading before readers so many disparate historical figures, appending to their names encomia so pithy as to be all but impenetrable? How important did Yang Xiong think consistency of message?[5] And what lessons does Yang Xiong want readers to take away from his work?

The structure of the *Fayan* illuminates none of these questions, which is distinctly odd, given that one of Yang Xiong's one masterworks, the *Taixuan* 太玄 (composed before the *Fayan*) seems utterly reliant on the exposure of an exostructure relying on yin, yang, and the Five Phases *qi*. What strikes most readers initially about the *Fayan* is its apparent lack of structure. How did Yang Xiong ever conclude that the work was done? Arguably, Yang's apparent casting off of structure may serve a useful purpose: readers are led to attend obsessively to the several preoccupations of the *Fayan*, in the hopes of piecing items painstakingly together, more by insight and intuition than by logical connection. Readers fully alive to the complexities of the text are more apt to reflect upon their own confusion, even as they grope their way toward a heightened appreciation of the extraordinary erudition and style displayed by Yang as classical master. They are more apt to see how firmly Yang occupies centre stage throughout the text, since Yang is the Master to whom all matters are referred. Several times in the *Fayan*, Yang explains with some asperity why a true Classic cannot be made "simple and easy" in the ordinary sense of those words, but only "simple and easy" in the sense of being "without deceit or treachery" (a phrase implying a measure of coherence).[6] In Yang's view, the readily

---

5 The question of coherence in Yang's masterwork is a subject that has long troubled students of Yang. Su Shi 蘇軾 (1036–1101) complained in a famous letter to a friend about the complicated arguments and ambiguous expressions in the *Fayan*. See his "Da Xie Minshi shu" 答謝民師書 [Reply to Mr. Xie], which also criticizes Yang Xiong's propensity to use unusual vocabulary, in Han Zhaoqi 韓兆琦 and Zhao Guohua 趙國華, *Qin Han shi shi wu jiang* 秦漢史十五講 [Fifteen Lectures on Qin-Han History] (Nanjing: Fenghuang chubanshe, 2010), 262–266. See Andrew Colvin, "Patterns of Coherence in the *Fayan* of Yang Xiong" (Ph.D. thesis, University of Hawaii, 2001). Colvin, to me, seems to conclude that there ought to be coherence in the *Fayan*, but Yang's principles of coherence are elusive at best. L'Haridon also takes up this question. See Béatrice L'Haridon, *Yang Xiong, Maîtres mots* (Paris: Éditions les Belles-Lettres, 2010).

6 See, e.g., *Fayan* 2/9, 7/8, 8/8, 8/11.

accessible ideas in life are of little or no value to the eager student seeking an integrated vision of the moral and cosmic Way that Yang dubs 'the Mystery.' That is a good entry point into Yang's meaning.

As no one single essay is likely to plumb the full depth of meaning constructed by Yang Xiong's *Fayan*, this essay will focus on a second problem that cannot but intrigue readers who hope to understand the ardent devotion Yang inspired in self-proclaimed disciples over long centuries: the stark tension between two constructions of the exemplary master that are traced in the *Fayan*. Careful reading of the *Fayan* presents readers not with one, but with two portraits of masters competing for the readers' attention: the conventional master of dazzling erudition and lofty character responding to potentially promising interlocutors (the type who appears in quite a few earlier texts cited by Yang Xiong, including the *Zuo zhuan*, the *Mencius*, and the *Xunzi*) versus the Other master, the harsh gadfly whose tyrannical thrusts and parries frequently reduce others to silence. I will argue that it is not mere coincidence or a bubbling up of the unseemly unconscious that these two portraits of the master Yang vie for our attention. In my working hypothesis, Yang both covets and despises the title of "great master of classical learning" (*da Ru* 大儒), insofar as he suspects that good models are "very heaven" for the hesitant beginner, yet reliance on their teachings is woefully inadequate to the task of attaining supreme virtuosity.

The plausibility of this essay rests on two claims, at least: that Yang is relentless in his insistence that he remain at centre stage in the *Fayan*, also that Yang highlights (and is almost certainly cognizant of) conflicting views about what it means to be an ideal classical master. Up to now nearly all scholarly discussions of the *Fayan*'s content have zeroed in on the dialogues constructed by Yang in purported imitation of the *Analects*, but Yang actually appears in the *Fayan* in no fewer than eight logically separable guises: (1) as compiler of the brief verse summaries appended as postfaces or prefaces to the thirteen *Fayan* chapters, (2) as 'wisdom bag' never at a loss when confronting multiple queries posed by one or more unnamed interlocutors in short dialogues, (3) as purveyor of a number of sayings or maxims, some almost certainly proverbial,[7] that do not demand an answer or a comment, but instead function as slogans

---

7 Given the absence of graphic means to mark citations in classical Chinese, we can only tag the passages that seem to cite proverbs. For the history of early punctuation, see Guan Xihua 管錫華, *Zhongguo gudai biaodian fuhao fazhanshi* [The History of Development of Punctuation Marks in Early China] (Chengdu: Ba Shu shushe, 2002). See also Enno Giele, "Signatures in Early Imperial China," *Asiatische Studien/Études Asiatiques* 59:1 (2005): 353–387. Guan speculates that controversies over *zhangju* during Han often concerned punctuation.

or touchstones handed down *ex cathedra* (or rather *ex traditione*) for the readers' delectation, (4) as 'objective' literary critic stepping out of his carefully styled persona as classical master to directly address the reader on the merits of a wide range of texts, including the Five Classics, lexicons, master texts, and *fu* 賦, (5) as faithful historian offering appraisals—cryptic and clear—of prominent Qin (221–206 BC) and Western Han (206 BC–AD 9) figures, in the manner of a latter-day *Chunqiu* 'master,'[8] (6) as editor culling the best parts of a long tradition (singular) handed down from the sage-kings of legend, in order to help prepare lesser men to undertake successive acts of cultural reproduction in conformity with that tradition,[9] (7) as historical figure pontificating on the coherence, relevance, and absolute exemplarity of his own moral progress in cultivation of the Way, not primarily in relation to his own era but for the edification of later generations; and (8) as textual critic looking to establish a better, and more scientific way to interpret texts of genuine antiquity.[10] Of course, Yang even in the same passage slips easily in and out of these related personae.

Outside the *Fayan*, Yang also weighs the quality and effectiveness of his own literary efforts, in his autobiography included in his *Han shu* biography, for example, as well as in his *fu*. Yang was the first to compose a lengthy autobiography wherein he figures as a remarkable, self-made, man of letters. (Readers will recall that the authors of the *Shiji* had been heirs to a long line of historians stretching back to Western Zhou times, and such authority as they commanded was a function of their office.)[11] Significantly, it was also Yang whose major innovations in the form of the grand display *fu* allowed him to effectively supplant the emperor from centre stage.[12] And despite the reality that Yang

---

8   For the difficulties entailed in making sense of Kongzi's "subtle words," see Eric Henry, "'Junzi yue' versus 'Zhongni yue' in *Zuozhuan*," *Harvard Journal of Asiatic Studies* 59.1 (1999): 125–161. On Yang's important role in the condemnation of "harsh Qin," see Nylan, "Han Views of the Qin Legacy and the Late Western Han 'Classical Turn',' forthcoming in *Bulletin of the Museum of Far Eastern Antiquities* 79.

9   My feminist soul wishes that I could write "men and women" here and below, but my historian's soul will not allow me to hazard anything beyond Yang's keen interest in converting other men of the governing elites to his views.

10 Cf. Kongzi's acts "for later generations," as described in *Fayan* 8/7. This is a *Gongyang* topos found in the last entry for Lord Ai 14.1, that also appears in the *Chunqiu fanlu* and *Shiji*.

11 *Shiji* 130. 3285-86. The Simas were Directors of Archives, but there was no Bureau of History in Western Han.

12 A comparison of the *fu* ascribed to Sima Xiangru with those included in Yang's autobiography shows just how skilfully Yang accomplished this daring act of substitution, and showcased his low bureaucratic rank and social status so as to avoid being seen as a substantial threat to the Han ruling line. While Sima Xiangru invariably styled himself "an

continued to compose set poetical pieces on command for the rest of his days, in his later years he adopted the air of one who was the sole creator of and inspiration for his writings, except when co-writing a piece with a beloved son.[13] Supposedly his mature works had been conceived in complex response to feelings that had arisen within his own person—his genius being in no way dependent on external phenomena or people.[14] To interpret his most mature works, Yang proffered prefaces, auto-commentaries, or 'explanations' (*jie* 解), each of which was designed to minimize damage to his works from interpolations and emendations or worse, uncongenial readings, in effect devising complex textual tools that could forestall the propensity of the activist editors of Yang's day to 'fix' the difficult prose and thereby flatten the effect.[15] Yang was the first to criticize a specific mode of writing, the *fu*, in which he had made a

honoured guest" of his powerful ruler, spinning variations on old conceits borrowed from the Zhanguo *fu*, Yang preferred to play the roles of omniscient narrator (in his early *fu*) or host to unnamed interlocutors confounded by recent events (in most of his later *fu*). Hence the construction of the so-called 'hypothetical discourses' (or *shelun* 設論) that are the major topic of the fine book by Dominik Declercq. See his *Writing Against the State: Political Rhetorics in Third and Fourth Century China* (Leiden: Brill, 1998). To see how far this trend went during Eastern Han, one might look at the writing of Feng Yan 馮衍, whose *Hou Hanshu* (28A.962–78) biography has Feng styling himself Master Feng (i.e., Fengzi). Feng Yan claims to have the character of a lady, to be like jade; to float with the Dao, etc., he becomes the central character in a *fu* that treats him with all the solemnity of a ritual object or sacrifice.

13   Of course, Yang lived on his official salary of 600 bushels/year (the lowest tier in the upper stratum of the Han bureaucracy, where salaries went up to two thousand bushels/year). For further details, see Michael Nylan, *Yang Xiong and the Pleasures of Reading and Classical Learning* (New Haven: American Oriental Society, 2011), chap. 1. There are prefaces attached to *fu* supposedly written by Yang Xiong, but many scholars dispute that such prefaces (e.g., to the "Gaotang *fu*" or the "Luo shen *fu*") are Han works. Cui Shu 崔述 in his *Kaogu xushuo* 考古續說 [Examination into Antiquity, Continued] (Shanghai: Gushu liutong chu, 1924), juan 1, pronounced them literary impersonations of the Six Dynasties period, for example.

14   For Yang's independent stance, see below.

15   Taniguchi Hiroshi 谷口洋, "Fu ni jijo o tsukeru koto: RyōKan no majiwari ni okeru sakusha no mezame" 賦に自序をつけること：兩漢の交における作者のめざめ [English title by author: The Addition of Author's Prefaces to Rhapsodies: The Awakening of the 'Writer' During the Transition from Former to Later Han], *Tōhōgaku* 東方學 119 (Jan., 2010): 22–39, esp. 28–30, makes this observation. As editor and collator employed in the imperial libraries, it could hardly have escaped his attention that the vast majority of writings from the distant past had been shortened, emended, or discarded during the long years of transmission, and the rest subjected to activist editing processes. For further information, see Nylan, *Yang Xiong and the Pleasures*, esp. chap. 4.

name for himself as a younger man.¹⁶ Taken together, these several authorial moves provided Yang with the opportunity to step outside the subservient role of court-appointed poet to assume the multiple roles of independent author and classical master, social critic and historian. Arguably, Yang Xiong was the first to establish himself as a classical master whose principal authority stemmed from his superior knowledge of texts, his compilation of reliably superior texts, and his superior understanding of what to do with texts (see below).¹⁷ It should come as no surprise, then, that it was Yang who began the practice of 'imitating Classics' (*nijing* 擬經)—an act that itself came to be imitated over and over again in later eras, despite attracting some criticism.¹⁸

In the *Fayan* allusions to all these authorial voices are unified in the single extraordinary literary construction, Yang-the-Double-Master, made particularly memorable by Yang's unusual willingness to signal his abrupt departures from both the common wisdom of his day and the imperial policy and personnel stances during Han.¹⁹ The result: Yang handily establishes for himself a dis-

---

16 *Fayan* 2/1, where Yang disparages the writing of *fu*. Yang ostensibly rejected the *fu* form, on the grounds that it lost all value as a tool for remonstrance, yet we know that he kept on writing *fu* on demand for the emperor (and was handsomely rewarded for doing so). Taniguchi, "Fu ni jijo," 31, argues that while Yang Xiong's autobiography and Huan Tan's *Xinlun* include *fu* in their contents, those *fu* are put to a new use: to supply more context for the authorial stance.

17 Taniguchi, "Fu ni jijo," passim makes much of the fact that Yang carefully arranged his own writings in chronological order, the better to allow readers to view them from a retrospective vantage point that lent Yang and his work the air of objective greatness.

18 Imitations of Yang during Eastern Han and Six Dynasties is the subject of an unpublished conference paper produced in Dec., 2010, entitled "Looking For Yang In All the Wrong Places: the Afterlife of Yang Xiong 揚雄, the Historian, from Late Eastern Han to the End of Six Dynasties." By Eastern Han, ambitious authors hoping to establish their names as classical masters and independent thinkers tended to cite Yang as their principal model when writing. Among Yang's admirers were other ambitious writers, including Huan Tan, Ban Gu, Zhang Heng, and Wang Chong and Liu Zhiji, all of whom treated Yang Xiong as their most important model. For further details, see Mark Pitner, "Embodied Geographies of Han Dynasty China: Yang Xiong and his Reception" (Ph. D thesis, University of Washington at Seattle, 2010).

19 By my rough count, some seventy-five Western Han figures are named, and a clear majority of those were figures suspected of crimes by the court (the names would include Bing Ji, Dong Zhongshu, Dou Ying, Guan Ying, Han Yanshou, Jia Yi, Jia Juanzhi, Li Guangli, Luan Bu, Shen Pei, Master Yuangu, Shi Qing, Sima Qian, Wang Zun, Wei Qing, Xiahou Sheng, and Zhi Buyi); executed by the court (the names here include Chao Cuo, Han Xin, Han Yanshou, Jing Fang, Liu An, Sang Hongyang, Shangguan Jie, Yuan Ang, and Zhao Guanghan); wrongly favored by the court (including Chen Tang, Dongfang Shuo, and Gongsun Hong), or figures playing more ambiguous roles than they should have, given

tinctive character in command of the qualities required for the elevated status of philosophical and ethical master. Thus the soundness of Taniguchi Hiroshi's 谷口洋 recent argument that it is Yang, not Sima Qian 司馬遷 (*circa* 145/135 – 86 BC), who is the first author to express "conscious self-awareness."[20] The task confronting readers of the *Fayan* is, therefore, to interpret the multiple voices and registers that Yang employed while fashioning this persona as master of all the phenomena worth knowing,[21] when Yang alerts us to the fact that an overly literal reading of any text composed by him is bound to end in a misreading.[22]

On the presumed structure of the *Fayan*

Readers unfamiliar with the *Fayan* will probably find it helpful to review some features of the text that earlier commentators have noted. Let us begin with what readers new to the *Fayan* tend to find the most puzzling feature of Yang's self-construction: Yang's claim in several chapters of the *Fayan* that he is a classical master of equal stature with Kongzi. Already in chapter 2 Yang provides the dialogue below between himself and an unnamed interlocutor:

"As the saying goes, 'A trail through the mountains is too narrow a path to follow,' and 'a door facing the wall' leaves too little space to enter."

> How is a person to go in, then?
> Kongzi. Kongzi is the door.
> Are you, master, a door?
> A door! What a door! How could I possibly fail to be a door![23]

---

the trust invested in them by the Han court (e.g., Chen Ping, Zhou Bo, and Huo Guang). By my count, only fourteen people were more or less correctly judged by the Han court, according to Yang: Fan Kuai, Feng Tang (?), the Four Greybeards, Guan Fu, Juan Buyi, Lou Jing, Lu Jia, Su Wu, Xiahou Ying, Yin Wenggu, and Zhang Anshi.

20   Taniguchi, "Fu ni jijo," *passim*.
21   For this reason, unlike L'Haridon, I have rendered in my English translation *huo yue* as 'Someone asked me.'
22   Yang supplied an astonishing hermeneutical key to his *fu*, wherein the more overwrought and exaggerated his praise of a given phenomenon, the more profound his actual rejection of it. See *Han shu* 87A.3535; DRK 24.
23   *Fayan* 2/10. In this company of sages and near-sages, Yang places himself on a par with Xun Qing (Xunzi) and Mencius. See *Fayan* 12/4–5, where the analogy of 'door' is repeated.

Yang's claim to provide an entry into a higher, and more capacious mode of seeing and thinking is repeated throughout the *Fayan*. For instance, the verse preface to Chapter 10 says,

> Since the time of Zhongni [ie., Kongzi], rulers, generals, chancellors, ministers, men in service, and famous officers have been judged by non-uniform standards. I judge them by a single standard, that of the sages.

Similarly, the preface to Chapter 11 states,

> There have been the exemplary men of virtuous conduct, [virtual] Yan Huis and Min Ziqians, and exemplary right hand men, [virtual] Xiao Hes and Cao Shens, not to mention generals. Ranking their eminence, I weigh and relate their types and qualities.

Through such summaries for the historical chapters, Yang principally identifies himself with Kongzi, and casts his *Fayan* as a latter-day *Chunqiu*. At the same time, Yang in no way denies that his authority derives from his unusual ability to grasp the centrality, utility, and intelligibility of Kongzi's message (itself distilled from earlier sages),[24] and then faithfully pass on those teachings to later followers. Note that Yang's willingness to credit Kongzi as his chief model and inspiration in no way implies that he, Yang, is an inferior copy, belying the routine presumptions about original vs. copy in the classical Western tradition.[25] It remains for us, then, to understand how the *Fayan* made such claims plausible.

Early on in chapter 1, Yang identifies his target readership for the *Fayan* as those who are "dense and dim-witted,… giving free rein to their own instincts, with their faculties of sight and hearing quite undeveloped."[26] Just as quickly he identifies himself as one who "loves learning," does not "covet long life" or wealth or an official career, someone with the requisite erudition and insight to "give voice to" the way transmitted by Kongzi.[27] By his own account, Yang has mastered, improved, and finally ennobled his original endowment, all through his own efforts and the same "unflagging determination" supposedly exhibited by Kongzi.[28] Having mastered himself, he is ready to act as master to others, enlightening them so that they can be lifted out of their present sorry

---

24   *Fayan* 2/14, 2/15, 6/3.
25   *Fayan* 1/18.
26   Preface, Chapter 1.
27   *Fayan* ½–3. For Yang's disdain for high office, see, e.g., *Fayan* 1/15.
28   *Fayan* 1/6, 1/8, 1/24.

condition as benighted souls.[29] Hence Yang's unparalleled importance as a 'true teacher' and 'model.' Still in the first chapter of the *Fayan*, for example, Yang asserts that,

> The model teacher; the model teacher—he it is who represents the very fate of the ignorant stripling. To work hard at study is less important than working hard at finding the right teacher, for the teacher is the very model and standard for people. In quite a few cases, of course, the model is no model, and the standard no standard at all.
>
> Just as countless numbers of ideas exist in a single alleyway's market, so, too, innumerable arguments may co-exist in any single scroll of writing. And just as a balance must be set up for each little market, so, too, must a teacher be set up even for a text one scroll in length.[30]

That things—and above all people—are unequal by nature is a lesson that Yang hammers home repeatedly.[31] Moreover, only fools who have not accepted tutelage by Yang accept the common wisdom regarding the correct assessment of value. Since Yang's writings match the spirit of the Classics "in form, style, and quality," they must be honoured as latter-day Classics, regardless of their author's standing at court.[32] For Yang himself has a pearl beyond price—his unique knowledge and understanding of the connoisseur's Way of learning and practice.[33] Adherence to this Way that Yang favours will ensure that a person comes to possess the sort of charismatic authority that will allow him, at least in social relations, "to align his stance" with the prevailing patterns in such a way that his every action reliably "hits the target."[34]

A summary of the main themes in the *Fayan* may give readers unfamiliar with the text some idea of its riches. Chapters 1–3 of the *Fayan* describe the basic human condition (what constraints exist on human nature, and what capacities inhere in the original endowment, including the sensory capacities). The early chapters also explain why love of learning proves, over the long haul, to be hugely more satisfying than the pursuit of more conventional goals. While a love of learning can never ensure success in bureaucratic careers or in moneymaking ventures, that love eventually transforms the person into a

---

29   *Fayan* 3/14.
30   *Fayan* 1/10–11.
31   *Fayan* 1/7, 1/12, 1/16, 1/19, 2/8, 2/9, 2/13, 2/20, 3/10. Yang continues to remind readers of this basic fact, as, for instance, in *Fayan* 6/6.
32   *Fayan* 1/19.
33   *Fayan* 1/21–23, where Yang and Yan Hui are conflated; also ibid., 2/9, for connoisseurship.
34   *Fayan* 3/1. For Yang's assurances of reliable success in the Way, cf. *Fayan* 3/12.

connoisseur of the Way, which introduces its own exquisite pleasures. No less importantly, the same habits of mind developed through love of learning allow the discerning person to apply his distinctive human capacities to the task of ascertaining the relative value of the claims made upon his attention, with the inevitable result that he chooses to interact with other men who are worthy of emulation.[35] (To fail to interact in this way, in Yang's view, is to accept an inferior life where the primary human capacities for superb sociality wither and die.)[36] Self-mastery is the supreme goal, where 'mastery' is predicated on concentrating the will on the radical expansion of one's own inherent capacities as human being.[37]

Chapters 1–3 immediately confront readers with the potential division between statements that Yang has chosen to argue via constructed dialogues and maxims that he simply pronounces. The first three chapters of the *Fayan* registers no fewer than five assertions not liable to dispute, dialogue, or discussion. These describe the basic human condition, allege the manifest superiority of the sages' teachings over all others, insist upon the superiority of practice over mere study and erudition, aver the necessity to locate a good teacher and model,[38] and equate study of the writings a teacher has left behind with tutelage under that same teacher when he was alive. That several of these assertions were hotly debated in Yang's era should be obvious even to the beginning student of Chinese thought. Many thinkers in early China debated the essential features of human nature and the degree to which those features were shared with members of the animal kingdom, for instance. The statement that a teacher and his writings are "one and the same"[39] is no less curious, given the frequent characterization, by which any transcription of ideas—in even the

---

35   *Fayan* 2/20, *Fayan* 3/14. The dead are known chiefly through the writings they have left behind. I regret to say that Yang appears to have men and men only in mind.

36   *Fayan* 3/8–9: "Someone asked me, 'Since the noble man is to guard his integrity, why would he engage in social relations at all?' Through the comingling of heaven and earth the myriad sorts of creatures are born. Through human interactions great achievements may be realized. What good is preservation, if it threatens that?"

37   *Fayan* 3/14–15.

38   For the superiority of practice over study, see *Fayan* 1/1, 1/6, etc. Assertions regarding the superiority of the sage's teachings begin with *Fayan* 1/3, and continue throughout the chapters (e.g., in *Fayan* 2/9, 2/14, 3/20). For descriptions of the basic human condition, see, e.g., *Fayan* 1/9, 3/1–3, 3/12, etc. For the necessity to find a good teacher, see *Fayan* 1/10–11.

39   *Fayan* 2/20 has the interlocutor ask, "Someone asked me, 'But how is one to spot a sage, so as to judge them?' If he be alive, one takes the person as model, but if he be dead, one consults his writings. The principle is one and the same."

most authoritative writing—is the "dregs of the sages."[40] Readers should therefore entertain the suspicion that Yang does not seek to defend such maxims because it would be rhetorically risky, if not impossible to do so.

As Yang has already, in chapter 2, openly identified himself as a superb teacher on a par with Kongzi himself, he needs only to show us what sort of lessons he would propagate to his would-be followers. This he proceeds to do, in Chapters 4–6, where he explains first the near miraculous benefits to be derived from adherence to his model (it being identical with that proposed by the sages of yore),[41] and second, what he borrows or rejects from earlier thinkers (e.g., from Laozi, from Zhuangzi, and from the military strategists).[42] Yang cheerfully discounts the work of each and every one of the main pre-imperial thinkers whose theories have been touted at the various Western Han courts, identifying their theories as markedly inferior to his own Way. In the course of outlining his objections to the various philosophical masters, Yang goes so far as to stipulate what is or is not "permissible" for the rulers to do.[43] Yang then identifies the problem with all writings transmitted down through the ages: even the best pieces of writing, such as the Five Classics, have suffered losses and interpolations.[44] That being the case, it is all the more important that latter-day sages like Yang continue to supplement and elucidate the store of Classics via their own writings.[45]

Chapters 4–6, Yang's second block of text, also take for their subject the true nature of wisdom, an inexhaustible store when it comes to identifying and then rendering intelligible the constant patterns of the universe.[46] Yang then claims that he commands "a thorough understanding of the reasoning behind the invention of such utensils, tools, and contraptions as boats and carts, houses and chambers," with the implication that he has what it takes to devise new rules for the rites.[47] Hence Yang's grand claims that another of his masterworks, the *Taixuan* 太玄 or *Supreme Mystery*, manages to straddle humble

---

40   The *Zhuangzi*'s famous story about Wheelwright Bian is repeated in *Hanshi waizhuan* 韓詩外傳 5/6 with no objection registered, which suggests that it is not merely a 'proto-Daoist' story. See James Robert Hightower, *Han Shih Wai Chuan: Han Ying's Illustrations of the Didactic Application of the Classic of Songs* (Cambridge: Harvard University Press, 1952), 167.
41   *Fayan* 4/7–9.
42   See *Fayan* 4/6, 4/18, 4/21, 4/22, 4/23–45, 4/26, and 5/27, for example.
43   *Fayan* 4/21.
44   *Fayan* 5/6–8.
45   *Fayan* 5/6.
46   *Fayan* 4/7–9, *Fayan* 4/13–14.
47   *Fayan* 4/14.

transmission and godlike creation in a way that surpasses even the works of Kongzi.[48] Chapters 4–6 go on to describe the powers of heaven as model for human action,[49] as well as the powers of writing (as opposed to speech) to transmit heaven's will.[50]

As before, it is crucial to notice for which propositions Yang does not mount a defence, perhaps because no logical defence is possible. These include Yang's understanding of the distinctive strengths of direct speech vs. writing,[51] as well as the importance of good timing and discrimination.[52] Largely without resort to the dialogue format, Yang also troubles to define a host of common words that would hardly seem to merit any effort on his part. These terms include the Way (*dao* 道), charismatic power (*de* 德), ritual decorum (*li* 禮), wisdom, long-lasting reputation,[53] the Central States or Zhongguo (中國),[54] the Decree or Mandate (*ming* 命),[55] definitions of old versus new[56] and of the divine aspects within people,[57] eloquence in rhetoric,[58] and reckless behaviour. It is as if Yang sees the necessity for men of erudition and standing to start from fresh premises, forgetting virtually everything they have learnt, if they are to reorder their priorities. But through such definitions, Yang can construct himself as a figure who remains, like the sages of old, quite impervious to the court's approbation

---

48 *Fayan* 5/18.
49 *Fayan* 4/5.
50 The power of writing—far from being taken for granted long before Yang's time, as some had opined—is asserted for the first time in a positive way by Yang's *Fayan*; for Yang, writing is the only power that remains intact over long periods of time, when all else fades. See *Fayan* 5/12–13, 12/11, with the latter contrasting paintings whose colours fade with writings that do not. Sima Qian, of course, had asserted writing's power in negative ways, saying that writing providing an emotional outlet for good and talented men who had been frustrated in their careers. But Yang credits writing with powers well beyond this therapeutic potential. He sees writing as a tool capable of breaking through the usual barriers of time and space, communicating one's message to communities in ages hence, in ways that allow for "no-death" and triumph over the limitations of one's short lifespan. After all, Kongzi's words, like those of Yang's other hero Mencius, still appear quite fresh and new after the passage of five centuries (*Fayan* 5/13, 7/6). They are models of perfection that have withstood the test of time.
51 *Fayan* 5/13.
52 See *Fayan* 6/13 for timing; ibid., 6/14–15, 6/17, for discrimination.
53 *Fayan* 4/15.
54 See *Fayan* 4/11, for Yang's complex definition of 'Zhongguo.'
55 *Fayan* 6/11.
56 *Fayan* 4/19.
57 *Fayan* 5/1–4.
58 *Fayan* 5/14.

or disapproval,[59] in large part because he has perfected his innate capacities and attuned his inner nature to the dictates of outer decorum. Risking the ruler's pleasure or displeasure "is hardly a matter for concern" to Yang (不憂其不合也),[60] with the result that Yang asserts a special authority quite apart from the four interlocking systems of ranks and honour mandated by the Han court[61]—an authority said emphatically to exist, whether others recognize it or not.[62] By Yang's account, the same was true of Kongzi in earlier times.[63] Thus Yang constructs his particular Way as one that allows people to perform at their absolute peak,[64] even as he aligns his own efforts with those of the sages of legend.[65]

More importantly, perhaps, in identifying the flawed character of what passes for hallowed traditions, Yang prepares readers to accept his own masterworks as crucial supplements and correctives to the classical teachings.[66] The conventional notion that a true Classic ought to be somehow "simple and easy" to understand he ably counters.[67] And he meanwhile shows us that exemplary writings like his own have the potential to survive the ravages of time and transmission over long distances.[68] From there Yang proceeds in three short dialogues to discuss his own work as if he were reflecting upon it from altogether a higher plane:

> Someone asked me, "Given [Kongzi's] model of 'transmitting and not creating,' how is it that you came to create the *Mystery*?"
> "The traditions have been transmitted through the ages, though the writing is newly done."[69]

---

59 *Fayan* 6/16. Cf. ibid., 6/17, 6/22.
60 *Fayan* 6/22.
61 Four interlocking types of systems: (1) orders of honour; (2) bureaucratic rank; (3) status; and (4) wealth or class.
62 *Fayan* 5/24.
63 *Fayan* 6/9.
64 *Fayan* 4/7, which says that without Yang's way, a person "cannot see clearly into a space delimited by four walls."
65 See *Fayan* 4/1. Note also the explicit parallels between the way of Heaven, which has no explicit aim (*Fayan* 4/3), and Yang's love of learning, which does not seek a single goal extraneous to itself (*Fayan* 1/2).
66 *Fayan* 5/5–8.
67 *Fayan* 5/10–11.
68 *Fayan* 5/13. At the beginning of the passage, Yang argues against one common understanding of claims made in the "Xici" (shang/ 12), introduced by the phrase 'They say...'
69 *Fayan* 5/18.

The phrase "raised but never sprouted"—does this not apply to my own child, Tongwu? At the age of nine *sui*, he joined me in composing the *Mystery*.⁷⁰

Someone asked me, "Why write the *Mystery*?"
"For the sake of humaneness and a sense of duty."
"But who *isn't* in favour of these two virtues? Who *isn't*?"
"The point is not to have other messages mixed in—that's all."⁷¹

The enviable result of not mixing inferior messages into one's writing: the man of illumined wisdom, resplendent and bright, shines everywhere like a torch.⁷²

Chapters 7–9, constituting the third block of text, build upon earlier arguments to explain why the Classics, no less than Yang Xiong's neo-Classics, are "Far-ranging words from the remote eras [that] encompass heaven and earth, giving aid to divine insight."⁷³ Yang in these chapters reiterates his earlier point that superficial, unwitting, or reluctant conformity with the model of the Classics—such as is typically undertaken by those calling themselves "Ru" who are actually motivated by careerist ambitions—is distinctly inferior to profound, conscious, and whole-hearted commitment to the classical models.⁷⁴ In these chapters, Yang works to disassociate himself from the less committed classicists, those who have neither the will nor the discrimination necessary to adhere to his Way (it being identical to the Way of the sages).⁷⁵ One key argument of chapter 7 depends on wordplays to establish the relation between 'disputation' (and, by implication, the disputatiousness of which Yang could be accused) and 'eloquent rhetoric,' on the dual grounds that the same term *bian* 辯 connotes both ideas in Chinese, and both implicit disputation and explicit eloquence define the Classics.⁷⁶ That bit of wordplay then spurs the observation that it has been five hundred years since the time of Kongzi, with the strong implication that Yang is the sage destined to succeed him, according to one prevailing theory of the cyclical appearance of sages.⁷⁷ Yang accordingly

---

70 *Fayan* 5/19.
71 *Fayan* 5/20.
72 *Fayan*, chap. 6, verse preface.
73 *Fayan*, chap. 7, verse preface.
74 E.g., *Fayan* 7/1.
75 *Fayan* 7/2, speaks of not having the will to apply themselves; and ibid., 7/3, of not having discernment, for example.
76 *Fayan* 7/5.
77 *Fayan* 7/6, referring to *Mengzi* 7B38. That Yang, like Mengzi, is making a point more about his own merits than the cyclical appearance of sages becomes clear in ibid. 8/1, which disputes the existence of such cycles.

launches into a defence of himself and his work against a series of charges levelled by his peers, judging from external evidence in Yang's *fu*: Yang's work was *not* over-elaborate.[78] It was *not* designed with ulterior motives in mind, such as the desire for career advancement.[79] It did not pander to princes.[80] In Yang's view, remarkably few things, events, and people prove to be worthy of steady contemplation,[81] but Yang's writings are of sufficient quality.

In general, Chapter 8 sets out to refine the grand claims that ignorant men make for the sages, a theme broached earlier but there fully explored.[82] While "the sages have what it takes to embody the patterns of heaven-and-earth,[83] and make of their persons the Third in the triad of sacred powers," they are humans nonetheless, and so they experience the ordinary setbacks and travails of human existence. The powerful can force them to accommodate power,[84] or ignore them (though they do so at their peril).[85] Sages have to be on the lookout for slanders and false friends,[86] and they may not live to see their aims fulfilled," if "the times are out of joint."[87] Faced with the certain prospect of death, they must accept the fact that their posthumous fame relies solely on men of "refined sensibilities in later generations."[88] Despite such practical constraints, the sages are never inclined to grovel or demean themselves,[89] lest they sully the inherent dignity conferred upon them by the Way. That said, the sages surpass lesser men of undeveloped capacities in their stunning powers of imagination and insight, as well as in the profound pleasure they experience when they have found the *mot juste* likely to impress

---

[78] *Fayan* 7/7.
[79] *Fayan* 7.8.
[80] *Fayan* 7/9.
[81] *Fayan* 7/15.
[82] *Fayan* 5/5.
[83] *Fayan* 8/2. Li Gui 李軌 (Jin dynasty *Fayan*-commentator, fl. 317 CE) believes that the human parts are modelled on aspects of the cosmos (e.g., the four limbs correspond to the Four Seasons, etc.), but this observation probably does not correspond to Yang's observation that the sages model themselves as patterns worthy of emulation on the cosmic processes or phenomenal existence ("heaven and earth"); that explains why the sages were be co-adjutors of heaven-and-earth in important sacrifices (see above).
[84] *Fayan* 8/3.
[85] *Fayan* 8/6–7.
[86] *Fayan* 8/13–14.
[87] *Fayan* 8/7.
[88] *Fayan* 8/7, modifying the phrase "Awaiting expectantly sages of future generations," from the *Gongyang zhuan* Lord Ai 14.1: 所以俟後聖.
[89] *Fayan* 8/8.

others.[90] And in the end, the sages can "act as they please," for the simple reason that they invariably choose to proceed in constructive ways.[91] Therefore, the sage comes, by dint of hard work or by his great good fortune, to enjoy a second nature that does not fret over the mundane impositions in life.[92] Knowing what to do, he then does it, without agonizing over decisions. But this does not mean that the sage willingly flouts polite conventions.[93]

The next chapter, Chapter 9, takes up the subject of prescience versus foresight, the first being impossible for any human being, but the second eminently possible for superior men such as Yang.[94] For most of the rest of the chapter, Yang seeks to show how foresight can be applied to the administration of the realm. Good rule Yang first defines in terms of the ideal relation between the ruler and his officers, on the one hand, and the ruler and his people, on the other.[95] In consequence, he soon considers what proper incentives good governments should provide for their officers and commoners.[96] He disputes the prevailing assumption that the classical system of rites and music functions as a virtual straitjacket on rulers, officers, and commoners alike.[97] And he insists that the ruler's main job is to provide a suasive model for "those below," not to administer the realm through laws and institutions.[98] When the unnamed interlocutor finally lobs questions about Yang's own suitability for high office, Yang declines any comparison with good administrators or harsh legalists, even as he identifies the key to good rule as finding the correct balance between punishments and rewards, and in rates of taxation.[99] Such lessons are basic, he says, for any who would administer the realm at any level. Chapter 9 moreover provides the first rationale for the study of history, in the form of a pronouncement (not a dialogue): "Certainly no mirror could give a closer and more accurate reflection than listening attentively to earlier generations and seeing what happened afterwards."[100]

Yang's last block of *Fayan* text, composed of Chapters 10–13, opens with allusions to the historian's offices and duties (tied to the astronomers and archi-

---

90   *Fayan* 8/18.
91   *Fayan* 8/19.
92   *Fayan* 8/24.
93   *Fayan* 8/3.
94   *Fayan* 9/1.
95   *Fayan* 9/2–5.
96   *Fayan* 9/5, 9/8.
97   *Fayan* 9/8.
98   *Fayan* 9/9–10.
99   *Fayan* 9/22–24, 9/25–26.
100 *Fayan* 8/22.

vists of hoary antiquity) and to the historical cycles posited in some authoritative texts,[101] while alluding to current controversies during Wang Mang's regency and reign tied to the *haogu* 好古 ('loving antiquity') movement.[102] The question of intentional fakery is mentioned in connection with pseudo-historical claims,[103] but very quickly Yang's *Fayan* turns to the all-important task of weighing the respective merits of a host of figures deemed 'heroes' in legend. *Fayan* 10/3 is a typical entry in the 'historical chapters,' in that it compares several contenders for fame and judges them largely according to the standards they claimed to uphold themselves:

> Someone asks who was more capable, Wu Zixu [the martial hero], Wen Zhong, or Fan Li?
>
> "Wu Zixu engineered a coup in Wu, broke Chu, and invaded the capital of Ying. He whipped the corpse of King Ping of Chu, and he occupied the Chu official residences. In no case did he follow the course of virtue. But Wu Zixu's advice was ignored when he plotted against Yue and advised against attacking Qi. And since he found himself unable to leave Wu, in the end he 'eyeballed' it. As for Wen Zhong and Fan Li, they failed to remonstrate forcefully. Instead they perched high up on the mountainside. They caused their lord to be humbled before the gods of the soil and grain, and reduced to the status of mere houseboy. What was still worse: in the end, they destroyed Wu. As to being capable and wise, none of the three deserves high praise. And as for Fan Li's sending a letter to Wen Zhong urging him to go into hiding like Fan—that was certainly rich!"

Very much as he did in the *Taixuan*,[104] Yang in his *Fayan* historical chapters ascribes multiple factors operating throughout human history, only one of which roughly approximates the modern notion of 'personal agency.' That a person's best efforts can be thwarted by bad timing is a notion that Yang takes for granted. Yet Yang consistently denies the effect the conjunctions of the stars may have on men's fortunes, leaving the reader in some doubt as to how Yang functioned as resident omen expert at the Han court. *Fayan* 10/7, one representative passage explicating the interplay of diverse historical factors, assigns certain roles to different factors underlying the unification under Qin and Han, in order to prove Yang's contention that all major events unfold as the

---

101   See *Fayan* 10/1–2.
102   For more on the *haogu* movement, see Nylan, *Yang Xiong and the Pleasures*, esp. chap. 4.
103   *Fayan* 10/2.
104   See Nylan's Introduction to *The Canon of Supreme Mystery* (Albany: SUNY Press, 1993), 41–44, where Yang's *Taixuan* names four factors operating in human history as timing/fate (*shi* 時), strategic position (*shi* 勢), tools (*qi* 器) and human agency and choice, called 'virtue' (*de* 德).

result of a complex convergence of multiple factors. Given the complexity with which human events arise, individual actors with any access to power cannot excuse their failures on the grounds that they were powerless to change the course of events. Though heaven intervenes in human affairs, to "strike down those with obvious faults" and to bless men of virtue,[105] its intervention is not necessarily more decisive than actions by leading figures, as *Fayan* 10/9-10 explains. When great talents are put to petty ends, the historical agent deserves to be blamed, as Yang shows in the cases of Chunyu Yue and others.[106] Yang also condemns those who failed to see that their responsibility as advisors to remonstrate does not entail wasting their breath or risking their lives rebuking unreceptive rulers.[107] No less blameworthy, in Yang's view, are the towering figures who failed in later life to 'guard their virtue till the end.'[108] A man's character and worth are ultimately defined by one criterion and one only: what actions he cannot bring himself to do.[109] At the same time, the ability to keep a cool head in a crisis merits strong praise from Yang,[110] who scoffs at the propensity of people to admire acts of reckless derring-do, regardless of the consequences.[111] The same goes for defiant speeches, for, as Yang astutely remarks, "the phrase 'powers of persuasion' [should] refer to persuading yourself to undertake the right course of action. Persuading others of something—now that's really dangerous!"[112]

Having loftily meted out some praise and blame, Yang then takes up the thorny issue of why Kongzi, despite his perfect exemplarity, was nonetheless incapable of assuming the throne in his own day. Yang comes to a plausible conclusion: that Kongzi lacked the requisite land base from which to begin an ascent to power.[113] Still, any sceptic worth his salt would have pressed Yang on this particular issue, for how, then, had Liu Bang managed to occupy the throne, given that he had no land initially? This tricky question Yang neatly evades in his constructed dialogues, preferring to pit Liu Bang, the larger-than-life figure, against Xiang Yu or the First Emperor of Qin. In any case, Chapter 10's focus on the history of events leading up to unification concludes, quite fittingly, with laudatory comments on three masterworks whose putative

---

105　*Fayan* 10/11.
106　*Fayan* 10/16. Cf. ibid., 11/8, where magnificent talents are put to a petty end.
107　*Fayan* 10/17.
108　*Fayan* 10/15, 10/21.
109　*Fayan* 10/26.
110　*Fayan* 10/27.
111　E.g., *Fayan* 10/22.
112　*Fayan* 10/19.
113　*Fayan* 10/12.

authors guided the eras in which they lived: the Duke of Zhou's *Zhouguan* 周官 (also *Zhouli* 周禮, admired for its clear organization of bureaucratic ranks), Zuo Qiuming's *Zuo zhuan* (admired for its clear ranking of rulers and officers at court),[114] and Sima Qian's *Shiji* (admired for the veracity of its record).[115] (Small wonder that Yang was instrumental in the elevation of the *Shiji* to the status of classic.)[116]

After Chapter 10's outline of the decisive factors in history, Chapter 11 takes up the more complicated task of assessing the historical influence of secondary figures who are not rulers and kings, again with the view to weighing which models are worthy of emulation by members of the governing elite. True, Chapter 11 first names the sage-kings as the right models for virtuous men without high rank; Shun, for example, is a good model for men who would be filial, and Yu, for the diligent.[117] But men who are far below the kings in rank are also to be sorted into great and small, according to their just desserts. This suggests that there is no real limitation to the degree of perfection a man of sufficient cultivation can attain, despite the obvious limits on the degree of power such a man may achieve. (One thinks again of Yang.) Yang then supplies several rules for judging men: It is equally bad to be preyed upon as to prey upon others.[118] And to adopt a pose merely for the sake of acquiring fame is to deceive others—and deceit is never to be applauded.[119] In the final analysis, men are to be judged by their contributions to society, which can come in many forms.[120] Thus perfect models can exist aside from that of Zhongni/Kongzi or the sage-kings. For example, one Li Zhongyuan of Shu, Yang's own teacher, is pronounced a "shining star" for his age, whether or not he won renown at court:

> When one saw his demeanour, it was reverent. When one heard his talk, it was eloquent. When one observed his actions, they were imposing and compelling. I have only heard that one uses virtue to make others submit. I have never heard that one uses virtue in order to submit to others.[121]

---

114 Of course, modern historians would not ascribe the composition of this text to Zuo Qiuming.
115 *Fayan* 10/30.
116 As was his mentor Liu Xiang. This story is told by Yang Haizheng 楊海崢, *Han Tang Shiji yanjiu lungao* 漢唐史記研究論稿 (Jinan: Qi Lu shushe, 2003), esp. 21–32.
117 *Fayan* 11/6.
118 *Fayan* 11/9.
119 *Fayan* 11/21.
120 Hence, *Fayan* 11/6 extolling Shun for one aspect and Yu for another.
121 *Fayan* 11/23.

Chapter 12 adds further historical examples, but not before reviewing the respective achievements of Kongzi, Mencius, and Xunzi.[122] Master Huainan is rated lower than Sima Qian, from whose work "even a sage can draw some inspiration and erudition."[123] Clearly, the sage expresses himself not only through "speech and conduct" but also through memorable writings.[124] Yang Xiong therefore eventually circles back to the larger principles that his exemplary figures epitomize, drawing as often upon metaphors as upon specific historical figures to illustrate his points. He concludes Chapter 12 with a series of dialogues that bring home the total futility of the conventional searches for official fame, for eternal life, and for the other goals that spell success to so many. That paves the way for an extended treatment in Chapter 13 of the two larger entities, family line and political realm, whose welfare the noble man would promote.

The main argument constructed in Chapter 13 concerns filial duty broadly defined as the repayment of one's obligations to one's superiors, visible and invisible, living and dead, through the faithful provision of food or food offerings and loyal service.[125] For the Son of Heaven in particular, due care for the survival of his dynastic line requires that he aid and comfort his empire's subjects in such a way as to please the spirits, who will then bless those sitting on the throne.[126] No effort is too great when it comes to repaying one's debts to those who have either given us life or sustained us through life.[127] And so

---

122 *Fayan* 12/3–5, 12/8.

123 *Fayan* 12/9.

124 *Fayan* 12/12.

125 Duties to one's parents are discussed in *Fayan* 13/1–9. Feeding dead parents obviously means fasting and sacrifice. As early as *Fayan* 1/21–22, Yang had noted that filial reverence does not require great wealth on the part of the children. In *Fayan* 7/20, Yang explains the implicit *quid pro quo* or social contract: the people are to serve the ruler loyally, in return for which he is to reward them generously. How broad Yang's definition of 'the people' is, however, is uncertain. The term *min* 民 originally referred to 'the king's people' or 'king's men' (i.e., those at the court), as in certain *Documents* chapters that Yang knew well. By Han times, the term more generally denoted 'all the king's subjects, including commoners.'

126 *Fayan* 13/10 on, but esp. *Fayan* 13/31.

127 I will not discuss Chapter 13 at great length, as it constitutes the sole subject of an essay, "Yang Xiong's Final *Fayan* Chapter: Rhetoric to What End and for Whom?," in *Facing the Monarch: Modes of Advice in the Early Chinese Court*, ed. Garret P.S. Olberding (Cambridge: Harvard University Asia Center, 2013), 237–272. The main points made there are that the Chapter ending is hardly a ringing endorsement of Wang Mang (contra convention), and that the Chapter represents a strong vision of good rule as the key obligation owed the imperial ancestors, over and above cult offerings.

through incremental acts expressly designed to meet their subjects' needs, rather than by self-aggrandizing policies, the legendary sage-rulers exhibited in their own persons that level of perfection destined to elicit the admiration of the ages.[128] By stressing the hard-working and selfless character of those legendary figures, Yang confirms the justice of his earlier remark that "there is no real alternative to aiming so high!"[129] For unless those in power aim high with the goal of ennobling themselves and empowering others, there is really no way to "extend their [the ancestors' or the sage-kings'] shining glories to the present age."[130] On the other hand, in theory no position, even that of the Son of Heaven, is too high or mighty for one whose charismatic authority rests on compelling virtue accrued over time,[131] since patient efforts can tame even the most recalcitrant human beings,[132] leading to the moral transformation of the empire. Hence the wise ruler's careful cultivation of his suasive power to effect the good, a power whose level he gauges by portents, and doles out through substantive achievements[133] "to the very end" of his days.[134]

With the ruler's seemingly unlimited potential for good ensured by the simple fact that no act of appalling cruelty is nearly as compelling as an act of benevolence,[135] the wise ruler perceives the obvious advantages to be gained by retracting the borders of his empire, for this apparent diminution in his power will be more than compensated for by the ruler's enhanced ability to attend to his subjects once his borders become more defensible.[136] Most especially, "The [true] ruler of men works hard to make the people prosper and to increase their wealth, to clarify the Way and clearly exemplify it, and to extend a sense of justice and duty to all, so as to achieve efficacy in the Lordly

---

128　*Fayan* 13/9. Unfortunately, if Yang's account can be trusted, most of Yang's peers have forgotten the lesson relayed in the "Xici" and other classical works: charismatic virtue accrues very slowly through much effort and exertion. See *Fayan* 13/12; cf. "Xici" B (*xia* 下), section 4 (p. 47 in the Harvard-Yenching index); *The I ching; or Book of Changes*. Richard Wilhelm translation rendered into English by Cary F. Bayes (New York: Pantheon Books, 1950), 340, describing the Hexagram 21, "Shi he" 噬嗑.

129　*Fayan* 13/9.

130　*Fayan* 13/10.

131　*Fayan* 13/11.

132　*Fayan* 13/13, *Fayan* 13/16.

133　*Fayan* 13/20–22.

134　*Fayan* 13/17–18. The last block of text, chapters 10–13, uses something like this formulae no fewer than twenty times, reminding the reader of the ultimate ends of the good man with access to power.

135　*Fayan* 13/22–23, 27.

136　*Fayan* 13/29–31.

functions and so accomplish the transformation of all things in heaven-and-earth."[137]

On the Anti-structure of the *Fayan*

Unfortunately, the foregoing synopsis of the main claims advanced in Yang's text gives the utterly false impression that ideas in the text of the *Fayan* unfold quite neatly, one after the other, with the result that meaning can be constructed by reference to form. Blocks 1–4, however, cannot be accurately construed as building one upon the other. No reason can be adduced to explain why, for example, Block 4 (mainly devoted to 'historical figures' interspersed with comments about other subjects) should not be Block 2, nor is any given Block free of comments that diverge on the path laid by the immediately preceding remarks. Yang Xiong scatters syntactic units that most readers would group together over several different chapters and sections. Historical figures appear throughout Blocks 1–3, for instance, and assessments of the various thinkers are not confined to Block 4, as one might expect, since they played a role in history; instead, Zhuangzi, to take one example, pops up in Blocks 1 and 2, in Chapters 2 and 5. Likewise, definitions for ethical vocabulary items can be found in each and every Block. Nothing in the style of the *Fayan* recalls the writings of Mencius and Xunzi or Mozi, in other words, where the definition of key ethical terms comes with patient exposition of the implications that ensue from acceptance of those definitions. If moderns only knew the bamboo strips of an excavated *Fayan* manuscript whose silk binding strings had broken, they would find that the text itself offers few internal clues to help them in reconstruction.

Even more importantly, more than one statement made in one passage is flatly contradicted in another. For example, as noted above, Yang Xiong pointedly suggests in one passage in the *Fayan* that five hundred years have passed since the death of the sage Kongzi, with reference to the cyclical model in *Mengzi* 7B38 strongly implying that another sage—Yang himself—is due to arrive on the scene.[138] But a second passage pooh-poohs the very idea that the sages are born on any kind of cyclical cosmic schedule, pointing out that Kings Wen, and his sons King Wu and the Duke of Zhou, all lived in the same era, and

---

137   *Fayan* 13/31. Yang continues: "In this way, the ruler causes the sedentary grain-eaters [of the Central Plains] to laugh and feel at ease, so that when cult is offered to the spirits, the spirits will certainly accept them!"

138   *Fayan* 7/6.

first Yao and Shun and then Shun and Yu served one another as ruler and minister.[139] The Central States are presented both as an 'imagined community' that might spring up anywhere, if sufficient numbers of good men can be found in any society "between heaven and earth," and a location uniquely redolent with historical ties and traditions whose boundaries cannot usefully be extended.[140] Yang meanwhile presents himself by turns as timorous and brave, as cramped and soaring like a phoenix, as the butt of cruel jokes and a commanding authority.[141] Even some of Yang's assessments of historical figures are puzzling, where we might anticipate straightforward praise and blame from a lesser thinker.[142] Yang simultaneously belittles and commends Sima Qian and Zhuangzi, for example.[143] As a result, the reader inclined at one point to sigh, "Ah, now I've discovered where he's going!" immediately comes a cropper, unable to sustain a single train of thought over several successive lines.

Indeed, the single point of contact joining the units is the literary Yang himself, who passes on earlier sayings or judgments or answers questions. And so we readers are reduced to reading the *Fayan* obsessively, in the hopes of parsing the multiple moods of Yang-the-author. Elsewhere, as noted above, Yang has explicitly warned the reader that he often means the precise opposite of what he says (see above).[144] And while he does not repeat such a warning in the *Fayan*, Yang clearly means the reader to understand that his statements on what we might take to be a single subject are shaped by the context in which they are made and also his mood when replying to questions. Yang attacks and

---

139   *Fayan* 8/1.
140   *Fayan* 3/20, 4/11, 9/26, 11/14, 12/8, and 13.27.
141   Such contradictions abound in some of Yang's other writings, if they are rigorously kept out of the *Taixuan*. We know that Yang portrayed himself as a powerless figure at court, disdained as a mere entertainer, when we also learn that he (a) was brave enough to denounce his emperor as "but another Jie and Zhou," meaning, an archetypically bad ruler; and (b) had his advice on important policy matters accepted and rewarded. For more on this, see Nylan, *Yang Xiong and the Pleasures*, esp. chap. 1.
142   Here, of course, one might argue that the pronouncements by the *junzi* (taken to be Kongzi), as 'recorded' in the *Zuo zhuan*, are hardly straightforward (though the *Gongyang* commentaries tried to make them appear so, by providing certain hermeneutical keys to unlock meaning). On these pronouncements, see Henry, "Junzi yue."
143   *Fayan* 5/16, 7/8, 10/30, 12/9. Yang denounces Zhuangzi, comparing his works with those of Han Fei and Yang Zhu, while he concedes at another that he has borrowed much from Zhuangzi himself. See *Fayan* 4/26, 5/27.
144   See note 22 above. Yang wrote that "even if I wished to admonish, it was the wrong time. Yet even though I wished to remain silent, I could not, and so I elaborated and exalted them [the offending imperial structures and activities]," in hopes that the exaggeration would convey his 'subtle warning.'

retreats from various stances, modifying his assertions until the reader's head fairly swims. The lack of structure, therefore, only compounds the difficulty in establishing meaning, until ultimately the *Fayan* seems far more of a mystery than Yang's famous masterwork by that title. Often enough, Yang shows that "the interlocutor does not understand," or he "has not thought it through yet."[145] At times the interlocutor is said to be startled by Yang's response.[146] And the reader who comes to Yang hoping to pose many of the same questions as the interlocutor ultimately feels no less muddled. Chiefly the fact of some small measure of coherence in the various Blocks leads readers to keep the faith, on the presumption that Yang has something more important and deeper to convey, unlike the rival thinkers who have "used great erudition to produce mixed bags,"[147] "teachers with paltry bits of erudition,"[148] who are of little or no use to the ardent student of cultivation.

I would argue that there is a point to the apparent lack of organization in the *Fayan*, as Yang in earlier writings, including the *Supreme Mystery*, had already demonstrated a rigorously logical and systematic approach.[149] Yang means us to read his work obsessively, for the close readers' search to weave together syntactic units, in the effort to establish Yang's meaning, means that readers learn to discipline themselves in the process. Moreover, readers will refer matters continually to Yang's judgments, seeking his advice on sundry issues, rather than relying on their half-baked formulations (hence Yang's reiterations of the warning, "You have not thought it through yet!"). Finally, Yang through this seeming lack of structure helps readers grasp the subtle idea that no small part of learning and living well depends on divine insight and intuition, and cannot be grasped by strictly logical means. With his frequent references to the Mystery and the need for "spirit-like illumination,"[150] Yang paradoxically consigns far more to the Mystery (the Dao) in the *Fayan* than he ever did in the *Taixuan*, where talk of the Mystery tends to boil down to the regular alternation of the cosmic forces of yin and yang *qi* and the Five Phases, in constant interplay with human activities.[151]

---

145   See *Fayan* 6/16, for example, where both expressions are used.
146   *Fayan* 1/23.
147   *Fayan* 5/16.
148   *Fayan* 6/3.
149   That is why much of the verbiage expended on the issue of whether the early thinkers in China were capable of logical or rational thought is so silly. Different goals when writing called for different rhetorical modes.
150   This is the subject taken up repeatedly in chapter 6 of the *Fayan*, as well as elsewhere.
151   One wonders whether Yang's departures from Xunzi's more rational world view are not prompted by his profound awareness that many teachings in conflict with those of the

On Yang's Double Voice

The previous section hazards the notion that Yang Xiong's *Fayan* may be structured in such a way as to utilize a seeming lack of structure—or even an anti-structure, if you will—to reproduce the dizzying array of experiences and responses that humans inevitably generate in the social realm, and, more particularly, that stop-and-start, non-linear, and at points downright messy quality of the learning and living processes themselves, as students lobby follow-up questions after a topic has been raised, or pursue peripheral issues to satisfy their own curiosity. It beggars belief, the previous section argues, that Yang was unaware of what he chose to do with the *Fayan*, given the highly self-conscious authorial self crafted by Yang in all his extant works. Evidently Yang was determined to invent a new format that purposely retained one of the striking features of the *Analects*, its apparent lack of structure (an artefact, presumably, of the far less conscious processes by which the stories relating to Kongzi were incorporated into that earlier compilation by the disparate groups that preferred them.) Yang-the-constructed-Master, like the dragon of legend, is both constant and protean, endlessly liable to transformation.[152] By implication, the previous section also argues that Yang chose to make himself the principal subject of the *Fayan*, the person to whom all questions must be referred in the end, the person whose pronouncements (clear or ambiguous, partial or complete) the would-be learner was advised to mull over (and obsessively read), if he would become an able Yan Hui to Yang's own exemplary figure of the Master.[153]

This section turns to develop a second working hypothesis prompted by multiple readings of the *Fayan*: that Yang both accepts and deplores the conventional expectations of the Han governing elites about masters of classical learning, and thus the *Fayan* provides his authorial persona with a double

---

sages nonetheless command considerable authority in his time as 'hallowed traditions' passed on from antiquity. In consequence, the search for a good teacher capable of sorting the true from the false has become far more crucial to cultivation than discipline or diligence. For only the right sort of teacher is likely to persuade "those very men to put their trust in the teachings of Kongzi and the sage-kings." Yang to some degree has given up on rational appeals, and asks his best readers to have faith in his judgments. According to Yang, at the very least, one learns *something* from reading and reciting the sages, though a person of lesser ambitions and talents (we cannot be sure which of the two conditions is the more debilitating) may not learn nearly as much from close acquaintance with the sages and their writings as pupils of greater aptitude and determination.

152   See *Fayan* 6/18, for one of many times that Yang compares himself to the dragon.
153   *Fayan* 1/18.

voice capable of both satisfying and undercutting those conventional standards. With respect to quite another context—that of the Mediterranean world of thought taking shape in the centuries before and after Yang—Daniel Boyarin has pointed out that Plato's artful construction of Socrates foists a series of untenable propositions upon his all too easily addled Sophist interlocutors in 'dialogues' which function as virtual monologues, evincing none of the give-and-take of real conversations, and that this same construction of Socrates belongs to "a peculiar type of literature produced by and for intellectuals in which their own practices are both mocked and asserted at one and the same time."[154] After all, as Boyarin astutely observes, to acknowledge the limitations and failings of the main heroes of an intellectual community need not involve total "abandonment of the authority of [some of] the practices" within that community.[155] Much the same duality colours many of the portraits of the wisest rabbis known from the Talmudic tradition—and this by no means is coincidental, says Boyarin.

Following Boyarin's line of argument, the rest of this essay considers the possibility that the *Fayan* carefully interweaves diverse, even contradictory strands of meaning, the better to construct a Yang-the-Master that will satisfy readers at both the elementary and advanced levels of understanding.[156] After all, Yang insists that a true Classic be useful to men at any stage of cultivation: "Small men can use it to perfect themselves in small things, and the great in great."[157] So conventions positing the superhuman wisdom of true masters of classical learning may serve to lead people a little way on the path of cultivation, although hero worship and a disregard for the need for context-specific judgments are hardly likely to foster the development of that admirable degree of independence to be possessed by the fully-formed man of cultivation. Nor can an over-preoccupation with "correctness" allow a man of learning to rise above "the smugly parochial."[158] That the formation of an independent capacity for judgment is the final goal of classical learning is a point which Yang underscores repeatedly in the *Fayan*,[159] in which Yang names himself as that

---

154 Daniel Boyarin, *Socrates and the Fat Rabbis* (Chicago: The University of Chicago Press, 2009), 27.
155 In *Socrates,* Boyarin explicitly argues against readings that construe Socrates either as Plato's 'mouthpiece' or as a simulacrum of Socrates' historical self. I have added the material in the brackets.
156 *Fayan*
157 *Fayan* 8/12.
158 Compare *Fayan* 11/22 and *Analects* 17.13.
159 See, e.g., *Fayan* 6/22. Cf. *Fayan* 5/5: "The sage is a sage by virtue of his not being led around by the nose."

unusual figure, a "true recluse at court" who is utterly unlike false poseurs who have won a name for independence. Hence Yang's oddly extended denunciation of Dongfang Shuo[160] and the *Fayan*'s continual circling around other famous recluses, such as Xu You, Bo Yi and Shu Qi, Liuxia Hui and Fan Li, the Four Greybeards, Fan Li and Wen Zhong, and Yang's own classical masters, Yan Junping 嚴君平, Linlü Wengru 林閭翁孺, and Li Hong 李弘.[161] According to Yang, sages like himself have no desire to indulge in the sort of self-serving claims made by many would-be recluses at court; he "neither flees the world, nor detaches himself from the crowds."[162]

Admittedly, this second working hypothesis seems counter-intuitive at first. But the abrupt changes in tone throughout the *Fayan* merit further consideration. Yang is by turns encouraging and harsh, an overbearing know-it-all brooking no opposition and a consummate gentleman of infinite patience. A closer look at the *Fayan* suggests that the more elementary propositions Yang advances rather aggressively, whereas more advanced subjects receive a softer tone. On the one hand, many of the *Fayan* dialogues were framed in such a way to allow readers in Yang's own day or in later eras to become more comfortable with a long list of distinctly unpalatable truths, chief among them that a well-intended person may never see perfect justice in her own lifetime;[163] that supreme moral (as opposed to legal) authority is not invested always in a leader or his administrators, and that it can even reside in a figure who enjoys little standing, prestige, or privilege; that hallowed texts like the Five Classics are liable to tampering and loss, "to adding and subtracting," rendering some of their pronouncements suspect;[164] that many of the Ru traditions have been contaminated to the extent that they no longer provide adequate guidance to would-be seekers after the Way;[165] that hard-won erudition does not always

---

160   *Fayan* 11/21.
161   FY 11/23, for Yang's teachers; cf. Chang Qu 常璩, *Huayang guozhi* 華陽國志, *Huayang guozhi jiao bu tuzhu* 華陽國志校補圖注, ed. Ren Naichiang 任乃強 (Shanghai: Shanghai guji chubanshe, 1987), 10A.532–534. Ren Naiqiang's notes suggest that marriage ties bound Linlü Wengru and Yang Xiong, but no specifics are given (p. 543). The identification of Li Hong is tentative, since it is difficult to ascertain the dates for Li Hong's life, and perhaps Yang meant only that he modeled himself after Li, not that he was a pupil of Li's. For the other recluses, see, e.g., *Fayan* 6/19.
162   *Fayan* 9/19–20.
163   *Fayan* 5/25, 6/9.
164   *Fayan* 5/6–8.
165   *Fayan* 1/3, preface to Chap. 2, *Fayan* 2/13, etc.

translate into a greater facility for social interaction and communication;[166] and that death is inevitable and few can look forward to enjoying long-lasting reputations, unless they are fortunate enough to be either superb writers or the subjects of superb writing;[167] that true prescience about the future—as opposed to foresight about the course of human relations—is impossible;[168] and that the life Yang would impose on his adherents cannot ever be made "simple and easy" in the ordinary sense of those words.[169] On such issues, Yang Xiong brooks no opposition and his message rings out loud and clear.[170]

At the same time, Yang-the-constructed-Master is presented as far less opinionated whenever the subject turns to the far more difficult question of how and when a classical Master should act, speak, or write. Two alternatives could account for this: Either Yang Xiong deemed his construction of himself as classical Master to be so utterly compelling that he never anticipated any objections to his overbearing responses. Or Yang himself entertained nagging doubts about the typical claims and imputations that tended to be asserted by the most famous classical masters of his own day, though he occasionally deemed it prudent to borrow from these very claims and imputations when fashioning his own persona, the better to appeal to a greater number of potential followers. Quite tellingly, Yang undercuts his readers' expectations that true classical masters display perfection. He suggests, for instance, that he possesses a measure of foresight, but no miraculous foreknowledge or prescience at all.[171] And he positively waffles around the issue of whether he can transcend the usual human responses to life's vicissitudes.[172] The additional assertion that no huge gap separates the celebrated models of near-perfection from lesser mortals has Yang taking his own elevation down a notch.[173] Yang moreover says that he has

---

166   *Fayan* 6/23, for example, defines wisdom as "everywhere making clear one's thoughts and desires" and practical wisdom (shown in conduct) as "everywhere communicating one's virtue." *Fayan* 3/8–10 makes a strong case for virtue and wisdom as "communication" and "social exchange."

167   *Fayan* 12/20–23, 11/1, 1/23.

168   *Fayan* 6/1.

169   *Fayan* 5/10–11.

170   Cf. *Fayan* 1/3: "the best way of doing this [continuing the tradition of Kongzi] would be to cause all the classicists to make their voices ring out loud and clear, like wooden tongues giving voice to bells of bronze."

171   *Fayan* 9/1.

172   Contrast *Fayan* 12/11–12, with other passages, e.g., *Fayan* 6/16–17, 6/22.

173   *Fayan* 7/6, for example, says, "For a very long time the realm has been without a sage. But every mewling infant knows his or her own parents; and those armed with competing theories each emulates a teacher. If we would only refine and refine them [the competing

no control over which people have the capacity to recognize his sublime erudition and superlative cultivation.[174] Yang is not to be blamed if Yang's persuasions have not worked their consummate magic on the person's heart and soul. Simply put, most of those who profess themselves to be learners have not themselves developed the deliberative faculties sufficiently far enough to allow them, as true connoisseurs of men, to acquire a taste or even a yearning for proper action expressed in bodily decorum, artful speech, or compelling writing—fields of endeavour where Yang's authority would survive the annoying challenges.[175]

But what really should give careful readers pause is Yang's construction of himself as a classical master who is by turns hectoring, rude, and unlikeable—a construction distinctly at odds with unreflective if profound admiration for the classical master. When readers set aside the propositional content of the *Fayan* and examine the various poses at play in Yang's masterwork, it becomes immediately clear how often the one or more unnamed interlocutors who come to Yang appear not only to be confused, but also humiliated[176] when confronted with Yang's harsh teaching style. One of the rare verbatim repetitions in the dialogues of the *Fayan* illustrates the withering tone of voice that Yang is apt to adopt when exchanging remarks with his interlocutor: "You certainly have not thought it through yet!"[177] "What is really too bad is your own failure to understand anything at all!" he thunders. This literary construction in the *Fayan* positing Yang's bullying and condescending attitude may take modern readers by surprise, but given its prominence they can hardly afford to ignore this important feature of that masterwork. Yang obviously despises those who

---

theories advanced by teachers], then certainly the right Way would be in their midst." Cf. *Fayan* 1/18, where Yang says, "whoever, for his part, aspires to be a Yan Hui is in a class with Yan Hui." However, certain passages in the *Fayan* ascribe perfect potency to the model of the sages. See, e.g., *Fayan* 12/11–12.

174 Yang has already explained that any failures to persuade his unnamed interlocutor of the right Way cannot be Yang's fault or the fault of Five Classics rhetoric; the fault must lie in the ill-formed character of the interlocutor himself. For a sage like Yang can only explain things to would-be sages already in general agreement with Yang's ordering of the priorities and set of values. Yang aims to instruct others in the craft of the Way, but no craftsman, however skilful, can be expected to win over people who lack keen perceptual powers. See *Fayan* 5/10–11.

175 *Fayan* 2/9, 5/11, 6/1.

176 *Fayan* 5/21, for example, says, "[t]he interlocutor fails to understand."

177 Yang lambasts his hapless interlocutor this way no fewer than three times in the first half of the *Fayan* text and the dialogues feature similarly caustic remarks in the second half. See *Fayan* 1/4, 1/24.

have neither the wisdom nor the guts to follow his Way, due to their overweening ambitions or the mistaken belief that bits and pieces of ordinary learning will yet secure them high rank and good names. But Yang tends to berate all his students as "dense" and "uncomprehending"—they being grown men too immature to leave off their childish games.[178] He thumps the less-than-committed students of the Way, comparing them to "those despicable fellows who draw lines in the sand beyond which they refuse to budge"[179] in their cowardice and sloth. At one point, he goes so far as to compare his dim interlocutor to a blind man clumsily trying to locate the path with the end of his staff.[180] By his account, people reduced to a sub-human existence virtually indistinguishable from that of the birds and beasts are fully responsible for their lazy acquiescence in a range of habits that leave their uncontrolled desires firmly in control.[181]

It surely makes sense, then, to entertain the possibility that the second alternative is right—and not only because the principle of charity demands that readers impute any failures to understand to their own limitations rather than to the failures on the part of the eminent thinker whose work they would interpret. The unprecedented self-awareness that Yang seems to have brought to his own authorial role nearly forecloses any other explanation. How could Yang-the-supreme-stylist have been blind to the profusion of high-handed and occasionally preemptory stage directions or oblique answers that Yang himself inserted into the *Fayan* "exchanges?" Then, too, one must ask why Yang's *Fayan* dialogues occasionally permitted his unnamed interlocutors to protest his manner of teaching, if Yang did not intend his more advanced readers to wonder whether a more consensual approach to learning in general and moral learning in particular might not be preferable, along with less hero worship. In all likelihood, then, Yang, in a latter-day imitation of Kongzi's "subtle writing" (*wei yan* 微言) larded the *Fayan* with hints that would allow superior men unfazed by convention to discern the glaring contradictions imbedded in the conventional narratives about what a classical master should be and do. Yang could enjoy his triumph in the one way, acceding to the prevailing cultural

---

178 E.g., *Fayan* 2/1, and 6/16–17. In the latter set of units, the interlocutor "does not understand." This is the right context for Yang's famous remark disparaging the writing of grand display *fu*. Contrary to the impression given in many accounts, there is no doubt that Yang continued to write *fu* after composing the *Fayan*, so he does not eschew writing all *fu*; just the *fu* that ostensibly remonstrates but really encourages bad behaviour.
179 *Fayan* 1/19.
180 *Fayan* 3/14. Still other passages show the interlocutor as having trouble making sense of Yang's key propositions (e.g., *Fayan* 1/23).
181 For these remarks, *Fayan* 1/16–17.

norms, even as he covertly appealed to considerably more refined notions of mastery at irregular intervals within his own masterwork. Then and only then could Yang's masterwork itself become a Classic that "small men use to perfect themselves in small things, and the great in great."[182]

Yang's probable motive behind this employment of a double voice is easy to see, for Chapter One of the *Fayan* registers Yang's noisy complaints about the court Academicians and their examinations,[183] demonstrating that most of the current crop of men of learning (the Ru 儒) are *not* ethical followers of Kongzi, but mere pretenders to learning and wisdom, and this assertion becomes one of the leitmotifs threading throughout the *Fayan*.[184] When all was said and done, absolute dedication to the task of persuading men to undertake the study of classical learning did not preclude grave doubts about the wisdom of emulating the examples given by many contemporary classical masters—especially when Yang was trying to put classical learning on a new and sounder footing,[185] and when Yang was impatient with slavish panderers to convention.[186]

One suspects that Yang would have found it easier to establish the first voice, that of the superior classical master of convention outshining and dazzling most of his peers. Yang had merely to show himself to be vastly superior to his unnamed interlocutors in wit and erudition and, more importantly, in the ability to apply his knowledge of the cosmic and social patterns to deliberations on the most prudential course of action. And this Yang handily proceeds to do in the early chapters of the *Fayan*, besting his interlocutors (probable stand-ins for men of influence at court) with seeming effortlessness in all games of wit

---

182   *Fayan* 8/12.
183   *Fayan* 1/3 addresses the failings of the Ru, after the first two entries describe "true love of learning." *Fayan* 1/10–11 continues the complaints. *Fayan* 1/19 condemns the bureaucratic examination system, as does ibid., 7/8. The preface to Chapter One implies that Yang alone is fit to teach the people.
184   For example, *Fayan* 2/12, suggests that most other Ru are mere simulacra of true classicists, men who ape the outward mannerisms of Kongzi, but actually function at court as rapacious wolves who show little concern for anything but the mandating of harsh laws. Compare *Fayan* 3/20.
185   I have argued elsewhere, in *Yang Xiong and the Pleasures*, chap. 4, Yang in his later years was seeking to devise a way to 'correct' the Classics by resort to word lists, such as the *Erya* and *Fangyan*.
186   See, e.g., *Fayan* 7/8, where Yang condemns the careerist ambitions of the court Ru. This he also does with several pejorative remarks about the examination system (e.g., ibid., also *Fayan* 1/19, 7/8). Yang seems in part to have downgraded Dongfang Shuo's reputation because Dong supposedly "cautioned his sons to always go along with others." See *Fayan* 11/21. Cf. *Fayan* 11/22, which decries the village gossip and the "smugly parochial."

STRUCTURE AND ANTI-STRUCTURE, CONVENTION AND COUNTER-CONVENTION 233

and erudition, however serious the topic under discussion. As an example of Yang's absolute facility in these rhetorical contests, I cite a single extended passage from Chapter One in the *Fayan*, which makes the case that great wealth is by no means a prerequisite for the performance of one's filial duty:

> Someone remarked, "The assets that you have managed to amass cannot compare with Cinnabar Gui's wealth."
> I said: "I have heard that gentlemen, in conversing with one another, talk of humaneness and a sense of duty, while merchants talk of wealth and profit. So much for riches! so much for riches!"
> Someone asked me, "But if you are poor, in life you have nothing to live on, and when you die, there will be nothing to bury you with. What about that?"
> I said: "To have whatever is appropriate to nourish oneself—that's the very best sort of nourishment. To use whatever is appropriate for burial—that's the finest sort of burial."
> Someone objected: "But if you took Yidun's wealth and used it to fulfil your filial duty, would that not be the very best kind of filiality? Surely Yan Hui often went hungry!"
> I said: "The former used his own crude methods, while Yan Hui used his refined sensibilities. The former employed a bent and partial way, in contrast to Yan, who used the most reliable, upright, and true method. In what way was Yan Hui inferior? In what way, pray tell?"
> Someone said to me, "Were I to have crimson sashes and stores of gold—the pleasure would be infinite!"
> I said: "Crimson sashes and stores of gold—the pleasures that come with those are inferior to those known by Yan Hui. For Yan Hui's pleasures were internal while high rank and wealth are external."
> Someone asked me, "I beg to ask about the inner happiness that you think comes from 'repeatedly going hungry'."
> I said: "If Yan Hui could not become another Kongzi, he would not have thought even possession of the empire enough to make him happy."
> "But did he not, for all that, have his bitter sorrows?"
> I said: "Yan Hui was deeply troubled by the perfection of Kongzi."
> The interlocutor was startled. "That particular form of trouble—was it not the very means by which Yan made himself truly happy?"[187]

As is true of many dialogues in the *Fayan*, Yang has gone well beyond proving the justice of his main assertion; he has also laid the groundwork for a second assertion that is hardly liable to proof at all: that the grave discomfort occasioned by a sensitivity to one's own failings is the first step on the path to seek-

---

187   *Fayan* 1/21–23.

ing those very improvements in one's own character that will eventually insure the greatest happiness in life.

Having trounced his opponents in these contests of wit that surely mimicked competitions and contests at court, it remains for Yang simply to demonstrate that he has applied his wits and energy to matters of supreme import, rather than frittering away his magnificent talents and store of learning in useless or insignificant projects. To the degree that he can assert his mastery of the central issues through his lofty and comprehensive overview, Yang may fairly insist that his tutelage is vital to the moral and intellectual development of every one in his circle of peers and rivals, not to mention later readers.[188] And so Yang spends much of his first three chapters showing that he is one of the few masters—perhaps the only one alive—to have recognized what is truly important and so discounted the undeniable appeals of more conventional claims and goals, in order to achieve a panoptic view expressing the highest level of broad concerns. As Yang puts it,

> In the world we know "under heaven," there are three sorts of preferences [expressed by people]. The ordinary people like to follow their own whims. The worthy people like to correct their persons. The sages like to make themselves into proper teachers and models. The ordinary people are bound by family concerns; the worthy, by those of their own countries; and the sages, only by larger concerns about the entire world.[189]

That his preoccupation with larger concerns is clearly *not* shared by the current crop of classicists or encouraged by the current examination system he notes with exasperation.

Once Yang has successfully asserted his breadth of vision and its unerring quality, no ruler or minister has the grounds on which to object to Yang's arrogation of the privilege (usually reserved for the ruler or the sage) to employ the same "praise and blame" style of pithy historical judgments as Kongzi with respect to prominent figures of the recent past. And this Yang proceeds to do, with brilliance and verve, in his historical chapters, as recounted above. Having asserted his authority over both his unnamed interlocutors and the most important figures in recent history, Yang then ups the ante, as it were, in declaring himself as perfectly attuned to "heaven and fate" as the legendary sages of old. His exceptional, "unflagging" devotion to the Way he traces to his enviable position as a true *voluptuary* of the Way—a role projected onto Kongzi in a few

---

188   For Yang's claims to centrality and comprehensiveness, see, e.g., *Fayan* 2/4.
189   *Fayan* 3/21.

brief *Analects* passages,[190] but sustained throughout the *Fayan*. As early as Chapter One, Yang's *Fayan* portrays Yang as perhaps the only living master to fully understand the complex passions propelling the noble man's rise, passions that sometimes begin with a mere "love of books" but can rapidly flower into a true "love of learning" that in turn paves the way, with steady application, for the profound thrill experienced by the masters who can effortlessly put into practice what they have learnt. In Yang's picture, the abiding sense of pleasure produced by the knowledge that one is reliably good at one's chosen endeavours is duly magnified again by the sage's realization that the same moral acts that ultimately satisfy his yearning to radically expand his capacities for pleasurable sociality simultaneously help others achieve many of their interim goals as well.[191] Yang conveys his passion for the moral Way through metaphors and similes, the most memorable of which compare the lure of learning with the indefinable allure of sexy women and speak of the yearning even ordinary men feel for contact with the truly great.[192] The passion ascribed to Yang by Yang himself stems from his exquisitely refined taste for what is classical in its proportions and thus beautifully disciplined in its patterns and variations.[193] Such a passion is not easily reduced to a mere fondness for aesthetic order, since a highly self-conscious pleasure in doing good informs and dignifies every action of a sage, as is evident from Yang's own life.[194] The sheer thrill of creation—when the material begging to be recast or remoulded is other social beings inhabiting the Central States—provides the ultimate justification for the voluptuary addicted to carrying out the Way.[195]

Almost certainly the historical Yang found it much more difficult to provide in the *Fayan* a second, convincing portrait of the ideal classical master that could supplement the first, for the second portrait of Yang revealed a classical master resigned to his unhappy fate and inured to his own low status and fallibility. Such a demanding counter-cultural sketch of the classical master's intangible rewards was hardly likely to prove much of a draw to the majority of the Han court; it could only appeal to the more clear-eyed classicists of sturdier stock. Indeed, Yang would not have been able to devise such a second voice, were it not for his independent and even stunningly arrogant habits of

---

190   E.g., *Analects* 7/2.
191   *Fayan* 2/13–14.
192   For the first comparison, see *Fayan* 2/5. For the second, see *Fayan* 9/4.
193   See, e.g., *Fayan* 2/2–3, 2/5.
194   *Fayan* 6/5. Much the same is said in *Fayan* 3/3, which claims Kongzi neither toiled nor worried, since he so enjoyed what he did.
195   *Fayan* 1/8.

mind. Small wonder, then, that Yang's *Fayan* offered a most curious portrait of Mencius, one that emphasized Mencius' courage in positing the fundamental goodness of at least some of the impulses of men.[196]

Even dolts and dullards can see how every monologue found in the *Fayan* 'dialogues' centres on Yang-the-Master, with most of the popular propositions put forward by earlier masters dismissed out of hand, and the views held by Yang's unnamed interlocutors continually demolished. But if Yang was determined to simultaneously appropriate and challenge the prevailing conventions in Han court scholarship, he knew he would have to supply enough subtle clues in the *Fayan* to make his brighter readers bristle at the domineering pose adopted by Yang-the-Master in the majority of the *Fayan's* dialogues. Meanwhile, Yang seeds the *Fayan* pages with a number of intriguing hints indicating a preference for a more consensual and less domineering model for classical learning than that which dominated court life.[197] These clues begin with Yang's curious assertion in the *Fayan* that he composed his earlier masterwork, the *Taixuan*, in 'collaboration' with his young son, who was a prodigy. Yang's willingness to credit a nine year-old with at least partial authorship of his *Taixuan*—a work that Yang hails as a neo-Classic in no uncertain terms—suggests Yang's belief in a potential for collaboration and communication outside the strict hierarchy that usually defined master-disciple relations in Han.[198] Two further observations underscore the same message: Yang's insistence on the crucial role played by reciprocity in the building of authority,[199] and his equal insistence on the propensity of the noble man (not to mention the sage) to forget his own excellent qualities, so long as he is fully sensible of the need to

---

196   *Fayan* 11/4.

197   Note that at this time, we have no evidence that private academies outside the court existed. Schools at the commandery, kingdom, and county levels presumably took their lead from the court, as they did in so many other institutional matters.

198   *Fayan* 5/18–19. The two classic stories of master-disciple relations in Han times concern Dong Zhongshu and Ma Rong. According to legend, neither of these teachers saw a majority of their 'disciples' in the course of their teaching. If the stories are to be believed, only a small circle of disciples reached the 'inner sanctum' and so had direct contact with their classical masters. For further information, see Nylan, "Textual Authority in pre-Han and Han," *Early China* 25 (2001): 1–54. Yang's acceptance of child prodigies is confirmed in *Fayan* 10/18.

199   *Fayan* 8/23: "Someone asked me how to act so as to be regarded with awe." "Regard others with awe." "And to be reviled?" "Revile others. As we all know, awesome authority and insults in all cases stem from one's own actions." Cf. *Fayan* 9/4 on the crucial importance of reciprocity to good rule. Cf. ibid. 9/9–10.

acknowledge the excellent points in the characters of others.[200] Yang's identification of the human potential for communication and exchange as the single trait separating people from the birds and beasts is certainly germane here as well,[201] as is Yang's persistent allusion in his historical examples to the fact that no man, however fine, can lay claim to absolute perfection in every aspect of his character.[202] Contrary to all expectations, Yang doesn't even require absolute fidelity to his loftier visions in those he would praise.[203] Even sages and near-sages—and, by implication, Yang himself—were prone to particular strengths and weaknesses when operating at the court.[204]

It is surely significant that the model for true teaching and emulation, as presented in Yang's masterwork, depends far less on a rigid subordination to a classical master than a disciple's willing immersion into the heart and soul of the Master—an intuitive process akin to falling in love, a process said to be facilitated by familiarity with the Classics but one that can never be accomplished by textual mastery alone, no matter how persuasive the models presented by the Classics and masterworks:[205]

---

200 *Fayan* 12/14. But see *Fayan* 12/18, which emphasizes the noble man's secure sense of his own worth.

201 *Fayan* 3/8 identifies 'exchange' as the identifying characteristic of human beings—something that cannot be lost or foregone, if men's souls are to be preserved at all. Ibid., 9/19 reiterates that the sages "neither flee the world, nor detach themselves from the crowds," because they need other people on whom to work.

202 Significantly, the *Fayan* consistently celebrates its exemplary figures for one characteristic, rather than for comprehensive virtues. See, e.g., *Fayan* 10/24, 10/26, 10/27. In the *Fayan* each role or virtue has its exemplary figures, but it takes a composite figure parsed from many exemplary lives to adequately represent the sum of all perfections, even when the sages are involved. *Fayan* 11/6, 11/18–19. Thus Yang's remark, in *Fayan* 11/13, that "the last word in virtue" would be "Shun for filial duty; Yu for hard work and achievements; and Gao Yao for wise counsels."

203 For Yang's view of Sima Qian, see, e.g., *Fayan* 12/9; for Yang's view of Dong, see *Fayan* 3/11, 11/16. Equally notable is Yang's occasional willingness to say what he has borrowed from previous sages and Zhanguo masters (most of whose proposals and propositions he disagrees with).

204 *Fayan* 11/23. Perhaps only the practitioners of classical learning who kept aloof from the court are sufficient unto the limited tasks they have set themselves. After all, even the estimable Kongzi faced many constraints and acknowledged certain limitations over the course of his life. See *Fayan* 8/3, for example.

205 That erudition is not the key to the powerful authority of Kongzi—though Kongzi was undoubtedly learned—is the argument made in *Fayan* 5/16. See ibid., 11/2 for the awe and love the disciples brought to their master. See also *Fayan* 2/12.

Long ago, Kongzi certainly immersed himself, heart and soul, in King Wen, and he fully apprehended him. Certainly Yan Hui, for his part, also immersed himself, heart and soul, in Kongzi, and he apprehended all but a very little. Clearly, divine insight depends solely upon immersion!"(5/1)

As "the noble man is defined by his desire to apply his whole heart and mind to the Way of the sages,"[206] that attitude is the precondition qualifying a man to attain the coveted title of ideal classical master with true authority, in Yang's counter-cultural view—not the usual trappings of the Ru teacher wearing special clothes and hats, intoning a special sort of court language, condescending to his students, or aspiring to enter the court's highest reaches after gaining his Academician's post.[207] When immersion is the goal, can it be right, readers are gently schooled to ask, that classical masters brook no opposition when instructing others in the Way? Without a good model of back-and-forth, how could pupils less advanced in the Way ever come to intuit the pleasures enjoyed by those discerning exemplary figures, living and dead—pleasures far superior to any satisfactions that could be wrested from temporary alliances with "fair-weather" allies and patrons?[208] To pose such questions was but the prelude to posing still more sophisticated questions about relative values and worth—the sorts of questions that resist easy answers, even where sages are concerned.

A book devoted to literary structures should acknowledge one important fact: that the creation of a double voice able to convey conventional and less conventional messages about the life and practices of the superlative classical master, like a literary intimation of the learning process, calls for rhetorical devices that successfully conceal or confound the structure of the text. The more tried-and-true formats, including the chronicle and expository essay, must be avoided at all cost. For it is hard to imagine how one could deliver a sense of two different, if related personae, if not through a series of strictly segmented dramatic exchanges arranged in seemingly haphazard fashion. Were Yang to employ the expository essay, he would have had, sooner or later, to identify one model of classical master as superior to the other. Had Yang tried out the chronicle format in the *Fayan*, he might well have risked charges of treason, given his propensity to supplant the ruler as organizing principle of his texts. No less importantly, the chronicle by its very nature conveys a sense

---

206   *Fayan* 7/2.
207   For the usual attributes of the Ru, see Robert Eno, *The Confucian Construction of Heaven* (Albany: SUNY Press, 1990), chap. 1.
208   *Fayan* 1/6 explains the advantages of true friendship; ibid., 1/20, the uselessness or outright harm of alliances forged for convenience.

of progression not necessarily linked in any way to progression in the Way (identified with progress in emulating Yang), the only sort of advance that Yang professes an interest in.[209] No, only a series of short bursts of dramatized communication between a master in various moods and an unnamed interlocutor, by turns puzzled and mistaken, was likely to impart a sense of the difficulties, as well as the joys attendant upon learning to compose the artful self.

Conclusion

Previous readers have brought certain expectations to reading the *Fayan* that encouraged them to see Yang as modelling himself on the Supreme Master, Confucius (aka Kongzi). Earlier readings, therefore, have stressed the lines in Yang's *Fayan* that first query the conventions of value and then establish new definitions of moral worth via new definitions for key concepts framed both positively and negatively, and finally mete out "praise and blame" to groups of people commonly cast as exemplary figures, reserving special praise for a handful of figures (many of them relatively obscure) said to deserve lasting fame. Michael Loewe is one of several scholars to suggest that Kongzi was not yet in Han the Supreme Master we find in the True Way Learning movement of late imperial China.[210] Thus the present exercise in retrieval is destined to fail if readers remain wedded to the outmoded presumption that men for centuries before, during, and after Yang's creation accorded Kongzi a unique status as Supreme Sage "for all the ages."

This paradigm ignores quite a number of inconvenient facts on the ground, including: (1) in the classical era in China (323 BC–AD 316), Kongzi's name was frequently coupled with those of other masters of classical erudition, including Mozi, Laozi, and Zhuangzi;[211] (2) Both Mencius and Xunzi cast themselves as classical masters equal to Kongzi, if arguably more successful than the earlier master from Lu;[212] (3) Eastern Han stelae routinely proclaimed

---

[209] *Fayan* 1/14, 1/19, 6/22, 12/15.

[210] Loewe, *Men who Governed* China: *Companion to A Biographical Dictionary of the Qin, Former Han and Xin Periods* (Leiden: Brill, 2004), 337–339.

[211] See, for example, Michael Nylan, "Kongzi 孔子 and Mozi 墨子, the Classicists (Ru 儒) and the Mohists 墨, in Classical-Era Thinking," *Oriens Extremus* (2009): 5–20; also Michael Nylan and Thomas Wilson, *Lives of Confucius* (New York: Random House/Doubleday, 2010), chap. 3.

[212] For example, the beginning of the "Eulogy" in the *Xunzi* (either the end of juan 32 or a separate juan) says, "[t]he persuaders say, 'Xun Qing [Xunzi] is not the equal of Confucius.' This is not true… If one closely inspects his good works, one would see that

that the honoured dead whom they commemorate outshone the sage Kongzi himself;[213] and (4) for nearly the whole of Western Han, cult was never offered directly to Kongzi, but only indirectly as representative for an older, established ruling line, either that of the Shang kings or of the Duke of Zhou.[214] Thus it is hardly inconceivable either that others would deem Yang Xiong the equal of Kongzi (as Huan Tan clearly did) or that Yang himself would claim equality with Kongzi,[215] as in *Fayan* 2/10.

No commentators, to my knowledge, have adequately accounted for two features of the *Fayan*: its apparent lack of structure and the curious twists and turns displayed by the dual personae of Yang-the-Master. While the two tentative hypotheses hazarded in this essay are not sufficient for absolute proof, they have the signal advantage of letting us account for far more of what enlivens the *Fayan* text than earlier readings informed by pious presumptions. Furthermore, they retroject a measure of play into Yang's persona—and certainly the pleasures of playful erudition is an important theme in the *Fayan* that the moralizers ignore at their peril. The goal, for Yang as for Zhuangzi, was to "occupy the narrow space between the permissible and the impermissible."[216] We would do him honour were we to locate and dwell in that felicitous space ourselves.

---

even Confucius did not surpass him." This translation modifies that found in John Knoblock, *Xunzi: a Translation and Study of the Complete Works*, vol. III, Books 17–32 (Stanford: Stanford University Press, 1994), 269.

213 Eastern Han stele inscriptions repeatedly compare the least impressive people—including those who died prematurely, without achieving much success—to Kongzi and the sage-king Shun. While those inscriptions generally date from Eastern Han, their style of rhetoric—praise for the dead—is likely to be relatively conservative. For instance, Jing Yun 景雲, a local magistrate of Quren, was supposedly both a Confucius and a Shun, according to stele erected in his honor in AD 173, published in "Bajun Quren ling Jing Yun bei" 巴郡朐忍令景雲碑 [Short Report on the Stele of Jing Yun, county magistrate of Quren, Ba county], Chongqing Zhongguo Sanxia bowuguan-Chongqing bowuguan 重庆中国三峡博物館, 重庆博物館 [China Three Gorges Museum Chongqing, Chongqing Museum] (Beijing: Wenwu chubanshe, 2005), 96–97, entry 30.

214 See Loewe, *Men who Governed*, 337–339.

215 For Huan Tan's remark that Yang was the equal of Kongzi (and not just a virtual Kongzi "of the West"), see Jiao Yanshou 焦延壽, *Yilin* 易林 [Forest of Changes] (Taipei: Yiwen yinshuguan, 1960), 3/9a.

216 *Fayan* 11/23.

References

"Bajun Quren ling Jing Yun bei" 巴郡朐忍令景雲碑 (The Stele of Jing Yun, county magistrate of Quren, Ba county). In *Chongqing Zhongguo Sanxia bowuguan-Chongqing bowuguan* 重庆中国三峡博物馆，重庆博物馆 (China Three Gorges Museum Chongqing, Chongqing Museum), edited by Wang Chuanping 王川平. Beijing: Wenwu chubanshe, 2005: 96–97.

Boyarin, Daniel. *Socrates and the Fat Rabbis*. Chicago: The University of Chicago Press, 2009.

Chang Qu 常璩. *Huayang guozhi* 華陽國志. In *Huayang guozhi jiao bu tuzhu* 華陽國志校補圖注, edited by Ren Naiqiang 任乃強. Shanghai: Shanghai guji chubanshe, 1987.

Colvin, Andrew. "Patterns of Coherence in the *Fayan* of Yang Xiong." PhD diss., University of Hawaii, 2001.

Cui Shu 崔述. *Kaogu xushuo* 考古續說 (Examination into Antiquity, Continued). Shanghai: Gushu liutong chu, 1924.

Declercq, Dominik. *Writing Against the State: Political Rhetorics in Third and Fourth Century China*. Leiden: Brill, 1998.

Eno, Robert. *The Confucian Creation of Heaven*. Albany: SUNY Press, 1990.

Giele, Enno. "Signatures in Early Imperial China." *Asiatische Studien / Études asiatiques* 59.1 (2005): 353–387.

Guan Xihua 管錫華. *Zhongguo gudai biaodian fuhao fazhanshi* (The History of Development of Punctuation Marks in Early China). Chengdu: Ba Shu shushe, 2002.

Han Jing 韓敬. *Fayan zhu* 法言注 (Fayan Commentary). Beijing: Zhonghua shuju, 1992.

Henry, Eric. "'Junzi yue' versus 'Zhongni yue' in *Zuozhuan*." *Harvard Journal of Asiatic Studies* 59.1 (1999): 125–161.

Hightower, James Robert. *Han Shih Wai Chuan: Han Ying's Illustrations of the Didactic Application of the Classic of Songs*. Cambridge: Harvard University Press, 1952.

Jiao Yanshou 焦延壽. *Yilin* 易林 (Forest of Changes). Taipei: Yiwen yinshuguan, 1960.

Knoblock, John. *Xunzi: a Translation and Study of the Complete Works*. Vol. III, Books 17–32. Stanford: Stanford University Press, 1994.

Loewe, Michael. *Men who Governed China: Companion to A Biographical Dictionary of the Qin, Former Han and Xin Periods*. Leiden: Brill, 2004.

Matsukawa Kenji 松川健二. *Rongo no shisōshi* 論語の思想史 (History of Thinking about the Analects). Tokyo: Kyūko Shoin, 1994; translated as *Lunyu sixiang shi* 論語思想史, by Lin Qingzhang 林慶彰. Taipei: Wanjuan lou tushu, 2006.

L'Haridon, Béatrice. *Yang Xiong, Maîtres mots*. Paris: Éditions les Belles-Lettres, 2010.

Nylan, Michael. "Introduction." In id. *The Canon of Supreme Mystery*, by Yang Xiong, translated and commentated by Michael Nylan. Albany: SUNY Press, 1993: 1–79.

———. "Textual Authority in pre-Han and Han." *Early China* 25 (2001): 1–54.

———. "Kongzi 孔子 and Mozi 墨子, the Classicists (Ru 儒) and the Mohists 墨, in Classical-Era Thinking." *Oriens Extremus* (2009): 5–20.

———. "Looking For Yang In All the Wrong Places: the Afterlife of Yang Xiong 揚雄, the Historian, from Late Eastern Han to the End of Six Dynasties." Unpublished conference paper, Dec. 2010.

———. *Yang Xiong and the Pleasures of Reading and Classical Learning*. New Haven: American Oriental Society, 2011.

———, transl. *Exemplary Figures: a complete translation of Yang Xiong's Fayan*. Seattle: University of Washington Press, 2013.

———. "Yang Xiong's Final *Fayan* Chapter: Rhetoric to What End and for Whom?" In *Facing the Monarch: Modes of Advice in the Early Chinese Court*, edited by Garret P.S. Olberding. Cambridge: Harvard University Asia Center, 2013: 237–272.

———. "Han Views of the Qin Legacy and the Late Western Han 'Classical Turn'." *Bulletin of the Museum of Far Eastern Antiquities* 79, forthcoming.

Nylan, Michael, and Thomas Wilson. *Lives of Confucius*. New York: Random House / Doubleday, 2010.

Pitner, Mark. "Embodied Geographies of Han Dynasty China: Yang Xiong and his Reception." PhD diss., University of Washington at Seattle, 2010.

Su Shi 蘇軾 (1036–1101). "Da Xie Minshi shu" 答謝民師書 (Reply to Mr. Xie). In *Qin Han shi shiwu jiang* 秦漢史十五講 (Fifteen Lectures on Qin-Han History), by Han Zhaoqi 韓兆琦 and Zhao Guohua 趙國華. Nanjing: Fenghuang chubanshe, 2010: 262–266.

Taniguchi Hiroshi 谷口洋. "Fu ni jijo o tsukeru koto: Ryō Kan no majiwari ni okeru sakusha no mezame" 賦に自序をつけること：兩漢の交における作者のめざめ (English title by author: The Addition of Author's Prefaces to Rhapsodies: The Awakening of the 'Writer' During the Transition from Former to Later Han). *Tōhōgaku* 東方學 119 (2010): 22–39.

Wang Rongbao 汪榮寶. *Fayan yishu* 法言義疏 (Fayan, Interpretations), 2 vols. Beijing: Zhonghua shuju, 1987 [1933]; compiled 1899, with more complete notes in 1911.

Wilhelm, Richard. *The I Ching; or Book of Changes*. Translated by Cary F. Bayes. New York: Pantheon Books, 1950.

Yang Haizheng 楊海崢. *Han Tang Shiji yanjiu lungao* 漢唐史記研究論稿. Jinan: Qi Lu shushe, 2003.

CHAPTER 8

A Ragbag of Odds and Ends? Argument Structure and Philosophical Coherence in *Zhuangzi* 26

Wim De Reu

This paper challenges the common reading of *Zhuangzi* 26 as a ragbag of odds and ends. I argue that the sections of this chapter may be read as making a coherent exposition. By offering a specific reading of the chapter's argumentative structure, I not only illuminate the philosophical relevance of previously neglected material, but also revise the interpretation of its well-known final section. I argue that this section does not—as is often assumed—deal with the dynamics of the relationship between 'language' and 'meaning,' but rather that it is better explained as making a distinction between two very different modes of linguistic engagement with any given social context. The chapter as a whole can plausibly be read as a critique both of patterned linguistic interactions and of the process of model emulation on which such interactions are based. I start my analysis by summarizing the current state of research on the later *Zhuangzi* chapters. In the second part of my analysis, I set forth preliminary evidence that suggests the plausibility of contextualizing the final section of the chapter against information from other sections. This evidence takes the form of three sets of explicit verbal connections that tie together the final and other sections. The third part of my analysis involves a close examination of the key terms of these connections as they appear in their contexts of utterance. From this basis, I proceed in part four to offer a contextually-grounded interpretation of the chapter's final section. Part five traces the main ideas of the chapter as they build from section to section. As a result, the chapter-level coherence of *Zhuangzi* 26 is established, thereby invalidating the so-called ragbag hypothesis. In the conclusion, I sum up my findings and briefly examine the chapter's literary form in relation to its philosophical position.

The Ragbag Hypothesis

This paper[1] examines "Waiwu" 外物 ("Things External," ch. 26), one of the Miscellaneous Chapters (*za pian* 雜篇) of the *Zhuangzi* 莊子. This chapter is lacking in manifest organization and contains a variety of writing styles. Moreover, the subject matter of its respective component sections appears to be unrelated. In view of this, "Waiwu" is regularly grouped with other enigmatic chapters from the later part of the *Zhuangzi* (particularly chapters 23–25, 27 and 32). Together, these chapters are commonly regarded as nothing more than "heterogeneous collections of fragments."[2] Angus C. Graham, who is the most influential proponent of this view in Western scholarship, maintains that they are "ragbags of odds and ends,"[3] while Chen Guying 陳鼓應 on the Chinese side frequently invokes phrases such as "resulting from mixed compilation" (雜纂而成) and "the various sections are unrelated in meaning" (各章意義不相關聯) to capture their perceived lack of coherence.[4] Overall, mainstream opinion holds that these chapters are made up of scraps that have been put together at random.

Reflective of this widely-held view is the fact that there is hardly any systematic research that has been undertaken on the later *Zhuangzi* chapters. Typically, sections of these later chapters are merely drawn upon to support or clarify ideas identified in other writings, either the Inner Chapters (*nei pian* 內篇) of the *Zhuangzi* or altogether different texts.[5] Even when subjected to

---

1 Research for this article was supported by grants from the Ministry of Science and Technology (Taiwan, R.O.C.). Reference numbers NSC 98-2410-H-002-148, NSC 99-2911-I-002-128, and NSC 100-2628-H-002-135-MY3. An earlier form of the article was presented at the conference "New Perspectives on Chinese Culture and Society: Literary Forms of Argument in Pre-modern China," held at The Queen's College, University of Oxford, 16–18 September 2009. I also benefited from discussing part of the primary text in a reading group whose participants included Dirk Meyer, C. Lynne Hong 洪嘉琳, and Larson Di Fiori.

2 Harold D. Roth, "*Chuang tzu*," In *Early Chinese Texts: A Bibliographical Guide*, ed. Michael Loewe (Berkeley, CA: Society for the Study of Early China and Institute of East Asian Studies, 1993), 57.

3 Angus C. Graham, trans. *Chuang-tzŭ: The Seven Inner Chapters and Other Writings from the Book "Chuang-tzŭ"* (London: Allen & Unwin, 1981), 28; Graham, *Disputers of the Tao: Philosophical Argument in Ancient China* (La Salle, Ill.: Open Court, 1989), 173.

4 See, for instance, Chen Guying 陳鼓應, comm. and trans., *Zhuangzi jinzhu jinyi* 莊子今註今譯. Rev. ed. (Taibei: Taiwan Shangwu, 1999), vol. 2: 643, 719, 745, 846.

5 The affinity between these chapters and the Inner Chapters (*nei pian* 內篇) has long been noted. Liu Xiaogan 劉笑敢 subsumes chapters 23–27 and 32 into the category of "*shu Zhuang pai*" 述莊派 (his label for chapters that most closely follow the thought of the Inner Chapters), while Graham not only lists a number of fragments as related to the Inner Chapters, but even

greater scrutiny, the later *Zhuangzi* chapters are not treated as meaningful entities in and of themselves. For instance, Liu Rongxian 劉榮賢 maintains in one comprehensive study that most of the Outer and Miscellaneous Chapters (*wai za pian* 外雜篇) of the *Zhuangzi*—and especially chapters such as "Waiwu"—lack central and unifying ideas. Liu suggests that research ought to proceed by taking the self-contained section as the basic unit of meaning,[6] and that the task of the text's interpreter is to break up chapters into sections and reorganize these sections into a new hierarchy of ideas.[7] This process of textual rearrangement can also be witnessed to a lesser extent in Graham's translation.[8] In short, the scholarship is characterized by a tendency to reduce later *Zhuangzi* chapters to convenient supporting material and by attempts to render these chapters meaningful through substantial textual rearrangement.

The ragbag view and its associated conventions for reading the later *Zhuangzi* chapters are—it needs to be stressed—not the product of an unsuccessful attempt to find coherence on the chapter level. Rather, apart from impressions regarding the varied outlook of individual chapters mentioned at the very beginning, this ragbag view—the standard hermeneutical position—is mainly inspired by text-historical factors.[9] It is not my concern in this paper to analyze the complicated and often conjectural issues surrounding text-historical fac-

---

incorporates some fragments into his reconstruction of those Inner Chapters. Their views are largely based on textual parallels and on corresponding technical terminology rather than on careful readings of the later chapters as meaningful wholes. See Liu Xiaogan, *Zhuangzi zhexue ji qi yanbian* 莊子哲學及其演變 (Beijing: Zhongguo shehui kexue chubanshe, 1987), 62–78; Graham, *Chuang-tzŭ*, 36–37; and Graham, "How Much of *Chuang-tzŭ* Did Chuang-tzŭ Write?" in *Studies in Chinese Philosophy and Philosophical Literature*, ed. Angus C. Graham (Singapore: Institute of East Asian Philosophies, National University of Singapore, 1986), 283–301.

6   Liu Rongxian 劉榮賢, *Zhuangzi wai za pian yanjiu* 莊子外雜篇研究 (Taibei: Lianjing, 2004), 19–21.
7   Ibid., 87–118.
8   See especially the "School of Chuang-tzŭ" part of his translation. Graham, *Chuang-tzŭ*, 37–38.
9   Regardless of the material that was circulating during the Warring States (ca. 481–222 BC) period, the *Zhuangzi* 莊子 was probably first compiled as a 52-*pian* 篇 work during the early Western Han 西漢 (206 BC–AD 8). It was edited by several scholars during the 3rd and 4th centuries, and assumed its current 33-*pian* length after a revision by Guo Xiang 郭象 (d. 312). For basic information and references on text-historical issues, please refer to Harold D. Roth, "Chuang tzu," in *Early Chinese Texts: A Bibliographical Guide*, ed. M. Loewe (Berkeley, CA: Society for the Study of Early China and Institute of East Asian Studies, 1993), 56–66. For recent work and additional references, see Liu, *Zhuangzi wai za pian yanjiu*, 1–74; and Esther Klein, "Were there 'Inner Chapters' in the Warring States? A New Examination of Evidence about the *Zhuangzi*," *T'oung Pao* 96 (2011): 299–369.

tors, since such research would itself require a dedicated lengthy study. What I do wish to point out at this juncture, however, is that text-historical factors can never settle a debate on the question of a text's coherence. Neither should text-historical factors divert our attention from the task of interpreting the content of a text. The question of coherence can only be settled by taking the text at face value and by trying to uncover its internal architecture. Thus, as I proceed to dispute the ragbag hypothesis for *Zhuangzi* 26, I will not be doing so by taking issue with text-historical factors. Instead, I will do so by showing how the sections of this chapter may be read as forming a coherent philosophical treatise. While I do believe that the chapter is compiled and edited in part from pre-existing material, I am not committed to any further position on the issue of dating and authorship. Even if the current "Waiwu" were the product of extensive later rearrangement, it should not be treated as a less-valuable remnant of past intellectual endeavors because of this fact.

Initial Plausibility: Explicit Verbal Connections

I divide "Waiwu" into twelve sections. The first eight sections are stable and generally agreed upon; it is on little less than the last quarter of the chapter where opinions diverge. This part of the chapter consists of several units. Based on structural considerations that will become evident in due course, I group these units into four sections, thus arriving at a total number of twelve sections for the chapter as a whole.[10]

The content of the sections can be briefly outlined as follows. Section 1 states that one should not interact with the world in a patterned or invariable manner. Sections 2 and 3 jointly enact the concern of section 1 by presenting antithetical evaluations of a single policy in the domain of politics. Sections 4 and 5 further this concern by problematizing the cultivation of set dispositions within master-disciple communities. Sections 6 and 7 turn to the subject of language and target strict categorization in favour of a more open, untutored and inclusive use of language. Section 8 contrasts the wandering of the ideal persona to the commitment of those who identify themselves with a particular

---

10   For alternative ways of grouping the final units, compare with Wang Shumin 王叔岷, ed. and annot. *Zhuangzi jiaoquan* 莊子校詮 (Taibei: Zhongyang yanjiuyuan lishi yuyan yanjiusuo, 1994), vol. 2: 1076–1088; and Chen, *Zhuangzi jinzhu jinyi*, vol. 2: 738–744. The validity of my interpretation does not depend on a particular grouping of these units. An overview of section divisions against the *Zhuangzi*'s two main concordances can be found in the appendix.

political or intellectual position; section 9 associates wandering with a cleared internal state in contrast to perceptive and cognitive obstruction. Sections 10 and 11 discuss the subject of patterned behaviour in concrete terms. They contrast those who are obsessively concerned with tools and standard remedies to the person uninterested in such methods. Section 12, finally, closes the chapter with a call to disregard patterns of linguistic interaction.

The final section plays a pivotal role in my exposition. It may be regarded as the culmination of the entire chapter. Incidentally, it is also one of the *Zhuangzi*'s more famous passages, and it occupies a prized position in the history of Chinese philosophy. At this point, I simply offer the Chinese text along with what may suffice for a standard translation, followed by a brief discussion.

> 12 (ICS 26/79/12-14; HY 26/75/48-49)[11]
> 荃者所以在魚，得魚而忘荃
> Traps are means to catch fishes; forget the traps once you've got the fishes.
>
> 蹄者所以在兔，得兔而忘蹄
> Snares are means to catch rabbits; forget the snares once you've got the rabbits.
>
> 言者所以在意，得意而忘言
> Words are means to catch ideas; forget the words once you've got the ideas.
>
> 吾安得夫忘言之人而與之言哉
> Where can one get that person who has forgotten words and have a word with him?

This passage owes its prominence to Wang Bi 王弼 (226–249), who appropriated the first three parallel lines to aid in expounding his view on the semiotic

---

11   Quotations from and references to the *Zhuangzi* are based on *Zhuangzi zhuzi suoyin* 莊子逐字索引, ICS Ancient Chinese Text Concordance Series 43 (Hong Kong: Commercial Press, 2000). I have taken liberties in changing punctuation. Textual variants and emendations are considered only insofar as significant and necessary, and important changes adopted will be justified in the footnotes. I also include the reference to *Zhuangzi yinde* 莊子引得, Harvard-Yenching Institute Sinological Index Series Supplement No. 20 (Cambridge MA: Harvard University Press, 1956). The syntax of the reference to both concordances follows the "chapter/page/line" pattern.

structure and interpretation of the *Zhouyi* 周易 (*Changes of Zhou*).¹² Wang Bi's borrowing also typifies (and perhaps initiated) a reading strategy that favours treatment of this passage in isolation, without its preceding sections. This decontextualized reading strategy of this passage understands the central relationship between *yan* 言 ("words," "language") and *yi* 意 ("ideas," "meanings," or, in some interpretations, *Dao*) in the third line solely on the basis of its analogy with traps/fishes and snares/rabbits, as set forth in the first two lines. The standard explanation that typically results from this reading strategy holds that language is a tool for catching elusive ideas; once those are got hold of, language can be dispensed with.¹³

This standard reading of the allegory is intuitively plausible and connects well with common assumptions about the predominance of content over mere linguistic expression. Other readings, however, remain possible. Notably, Hans-Georg Moeller has argued in detail that the third line contains a play-on-words that upsets the standard interpretation.¹⁴ He holds that the phrase "*de yi*" 得意 not only carries the literal sense of "to get the meaning/idea," but also the more idiomatic sense of "to get one's desires" and "to be content/satisfied." This satisfaction, he argues, consists in a Daoist context paradoxically in *not* having (or, in having eaten up) desires, meanings or ideas. In contrast to the standard interpretation, according to which one is left with meanings and ideas once words are forgotten, Moeller's position is that "the sage should *neither be stuck with words nor with ideas or meanings.*"¹⁵

Moeller deserves credit for proposing a critical re-evaluation of a stock passage. I agree with his view that Wang Bi instrumentalized rather than interpreted the allegory, and that he did so by disregarding the context in which the allegory arose.¹⁶ My position differs from Moeller's, however, on the matter of *how* to contextualize the allegory. With the exception of a number of *Zhuangzi* quotations that serve to cast initial doubt on the standard interpretation, Moeller's argument for interpreting "*de yi*" as "giving up" rather than "getting at" meanings/ideas heavily relies on Guo Xiang's 郭象 (d. 312) reading of the allegory, as well as on two *Liezi* 列子 passages, along with the commentary of

---

12 See the "Ming xiang" 明象 section of his *Zhouyi lüeli* 周易略例 included in Lou Yulie 樓宇烈, *Wang Bi ji jiaoshi* 王弼集校釋 (Taibei: Huazheng shuju, 1992), 597–609.
13 For a basic overview of the standard interpretation and its genesis, see Hans-Georg Möller, "Zhuangzi's Fishnet Allegory: A Text-Critical Analysis," *Journal of Chinese Philosophy* 27.4 (2000): 490–492.
14 See Möller, "Zhuangzi's Fishnet Allegory" and Moeller, *Daoism Explained: From the Dream of the Butterfly to the Fishnet Allegory* (Chicago/La Salle, Ill.: Open Court, 2004), 55–62.
15 Ibid., 57.
16 Möller, "Zhuangzi's Fishnet Allegory," 491–492.

Zhang Zhan 張湛 (4th century). Like other scholars, Moeller overlooks the scope for interpreting the allegory in its direct textual context. In the absence of a local anchor of interpretation, he resorts to a broader narrative in Daoist philosophy.

Contrary to both Moeller's reading and the standard reading, I conjecture that the meaning of the fishnet allegory is grounded in the context of *Zhuangzi* 26, and that the allegory may be read as the culmination or closure of the entire chapter. In order to demonstrate the initial plausibility of this interpretation, we can start by noticing that it is precisely this final section that contains the largest number of explicit verbal connections with the chapter's other sections. These explicit verbal connections can be divided into three sets:

- *Suoyi* 所以 (lit. "that-by-which," also "tools," "remedies," "methods") appears in the first half of each of the three parallel lines. While the phrase "*suoyi*" typically functions as a common grammatical device, it is semantically charged in this chapter: *suoyi* (methods) are the topic of discussion in the second unit of section 10. In addition, the use of "*suoyi*" in reference to tools in section 12 (*quan* 筌 'traps,' *ti* 蹄 'snares') is adumbrated by a focus on tools and remedies at the very end of section 9 and in the first unit of section 10, respectively.
- *Yan* 言 shows up in sections 6 and 7. In section 12, it resurfaces as a tool that needs to be disregarded (*wang* 忘). The term "*wang*" also appears in section 5 as part of the phrase "*liang wang*" 兩忘 ('to disregard on both sides').
- *Yi* 意 appears once more in section 8 as the object of "*cheng*" 承 ('to accept'). Interestingly, this leaves us with three verb-object combinations containing the term "*yi*" as object. The other two, found in section 12, are "*zai yi*" 在意 and "*de yi*" 得意, commonly interpreted similarly as 'catching ideas' and 'getting ideas' respectively.

While these explicit verbal connections stand in need of further elaboration, they do suggest that chapter 26 may be more than a mere collection of unrelated fragments. The repetition of key terms and key verbal units is a technique that is widely and deliberately used to enhance textual coherence in all sorts of writings. We have to entertain the possibility that the verbal connections listed above perform such a function of enhancing coherence in chapter 26 of the *Zhuangzi*—a chapter which, after all, consists of a mere 49 lines of text.[17] In what follows, I will try to show that these explicit verbal connections are

---

17 According to the line count included in Harvard-Yenching's *Zhuangzi yinde*.

meaningful rather than coincidental. In doing so, I will occasionally construct bridges of interpretation to get to a contextually informed reading that would otherwise not be achievable. As a methodological contribution to this volume my interpretation of this text might also show, in a more general way, how the reconstruction of a text's coherent internal structure and the construction of interpretative links between textual parts go hand in hand and have to be related.

Fleshing out the Connections: Key Terms and Contexts

In this part, I provide detailed discussions of the key terms identified in the three sets of explicit verbal connections introduced above. I do this by closely scrutinizing the textual contexts in which these terms appear. I will argue, firstly, that *suoyi* are deeply ingrained and harmful patterns of interaction; secondly, that "*yan*" primarily refers to term judgments, that we can distinguish between two differently-evaluated modes of using these term judgments, and that "*wang*" stands for a process or practice of disregarding (linguistic) conventions; and thirdly, that "*yi*" simply stands for opinions or views current within society. In addition, I will point out a twofold contrast underlying each of the three sets of explicit verbal connections. I begin here first by discussing the context related to the phrase "*suoyi*."

First Set of Explicit Verbal Connections: Suoyi *or "That-by-which"*

Section 9 consists of two units with contrasting content in their correlated opening lines. As we will see further on, the opening line of the first unit (9.1) describes a wholesome and unobstructed state that is characterized by the keenness of the sensory organs and the cognitive faculties. The opening line of the second unit (9.2) lists instances of corruptive human tendencies. Segment 9.2.2 below follows on right after the opening line of the second unit, concludes the section, and functions as a point of transition into the next section. It relates a simple sequence of events, followed by an observation revealing the author's stance.

9.2.2 (ICS 26/79/5-6; HY 26/75/42/42-43)
春雨日時，草木怒生，銚鎒於是乎始脩。草木之到植者過半而不知其然。
When spring rains are timely, weeds grow vigorously, and at that point weeding tools start to be applied. More than half of the weeds will shoot back up, yet [weeders] are not aware that this is so.[18]

---

18   The second part of the final sentence requires a change of subject, unless one would like

Segment 9.2.2 describes the use of a certain method (the application of weeding tools) to cope with an undesirable situation (fast-growing weeds). The author is sceptical of the long-term benefit of this method—most weeds will shoot back up—and is critical of those putting the tools to use: the weeders do not realize how stubborn the weeds are. The image conveyed is one of subjects diligently tending to a situation, unaware of the limited impact of their efforts.

Within the context of section 9, the use of tools and methods may be viewed as unwholesome. They are symbols of human activity. Unit 9.1 emphasizes that human activity, not Heaven, is to be blamed for a decrease in perceptive and cognitive clarity (infra). Convenient solutions, we may surmise, are readily transformed into habitual and mindless patterns of action, and thereby obstruct one's grasp and limit one's responsiveness to the situation at hand.

10.1 (ICS 26/79/8-9; HY 26/75/43-44)
靜然可以補病；眥搣可以休老；寧可以止遽。雖然，若是，勞者之務也，非佚者之所嘗過而問焉。[19]
Resting can be used to make up for an illness; eye-massage can be used to ease [symptoms of] ageing; relaxation can be used to stop anxiety. Even though this is so, such things are affairs of those who strain themselves; [these things are] not what the person at ease has ever gone to ask them [i.e. those who strain themselves] about.[20]

---

to maintain that the weeds themselves are unaware of their own vitality. This is unlikely. One could focus on natural phenomena without any reference to weeding tools. The reference to such tools indicates that human activity is the topic of segment 9.2.2, and it is this that necessitates a change of subject. "Weeders" is the most obvious candidate for the vacant subject position. The context of section 9 further establishes *bu zhi* 不知 (not being aware) as a negative quality (infra).

19 Traditional editions contain the negative "*wei*" 未 ('not yet') in front of the past tense indicator "*chang*" 嘗 ('once', 'ever') to form the combination "*wei chang*" 未嘗 ('never'). This results in the final phrase containing a double negation (the other negative being the noun phrase negator "*fei*" "非"). The effect of this double negation is that the *yizhe* 佚者 (person at ease) *has* at one point gone to ask the *laozhe* (those straining themselves) about the remedies they apply. On this reading, any separate mention of a contrastive *yizhe* loses its relevance. I therefore agree with a number of other scholars that the traditional editions contain one redundant negation (see Chen, *Zhuangzi jinzhu jinyi*, vol. 2: 743, n. 3; Wang, *Zhuangzi jiaoquan*, vol. 2: 1084-1085, n. 3). Despite the repeated use of the phrase "*wei chang guo er wen yan*" 未嘗過而問焉 in unit 10.2, I choose to omit "*wei*" in favour of "*fei*" because keeping "*fei*" better brings out the overall noun phrase structure of the final phrases.

20 Note that "*wen yan*" 問焉 should be understood as "to ask [something] of someone," rather than as "to ask about something." Since the particle "*yan*" 焉 is a compound of "*yu zhi*" 於之, "*wen yan*" equals "*wen yu zhi*" 問於之. The direct object of the ditransitive verb "*wen*" 問 is in the present phrase expressed by the pronoun "*suo*" 所. The implicit prepo-

Unit 10.1 starts by listing three remedies recognized as effective in treating various forms of physical discomfort. These remedies are similar to the weeding tools, in that both are applied in an effort to relieve undesirable conditions. The parallel with segment 9.2.2 becomes more sophisticated when we note that remedies, too, have a temporally-limited impact, and that these remedies may be administered without fully recognizing that symptoms are likely to recur, just like weeding.

Unit 10.1 does more, however, than merely present additional examples of patterned behaviour from another sphere of human activity. The description of remedies is followed by a novel element: the contrast between *laozhe* 勞者 ("those straining themselves") and *yizhe* 佚者 ("person at ease"). The former, the *laozhe*, are dedicated to the routine application of prescriptive methods. Their designation as "*laozhe*" may be explained by the need for continuous effort, aggravated by the strain they put upon declining perceptive and cognitive faculties.[21] The *yizhe*, by contrast, stands as the positive counterimage of the *laozhe*. Not only can we infer that this *yizhe* is not committed to the use of methods, his non-commitment is also phrased in terms that suggest that methods are consciously learned (過而問焉). The *yizhe*, then, is a wholesome individual who does not subject himself to the mastery and routine application of prescriptive techniques.

10.2 (ICS 26/79/9-10; HY 26/75/44-45)

聖人之所以駴天下，神人未嘗過而問焉；
賢人所以駴世，聖人未嘗過而問焉；
君子所以駴國，賢人未嘗過而問焉；
小人所以合時，君子未嘗過而問焉。

That by which the sagacious person drums up the world, the numinous person has never gone to ask him [i.e. the sagacious person] about.

That by which the talented person drums up the generation, the sagacious person has never gone to ask him [i.e. the talented person] about.

That by which the person of high calibre drums up the state, the talented person has never gone to ask him [i.e. the person of high calibre] about.

That by which the person of low calibre confines the times, the person of high calibre has never gone to ask him [i.e. the one of low calibre] about.[22]

---

sitional object "*zhi*" 之 therefore unambiguously refers to the one to whom a question is posed. Within the context of unit 10.1, the referent of "*zhi*" is most likely the *laozhe*.

21 Note the irony of introducing the *laozhe* in a context concerned with health. In trying to relieve discomfort, they create discomfort for themselves.

22 As in unit 10.1, "*wen yan*" should be understood as "to ask [something] of someone." The referent of "someone" changes here with every new line.

On a textual level, unit 10.2 accomplishes two things. Firstly, it explicitly picks up (yet directly negates) *"chang guo er wen yan"* 嘗過而問焉 from the previous unit, 10.1, and merges concrete methods into *"suoyi."*[23] These connections import the contrast between the *laozhe* and the *yizhe* from the previous unit into the current unit. These connections are also the main reason for considering the two units, 10.1 and 10.2, as a single section. Secondly, this unit introduces a five-level scale with the numinous person (*shenren* 神人) at the top and the person of low calibre (*xiaoren* 小人) at the bottom. In comparison with the other types of persons, the defining features of the *shenren* are the absence both of *suoyi* and of a corresponding object of projected change. These features characterize the *shenren* as a perfect *yizhe*. At the opposite end of the scale, the *xiaoren* only engages with things by taking recourse to *suoyi*. He is the ultimate *laozhe*. In between the two extremes of *shenren* and *xiaoren*, we find three more types of persons. They are both *lao* and *yi*, relative to gradually narrowing spatio-temporal scopes. The sagacious person (*shengren* 聖人), the talented person (*xianren* 賢人), and the person of high calibre (*junzi* 君子) each strain themselves in handling affairs on their own level, while taking no interest in the methods applied on the next level down.[24] Since the *yizhe* can only be described negatively in comparison to a previously established point of reference, the scale is composed in reverse linear order.

The above analysis goes a long way in shedding light on unit 10.2. Producing a more complete grasp of its content, however, requires us to fully exploit the connections and to spell out the novel elements that the unit contributes. The interpretation of unit 10.1 above benefited from a parallel reading with segment 9.2.2. The existing connections between 10.1 and 10.2 also mean that a contextual reading of 10.2 is needed. The implication here is that the measures employed on each stratum are only temporarily effective and are subject to continued renewal. The main actors, for their part, are oblivious to the limited use of their efforts. They are caught up in the action and strain themselves in their attempts to handle their surroundings. What unit 10.2 adds is, firstly, the projection of corrective measures onto the socio-political sphere, and secondly, a heightened awareness that these measures, although employed to bring about change for the better, create discomfort for the objects they are intended to change. Not only do they drum up or alarm/distress (*xie* 駴) society, but

---

23 In unit 10.1, the overall noun phrase structure required the noun phrase negator *"fei."* Here, in unit 10.2, the absence of a noun phrase structure in the final phrase of each line prompts the negative *"wei"* to directly precede *"chang guo er wen yan."*

24 The import of this classification is limited to the present unit. Section 6, for example, criticizes the numinous (*shen* 神), while section 5 presents the sagacious person (*shengren* 聖人) as a positive counterimage.

their application to increasingly limited spatio-temporal scopes eventually leads to communities that are confined and closed off (*he* 合).[25] These measures, then, not only strain those who apply them, but they also adversely impact those to whom they are applied.

We could conclude our discussion of the first set of connections at this point, for section 11 seems to consist merely of semi-legendary anecdote unconnected to the previous units. Nevertheless, as it is positioned between sections 10 and 12, both of which refer to methods, it may prove instructive to attempt a contextual reading. In what follows, I will first plainly describe the content of section 11, and then on that basis construct a bridge between section 11 and the preceding units by suggesting that it is possible to read section 11 in terms of the emergence of *suoyi* and the distinction between the *yizhe* and the *laozhe*. Such a reading will sharpen our understanding of the issues at hand.

> **11** (ICS 26/79/10-12; HY 26/75/46-48)
> 演門有親死者，以善毀爵為官師。其黨人毀而死者半。
> By the Yan gate, there was someone whose parents had died and who was honoured with the rank of unit head on the basis of his excellence at emaciating himself. Half of his fellow villagers died while emaciating themselves.
> 堯與許由天下，許由逃之；湯與務光，務光怒之；紀他聞之，帥弟子而踆於窾水，諸侯弔之三年，申徒狄因以踣河。
> Yao offered the empire to Xu You; Xu You fled from him. Tang offered [the empire] to Wu Guang; Wu Guang took offence at him. Ji Tuo heard about this and led his disciples to retreat at the Kuan River, [yet] the feudal lords implored him for three years. Shentu Di, because of this, threw himself into the Yellow River.

Section 11 consists of two contrastive strains. The first strain describes an act of acceptance (the person at the Yan 演 gate accepting the honour and rank conferred upon him), whereas the second strain consists of several acts of refusal (starting with Xu You 許由 declining the empire given to him).[26] This contrast is readily visible. What is harder to spot, however, is a second kind of contrast present *within* each of the individual strains. Fully identifying this contrast requires us to analyze the two strains in more detail.

---

25 "*Xie*" 虩 means 'to strike a drum with the sound of a thunderstrike' (*Hanyu da zidan* 漢語大字典 [Hubei cishu chubanshe/Sichuan cishu chubanshe, 1986–1990], vol. 7: 4556). It is interchangeable with "*hai*" 駭 ('frightened horse,' ibid., vol. 7: 4555). *He* 合 carries the meaning of 'to move things together' as when one brings the lips together to close the mouth (ibid., vol. 1: 581). It has here, I submit, a negative connotation: an activity resulting in a suffocating internal unity.

26 For the theme of throne refusal in ancient Chinese legend, see Sarah Allan, *The Heir and the Sage: Dynastic Legend in Early China* (San Francisco: Chinese Materials Center, 1981). By not opposing Xu You 許由 to Shun 舜 (who accepted the throne from Yao 堯), section 11 bypasses the heir-sage-mediator complex.

The first strain consists of three elements: the act of self-emaciation of the initially-anonymous person at the Yan gate, this person's being awarded the rank of "unit head" (*guan shi* 官師), and the fatal outcome for the villagers who emulate him.[27] The second element plays a pivotal role: it is the person at the Yan gate's official status that prompts his villagers to take emaciation as a reliable measure that one can take to secure success. They regard their now-famous fellow as a worthy model, and hyperbolically imitate his act. Eager for success and recognition, they become *too* good at emaciating themselves. By contrast, the original act of the person at the Yan gate seems to have been performed spontaneously without any modeling or specific purpose in mind. It is simply what he did in response to the death of his parents.

The second strain chronicles a chain of copycat behaviour modelled upon Xu You's original act of refusal. The case of Ji Tuo 紀他 is particularly instructive. Not only does he hear/learn about (*wen* 聞) the previous instance, but he also sets an example for his disciples by taking his act of refusal to a new level: he flees away *prior* to being approached.[28] Aware that the feudal lords still managed to locate Ji Tuo—and perhaps secretly aspiring to the recognition and fame that Ji Tuo gained for his failed escape—the final actor on the stage, Shentu Di 申徒狄, resorts to the most drastic act of refusal: he commits suicide. Here, as in the previous strain, we bear witness to hyperbolic imitations of an original act that eventually lead to self-inflicted death. We also see the presence of a role-model in the process of emulation.

My suggestion is that the contrast within each of both strains illustrates the distinction between the *yizhe* and the *laozhe*, as well as signposts the emergence of *suoyi* as representative of concrete methods. Both the anonymous person at the Yan gate and Xu You may be regarded as *yizhe*. The former does not appear to perform his act with an external goal in mind, nor is his emaciation described as consciously learned and applied. The latter is known as the first figure to refuse the throne, and as such his act is truly original. The other figures (the villagers, Ji Tuo, and Shentu Di), by contrast, can be construed as *laozhe*. They regard emaciation and refusal as default responses or methods (*suoyi*) to cope with a given situation. Developing such *suoyi* consists in the hyperbolic and mechanical imitation of an original act. This can take a sudden

---

27 "*Guanshi*" 官師 either generically refers to lower-level officials or to someone at the head (*shi* 師) of a unit of such officials. See *Hanyu da cidan* 漢語大詞典 (Shanghai: Shanghai cishu chubanshe/Hanyu da cidian chubanshe, 1986–1993), vol. 3: 1388 for examples.

28 Note also that the rulers reaching out to Ji Tuo 紀他 are mere feudal lords (*zhuhou* 諸侯), in contrast to the elevated sage-ruler Yao who approached Xu You. While this feature corresponds to a change in historical reality, it is consistent with the notion of hyperbolic imitation, and may have been employed for this very reason.

(first strain) or gradual (second strain) form. In both cases, however, a pivotal role is played by a figure of authority. Imitating the example leads to a strained response and, ultimately, a disastrous outcome.

This contextual reading of section 11 turns apparently trivial, semi-legendary narratives into illustrations of the adverse consequences of *suoyi*-methods. It also enriches our understanding of the preceding discussion in two ways. Firstly, the *yizhe* (the anonymous person at the Yan gate and Xu You) are not contrasted to the *laozhe* in terms of non-action: they engage themselves in the same actions as the *laozhe* (here, emaciation and refusal). The contrast has rather to be found in social organization and in the way that actions are performed. The *yizhe* is not part of a group surrounding a role model; he acts on his own initiative and is not intent on a particular outcome. Nevertheless, his actions apparently match the situation. The *laozhe* takes the contextualized action of the *yizhe* and develops this into a pattern or method (*suoyi*) to be applied more generally and mechanically across situations.[29] These methods become the 'proper' thing to do. They are turned into objects of learning and are strictly and unquestioningly adhered to, yet seem out of touch with reality. Secondly, the presence of the *yizhe-laozhe* distinction within *both* strains indicates that the target of these strains' criticism is neither the act of acceptance nor the act of refusal per se. Rather, criticism is directed against patterned response irrespective of its content. This point is relevant because unit 10.2 in particular could leave one with the impression that commitment to the mechanical application of methods only occurs in a context of practising politics. While the application of methods is perhaps more typical in such a setting, the second strain of section 11 makes it clear that patterned response also takes place in circles of political refusers. They wish to remedy a situation just as their politically-active counterparts do (for example, when being offered the throne or a high position). Their *suoyi*-response consists in refusal.

I will presently conclude my findings regarding the first set of explicit verbal connections. Firstly, on a structural level, we may see section 10 as the centerpiece of the that-by-which (*suoyi*) set. The two units of this section are internally linked via the expression "(*wei*) *chang guo er wen yan*" and the implosion

---

29   This focuses unit 10.2. It is not that the *shenren* does not do anything at all. He does perform some actions, which the *shengren* develops into harmful methods. The *shenren* is not interested in these methods. The *shengren* also possesses some authenticity. His acts are developed into methods on the next lower level, and so on. Significantly, unit 10.2 avoids associating *yizhe* with *suoyi*. It does not, for instance, state: "the *suoyi* by which the *shenren* does things is further developed by the *shengren*." The *yizhe* does do something, but the harmful *suoyi* development properly belongs with the *laozhe*.

of remedies into the term "*suoyi*." In addition, section 10 is connected to its surrounding sections. Segment 9.2.2 and unit 10.1 both list standard methods of interaction—*suoyi*—which allows for the cross-projection of features between them. Section 11 can be understood to be illustrating the *yizhe-laozhe* distinction introduced in section 10. Secondly, in terms of its content, the "that-by-which" set of connections contains three main elements. They are summed up as follows:

> SUOYI. Ingrained patterns/methods mechanically applied across situations; learned by imitation to a degree that is excessive or hyperbolic; provide some benefit, yet adversely impact both agents and objects of change; performed without full understanding of situation.
> LAOZHE. Those committed to *suoyi*. The category '*laozhe*' is complex as it may incorporate people with contrastive values and worldviews, such as political refusers and the politically active. I will refer to this contrast as 'content-contrast.'
> YIZHE. Those *not* committed to *suoyi*. They differ from the *laozhe* not in the content but in the *mode* of their actions, that is, the way their actions are performed. I will refer to this contrast as 'mode-contrast.'

Second Set of Connections: YAN or 'Term Judgments'

Sections 6 and 7 contain valuable material for understanding the nature and function of *yan*. They will take up most of our attention. We start, however, by taking a brief look at the phrase "*liang wang*" in section 5. This phrase not only relates to the following discussion, but also contextualizes the expression "*wang yan*" 忘言 in the final section.

The final part of section 5 contains a critique of Zhongni 仲尼 (Confucius) and Lao Laizi 老萊子 (infra). Though being different in their stances towards society—these two characters vie for a position and lead a life of reclusion, respectively—both Zhongni and Lao Laizi gather a following of disciples and hence qualify as masters. The final part of section 5 contrasts them with the sagacious person.

> 5 (ICS 26/78/7-8; HY 26/74/22-23)
> 與其譽堯而非桀，不如兩忘而閉其所譽，反無非傷也，動無非邪也。聖人躊躇以興事，以每成功。
> Compared to their praising Yao and condemning Jie, it would be better to "disregard on both sides" and to [thereby] block the objects of their praise, [since] in opposing there is nothing but harm, and in stimulating there is nothing but wickedness. The sagacious person is wavering in initiating affairs so as to aim for accomplishment.

Zhongni and Lao Laizi are experts at praising-stimulating (*yu* 譽, *dong* 動) and condemning-opposing (*fei* 非, *fan* 反). Praise is reserved exclusively for the good (Yao), while so-called evil (Jie) is invariably condemned. This praising/condemning creates a sharp cognitive distinction and instils fixed patterns of preference in themselves and in their disciples. It also turns "the good" into a dominant presence. Contrary to the constructive projects of Zhongni and Lao Laizi, the narrator calls for an end to the dominance of the moral paragon through a process or practice of deconstruction called *"liang wang"* 兩忘 ('disregarding on both sides'). The proposed alternative is the *chouchu* 躊躇 (lit. 'strolling back and forth,' hence 'wavering,' or 'hesitant') mindset of the sagacious person. The sagacious person, it appears, does not rely on the quick responses that are associated with masters and their followers. He is not as clear-cut and predictable, he contemplates various possibilities and, the text suggests, he accomplishes more.

Within the context of section 5, *"liang wang"* refers to a process or practice of disregarding both of the formerly acquired associations of "praise-good" and "condemn-evil."[30] The unlearning of such social conventions results in a wavering perspective: preference-based discriminations once taken for granted are forsaken, and the dominance of the moral paragon is brought to an end. As such, we may surmise that the phrase *"wang yan"* in the final section refers to the process or practice of disregarding ingrained linguistic conventions. I now move on to the discussion of *yan* in sections 6 and 7.

Section 6 consists of two units: 6.1 is a description of events and 6.2 is an evaluation of these events. The concern with language does not become explicit until the final statement of the evaluation at the end of the entire section: "Little children, despite not having had master-teachers since birth, are able to *yan*. This is because they dwell with those who are able to *yan*" (嬰兒生无石師而能言，與能言者處也). A plausible reading should explain this statement in relation to the context of its utterance. Below is unit 6.1.

6.1 (ICS 26/78/11-17; HY 26/74/24-28)
宋元君夜半而夢人被髮闚阿門，曰：「予自宰路之淵，予為清江使河伯之所，漁者余且得予。」元君覺，使人占之，曰：「此神龜也。」君曰：「漁者有余且乎？」左右曰：「有。」君曰：「令余且會朝。」明日，余且朝。君曰：「漁何得？」對曰：「且之網得白龜焉，其圓五尺。」君曰：「獻若之龜。」龜至，君再欲殺之，再欲活之，心疑，卜之，曰：「殺龜以卜吉。」乃刳龜，七十二鑽而无遺筴。

---

30 It is worth mentioning the expression cognate to this, which is *"liang xing"* 兩行 (*Zhuangzi* ICS 2/5/5-6). In chapter 2, *"liang xing"* refers to walking both of two alternative paths. Arguably, *liang wang* is the mental counterpart of (and precedes) *liang xing*.

> Lord Yuan of Song, in the midst of night, dreamed of a man with hair hanging over his shoulders, peering through the side door, and saying: "I come from the Zailu currents. I was sent to the residence of the earl of the Yellow River by Clear Yangzi. The fisherman Yu Ju caught me." When Lord Yuan woke up, he had someone interpret it. [The interpreter] said: "This is a numinous turtle." The lord said: "Is there a Yu Ju among the fishermen?" The attendants said: "There is." The lord said: "Order Yu Ju to come to court." The next day, Yu Ju appeared at court. The lord said: "What did you catch, fisherman?" [The fisherman] replied: "My nets caught a white turtle, its girth is five feet." The lord said: "Present that turtle." After the turtle had arrived, the lord now wanted to kill it, then wanted to keep it alive. [His] heart-mind was in doubt, and he had the matter divined. [The diviner] said: "Kill the turtle so as to use it in divining fortune." The turtle was thereupon scraped out. It was drilled seventy-two times without any failed yarrow stalks.[31]

Following the account of the lord's dream, this unit may be analyzed against its two central questions, both of which need the help of an expert in order to be resolved. The first question deals with the nature of the creature that appeared in the dream. It is probably prompted by the confusing experience of the dream itself where, strangely enough, a human being (*ren* 人) introduces himself as if he were a water creature. A dream expert is consulted and interprets that it is a numinous turtle (*shen gui* 神龜). The second question addresses the issue of what to do with the turtle once it has been presented at court. The dilemma is framed as a choice between killing (*sha* 殺) the turtle and keeping it alive (*huo* 活). The lord's heart-mind is in a state of doubt (*xin yi* 心疑) and the matter is settled by an expert who divines that the turtle is to be killed for use in divination.

The story contains valuable information concerning divination practices. As it is presented in the two instances of this paragraph, divination serves to remove confusion or uncertainty, whether about a state of affairs or about a future course of action. Eliminating ambivalence requires one to make a clear and irrevocable choice among alternative possibilities, 'human being' versus

---

31 *Ce* 筴 are yarrow stalks used in divination. Marc Kalinowski observes that they may be used in combination with turtle divination, and describes a case exhibiting both turtle and yarrow stalk divination where yarrow stalks are used to verify a prediction made through turtle consultation. The phrase "*wu yi ce*" 無遺筴 in the present context implies that all of the turtle's predictions are subsequently confirmed by yarrow stalk divination. Marc Kalinowski, "Diviners and Astrologers under the Eastern Zhou: Transmitted Texts and Recent Archaeological Discoveries," in *Early Chinese Religion: Part One: Shang though Han (1250 BC 220 AD)*, ed. John Lagerwey and Marc Kalinowski (Leiden: Brill, 2009), vol. 1: 351–356.

'turtle' in the first instance, and 'killing' versus 'keeping alive' in the second instance. The choice, uttered as a statement by an expert, is understood as a prediction open to verification. In the former case, the dream expert's statement leads the lord to reason through to the 'turtle' alternative, prompting him to make inquiries about the existence of the fisherman and his catch, both of which are brought to court in succession. In the latter case, the turtle, after being killed and scraped, indeed proves expert at prediction, which in turn gives credence to the foresight of the diviner.

Given these multiple confirmations, divination appears to be a highly reliable practice, providing guidance. This definitive measure of success, combined with the function of satisfying a craving for definite answers, would seem to account for the lord's dependence on such practices. A good case could be made, then, for the claim that divination is valuable and useful. Nevertheless, it is precisely this claim that is questioned in the subsequent evaluation in unit 6.2.

6.2 (ICS 26/78/17-20; HY 26/74/28-31)

1C 仲尼曰

2A 神龜能見夢於元君而
不能避余且之網

3B 知能七十二鑽而无遺筴
不能避剖腸之患

4C 如是則

5B 知有所困

6A 神有所不及也

7C 雖有至知[至神]

8B 萬人謀之

9A 魚不畏網而畏鵜鶘

10B 去小知而大知明

11A 去善而自善矣

12C 嬰兒生无石師而能言
與能言者處也

Zhongni said: "The numinous turtle is capable of appearing in a dream to Lord Yuan, yet unable to avoid Yu Ju's nets. [Its] knowledge is capable of not failing any yarrow stalks despite being drilled seventy-two times, yet unable to avoid the disaster of having its intestines scraped out. As such, then, there are cases where knowledge encounters difficulties, and there are cases where the numinous falls short. Even if [the turtle] had ultimate knowledge, a myriad people would [still] consult it. [Even if it were

A RAGBAG OF ODDS AND ENDS? 261

ultimately numinous], as a water animal [it] would [still only] fear pelicans while being fearless of nets. In getting rid of small knowledge, great wisdom will become manifest. In getting rid of being sublime, you will become sublime-of-yourself. Little children, despite not having had master-teachers since birth, are able to *yan*. This is because they dwell with those who are able to *yan*."

While the narrative of unit 6.1 fixates on the questions posed by the lord, unit 6.2, narrated by Zhongni, focuses on the turtle.[32] It is composed in loose Interlocking Parallel Style (IPS), the two strains of which represent the turtle's central features. Strain A refers to the turtle's numinous qualities (*shen* 神), in particular its ability to appear in dreams. Strain B discusses its knack for knowledge (*zhi* 知).[33] Since knowledge is understood here as foresight in divination, strain B topically relates to unit 6.1. The remaining C-elements, of which line 7 is a clear instance of a *pars pro toto* construction, are related to both A and B strains.[34]

Let us take a first look at the argument. The paragraph starts by identifying a flaw (lines 2–6): although capable of amazing feats, the turtle's numinous and predictive abilities are surprisingly useless in offering basic protection, and their range of applications does have limits. The paragraph then continues by formulating a solution (lines 7–11). The shortcoming of the turtle's numinous and predictive features cannot be resolved by simply enhancing these features. On the contrary, the proposed solution consists in the very removal of those features. This implies that these otherwise impressive features are not

---

32 Interestingly, Zhongni 仲尼 is here staged as a mouthpiece criticizing a view very much like his own (and commending a position very much unlike his own). I will have more to say about this and other writing strategies later on.

33 For Interlocking Parallel Style, see Rudolf G. Wagner, *The Craft of a Chinese Commentator: Wang Bi on the Laozi* (Albany: State University of New York Press, 2000), 53–113. Each strain contains a mix of open (explicitly repeated) and closed (associated) terminology. As for the easier strain B, "*zhi*" 知 appears in lines 3B, 5B and 10B, while *mou* 謀 is the result of the turtle's *zhi* at making predictions (people wish to consult the turtle; this is also why the turtle is killed, which relates back to the second part of 3B). As for strain A, "*shen*" 神 appears in 2A and 6A; line 9A explicitly picks up the turtle's being netted (*wang* 網) from the second part of 2A; line 11, being parallel to 10B, properly belongs to strain A, and its key term "*shan*" 善 hence needs to be read in a way which brings out the connection to *shen* (I propose to translate "*shan*" as 'sublime').

34 For a description of *pars pro toto* constructions, see ibid., 69-72. If line 7C were not read as a *pars pro toto*, then the *sui you* 雖有 argument which introduces a possible solution to the shortcomings of the turtle's features (infra) would only relate to strain B. This would leave the remainder of strain A unaccounted for. Line 7 is hence most plausibly read as a *pars pro toto* C-element (with an explicit B and a supplemented A component). I also suggest to read line 12C as a *pars pro toto* (infra).

merely useless, but moreover that they constitute the very reason for the turtle's failure at self-preservation. The removal of these features will reveal qualitatively different—and presumably safer—kinds of talent and wisdom. The final statement (line 12) thereupon commends untutored yet able children as epitomising the viable alternative.

This outline provides a basic overview of the argument as it develops within unit 6.2. What, however, could be so forbidding about the turtle's features? Admittedly, these features put the turtle through much trouble: its numinous ability, evident from the dream as well as from its earlier service as envoy, exposed it to capture and to dream-interpretation, which in turn set off a series of events leading to its eventual death. The fatal result of the turtle's other feature—a knack for foresight—is equally clear, since its talent at divination, recognized by the diviner, was the precise reason for killing it. Yet, why could no increase in ability have prevented such an outcome? All that would have been needed, one could argue, was for the turtle to make a prediction about its own knack for divination and to extend its numinous ability to include a fear of fishing nets. Why could no increase in ability have prompted the turtle to do so?

This question is not directly addressed in the text as it stands. Nevertheless, it is an important question in that it probes into the very core of what is problematic about the turtle's features. I propose to understand the trouble with the turtle's qualities in terms of the obstacles that they pose to critical self-reflection. The first paragraph presents diviners as experts not at asking questions but at answering them; they eliminate other people's doubt without themselves showing any signs of doubt. The turtle, as an expert at divination, does not doubt. By extension, the turtle's talent prevents it from reflecting upon its own predictive ability. As reflection and doubt are prerequisites for any call for a prediction, the turtle is unable to make a prediction about its own knack at making predictions. Its numinous quality suffers from the same shortcoming. As a numinous creature, the turtle is not predisposed to questioning itself. This can be gleaned from its post-capture report in the lord's dream, where it does not appear to entertain the possibility that it may to be blamed for its own capture. Critical reflection upon one's capacity to deal with unforeseen circumstances is a prerequisite for fear, and as such the turtle's numinous quality precludes the turtle from fearing anything beyond what it already fears by its nature. Since its numinous and predictive abilities thus seem to obstruct the turtle in questioning and reflecting upon the downside of its abilities, no quantitative increase in its genius could possibly make any difference. Hence, we may conclude, the text calls for a radical transformation of the self.

We now come to the final statement. Two related issues need to be addressed, the first being the issue of learning. Little children, the text states, have no need for master-teachers (*shi shi* 石師). They learn through natural interaction. Since the motif of the untutored child functions as a positive counter-image, the statement implies that formal instruction distorts. The rationale for this notion that formal instruction distorts can be found in the problems with the turtle's features that are outlined above: even though instruction by master-teachers instills formidable qualities, it decreases one's capacity to question and doubt. The final statement hence refocuses the narrative of the turtle from the natural to the human. The target of the paragraph is those who cultivate master-enhanced abilities and thereby cancel out critical self-reflection.

The second issue centers on the interpretation of *"yan."* The choice of *yan* as a topic is, I submit, not random. *"Yan"* can be semantically related to the divinatory utterances of unit 6.1, and is thereby also related to strain B of unit 6.2. Corresponding to line 7, the concluding statement stands as a *pars pro toto* construction that picks up strain B (here, in so-called closed form).[35] This reading is significant for the interpretation of *"yan."* Although one may be inclined to interpret *"yan"* as simply 'to speak,' the context leads me to favour a more precise identification of *"yan"* as "speech equal to or containing a term judgment," where 'term judgment' stands for "any side of a pair of binary opposites." Moreover, the qualitative contrast between the diviner-turtle and the untutored child entails a difference in how each uses these term judgements. Not having learned to *yan* under a master-teacher, untutored children are bound to be far less decisive and more open to alternative options than diviner-turtles are. Parallel to this contrast and in line with the two kinds of *zhi* 知 (small knowledge versus great wisdom) mentioned in line 10, we may hypothesize the existence of two modes of *yan*: the divination mode and the children mode. It is the latter mode that is characteristic of "those who are [really] able to *yan*" (*neng yan zhe* 能言者).

Unit 6.1 started off with a description of events that demonstrated the usefulness of divination. The evaluation in unit 6.2, while not denying the value of divination in the cases referred to in the description, focuses on the turtle's failure at self-preservation. By implicitly attributing the reason for this failure to the nature of the turtle's numinous and predictive abilities, the evaluation

---

35 Due to the open (explicit) form of the connection between lines 5 and 7, it is clear that the element in need of being supplied in line 7 is *"zhi shen"* 至神. The closed (implicit) nature of the link between lines 10 and 12 makes it tricky to supply the missing element in line 12. I refrain from doing so. Note also that the *pars pro toto* constructions in lines 7 and 12 establish strain B as the primary strain. The language topic related to strain B is taken further in section 7.

demonstrates the useless and even harmful side of divination. The text then presents the children mode of *yan* in contrast. Section 7 continues as follows:

7 (ICS 26/78/22-24; HY 26/74/31-33)
惠子謂莊子曰：「子言无用。」莊子曰：「知无用而始可與言用矣。夫地非不廣且大也，人之所用容足耳。然則廁足而墊之致黃泉，人尚有用乎？」惠子曰：「无用。」莊子曰：「然則无用之為用也亦明矣。」

Huizi said to Zhuangzi: "Your *yan* are useless." Zhuangzi said: "It is when [someone] knows the useless that one can first talk to him about use. The earth, for sure, is wide and big, yet what man uses is only [the space needed to] hold [his] feet. So then, if one were to dig away what is beside the feet and reach all the way down to the netherworld, would [the space occupied by] man still be useful?" Huizi said: "[It would be] useless." Zhuangzi said: "If so, then, it is also clear that the useless counts as useful."

Understanding this section in a way that maximizes coherence with the preceding section hinges, I believe, on two initial observations. Firstly, that the section is about *yan*, and secondly, that the opposite predicates 'useful' (*yong* 用) and 'useless' (*wu yong* 无用) are instances of *yan*. Both of these elements are present in Huizi's opening statement: "Your *yan* are useless" (*zi yan wu yong* 子言无用). The subsequent exchange between Huizi and Zhuangzi is a straightforward case of analogical reasoning, and this constitutes the main argument. In order to understand the argument, we need to unpack the analogy.

Zhuangzi sets up a space in which he contrasts the soil we stand on with the surrounding soil. These plots of soil are staged as objects of judgment. Huizi is implicitly portrayed as reserving the term 'useful' for the soil supporting his feet, while judging the surrounding soil as 'useless.' Each object is associated with only one of these two alternative term judgments. These term judgments would seem intuitively justifiable: we indeed often affirm and deny the usefulness of things in terms of their proximity to us. Against this background, Zhuangzi introduces a hypothetical situation: what if the surrounding soil were dug away? This novel element prompts Huizi to reverse the first of his initial intuitive judgements: in comparison to the massive amount of surrounding soil that enables movement, the soil supporting his feet now appears rather useless. Without the surrounding soil, this supporting soil confines us to our tiny spot. From Huizi's acknowledgment of this, Zhuangzi can at last conclude that it is, conversely, also clear that "the useless [i.e. the surrounding soil] counts as useful" (*wu yong zhi wei yong* 无用之為用).

This reasoning is likely to unsettle Huizi. He is made to consider, at least for a brief moment, a previously neglected alternative. Yet, we may still note a subtle difference between Huizi's final reply and Zhuangzi's concluding statement. Huizi's reply is phrased as a mere reversal of his original position that the supporting soil is useful. On the verbal level, this reply is as one-sided as his earlier implicit pronouncement concerning the supporting soil. Zhuangzi's conclusion, on the other hand, takes a paradoxical form by coordinating both positions. It does not squarely refute the position regarding the surrounding soil that is implicitly attributed to Huizi. By instead retaining the pronouncement 'useless' and adding 'useful' to it, the conclusion contains *both* judgments as predicates of the same object. The terms 'useful' and 'useless' are not, in the final statement, viewed as mutually exclusive. Both alternatives are simultaneously entertained.

Ultimately, this analogy is not about different plots of soil but about *yan*. It makes an argument about language. The two plots of soil make it clear that *yan* is not a singular concept: there are two kinds of *yan*. The section contains implicit clues to what these two kinds of *yan* are. Huizi's opening statement pronounces a judgement on Zhuangzi's *yan*, suggesting a contrast between himself and Zhuangzi regarding *yan*. Implicitly, then, Huizi considers his own *yan* useful. In the analogy, Huizi's *yan* maps onto the soil supporting the feet (both of which are initially deemed useful), while Zhuangzi's variety of *yan* relates to the surrounding soil. Crucially, the conversation itself showcases the difference between these two kinds of *yan*. As we saw, Huizi's use of the term judgments 'useful'/'useless' is exclusive, while Zhuangzi's concluding statement coordinates both of these alternatives simultaneously. The argument as a whole is designed to show that there is a viewpoint from which Huizi's *yan* are useless, and more importantly, from which Zhuangzi's *yan* are useful.

We have now come to understand the analogy. Yet, what does it mean for Zhuangzi's or Huizi's *yan* to be useful or useless? By referring to the standards of support and movement implied in judging the usefulness of the two plots of soil, one could argue that Huizi's exclusive use of *yan*, though supportive, constitutes a narrowed-down form of *yan*, and that this narrowed-down form of *yan* is functionally different from and more constraining than Zhuangzi's encompassing use of language. A compatible and more concrete understanding of these two forms of *yan* is suggested by some of the similarities that exist between sections 6 and 7. Not only do both sections exhibit two kinds of *yan*, but they also each contain two standards of judgment, and they both deal with the motif of being useful/useless. The similarities between the two sections enable us to cross-reference their content within a unifying framework: Huizi is associated with the divination mode and Zhuangzi finds a parallel in the children mode. According to this unifying framework, the one-sidedness of Huizi's *yan* is impressive in specific cases yet useless in offering basic protection. Conversely, although Zhuangzi's *yan* would be less impressive due to its undecided nature, it would save one from running blindly into difficulties, on account of its underlying openness and self-reflection.³⁶

There is one final topic of broader significance that needs to be addressed. The argument segment of section 7 contains two components that, due to their contrastive movements, form what I will refer to as 'dynamic mirror images.' Phrased in terms of the two modes of *yan*, this dynamic mirror images writing form works as follows: firstly, we see a movement from *useful* to *useless* for the divination mode; secondly, and as a result of this, the children mode undergoes an opposite movement from *useless* to *useful*. This argumentative pattern is adumbrated in Zhuangzi's initial response. Situated in between the opening statement and the main argument, Zhuangzi's response ironically takes up Huizi's statement and transforms it as part of an introduction to what then follows. The first half of Zhuangzi's response (*zhi wu yong* 知无用) relates to the result of the movement concerning the divination mode, while the second half (*yan yong* 言用) relates to the result of the movement concerning the children mode. The order of the two components, moreover, is not random: it is only when Huizi has been made to realize that the divination mode is useless that one can begin to (*shi* 始) talk to him about the useful aspects of the children mode. This 'talking' (*yan*) is exemplified by the coordinating or inclusive use of language in the concluding statement, which, as we noted earlier on, is itself an example of Zhuangzi's *yan* in action.

The full impact of this 'dynamic mirror images' writing form becomes clear upon observing that it is duplicated on the level of section-pair 6/7, and that it not only directs the reader towards the children mode of *yan*, but moreover does so by embodying this very mode of *yan*. Let me discuss these two issues separately. Firstly, based on our discussion so far, it is clear that sections 6 and 7, considered together, form dynamic mirror images. Section 6 focuses on the divination mode, and its discussion moves from recognizing the *usefulness* of this mode to an acknowledgment of its *uselesness*. Section 7 topicalizes the children mode; starting from the initial statement that this mode is *useless*, the section progresses to the concluding insight that we may also regard it as *useful*. This writing form establishes section-pair 6/7 as a single meaningful unit composed of two components, of which the latter properly follows the former.

---

36 A similar dialogue between Huizi and Zhuangzi also dealing with issues of *yan*, use, and self-preservation appears at the very end of the first chapter of the *Zhuangzi* (ICS 1/3/4-10). For a discussion of this passage and its embedded language views, as well as an analysis of related artisan tool metaphors, see Wim De Reu, "How to Throw a Pot: The Centrality of the Potter's Wheel in the *Zhuangzi*," *Asian Philosophy* 20.1 (2000): 32–66.

Secondly, the dynamic mirror images writing form may be seen as actively embodying the very message of inclusiveness that it is deployed to promote. This insight initially comes from observing how the paradoxical form of the concluding statement in section 7 is not just (as already noted) an example of Zhuangzi's inclusive use of language, but that it also describes the "useless to useful" movement regarding the children mode of *yan*. It follows that this movement, too, is part of the inventory of inclusive *yan* forms. Extrapolating from this, we may observe that such movements are generally characterized by inclusiveness. They lead us from one alternative to another in such a way that the result of the movement does not imply a flat-out negation of the starting position. Even after pointing out the uselessness of the divination mode in the task of self-preservation, the text yet maintains that divination was impressive in the individual cases offered (and vice versa for the children mode). As the movements that constitute the dynamic mirror image are themselves characterized by an inclusiveness of apparent opposites, so the dynamic mirror images writing form enacts or performs the very kind of *yan* that it is deployed to promote.

At this juncture, I will pull together some of the separate threads of my analysis so far. Sections 6 and 7 form a single meaningful unit: not only do they function as dynamic mirror images, they also share, among others, an explicit concern with language. Section 5 adumbrates this concern; masters (sec. 5) instill sharp good/evil distinctions in their followers and these distinctions are similar to the binary positive/negative divinatory utterances of diviner-turtles (sec. 6). Both masters and diviner-turtles, moreover, are encouraged to give up their ways in processes referred to as 'disregarding' (*wang*) and 'getting rid of' (*qu* 去), respectively. The alternative image of the sagacious person who is wavering and hesitant (sec. 5) in turn parallels the image of the children who have never had master-teachers and yet are able to *yan* (sec. 6). The image of the untutored children, moreover, makes it clear that the outcome aspired to is not a specifically pre- or post-linguistic state, but an altogether different kind of engagement with language. We may summarize this point by referring once more to the divination and children modes of *yan*:

> DIVINATION MODE. Clear and one-sided binary judgments; absence of reflection and doubt; initially impressive yet ultimately self-defeating; associated with masters; deeply ingrained. Examples: good/bad, divinatory utterances, Huizi's exclusive term judgments.
>
> CHILDREN MODE. Hesitant and wavering; inclusive; disassociated from masters; open to alternative possibilities. Examples: paradoxical form of Zhuangzi's final statement, dynamic mirror images writing form.

Third Set of Explicit Verbal Connections: Yi or 'Opinions'

The term "*yi*" only appears once outside of the final section. This is in section 8, which consists of an introductory statement followed by two structurally similar units. Below is the relevant unit, 8.3.

8.3 (ICS 26/78/28-29; HY 26/74/36-37)
                1C 夫

2A 尊古而卑今   3B 且以狶韋氏之流觀今之世
    學者之流也   夫孰能不波

             4C 唯至人乃能

5A 遊於世而不僻   6B 順人而不失己
                               7B 彼教不學

8A 承意不彼

In general, to look down upon the present in revering the past is the fashion of scholars; to observe the present age after the fashion of clansman Xiwei, who is able not to be washed away? Only the ultimate person, by contrast, is able not to be aloof in wandering through the world, not to lose himself in following along with others. "Reject teachings" [he] does not learn; "accept opinions" [he] does not reject.

The juxtaposition of the formal parallelisms 5/6 and 7/8 alongside the non-parallel elements in lines 1 and 4 strongly suggests that unit 8.3 is composed in Interlocking Parallel Style, or IPS (with two strains, A and B, and C elements related to both). Simplicity is gained by assigning lines 2 and 3 to separate strains. Though not formally parallel, these lines may be construed as representing two different stances towards society: that of the scholars (lit. 'those who learn' *xuezhe* 學者) and that attributed to clansman Xiwei (狶韋氏).[37] Lines 4–6 portray the ultimate person (*zhiren* 至人) as avoiding the pitfalls of either stance, followed in lines 7–8 by a description of his position towards two major precepts (infra). In the following paragraphs, I clarify the distinction between the two strains, identify the position of the ultimate person, and propose an interpretation of "*yi*" that will be pertinent to our reading of the final section.

One of the challenges in interpreting unit 8.3 lies in understanding what those inspired by clansman Xiwei in strain B stand for and understanding how their stance compares to that of the scholars in strain A. Despite a virtual lack

---

37 Any alternative placement of line 3B would destabilize the structure of the entire fragment. Accepting the anomaly of 3B is therefore the more elegant solution. The possibility of coherent interpretation (infra) gives further credit to the IPS arrangement.

of information concerning clansman Xiwei, the structural grid provided by IPS enables us to form a clear picture.[38] Two characteristics of IPS are crucial in building this picture. Firstly, as a rule, the two strains of a passage composed in IPS constitute complementary opposites. Secondly, each strain is internally related in terms of content. Starting with the easier strain A, we can be confident in stating that the scholars, in identifying with the past, look down upon (*bei* 卑) or are aloof towards (*pi* 僻) contemporary society. They have a strong sense of cultural belonging towards the past and disdainfully set themselves apart from the present times. Not fitting into society and aspiring to find an audience for their teachings, they wander through the world (*you yu shi* 遊於世). Since strain B has been composed to stand in opposition to strain A, it then stands to reason that those taking inspiration from clansman Xiwei in strain B would not have a substantial identity and would be easily influenced. Indeed, in interacting with society they are washed away (*bo* 波) and lose themselves (*shi ji* 失己); they merely follow along with others (*shun ren* 順人). Clansman Xiwei's followers in strain B, then, epitomize a high degree of receptivity vis-à-vis contemporary society. Together, strains A and B constitute the totality of ordinary stances that one might take towards society.

The ultimate person occupies a unique position. In lines 5–6, he is portrayed as performing the activities associated with the groups represented in strains A and B, yet he does not manifest the shortcomings that they do. This distinction between the ultimate person and the strain A and B groups is crucial in two ways. Firstly, it makes the wandering and following of the ultimate person qualitatively different. Secondly, it enables him to be all-encompassing: since he is not aloof, he can also be receptive; since he does not lose himself in the present, he can still see the value in transmitted wisdom. This is consistent with lines 7–8, each of which consists of a topicalized verb-noun precept, in turn followed by a description of how the ultimate person's stance differs from those of the two other groups. The scholars, on the one hand, are predisposed to reject (*bi* 彼) 'accept opinions' (*cheng yi* 承意); granted that he does not lose himself in the present, the ultimate person does *not* reject this precept. Those inspired by Xiwei, on the other hand, are unified in learning (*xue* 學) 'reject

---

38 Throughout the early literature clansman Xiwei 狶韋氏 is only mentioned in two other *Zhuangzi* sections. In these he is portrayed as a ruler of ancient antiquity (ICS 6/17/3 and 22/63/20). In another *Zhuangzi* passage, someone named Xiwei appears as a Grand Historian (*taishi* 太史) consulted by Zhongni (25/75/20-25). These sections are of little relevance to the present discussion. I here presume the existence of a group of people inspired by the views ascribed to clansman Xiwei. Notice that even if clansman Xiwei were indeed a ruler of ancient antiquity, it does not therefore follow that he and his followers are culturally conservative. This separates them from the scholars.

teachings' (*bi jiao* 彼教), in spite of their lack of substantial identity; granted that he is not aloof in attitude, the ultimate person does *not* subscribe to this precept.[39] The ultimate person thus occupies a uniquely neutral position, which is spatially represented by the position of the C-strain within the IPS. The ultimate person acknowledges the value of the two other positions without being dogmatically bound to either of them.

Based on the above reading, I propose that the term "*yi*" simply refers to opinions or views current within society. The crucial issue is how to position oneself in relation to these opinions. The scholars, those inspired by Xiwei, and the ultimate person all take up different stances. Even so, the former two, while standing in opposition to one another, deal with opinions in a similarly fixed manner—rejecting and accepting—irrespective of the particular nature of the contingent situation. The ultimate person, by contrast, does not have a fixed response. Presumably, his approach is more situational, allowing him to follow teaching over opinion in some cases and accept opinion over teaching at other times.

In anticipation of my analysis of the text's final section, I wish to point out one significant correspondence among the three sets of explicit verbal connections. In summing up the SUOYI set of connections, we identified two types of contrast: a content contrast and a mode contrast. Significantly, this twofold contrast can also be found in the other sets of connections. A content-contrast holds between Zhongni and Lao Laizi in the YAN set, and between the community of scholars and the followers of Xiwei in the YI set. These figures are opposite with regards to the *content* of their positions. A mode-contrast, on the other hand, holds between the sagacious person/uneducated children and the masters/turtle-diviners in the YAN set, and again between the ultimate person and the two groups of intellectuals in the YI set. These characters contrast each other in terms of the *mode* of their actions. This twofold contrast, which is most obvious in the IPS arrangement of unit 8.3, imparts a common structure to the three sets of connections, and suggests a considerable degree of coherence underlying chapter 26.

---

39   The key to appreciating the parallel form of lines 7/8 lies in reading both instances of "*bi*" 彼 as full verbs ('reject'). "*Bi jiao*" 彼教 and "*cheng yi*" 承意 can be identified as precepts by virtue of their function as preposed objects in sentential topic positions. There are three further things to note in addition to this: firstly, the precepts themselves are both formulated from the perspective of the followers of clansman Xiwei; secondly, "*jiao*" 教 most likely refers to the teachings of the scholars and "*yi*" 意 therefore relates to strain B; and thirdly, the ultimate person as an implied subject who distances himself from the treatment of the precepts by the respective groups forces lines 5–8 into an ABBA pattern.

Revisiting the Fishnet Allegory

We have now arrived at an important intermediary step. What are the implications of the above analysis for interpreting the final section, section 12? First, I revisit the Chinese text.

12 (ICS 26/79/12-14; HY 26/75/48-49)
1　荃者所以在魚　得魚而忘荃
2　蹄者所以在兔　得兔而忘蹄
3　言者所以在意　得意而忘言
4　　　　　　　　吾安得夫忘言之人而與之言哉

Contextualizing section 12 against the above findings, the impact is immediately apparent. Consider, for example, the impact for the import and meaning of "*yi*" on line 3. The standard reading of line 3 holds that "*yi*" refers to elusive ideas or abstract meanings (or even, unfathomable *Dao*), and that these *yi* constitute the main philosophical concern of the section. These two aspects of the standard reading are at odds with the above findings. As unit 8.3 makes clear, the term "*yi*" refers to opinions held among members of society. These opinions are public, known, and non-problematic, rather than elusive. It appears that the main focus of line 3 is neither elusive and abstract entities nor the question of how to detect such entities. Compared to the standard reading, this finding deflates the relevance of "*yi*" to the point of being philosophically trivial. Let us see whether this finding can be incorporated into a coherent interpretation of section 12.

Section 12 does not merely function as a redundant rephrasing of the chapter's content; it creates a new narrative level. This is achieved by, among other strategies, the integration of key terminology. The most direct form of this kind of integration is the identification of *yan* (language) as a *suoyi* (tool). This identification establishes a language-tool complex that stands out quantitatively as the dominant theme of the chapter as introduced thus far. Significantly, the importance of this language-tool complex is echoed in the syntactic structure of line 3; not only does "*yan*" occupy the topic position in the first half of the third line, but it also appears in the main clause of the compound verbal sentence in the second half of the line. Conversely, "*yi*," which is the focus of the standard reading, appears in the subordinate and therefore less important clause of the second half.[40] Moreover, since the first two lines function merely

---

40　Moeller also recognizes that the first three lines attach more weight to the instruments (and to the issue of how one should not rely on them) than to any sort of catch. However, he develops this observation in a very different direction from me, arguing that line 3 is

as a rhetorical build-up to line 3, and since line 4 also singles out *yan*, it may be assumed that the entire section is predominantly concerned with language.

The previous discussions regarding *yan* and *suoyi*, as well as their present integration into a meaningful 'language-tool complex,' can be employed to develop the interpretation of section 12 one step further. There are three initial observations to be explored. Firstly, in line with the interpretation of *"yi"* proposed above, *yan* are not to be understood as heuristic devices. Since *yi* do not count as elusive or abstract entities, these *yi* do not stand in need of discovery. The alternative suggested earlier is that *yan* are better understood as having an interactive function, that is, as concerned with the question of how to engage linguistically with the world around oneself. A similar focus on interaction surfaced during my analysis of the sections on *suoyi* and, interestingly, even in the fragment containing *"yi."* Secondly, *"yan"* does not refer to language in general, but to the use of term judgments and, by extension, to longer equivalent utterances. Thirdly, even in its sense of 'term judgments,' *"yan"* is not a singular concept. There are, as argued at length, two kinds of differently-evaluated *yan*. This has significant implications. Not only does any instance of the term *"yan"* raise questions about which mode of *yan* is being referred to, but it also reduces the likelihood that any given section is targeting *yan* as such. These initial observations cast doubt on the standard reading according to which *yan*, understood as unspecified language, is a disposable tool of merely heuristic value. These observations point towards a different possibility in interpretation.

The term *"yan"* appears four times in section 12. Bearing in mind the ambiguity of the term, we may assign a value to each instance. In lines 3 and 4 below, (1) stands for the divination mode whereas (2) stands for the children mode.

```
      (1)                (1)
3   言者所以在意 得意而忘言
                                    (1)              (2)
4                        吾安得夫忘言之人而與之言哉
```

In line 3, *yan* is a tool that needs to be *wang*. The term *"wang,"* as we saw in section 5, refers to disregarding deeply ingrained distinctions. Such distinctions, it was argued, correspond to the divinatory-style utterances of diviner-turtles in section 6. What needs to be disregarded, then, is the divination mode of *yan*. It follows that the second and, by implication, also the first instance of *"yan"* are

---

suggesting that one is not (only) supposed to catch but also supposed to get rid of thoughts/ideas as a condition for arriving at "a perfect Daoist silence" (wherein one has also discarded the instrument of language). See Moeller, *Daoism Explained*, 59–61.

cases of the divination mode of *yan* (1). The explicit identification of this mode of *yan* as a *suoyi*, moreover, fits the analyses of *"yan"* and *"suoyi"* proposed earlier on. Like other *suoyi*, exclusive *yan* are actively mastered, become deeply ingrained and mechanically applied (with a total lack of doubt), and can initially prove reasonably successful yet, ultimately, are also harmful.

Line 4 contains the idea that one can *yan* with someone who has *wang yan*. The standard reading, I believe, is unable to make direct sense of this idea. In order to make sense of this idea, the standard reading needs to explain not only how one could talk with someone who has discarded language, but also why such a person would be interested in doing so in the first place. Reading *"wang yan"* not as *discarding* language, but as merely *disregarding* the conventions of socially induced linguistic habits, however, does make direct sense of this idea of talking with someone who has *wang yan*. Such a conversation would feature wavering, inclusive, and open-ended term use, not definite and exclusive judgments. While the first instance of *"yan"* in line 4 clearly stands for the divination mode (1), the latter instance of *"yan"* qualifies as an instance of the children mode (2). Significantly, this combination of different conceptualizations of *"yan"* within the space of a single line creates an utterance that is itself an example of the children mode of *yan* in action.

Having discussed *"yi," "yan"* and *"wang,"* we can now move on to analyze the verbal components of *"zai yi"* and *"de yi."* I start by bringing the meaning of *"zai"* into focus. In the context of line 3, *zai* is an activity characteristic of the divination-tool mode of *yan*. Hence, it follows that, while the activity of *zai* offers a certain measure of success (catching something), it also and more importantly stands for a non-ideal mode of interacting with a given reality (in casu, *yi*, or 'opinions'). In line with the discussion on *suoyi*, we can read *"zai"* as a term connoting some degree of control: socially-induced linguistic habits are tools used—almost compulsively—to get a hold on reality.[41]

Attempting to get a hold on reality is not the exclusive domain of those wanting to actively transform society. Indeed, as we saw, one of the chapter's original insights involves the identification of two opposite but equally dogmatic/compulsive positions. In the SUOYI set of explicit verbal connections, the *laozhe* include those who frantically strive for official position as well as

---

41 For a similar use of *"zai"* elsewhere in the *Zhuangzi*, consult ICS 11/26/9. *"Zai"* is there paired with the verb *"you"* 宥 (interchangeable with: *"you"* 囿). Bringing out the locative sense of *"zai"* and *"you,"* Graham renders them as "keeping in place" and "keeping within bounds," respectively. One feels the need to *zai* the world out of a fear that "everyone may indulge man's nature to excess" (Graham, *Chuang-tzǔ*, 211). Clearly, *"zai"* bears a connotation of restraint.

those actively trying to escape from it (section 11). Following a parallel line of reasoning, the YAN set of connections pairs Zhongni with the recluse Lao Laizi, both of whom are masters at inculcating divination-like patterns of judgment (section 5). And in the final set of connections, the YI set, the scholars and those inspired by clansman Xi Wei are stereotyped in a similar way: the former mechanically 'reject' opinions, while the latter invariably 'accept' them (*cheng yi*). This unchecked enthusiasm for accepting opinions, too, is a reductive way of understanding and interacting with a complex reality, and may be understood as a peculiar manifestation of "getting a hold on opinions" (*zai yi*).[42] Thus, the first half of line 3 subsumes the content-contrasts that appear in each of the three sets of explicit verbal connections.

How does the above understanding of "*zai*" relate to the second half of line 3? For the purposes of argument, I will distinguish between a weaker and a stronger interpretation of this second half of the line. Apart from obvious differences regarding the understanding of "*yi*," "*wang*" and "*yan*," the weaker interpretation runs parallel to the standard reading: "*wang yan* once you've got *yi*." This reading treats *de* as equivalent or compatible with *zai*, and typically construes *de yi* and *wang yan* as two actions that happen consecutively. We are urged to disregard linguistic habits after having first used them to catch/get opinions. While this reading seems plausible and may find support in the transformation of the self called for at the end of sections 5 and 6, it is not entirely satisfactory, for the following two reasons. First, the weaker reading attributes all pragmatic relevance to the language-tool complex. It portrays *wang yan* as pragmatically insignificant, and indirectly provides an argument to continue to rely on induced linguistic habits. However, we do know that *wang yan* does not point to the absence of language, but to a superior mode of language engagement. A reading that highlights this pragmatic dimension of *wang yan* is preferable to a reading that does not. Secondly, the weaker interpretation does not sit well with line 4, which mentions "*de*" in connection with the ideal person: "How can one get (*de*) such a person who disregards words?" (吾安得夫忘言之人). On the basis of its equivalent reading of "*de*" and "*zai*," the weaker interpretation answers this question straightforwardly: by using a tool or method. This answer, however, is implausible since it is unlikely that one is able to catch/get someone who disregards socially induced linguistic habits by relying on those very habits.

---

42 The ultimate person in unit 8.3, unlike the scholars, does not reject 'accept opinions.' This does not imply, however, that he takes this precept as his own. His response to opinions is qualified by the condition not to lose himself in the present and by a recognition of the value of transmitted wisdom. This sets him apart from the followers of clansman Xiwei.

In view of these two shortcomings, I propose instead a stronger interpretation of line 3. The key to developing this stronger interpretation lies in recognizing that the verbal conjunction "*er*" 而 allows not only for a consecutive but also for a *concurrent* reading of the two clauses that make up the compounded verbal sentence. Thus, instead of interpreting "A *er* B" as "B only once you've A," one is equally justified in reading it as "in A-ing, B," or "B in A-ing." To demonstrate the viability of this interpretation of the syntax, we can make an analogy between the process described on line 3 and other success-oriented activities, such as piano playing, teaching, and drawing. The ability to execute each of these tasks fluidly is gained by disregarding set patterns and habits: while adhering to socially-induced patterns may bring reasonable success, any such performance is also likely to appear stiff and strained (as in the first half of line 3). Truly successful and consummate performance, one may argue, requires one to develop a sensitivity unconstrained by socially induced patterns (as in the second half of line 3), and such unconstrained sensitivity is not something that comes after the performance. Rather, this unconstrained sensitivity needs to be developed during practice and is an essential working component of truly successful performance.

This change in perspective opens up a novel understanding of line 3 that eliminates the shortcomings of the weaker interpretation described above. With regard to the second half of the line, this novel understanding puts *wang yan* in the midst of interaction as an essential component of *de yi*.[43] This renders *wang yan* pragmatically significant, and turns *de yi* into an action that is fully congruent with *wang yan*. As for the line as a whole, it establishes a contrastive understanding of its two halves, and introduces a non-equivalent reading of "*zai*" and "*de*." The first half describes what people normally do: they employ socially-induced linguistic habits in trying to get a hold on other people's opinions. This is the perspective of the *laozhe*. The second half of the line, by contrast, offers the perspective of the *yizhe* (or, alternatively, the sagacious person/uneducated children of sections 5–6, or the ultimate person of unit 8.3). This half of the line emphasizes the importance of developing a sense for disregarding rule-like patterns whilst interacting with the world around one. Accordingly, "*de*" lacks the connotation of control attributed to "*zai*." While likewise carrying the meaning of 'to catch' or 'to get,' we need to think of "*de*"

---

43   One may wonder why "*wang yan*" does not precede "*de yi*" to form the sentence "*wang yan er de yi*." Indeed, in ordinary cases the way in which something is done precedes and is subordinate to what is done. Our reading thus far, however, reveals that the central concern of chapter 26 is not the 'what' (content) but the 'how' (mode) of one's actions. Accordingly, "*wang yan*" occupies the main clause of the compound verbal sentence.

differently and may for this purpose translate it as 'to attract' or 'to win over.' Recalling the analogy with piano playing, "*zai*" and "*de*" refer to the same kind of activity, but do so in very different ways: the former is effortful, rigid, and controlling, while the latter is effortless, dynamic, interactive, and ultimately more successful. This non-equivalence in interpreting "*zai*" and "*de*" makes better sense of line 4: it exempts us from the need to answer the embedded 'how' (*an* 安) question by referring back to induced linguistic habits. Indeed, in this alternative reading, it is no coincidence that line 4 employs "*de*" rather than "*zai*." By no means could one get an ideal person by relying on socially-induced habits. Rather, it is precisely by employing a mode of engagement that disregards rule-like patterns (which is the answer to the 'how' question) that one may win over a person who disregards these patterns. This idea has a relevance that transcends section 12, as we shall see later on.

Finally, I wish to explain how this interpretation is coherent with the first two lines of section 12. Fish traps and rabbit snares are instances of *suoyi*. Therefore, within the context of the preceding sections, they are not to be regarded neutrally. They are associated with a decrease in awareness, mere short-term efficacy, attempts that strain both the performer and the object, hyperbolic imitation, and an overall adverse impact. Though it is probable that an *yizhe* did at first use something like a trap or a snare, this needs to be viewed as a timely act that was, as can be seen in section 11, subsequently developed by others into a default mechanical treatment with a standard pattern of use. As with line 3, then, the first halves of lines 1-2 both portray *laozhe* who rely on default mechanisms to get a hold on reality. The positive alternative, suggested in the second halves of lines 1–2, is to act like an *yizhe*, that is, to disregard set patterns of usage in dealing with the world around one. Lines 1–3 contain a call for openness and variation, and not, as the standard reading would have it, a call for non-action or silence.

The following translation of section 12 incorporates key elements of my interpretation, most notably the contrast between the two halves of each line, the concurrent reading of the two components in the second halves of each line, and the specification of *yan* in the third line. For the purpose of preserving the original pun, I refrain from specifying *yan* in line 4.

1. Traps are that by which [those who strain themselves] get a hold on fishes. [Alternatively,] in attracting fishes, disregard traps!
2. Snares are that by which [those who strain themselves] get a hold on rabbits. [Alternatively,] in attracting rabbits, disregard snares!

3. [Divinatory-style] term-words are that by which [those who strain themselves] get a hold on opinions. [Alternatively,] in winning over opinions, disregard [divinatory-style] term-words!
4. How can one win over such a person who disregards term-words, and have a word with him?

In the preceding pages, I have proposed an interpretation of section 12 that differs markedly from earlier readings. Neither the standard interpretation nor the reading put forth by Moeller takes account of the contextual clues that are provided by the explicit verbal connections extending across section 12 and other parts of the chapter. When considered against the context that these explicit verbal connections create, the understanding of section 12 provided by Moeller and the standard interpretation is problematic, even if one merely adopts the weaker version described above. A contextual reading, in its strong version, is not merely possible but also plausible. Firstly, the strong interpretation described above offers a coherent reading of section 12. In this reading, the two halves of lines 1-3 each stand for differently-evaluated modes of dealing with reality, whereas line 4 actively performs the kind of linguistic play that is characteristic of the preferred mode of engagement. Secondly, the strong interpretation not only integrates those key terms (i.e. "*suoyi*," "*yan*," and "*wang*") whose interrelation may be gleaned from the earlier textual analysis, but it more importantly also draws on the double content/mode contrast introduced before. In terms of content, we identified a contrast between the two kinds of *laozhe*. Since this contrast is not of central importance, section 12 merges these two kinds of *laozhe* in the first halves of lines 1-3. In terms of mode, the *laozhe* contrast to the *yizhe*. This mode contrast bears greater significance than the content contrast between the different *laozhe*, and manifests in the text by way of an implied opposition between the two halves of lines 1-3. The very possibility of reading section 12 against the background of a recurring twofold contrast highlights the plausibility of a contextual reading of it. The plausibility of such a reading also further decreases the likelihood that chapter 26 is a mere ragbag of odds and ends.

The Case for Chapter Coherence

Our focus has thus far been directed towards the final section. We analyzed several passages explicitly related to this section, and have done so in minute detail. This analysis generated both a novel reading of section 12 and the realization that various parts of chapter 26 share a common structure and a common concern, and as such this analysis indirectly made a case for coherence on the chapter level. In the following pages, I will strengthen the case for overall coherence by tracing the development of the chapter's argument. If chapter 26 as a whole can be shown to proceed along identifiable common lines of argument that correspond to previously-identified topics and concerns, then this will invalidate the ragbag hypothesis and further substantiate the contextual interpretation of section 12.

As a substantial amount of chapter 26 has already been introduced, I will mainly focus upon the remaining sections and upon the position and function of the other sections within the argument as it unfolds. The present objective is to prove overall chapter coherence, and as such I will delve into the finer details of individual sections only in so far as is necessary in outlining the main picture. A total of six stages may be identified in the development of chapter 26.

Stage One: Introducing the Main Concerns (sec. 1)
Stage Two: Illustrations from Politics (sec. 2-3) and the Intelligentsia (sec. 4-5)
Stage Three: Zooming in on Language (sec. 6-7)
Stage Four: Social and Internal Wandering (sec. 8-9)
Stage Five: Discussion on Methods (sec. 10-11)
Stage Six: Closing the Argument (sec. 12)

Stage One: Introducing the Main Concerns (sec. 1)

Section 1 sets the scene. It consists of two units. The first unit (1.1) starts with a statement, supported with evidence, that instructs on how (not) to relate to reality. This statement is substantiated with two further observations. The second unit (1.2) introduces a series of psychological states in the context of analogies with nature.

> 1.1 (ICS 26/77/7-9; HY 26/73/1-3)
> 外物不可必；故龍逢誅，比干戮，箕子狂，惡來死，桀紂亡。
> Things external cannot be taken as invariable. Evidence: Longfeng was executed, Bi Gan was slain, Jizi went insane, E Lai was killed, and Jie and Zhou perished.
> 人主莫不欲其臣之忠，而忠未必信；故伍員流于江，萇弘死于蜀，藏其血三年而化為碧。人親莫不欲其子之孝，而孝未必愛；故孝己憂而曾參悲。
> None among lords do not wish their ministers to be loyal, yet loyalty is not invariably trusted. Evidence: Wu Yun drifted on the Yangzi, and Chang Hong was killed in Shu (after his blood was stored for three years, it turned into green jade).
> None among parents do not wish their sons to be filial, yet filial respect is not invariably treasured. Evidence: Xiaoji was distressed and Zeng Shen saddened.

Unit 1.1 targets a common tendency to *bi* 必, that is, to regard a correlation observed among certain phenomena as invariably holding true across a variety of situations. The opening line states that one should not regard and deal with the world—typically the social world—around one in this *bi* manner. This is the central message. This message is documented by a series of historical figures, ranging from models of virtue to ruthless tyrants, all of whom were struck by misfortune, presumably because their actions were guided by a tendency to *bi*.

The remainder of unit 1.1 consists of supportive material. History shows that, contrary to what one may be inclined to believe, loyal ministers are not invariably trusted, and filial sons are not invariably treasured. The presumed correlation between respect and recognition does not, it appears, actually manifest in all cases involving ministers/lords and sons/parents.

1.2 (ICS 26/77/9-12; HY 26/73/3-6)
木與木相摩則然；金與火相守則流；陰陽錯行則天地大絯，於是乎有雷有霆，水中有火，乃焚大槐。
If wood is rubbed against wood, it catches fire; if metal is held against fire, it melts. If *yin* and *yang* are mingled, heaven and earth are greatly disturbed: at that point, there is the crashing and rumbling of thunder, fire in the midst of water, and then big pagoda trees are burnt down.
有甚憂兩陷而无所逃，螴蜳不得成；心若縣於天地之間，慰暋沈屯；利害相摩，生火甚多，眾人焚和，月固不勝火，於是乎有僓然而道盡。
There are [the following cases]: greatly troubled by being entrapped on both accounts and having nowhere to escape to—apprehensive, unable to succeed; the heart-mind as if dangling in between heaven and earth—gloomy, sunken. [When] benefit and harm rub against each other, much fire is brought about, [and when] common men burn up [their] harmony, the [cold] moon surely does not overcome the fire: at that point, we have [the following situation]: deteriorating, the Way is depleted.

Unit 1.2, seen above, consists of two parallel segments. Both segments contain a pair of opening lines as well as a final line describing events of greater and more disastrous impact. Each of the final lines appears to draw on the first two lines, all while taking a more dramatic turn. The parallel nature of the two segments is further reinforced by their common use of fire imagery.[44]

The two segments set up an analogy between nature and the human heart-mind. Arguably, the analogy illustrates how common people inwardly respond

---

44 Note also the construction *"yu shi hu"* 於是乎 ('at that point') appearing in both of the final lines.

to the absence or breakdown of reliable patterns of action: in the face of alternative options, they become apprehensive or gloomy; the continuous friction experienced in weighing benefit against harm burns up their inner harmony and, ultimately, depletes their life force.[45]

Section 1 warns against patterned interaction (unit 1.1) and mental imbalance (unit 1.2). We may infer that flexibility and composure are two main concerns that are being argued for, and that the ideal person is someone who does not rely on default solutions and yet remains unperturbed. Looking at the entire chapter, however, the former of the two concerns mentioned is most prominent. Thus, even though the concern with inner stability has to be implicitly presumed and occasionally surfaces in the text, chapter 26 as a whole foremost concerns itself with patterns, with the emergence and development of these patterns, and, most importantly, with the need to free oneself from them.

Stage Two: Illustrations from Politics and the Intelligentsia (sec. 2-5)

Sections 2–5 draw upon the domains of politics and the intelligentsia to illustrate the concern(s) of section 1. The juxtaposition of these two domains in stage 2 corresponds to what is arguably a parallel arrangement between units 8.2 (politics) and 8.3 (intellectuals). Moreover, as the composers of the text are themselves part of an intellectual elite that, in early China, was never completely disinterested in political matters, the appearance of these two domains within the text is largely a reflection of its composers' own lifeworld.

Sections 2-3: Politics

<u>2</u> (ICS 26/77/14-19; HY 26/73/6-11)
莊周家貧，故往貸粟於監河侯。監河侯曰：「諾。我將得邑金，將貸子三百金，可乎？」莊周忿然作色曰：「周昨來，有中道而呼者。周顧視，車轍中有鮒魚焉。周問之曰：『鮒魚來，子何為者邪？』對曰：『我，東海之波臣也。君豈有斗升之水而活我哉？』周曰：『諾。我且南遊吳越之王，激西江之水而迎子，可乎？』鮒魚忿然作色曰：『吾失我常與，我无所處。吾得斗升之水然活耳，君乃言此，曾不如早索我於枯魚之肆！』」

Zhuang Zhou's household was poor, so he went to borrow grain from the marquis in charge of the river. The marquis in charge of the river said: "Sure! I am about to receive fief tribute [in the form of] precious metal. I will then lend you

---

45 The term *"dao"* 道 occurs three times in the whole chapter. Only two of those are philosophically significant. In section 9, *"dao"* refers to pathways of perception and cognition. In the present section, it seems to refer to an inner life force.

three hundred pieces of metal, alright?" Zhuang Zhou flushed with indignation and said: "When I, Zhou, was coming over yesterday, someone called out midway. I looked over. There was a crucian fish right there in the carriage ruts. I asked it: 'Crucian! What are you doing there?' It answered: 'I am a stray fellow from the East Sea. Would my lord perhaps have a bucket or ladleful of water so as to let me stay alive?' I said: 'Sure! I am just now travelling south to the kings of Wu and Yue. I will divert the waters of the West River and have them flow up to you, alright?' The crucian flushed with indignation and said: 'I have lost my regular setting! I have no place to dwell! I only need a bucket or ladleful of water to live. Now that you have spoken as such my lord, you might as well look for me at the dried fish stalls before long enough.'"

Section 2 narrates Zhuangzi's attempt to secure an urgently needed loan of grain. The marquis agrees but then puts it off with the suggestion of giving him a huge amount of cash in the near future instead. The account is made more powerful by an embedded story. This takes the form of a fictional account of Zhuangzi's conversation with a fish, which mimics the primary story in an inverted analogy.

We can look at this section from two angles: from that of Zhuangzi and from that of the marquis. Zhuangzi acts upon the expectation that his request for an urgently needed loan will be granted. This expectation is not met. Confronted with the loan refusal, he flushes with indignation. Against the background of section 1, Zhuangzi errs on two accounts: he puts too much trust in the correlation 'urgent request-immediate grant,' and he burns up his inner harmony. Yet, while the image of Zhuangzi is thus undermined, the didactic self-ridicule of the embedded story also draws a more positive picture: Zhuangzi clearly understands that it would have been more proper for the marquis to grant the request. If Zhuangzi were the marquis, he would have judged the situation better.

The portrayal of the marquis is coloured by its own share of ambivalence. As it runs against Zhuangzi's expectation, the marquis' unexpected response reveals that he is unconstrained by what may pass for a conventional pattern of interaction in a feudal society. He does not, it appears, act in a *bi* manner. Yet, while there are situations in which it is indeed good practice to postpone immediate satisfaction for the sake of a larger, later benefit, the case at hand clearly required instant micro-action. The marquis errs on the side of the extraordinary. He misreads the situation. This may be due to a pattern of his own.[46] Consider section 3.

---

46   The moral motivations of the marquis are irrelevant. As we will see, the marquis and the main character of the next section share a principle of action that does not require refer-

3 (ICS 26/77/21-26; HY 26/73/11-16)

3.1 任公子為大鉤巨緇，五十犗以為餌，蹲乎會稽，投竿東海，旦旦而釣，期年不得魚。已而大魚食之，牽巨鉤，錎沒而下，驚揚而奮鬐，白波若山，海水震蕩，聲侔鬼神，憚赫千里。任公子得若魚，離而腊之，自制河以東，蒼梧已北，莫不厭若魚者。已而後世輇才諷說之徒，皆驚而相告也。

The scion of the duke of Ren made a big hook with a giant fishing line attached, used fifty bullocks as bait, squatted at [Mount] Kuaiji, and cast his rod into the East Sea. He fished day after day, yet did not get a fish for a whole year. Thereafter, a big fish took a bite, dragged along the giant hook, dived down, and violently flapped its fins while throwing itself back up in the air: with white waves like mountains, the waters of the sea stirred and agitated, and with sounds equal to ghosts and spirits. It awed everything within a thousand miles. Once the scion of the duke of Ren got this fish, he cut and dried it. From the Zhi River east and [Mount] Cangwu north, there were none who did not eat their fill from this fish. Later on, tale-tellers of little talent in subsequent generations all narrated this to one another in surprise.

3.2 夫揭竿累，趣灌瀆，守鯢鮒，其於得大魚難矣；飾小說以干縣令，其於大達亦遠矣。是以未嘗聞任氏之風俗，其不可與經於世亦遠矣。

To carry rods and fishing lines and rush to irrigation streams to lay hold of salamanders and perches: it will be difficult to get big fish; to embellish small tales [in striving] to become a district magistrate: it is far off from succeeding on a grander level. As such, never having heard of the customs of the Ren clan: by far one cannot be engaged in governing the world.

Section 3 may be divided into two units. Unit 3.1 consists of a story describing the marvelous fishing exploits of the scion, followed by the observation that these exploits are only superficially understood by tale-tellers of little talent. Unit 3.2 lists a series of three statements highlighting the difference between short- and farsighted actions. The concluding statement most explicitly brings out the central socio-political message. The entire section is designed to bring home the following point: we need inventive and far-sighted rulers who create greater benefit than do rulers who are merely concerned with the immediate satisfaction of their desires. The scion belongs to the latter kind and moreover seems inwardly composed.

The positions of the scion in section 3 and the marquis in section 2 are surprisingly similar: both implicitly take "confer a big benefit, but not at once" as their principle of action. The evaluation of this principle, however, is different in each case. Whereas a farsighted response is appropriate in the case of the

---

ence to moral intentions. Equally, Zhuangzi's reply does not refer to the moral quality of the marquis or his proposal. The focus is on whether the proposal or action is appropriate to the situation.

scion, it was clearly not the right approach for the marquis, who should have opted for instant and small-scale intervention. These antithetical evaluations of a single principle juxtapose sections 2 and 3 in a relationship of mutual negation. Considered in isolation, either section is misleading. Section 2 could leave one with the impression that doing something extraordinary is always wrong (or, conversely, that the ordinary is always right); this is denied by section 3. For its part, section 3 could convince one that it is always good to be inventive (or, conversely, that it is always bad to do the ordinary); this is denied by section 2. The two sections must be understood in opposition to each other. They silently perform the insight that one cannot invariably apply what works in one situation to other situations. It also follows that the scion and his clan, to the extent that they, as the text suggests, have their own habitual or invariable pattern of action (*fengsu* 風俗), are not perfect either.[47]

Sections 4–5: Intelligentsia

Sections 4 and 5 stage persons without any real political influence. They are no commoners either, however, but represent the intellectual elite of their times. Section 4 mocks *Ru* 儒 literati, while section 5 builds on an encounter between the exemplary *Ru* master Zhongni and Lao Laizi.

4 (ICS 26/77/28-30; HY 26/73/16-74/18)
儒以詩禮發冢。大儒臚傳曰：「東方作矣，事之何若？」小儒曰：「未解裙襦，口中有珠。」「詩固有之曰：『青青之麥，生於陵陂；生不布施，死何含珠為！』接其鬢，壓其顬，儒以金椎控其頤，徐別其頰，无傷口中珠！」

The *Ru* open up graves in line with Odes and Rituals. The senior *Ru* instructed: "The east is dawning. How do things stand?" The junior *Ru* said: "The skirt and jacket are not yet stripped off. There is a pearl inside the mouth. The Odes of old contain the following saying: 'Lush wheat growing on hill slopes; if one does not share [the wheat] while alive, then how can one hold a pearl inside the mouth when dead!' Squeeze his temple hair and pull his beard. Gently stroke his chin with a metal mallet and slowly separate his jaws. Do not damage the pearl inside the mouth!"

Section 4 develops a story about *Ru* literati who justify the exhumation of a dead person's body by invoking an ode and by performing the whole process in a ritualistic manner. The exhumation is presented as a retribution for the dead person's failure to share his wealth while alive.

---

47 The same applies to those who hear/learn about (*wen* 聞) the scion insofar as they take his act as a generally valid principle.

The story mocks the self-image of *Ru*. It sets up external symbols associated with literati (ode, ritual, hierarchy), yet undermines both these symbols and the literati by staging them in what is readily construed as an act of grave robbery. The message, I believe, is this: symbolic codes and their embedded rules of conduct do not reliably produce morally-acceptable behaviour.

5 (ICS 26/78/1-9; HY 26/74/18-24)

5.1.1 老萊子之弟子出薪，遇仲尼，反以告，曰：「有人於彼：脩上而趨下，末僂而後耳，視若營四海，不知其誰氏之子。」老萊子曰：「是丘也。召而來。」仲尼至。曰：「丘！去汝躬矜與汝容知，斯為君子矣。」

A disciple of Lao Laizi went out to collect firewood and ran into Zhongni. He went back to report it, saying: "There is someone over there: [with] a long upper and short lower body, a hunched back and withdrawn ears, [with] a gaze as if overseeing the four seas. I do not know which clan he descends from." Lao Laizi said: "That is Qiu. Call him over." Zhongni arrived. [Lao Laizi] said: "Qiu! Get rid of your bodily miseries and your postured cleverness, and then you will count as a man of high calibre."

5.1.2 仲尼揖而退，蹙然改容而問曰：「業可得進乎？」老萊子曰：「夫不忍一世之傷而驁萬世之患：抑固窶邪，亡其略弗及邪？惠以歡為，驁終身之醜：中民之行進焉耳。」

Zhongni cupped his hands in retreating backwards, changed his posture with some distress, and asked: "Can [my] mission gain advancement?" Lao Laizi said: "Not [being able to] endure the harm done to a single age, yet speeding up the calamity of a myriad ages: is this due to inherent boorishness, or is it the wits that are not up to it? Extending kindness for the sake of enjoyment, [yet] quickly bringing about lifelong disgrace: only the walk of average people can be advanced by this."

5.2 相引以名，相結以隱：與其譽堯而非桀，不如兩忘而閉其所譽，反無非傷也，動無非邪也。聖人躊躇以興事，以每成功。奈何哉其載焉終矜爾！

Pulling one another in making a name, tying one another up in hiding away: compared to their praising Yao and condemning Jie, it would be better to disregard on both sides and to [thereby] block the objects of their praise, [since] in opposing there is nothing but harm, and in stimulating there is nothing but wickedness. The sagacious person is wavering in initiating affairs so as to aim for accomplishment. What to do? Their undertakings! In the end, nothing but misery!

Section 5 may be divided into two units (5.1 and 5.2). The first unit consists of two segments. In the first segment (5.1.1), Lao Laizi ridicules Zhongni's eccentric appearance and mindset. The second segment (5.1.2) starts when Zhongni uneasily asks about the implications of Lao Laizi's criticism for his mission (*ye* 業). Lao Laizi undermines the value of Zhongni's mission: though it involves a refined awareness towards what is near at hand, it creates greater damage for others and oneself. It can only advance (進 *jin*) persons of average quality. The second segment (and thus the first unit) ends here: Zhongni's question as to whether his mission can gain advancement (*jin*) has been answered.

The second unit (5.2), though commonly regarded as a continuation of Lao Laizi's answer, is more meaningfully construed as a critique of both protagonists. Such reading is plausible not only because the preceding dialogue has already reached its conclusion, but also because of three further considerations. Firstly, in the opening line of the entire section, Lao Laizi is explicitly portrayed as having disciples. This turns him into a master. On the basis of our discussion of model emulation in section 11 and the positive image of the children who never had master-teachers in section 6, this is a questionable aspect to his character. In serving as a model, Lao Laizi is similar to Zhongni. Secondly, the parallel opening phrases of unit 5.2 can be convincingly interpreted as referring to Zhongni and Lao Laizi (and their disciples) respectively. While Zhongni and his like encourage one another in attaining name/fame (*xiang yin yi ming* 相引以名) so as to receive official tenure, Lao Laizi is known to have renounced such position in favour of a life in reclusion, whence the pronouncement that he and his disciples bond together in hiding away (*xiang jie yi yin* 相結以隱). Thirdly, as we saw, such reading is consistent with the 'content contrast' identified in unit 8.3 and section 11.

One immediate implication of such a reading is that both Zhongni and Lao Laizi would be urged to disregard their group-based preferences in favour of what I previously identified as a more open and wavering attitude (*chouchu*). Beyond the present context, this reading also relates back to section 4. If direct criticism of Zhongni is not a token of great insight, then the criticism levelled at the literati in section 4 should not be interpreted as a mere anti-*Ru* position. Even though traditional wisdom is not to be taken for granted, it may still be valuable. Section 1, it is useful to keep in mind, only points out that traditional virtues do not reliably produce desired results. It does not make the very different claim that such virtues can, under no circumstances, effectively guide us.

Before moving on to the next stage, I will first outline the development of the chapter thus far. The primary assertion of section 1 is that one should not view or interact with the world in a *bi* manner. Sections 2 and 3 substantiate this idea with stories drawn from the domain of politics. These stories present cases of extraordinary action. Not only do the antithetical evaluations of a single principle silently perform the primary concern of section 1, but the particular sequence of the stories as well as the type of principle can also be accounted for. Since the two main examples in section 1 target traditional notions and associations, the reader may take it for granted that a conventional approach is unreliable and hence develop a tendency for what is surprising and novel. Such a tendency is immediately undermined by the negative example of an extraordinary act in section 2, after which section 3 counters with a positive evaluation. Sections 4 and 5 are situated within the lifeworld of the intellectual elite. Accordingly, the focus here is not on a concrete policy adopted by individuals, but on the cultivation of set dispositions within master-disciple communities. The writing strategy in sections 4-5 differs correspondingly. The mockery of *Ru* in section 4 is not followed by a positive appraisal of rule-following. Neither do we find a mere unilateral criticism of traditional groups. The meta-criticism of section 5 equalizes traditional and atypical groups, and indicates that the problem is not so much the content of their positions as the common tendency to instill preference-based discriminations. Antithetical evaluations of a single principle and the meta-criticism of competing groups serve the same purpose: they remind the reader not to regard observed correlations, actions, and positions as having universal validity. It is at the end of section 5 that we first find a positive description of the ideal: the sagacious person does not stick to a particular position, but strolls back and forth (*chouchu*). Unlike others, he does not take things invariably (*bi*).

Stage Three: Zooming in on Language (sec. 6-7)
The earlier discussion of sections 6 and 7 offered insight into the difference between the 'divination mode' and the 'children mode' of *yan*. The shortcoming of the divination mode of *yan* is, as we saw, the removal or absence of doubt. The position of section-pair 6/7 within the chapter establishes a plausible connection between this lack of doubt on the one hand and a tendency to take things as invariable on the other. The divination mode of *yan*, associated in section 6 with master-teachers, is hence closely intertwined with patterned interaction. By contrast, the children mode of *yan*, corresponding as it does to the wavering attitude of the sagacious person, stands for a more open and variable engagement.

While this grounds the divination and children modes of *yan* within the developing narrative, we may still wonder why the issue of language is given such prominence. Addressing this question requires us to recognize, I believe, the guiding function of language. Language, in the sense of term judgments, categorizes and carries implications for action, and hence directs our engagement with things. In light of this, it is significant that the language theme is first explicitly introduced in a context related to master-teachers. Rival masters transmit their values through a subtle patterning of the language use of their disciples. This process, we saw, involves the inculcation of preference-based discriminations. Arguably, it is this widespread tendency to instil naming-patterns along with the guiding role of naming in interaction that turns language into a natural and indeed even an inevitable topic of discussion for anyone concerned with pragmatic (in)variability. Such discussion, I will observe later on, necessitates for the composers of chapter 26 the creation of peculiar forms of discourse and argument, such as paradoxes and dynamic mirror images.

Stage Four: Social and Internal Wandering (sec. 8–9)

Sections 8 and 9 are framed in terms of wandering (*you* 遊). Not only is *you*, or more specifically 'Heaven's wandering' (*tian you* 天遊) in section 9 a positive quality of the heart-mind (*xin* 心), but the opening line of section 8, which I identify as unit 8.1, deals exclusively with the topic of *you*.

> 8.1 (ICS 26/78/26; HY 26/74/33-34)
> 莊子曰：人有能遊，且得不遊乎？人而不能遊，且得遊乎？
> Zhuangzi said: "Someone capable of wandering, could he get to [a state where] he does not wander? Someone not capable of wandering, could he get to wander?"

Unit 8.1 distinguishes people according to their ability to *you*. The nature of *you* may be understood in the light of what we have learned from unit 8.3. Of the two types of contrast embedded in unit 8.3, the mode contrast between the ultimate person and the two groups of intellectuals is the most important. The two groups of intellectuals strictly adhere to their viewpoints, whereas the ultimate person acknowledges the value of both groups' viewpoints without strictly adhering to either. His responses are not fixed. I take the notion of *you* as apt to project onto the ultimate person.[48] It follows that *you* indicates a movement between positions whereby each position is only temporarily adopted. Such an interpretation of *you* fits well with the preceding sections, notably with the strolling back and forth (*chouchu*) of the sagacious person, which, as we saw, corresponds to the children mode of *yan*. By contrast, those unable to *you* are represented by the groups of intellectuals who, we may infer, cultivate divinatory-style patterns of interaction. I now turn to unit 8.2.

---

48 Unit 8.3 uses the phrase "*you yu shi*" 遊於世 ("wander through the world") to describe the scholars' travels from one state to another. Although they wander in this physical sense, their rigid points of view cause them to be aloof (*pi* 僻) and to look down (*bei* 卑) on others. As such, they do not wander in the sense of "*you*" that is intended here.

8.2 (ICS 26/78/26-28; HY 26/74/34-36)

```
                          1C 夫
    2A 流遁之志                              3B 決絕之行
                       4C 噫其非
                    a 至知      b 厚德
                       之任與
                                          5B 覆墜而不反
6A 火馳而不顧
                       7C 雖相與為
                    a 君         b 臣
                         時也
                       易世而无以相賤
                       8C 故曰至人不
                    a 留         b 行
                         焉
```

In general, a runaway mindset and disciplined conduct, ah, these are not tokens of ultimate wisdom and profound prowess! [Those with disciplined conduct] topple over yet do not retrace; [those with a runaway mindset] are speedy as fire and do not look back. Though they may be set up as rulers and ministers, this would be due to the [peculiarities of a particular] time. Change the age and they would not be in a position to despise one another. Therefore it is said: the ultimate person does not run and conduct himself in such ways.[49]

Units 8.2 and 8.3 are structurally similar. Both are written in IPS and contrast the ultimate person to those referred to in strains A and B. The IPS arrangement of unit 8.2 indicates a significant difference between the two strains. This difference is found not only with regards to a focus on mindset (*zhi* 志) and conduct (*xing* 行) respectively, but more importantly is also found in descriptive varieties such as 'speedy as fire' (*huo chi* 火馳) versus 'toppling over' (*fu zhui* 覆墜). Possibly, the style of those in strain A is unrestrained (*liu dun* 流遁), while those in strain B are burdened by ascetic discipline (*jue jue* 決絕). Despite these differences, however, they appear equally unwavering in 'not looking back' (*bu gu* 不顧) and 'not retracing' (*bu fan* 不反). It is probably with respect to this radical tendency that the ultimate person is different from both. If so, then the ultimate person may well recognize the value of some

---

49 The closed nature of the IPS along with the embedded a/b elements makes the reading of this fragment tentative, albeit not arbitrary. I follow Xuan Ying 宣穎 (fl. early 18th century) in connecting lines 3/5 and 2/6 (quoted in Wang, *Zhuangzi jiaoquan*, vol. 2: 1074, nn. 5, 6) and read "*liu*" 留 in 8C as its 2A homophone "*liu*" 流 (see *Hanyu da zidian*, vol. 4: 2537 for attested cases).

degree of liberty and discipline, but does not, in thought or action, commit himself to either of these two positions.

While units 8.2 and 8.3 are structurally similar, they present the stance of the ultimate person within two different domains. Unit 8.3 deals with the intellectual elite, whereas line 7C with its embedded a/b elements above suggests that unit 8.2 concerns itself with politics, more specifically with the qualities that a politician should (not) have in withstanding the times. The suggestion is that only a non-linear person—the ultimate person in line 8—is capable of adapting to future changes. Viewed in this way, units 8.2 and 8.3 parallel the arrangement of sections 2–3 (politics) and 4–5 (intelligentsia).

9.1 (ICS 26/79/1-4; HY 26/74/37-75/41)
(9.1.1) 目徹為明，耳徹為聰；鼻徹為顫，口徹為甘；心徹為知，知徹為德。
Eyes when cleared are perceptive, ears when cleared are acute; the nose when cleared is discriminating, the mouth when cleared is sensitive; the heart-mind when cleared is aware; intelligence when cleared is judicious.
(9.1.2) 凡道不欲壅，壅則哽，哽而不止則跈，跈則眾害生。
Passages detest being obstructed. If obstructed, [they are] choked. If choked without end, movement is hampered. If movement is hampered, then numerous kinds of harm are generated.
(9.1.3) 物之有知者恃息，其不殷，非天之罪。天之穿之，日夜无降，人則顧塞其竇。
Those things that have intelligence rely on breathing. That [their breathing] is not profound is not the fault of Heaven. Heaven's piercing them through does not diminish day or night. It is [rather] man who blocks up his [own] cavities.
(9.1.4) 胞有重閬，心有天遊。室无空虛，則婦姑勃磎；心无天遊，則六鑿相攘。
The womb has double emptiness, the heart-mind has Heaven's wandering.[50] If a room contains no empty space, then the women inside quarrel; if the heart-mind does not have Heaven's wandering, then the six apertures are in disorder.
(9.1.5) 大林丘山之善於人也，亦神者不勝。
That big forests and tall mountains are good for people is precisely because [in those places, one's] spirit is not subdued.

Unit 9.1 is different from section 8 in that it does not deal with socio-political reality but with internal states. As noted before, the opening line of unit 9.1 describes a wholesome and unobstructed state characterized by the keenness of sense organs and cognitive faculties. The entire unit is organized around

---

[50] For the phrase *"bao you chong lang"* 胞有重閬 and a discussion of the womb/bladder in early Chinese medicine, see Elisabeth Hsu, *Pulse Diagnosis in Early Chinese Medicine: The Telling Touch* (Cambridge: Cambridge University Press, 2010), 216 ff., esp. n. 65.

spatial metaphors.[51] The main idea is that only cleared spaces, permeated with the breath of Heaven, realize their full potential (9.1.1 and 9.1.3). The heart-mind in particular needs to be empty, allowing for Heaven's wandering (9.1.4). If thus cleared, the heart-mind will be acutely aware (9.1.1). By contrast, problems are due to man-made obstructions (9.1.2 and 9.1.3). The unit ends by describing the wholesome impact of vast natural spaces on man's spirit (9.1.5).

The unobstructed state recommended in unit 9.1 may be regarded as a precondition for wandering on the socio-political level. Such, then, is the internal state of the ultimate person described in section 8. His clarity allows him to interact with an awareness that is devoid of automatic response patterns. Those committed to a particular position or response, it follows by contrast, block up their perceptive and cognitive faculties. Unit 9.2, the second segment (9.2.2) of which we have already discussed, elaborates on the emergence of man-made unwholesome developments. It opens with the following line.

> 9.2.1 (ICS 26/79/4-5; HY 26/75/41-42)
> 德溢乎名，名溢乎暴；謀稽乎誸，知出乎爭；柴生乎守官，事果乎眾宜。
> Judiciousness is spilled by [attention to one's] reputation, reputation is spilled by exposure; schemes are reached under pressure, knowledge emerges from strife; blockage is generated by shielding the faculties/offices, tasks are the result of making conveniences more numerous.[52]

Segment 9.2.1 consists of three pairs of phrases. This grouping both structurally parallels and evaluatively contrasts with the opening segment of unit 9.1. The final pair deserves a special mention. The term "*guan*" 官 carries the meaning

---

51 My understanding of this unit has benefited from an exposition by Chia-Lynne Hong on a spatial image schema related to non-obstruction that underlies this unit's various segments. Chia-Lynne Hong, "Seeing through the *Dao*: Image Schema Related to Non-obstruction in the *Zhuangzi* 26," Paper presented at the XIX Biennial Conference of the European Association of Chinese Studies (EACS), Paris, September 2012.

52 The last pair has baffled virtually all commentators and translators. It is common practice to punctuate after the "*shou*" 守, thus creating the combination "*guan shi*" 官事. For reasons of parallel, however, it is better to preserve the "5-5" and "2 乎 2" schemes of character balance. The verb-noun combination "*shou guan*" 守官 does appear in a number of other early texts and is moreover intelligible within the present context. This in turn forces us to read "*zhong yi*" 眾宜 as a verb-noun construct. I take "*yi*" 宜 to refer to the convenient tools/methods first mentioned in segment 9.2.2.

of both 'senses' and 'official/office'.⁵³ The former sense calls to mind the reference to the senses in unit 9.1, and the obstructed state suggested by the image of (putting up) defensive obstacles (*shou* 守, *zhai* 柴) relates the first phrase of this pair to the unwholesome condition of the senses described in the earlier unit. The latter sense of *"guan"* as 'official/office' accounts for pairing the first phrase with the one following it, with its mention of *shi* 事 ('tasks'). Interestingly, this second phrase immediately precedes the first reference to tools/methods in segment 9.2.2. It is arguably the proliferation of convenient tools/methods that keeps people busy and thus creates tasks standing in need of completion.

To sum up, unit 8.1 distinguishes people according to their ability to *you*. Units 8.2 and 8.3 substantiate this distinction by contrasting the ultimate person, who is able to *you*, to those committed to a particular political or intellectual position. Section 9 turns the focus inwards and explicitly associates *you* with perceptive and especially cognitive clarity, in contrast to those who block up their passages and cavities. Within the broader context, these two sections shift the more abstract discussion concerning *yan* in section-pair 6/7 towards social life and internal states. As a bridge to the following two sections, segment 9.2.2 ends with a concrete example of man-made tools/methods which, in line with unit 9.1, are applied with a lack of awareness and understanding.

Stage Five: Discussion on Methods (sec. 10–11)

Tools and methods are symbols of declining ability (section 9). They obstruct the perceptive and cognitive faculties of the *laozhe*. They are, as indicated before, consciously mastered and performed in imitation of an authentic act performed by an *yizhe*. Only *yizhe* are capable of the social and mental wandering described in sections 8 and 9.

Stage Six: Closing the Argument (sec. 12)

The final section integrates key elements of the preceding sections, and closes the argument. As argued at length, this section calls upon the reader to disregard rule-like patterns in interacting linguistically with the world around oneself. This "world around oneself" is specified as *yi* (opinions current in society). Arguably, opinions guide interaction with the world at large. As such, a proper stance towards opinions provides meta-leverage in dealing with the world. The

---

53   See Jane Geaney, *On the Epistemology of the Senses in Early Chinese Thought* (Honolulu: University of Hawai'i press, 2002), 17-22 for more on what she calls the "bureaucracy of the senses" metaphor in early Chinese philosophical texts.

choice for *yi* over *jiao* (traditional teachings), both of which are mentioned in unit 8.3, may be thought of as revealing the moderately progressive yet non-committed outlook of the chapter's composer(s).

In the preceding pages, I have attempted to show that the chapter develops along identifiable lines of argument. Establishing section-pair 6/7 as a single meaningful unit and establishing the introductory status of section 1 left us with four intermediary sections. These sections fall neatly into two pairs, dealing with political and intellectual life respectively. Sections 2 and 3 enact the central concern of section 1 regarding (in)variability (*bi*) by way of antithetical evaluations of a single policy, while sections 4 and 5 focus on group-sanctioned rule-following, culminating in a meta-criticism of competing groups. Section-pair 6/7 zooms in on the crucial role played by language in interaction. The lack of critical reflection and doubt characteristic of divinatory-style utterances corresponds to the patterned and invariable mode of engagement acquired under the guidance of master-teachers. As a viable alternative, the text recommends the language use of untutored children, which, by contrast, should be thought of as hesitant, open, and variable in nature. The contrast between these two modes of engagement, first explicated at the end of section 5, runs through the subsequent sections and further clarifies the image of the ideal person. Sections 8 and 9 jointly contrast the internally cleared state of the wandering person to the perceptive and cognitive obstruction of those obsessively holding on to their respective positions. Sections 10 and 11 contrast those performing authentic acts (*yizhe*) to those developing such acts into tools and methods (*laozhe*). Section 12, finally, makes a contrast between the tool-divinatory language mode of engagement and an alternative mode of interaction that hinges on disregarding acquired linguistic conventions. The ideal person, we may infer, is wavering-wandering, inclusive, untutored, perceptive and aware, unconstrained by methods, and disinterested in getting a hold on reality. Nevertheless, he is ultimately more responsive and able to avoid mental strain and physical harm both on his part and on the part of others.

Conclusion

Chapter 26 of the *Zhuangzi* is commonly conceived of as a ragbag of odds and ends. In this paper, I have offered a reading of chapter 26 that seeks to maximize coherence. While one does not have to read the text exactly in the way I suggest, the text does allow for a coherent interpretation, and when held against this light, the ragbag view appears mistaken.

I started off by observing that the final section of the chapter shares three sets of explicit verbal connections with other parts of the chapter. Spelling out the key terms of those connections in detail, we discovered that sections belonging to the same set are mutually coherent, that each of the sets contains a twofold contrast, and that a contextual reading of the final section is not only possible but indeed quite plausible. The chapter as a whole, moreover, can be shown to develop along identifiable lines of argument. These mutually reinforcing findings make it highly unlikely that chapter 26 is the kind of ragbag that we traditionally take it to be. This conclusion corroborates the contextual reading of the final section and warrants a reappraisal of the chapter's content and literary form.

In line with much of early Chinese philosophy, the most pressing concern of chapter 26 is the pragmatic question of how to position oneself in relation to the social world around oneself. More pointedly, this may be phrased as a question of how best to linguistically engage with guiding opinions and teachings as a part of that social world. The text highlights the internal strain and harm associated with patterned engagement and offers a critique of the model-emulation on which such engagement is based. In arguing against the ingrained and automatic responses of patterned interaction, it suggests the value of doubt and non-commitment. Such resistance to patterned interaction corresponds internally to the ability to perceive and understand with awareness, and allows for variable engagement.

The chapter lends itself very easily to further reflection on a host of related topics, ranging from the psychology and visualization of internal states to the value of ambivalence, to the function of imitation and mimesis. I will here briefly single out one issue that has a bearing on the literary form of chapter 26. Phrased in terms of the central concern with language, the issue may be formulated as follows: how can one avoid the contradiction of establishing a naming-pattern in targeting naming-patterns? It is not my intention to evaluate whether or not chapter 26 is, in the end, fully successful in avoiding this contradiction. Rather, I wish to point out that, firstly, anyone who holds views such as those expressed in chapter 26 would need to engage and even invent peculiar writing strategies and forms of discourse, and, secondly, that we do find such strategies and discourse forms in chapter 26. Earlier on, we noted the use of antithetical evaluations of a single principle, the meta-criticism of competing groups, the use of paradoxical expressions, and what was referred to as a 'dynamic mirror images' writing form. Arguably, these literary forms both perform and bring the reader closer to the central message of the text, all the while avoiding the divination mode of language. To these writing strategies,

I wish to add two more. On a lower textual level, we may see the ambivalent portrayal of figures such as Zhuangzi (section 2) and Zhongni (sections 5–6) as a deliberate strategy that undermines fixed views towards these figures on the reader's part. As for the chapter as a whole, the variety of writing styles, the seemingly unrelated topics, and the submerged organization of the overall argument fits in well with the chapter's emphasis on variability as its main theme. Having a message of their own yet facing the difficulty of conveying this message without doing exactly what they deem problematic, it may have seemed natural to the composer(s) of chapter 26 to turn to the literary form that they ultimately used. If so, then the final line of section 12 packs a witty surprise: it is only by composing a text that disregards rule-like patterns that one can win over someone who disregards such patterns. As such, the final line refers back to the entire chapter and establishes the chapter as a written guide that guides without direct guiding.

Looking beyond chapter 26, it would be exciting to see whether other later *Zhuangzi* chapters, despite their apparent erratic nature, contain a coherent message of their own. Such discoveries would significantly raise our understanding of this fascinating text. In performing such research, one would need to be sensitive to the contextual nature of meaning. That is, rather than rearranging sections into systems of ideas that match assumptions already taken for granted, it may be more worthwhile to look for connections and writing strategies within the texts as they stand. If any advice can be drawn from section 12, it is to disregard stock interpretations in interpreting texts.

Appendix

The table below includes the stage and section divisions in *Zhuangzi* 26 as used in this paper. Stage divisions are first introduced in Part Five ("The case for chapter coherence"). For lower-level unit and segment divisions, please refer to the main text.

References are based on *Zhuangzi zhuzi suoyin* 莊子逐字索引, ICS Ancient Chinese Text Concordance Series; and *Zhuangzi yinde* 莊子引得, Harvard-Yenching Institute Sinological Index Series. The syntax of the reference to both concordances follows the "chapter/page/line" pattern.

Stage	Section	ICS	HY
1	1	26/77/7–12	26/73/1–6
2	2	26/77/14–19	26/73/6–11
	3	26/77/21–26	26/73/11–16
	4	26/77/28–30	26/73/16–74/18
	5	26/78/1–9	26/74/18–24
3	6	26/78/11–20	26/74/24–31
	7	26/78/22–24	26/74/31–33
4	8	26/78/26–29	26/74/33–37
	9	26/79/1–6	26/74/37–75/43
5	10	26/79/8–10	26/75/43–45
	11	26/79/10–12	26/75/46–48
6	12	26/79/12–14	26/75/48–49

References

Allan, Sarah. *The Heir and the Sage: Dynastic Legend in Early China.* San Francisco: Chinese Materials Center, 1981.

Chen Guying 陳鼓應, comm. and trans. *Zhuangzi jinzhu jinyi* 莊子今註今譯. Revised edition. Taibei: Taiwan Shangwu, 1999.

De Reu, Wim. "How to Throw a Pot: The Centrality of the Potter's Wheel in the *Zhuangzi*." *Asian Philosophy* 20.1 (2000): 32–66.

Geaney, Jane. *On the Epistemology of the Senses in Early Chinese Thought.* Honolulu: University of Hawai'i Press, 2002.

Graham, Angus C., trans. *Chuang-tzŭ: The Seven Inner Chapters and Other Writings from the Book "Chuang-tzŭ."* London: Allen & Unwin, 1981.

———. *Disputers of the Tao: Philosophical Argument in Ancient China.* La Salle, Ill: Open Court, 1989.

———. "How Much of *Chuang-tzŭ* Did Chuang-tzŭ Write?" In idem. *Studies in Chinese Philosophy and Philosophical Literature.* Singapore: Institute of East Asian Philosophies, National University of Singapore, 1986: 283–301.

Hong, Chia-Lynne. "Seeing through the *Dao*: Image Schema Related to Non-obstruction in the *Zhuangzi* 26." Paper presented at the XIX Biennial Conference of the European Association of Chinese Studies (EACS), Paris, September 2012.

Hsu, Elisabeth. *Pulse Diagnosis in Early Chinese Medicine: The Telling Touch.* Cambridge: Cambridge University Press, 2010.

Hung, William et al., eds. *Zhuangzi yinde* 莊子引得, Harvard-Yenching Institute Sinological Index Series Supplement No. 20. Cambridge MA: Harvard University Press, 1956.

Kalinowski, Marc. "Diviners and Astrologers under the Eastern Zhou: Transmitted Texts and Recent Archaeological Discoveries." In *Early Chinese Religion: Part One: Shang through Han (1250 BC 220 AD)*, vol. 1, edited by John Lagerwey and Marc Kalinowski. Leiden: Brill, 2009: 341–396.

Klein, Esther. "Were there 'Inner Chapters' in the Warring States? A New Examination of Evidence about the *Zhuangzi*." *T'oung Pao* 96 (2011): 299–369.

Lau, D.C. *Zhuangzi zhuzi suoyin* 莊子逐字索引, ICS Ancient Chinese Text Concordance Series 43. Hong Kong: Commercial Press, 2000.

Liu Rongxian 劉榮賢. *Zhuangzi wai za pian yanjiu* 莊子外雜篇研究. Taibei: Lianjing, 2004.

Liu Xiaogan 劉笑敢. *Zhuangzi zhexue ji qi yanbian* 莊子哲學及其演變. Beijing: Zhongguo shehui kexue chubanshe, 1987.

Lou Yulie 樓宇烈. *Wang Bi ji jiaoshi* 王弼集校釋. Taibei: Huazheng shuju, 1992.

Luo Zhufeng 羅竹風 et al. *Hanyu da cidan* 漢語大詞典. 12 vols. Shanghai: Shanghai cishu chubanshe / Hanyu da cidian chubanshe, 1986–1993.

Möller, Hans-Georg. "Zhuangzi's Fishnet Allegory: A Text-Critical Analysis." *Journal of Chinese Philosophy* 27.4 (2000): 490–492.

———. *Daoism Explained: From the Dream of the Butterfly to the Fishnet Allegory*. Chicago / La Salle, Ill: Open Court, 2004.

Roth, Harold D. "*Chuang tzu*." In *Early Chinese Texts: A Bibliographical Guide*, edited by Michael Loewe. Berkeley, CA: Society for the Study of Early China and Institute of East Asian Studies, 1993: 56–66.

Wagner, Rudolf G. *The Craft of a Chinese Commentator: Wang Bi on the Laozi*. Albany: SUNY Press, 2000.

Wang Shumin 王叔岷, ed. and annot. *Zhuangzi jiaoquan* 莊子校詮. Taibei: Zhongyang yanjiuyuan lishi yuyan yanjiusuo, 1994.

Xu Zhongshu 徐中舒 et al., eds. *Hanyu da zidan* 漢語大字典. 8 vols. Chengdu, Wuhan: Hubei cishu chubanshe / Sichuan cishu chubanshe, 1986–1990.

CHAPTER 9

Truth Claim with no Claim to Truth: Text and Performance of the "Qiushui" Chapter of the *Zhuangzi*

Dirk Meyer

Many texts from early China bear witness to the way thinking was caught in a conflict between the realisation (*zhi* 知)[1] that the workings of Dao 道 pervade the world, on the one hand, and the desire to communicate this insight and its implications to the world, on the other. But the realisation of the truth and its philosophical communication to the world form two poles in that they are fundamentally separated by language: speaking of the Dao is always a reduction of Dao to an arbitrary definition and therefore a destruction of reality.[2]

With 'truth' and 'philosophy,' I use two concepts that are not undisputed in Chinese history of thought. I take experience of truth as the subjective grasp (*zhi* 知) of the workings of Dao, which may be realised in different ways. I talk about philosophy as the reasoned attempt to communicate this experience to a community, which may necessitate a process of intellectualisation and systematisation.[3] At the same time, I think of the philosophical in early China as

---

1 For a discussion of the concepts knowing and knowledge in early China, see Anne Birdwhistell, "Knowledge Heard and Seen: The Attempt in Early Chinese Philosophy to Analyze Experiential Knowledge," *Journal of Chinese Philosophy* 11 (1984): 67–82.
2 This problem is discussed in considerable detail in Rudolf Wagner, *The Craft of a Chinese Commentator: Wang Bi on the Laozi* (Albany: SUNY, 2000).
3 Here I am not concerned with the question as to whether we should describe the intellectual activities in early China as "philosophy." I agree with Geoffrey Lloyd that the word philosophy is a mere epistemological obstacle for the historian of thought who wishes to study the intellectual reality of the past, be it in China or Greece. See Geoffrey Lloyd, *The Ambitions of Curiosity* (Cambridge: Cambridge University, 2002); Lloyd and Nathan Sivin, *The Way and the Word* (Yale: Yale University, 2002). Lloyd's positions are as summarised succinctly in Anne Cheng, "'Y a-t-il une philosophie chinoise?' Est-ce une bonne question?" *Extrême-Orient, Extrême-Occident* 27 (2005): 5–12. Unlike Heiner Roetz, esp. id., *Die chinesische Ethik der Achsenzeit. Eine Rekonstruktion unter dem Aspekt des Durchbruchs zum postkonventionellen Denken* (Frankfurt: Suhrkamp, 1992), I have no intention of looking for the universality of philosophical activity. Instead, much in agreement with Lloyd, I hold that we should attempt to demonstrate the polymorphous nature of philosophising in early China. Note also that I do not refer to "truth" in the sense of the Judaic-Christian theological image of the divine that

something that carries an element of performance.[4] It is an *act* of philosophising. As praxis-oriented activity, it is a real-world experience rather than a purely theoretical undertaking, and this is where the paradox lies. While there is an urge to communicate the experience of truth to the world, that action generally requires intellectualisation, systematisation and categorisation. But systematising truth means putting it into a rigid framework, which bears the danger of reducing it to an arbitrary set of definitions.

Consequently, different strategies were chosen to escape the problem that, at the very moment one speaks of truth, it is already something else. In this chapter, I discuss one such attempt, the "Qiushui" chapter of the *Zhuangzi* 莊子[5] as put together by Guo Xiang 郭象 (d. 312 AD). I suggest that Guo Xiang collaged a philosophically coherent essay that aims at bridging the gap between philosophy and praxis of Dao by producing a text that creates an act of

---

is "bound to contingency through historical revelation." See Petra Bahr, "Religious Claims of Truth Versus Critical Method—Some Western Remarks on a Complex Relationship in Western Tradition," in *Historical Truth, Historical Criticism, and Ideology: Chinese Historiography and Historical Culture from a New Comparative Perspective*, eds. Helwig Schmidt-Glintzer, Achim Mittag and Jörn Rüsen (Leiden: Brill, 2005), 1, but of a felt reality of Dao in the world.

4   See also Dirk Meyer, "Bamboo and the Production of Philosophy: A Hypothesis about a Shift in Writing and Thought in Early China," in *History and Material Culture in Asian Religions*, eds. Benjamin Fleming and Richard Mann (Oxford and New York: Routledge, 2014): 21–38.

5   The dating of the *Zhuangzi*, but also the organisation of the work into 'inner' (*nei* 內), 'outer' (*wai* 外), and 'miscellaneous' (*za* 雜) chapters is highly problematic. Scholarship has long regarded the inner chapters as the "core" of the *Zhuangzi*, while the outer and miscellaneous chapters were commonly taken as the work of later followers, and the chapters have been categorised according to their supposed philosophical value. (For such attempts, see especially Angus Graham, "How much of Chuang-tzǔ did Chuang-tzǔ write?" (Repr. in Graham, ed., *Studies in Chinese Philosophy and Philosophical Literature*, Singapore: The Institute of East Asian Philosophies, National University of Singapore (1986), 283–321); Harold Roth, "Who Compiled the Chuang Tzu?" in *Chinese Texts and Philosophical Contexts: Essays Dedicated to A.C. Graham*, ed. Henry J. Rosemont Jr. (La Salle: Open Court, 1991), 79–128; Liu Xiaogan, *Classifying the Zhuangzi Chapters*, William E. Savage, transl. (Ann Arbor: Center for Chinese Studies, University of Michigan, 1994); id. *Zhuangzi zhexue jiqi yanbian* 莊子哲學及其演變 (Beijing: Zhongguo Renmin Daxue, 2010); David McCraw, *Stratifying Zhuangzi: Rhyme and Other Quantitative Evidence* (Taibei: Institute of Linguistics, Academia Sinica, 2010). More recently, Esther Klein has argued that the Inner Chapters probably are the result of a careful choice of what was considered the best material, but they do not represent the earliest stratum of the body of materials (in Esther Klein, "Were there 'Inner Chapters' in the Warring States? A New Examination of Evidence about the *Zhuangzi*", *T'oung Pao* 96 [2011]: 299–369). Although much of it is may still be late Warring States period production, all we can say with certainty is that its final compilation—and composition?—is the product of Guo Xiang 郭象 (d. 312 AD).

philosophical performance. Much of the *Zhuangzi* is concerned with seeking Dao through the everyday rehearsal of seemingly trivial activity, as exemplified in the story of Cook Ding 丁 that describes the cook's knack in carving meat,[6] or that of the wheelwright Bian 扁 and the chiselling of wheels.[7] Dao learning, these stories suggest, comes through skill learning, and vice versa.[8] The "Qiushui" reflects exactly this dynamic and its very existence, I argue, manifests a claim to truth despite the fact that no such claim is ever made explicitly in the text.

The "Qiushui"

1.
秋水時至，百川灌河。涇流之大，兩涘渚崖之間，不辯牛馬。於是焉河伯欣然自喜，以天下之美為盡在己。順流而東行，至於北海，東面而視，不見水端。於是焉河伯始旋其面目，望洋向若而嘆曰：「野語有之曰：『聞道百，以為莫己若者。』我之謂也。且夫我嘗聞少仲尼之聞，而輕伯夷之義者。始吾弗信，今我睹子之難窮也，吾非至於子之門則殆矣，吾長見笑於大方之家。」[p. 561][9]

> The Autumn Floods arrived at the usual seasonal time and the various streams all poured into the River. It swelled up so widely that from [the distance] between the cliffs and islets of the two shores, one could no longer differentiate oxen from horses. At this, the Lord of the River was decidedly pleased, thinking that the world's beauty was all within himself. Flowing along the River, he (the Lord) travelled east until he reached the Sea of the North where, when turning his face towards the east to look out, he could not see the further edge of the water. Only then did the Lord of the River turn his head. Looking up to the sea, he faced the God of the North Sea, Ruo, and said, with a sigh: "There is a folk proverb that says the following:
> 'Those who know a hundred paths, think there is no one like themselves.'
> This could [also] be said about me. Also, I have heard of those who were mocking the knowledge of Zhongni and ridiculing the integrity of Boyi. At first, I did not want to believe it; but now that I see your endless vastness [I realise that],

---

6 "Yangsheng zhu" 養生主 (Nourishing the Lord of Life)
7 "Tian Dao" 天道 (The Way of Heaven)
8 See Robert Eno, "Cook Ding's Dao and the Limits of Philosophy," in *Essays on Skepticism, Relativism, and Ethics in the Zhuangzi*, eds. Paul Kjellberg and Philip J. Ivanhoe (Albany: SUNY, 1996), 127–151, 136 ff.
9 The pagination refers to the *Zhuangzi jishi* 莊子集釋 (1894) edition by Guo Qingfan 郭慶藩 (1844–1896) and compiled in *Xinbian Zhuzi jicheng* 新編諸子集成 (Beijing: Zhonghua shuju, 1961).

had I not come to your gates [to learn from you], I would have been in danger forever of being laughed at by the masters of the Great Method."

This scene sets the stage for a tortuous narrative within the *Zhuangzi* that is all about perspective and self-realisation. Not much is known about the origins and the composition of the "Qiushui" and the aim of this essay is not to disentangle different chronological layers in the composition of this text that is collaged from different snippets and scenes. Instead, I here wish to follow the composition of the text as created most likely by Guo Xiang and take seriously the picture that is presented through that composition.

The "Qiushui" consists of altogether thirteen scenes, many of which would make a good context-dependent text in their own right.[10] Of these scenes, eight record an imagined dialogue between the Lord of the River and the God of the Northern Sea, Ruo, before five more stories complete the narrative and conclude with the realisation that the reality of the world cannot be expressed through language that takes propositional force.

The text responds to the idea that language, when taken in absolute terms, serves as a proper tool to express reality. The "Qiushui" sets out to undo that myth. Through the literary device of separate scenes, the recipient of the text is confronted with different positions and ideas. The text behaves like the bends and turns of a river—the river is in fact the introductory metaphor of the text—in that with each scene (or bend), a new reality manifests itself before the reader's eye, only to change again at the next turn. The storyline that is unfolding accordingly shows that everything material—and this includes language and perception—depends on perspective and hinders the process of self-realisation when mistaken as ultimate reality. The "Qiushui" as we know it now is therefore not just a collection of snippets of unrelated stories. Instead, close analysis suggests that it makes sense to read it as a carefully crafted collage where the different scenes and stories each take a new turn in the development of the overall narrative. When approached accordingly, the different scenes compound the literary form of the argument and form a crucial device for delivering the message of this text. With each scene the text recipient realises that the understanding gained though the previous scene was yet again tainted because it was only the manifestation of a limited account of a much more complex situation. The overall structure of the composition therefore reduplicates the water metaphor through the stream that runs through the text, in that each bend of that stream presents a new reality, and so a changed

---

10 For a discussion of context-dependent texts, see Dirk Meyer, *Philosophy on Bamboo: Text and The Production of Meaning in Early China* (Leiden: Brill, 2012), 194 ff.

insight on the part of the text recipient. Through the repeated use of the water metaphor as something that is at the same time both strong and pliant[11] and able to adapt to—and is in fact dependent on—varying situations, the different scenes, when understood together and in this way, serve as a strong literary device to express a multi-facetted, ever-changing reality.

In what follows, I provide a form analysis of the "Qiushui" both on the micro-level of the text and on the macro-level of composition by analysing the individual scenes of which the text is composed and by reviewing the strategies by which the different scenes are connected in one complex narrative where meaning is produced on different levels.

The first scene of the "Qiushui" already hints at the central dilemma of self-realisation that features in the entire narration: a state of affairs is taken as the expression of ultimate reality rather than a conditioned snippet of a much more complex situation. Autumn floods led to a rise of the level of the river to the point where from the two shores, one could "no longer differentiate oxen from horses." The fact that the "Qiushui" qualifies the size of the river indicates that this is yet again only a conditioned manifestation of a more complex reality, for size is in itself meaningless. It requires a perspective (in that ox and horse can no longer be differentiated) and only works in a particular context. However, the Lord of the River mistakes size for absolute value, thinking not only that "the world's beauty was all within himself" but moreover that "there is no-one like [himself]." Going yet one step further, through the water/river metaphor at this stage of the text, the "Qiushui" provides a key to the fundamental conflict inherent in understanding. Water—in this scene it takes the form of a river—is a common metaphor for Dao, and here it can be read in that way too. Dao is the one thing that pervades the world.[12] Although in itself impalpable, it nevertheless manifests the ultimate reality of the world by being "the substance of the cyclical and dynamic universe."[13] The river is similarly difficult to grasp in cognitive terms. The nature of the river is to be in constant flux. Each of its many and constantly changing manifestations is easily mistaken as its ultimate form of reality: in this case 'big'; in other cases 'shallow,' 'deep,' 'rushing,' 'still,' et cetera. When read as a metaphor, the river thus prompts the conclusion that the nature of the world is to be in constant flux too. But a world in constant flux easily creates confusion. This is because

---

11   For a good discussion of nature serving as root metaphor of early Chinese thought, see Sarah Allan, *The Way of Water and Sprouts of Virtue* (Albany: SUNY, 1997).

12   The earliest and most explicit mention of this idea is perhaps in the "Tai yi sheng shui" from tomb Guodian One.

13   Y.M. Chang, *The Thoughts of Lao Tzu* (Taipei: Li Ming, 1977), 27.

constant flux is not commonly seen as the underlying pattern of reality, but instead each of the moments within that circle of constant change is commonly mistaken for the ultimate reality itself, rather than just a snapshot of something more complex. Through the river metaphor it therefore becomes clear that it is inherent in the world's nature to be miscomprehended when its individual material manifestations are not seen as a circle of everlasting change, where each moment within that circle takes a different realisation, and where each realisation is in fact nothing but one constituent of the unchanging reality of constant change. The river, when taken as root metaphor, is therefore in itself at the same time the source of misconception, as well as ultimate reality, depending on how one sees it. Through this depiction, the first scene expresses at the same time the fundamental insight, as well as dilemma, of this text. That insight, however, can only be gained when going through the "Qiushui" as a whole. The first scene therefore exhibits that the world is a constant manifestation of change. Moreover, as I discuss below, this scene also reduplicates the act of comprehension on the part of the text recipient.

On the level of its language, the first scene displays a skilful playfulness, and the literary form of the text plays a crucial part in presenting it in vivid terms. The first forty graphs (from 秋水時至 to 以天下之美為盡在己[14]) set the scene, followed by seventeen graphs of four subsets in units of quick rhythm dominated by regular tetrasyllabic units (順流而東行，至於北海，東面而視，不見水端[15]) that describe the movement of the Lord of the River as he flows along rapidly in an ardour of self-satisfaction. This unit of quick progression, beautifully introduced by *shun* 順 and demonstrating the quick movement of the river, is then slowed down in two subsets of ten/seven graphs that break the rhythm of quick sentence patterns at the very point where an incredulous astonishment sets in on the part of the Lord of the River as he faces the vastness of the sea (於是焉河伯始旋其面目，望洋向若而嘆曰[16]). The moment of astonishment is beautifully exaggerated through elements of elongation, especially *shi* 始, thus giving form to the Lord of the River's disbelief on the level of language and rhythm. The compositional features of this scene thus mirror the

---

14 P. 561, l. 1/1–l. 2/10: "The Autumn Floods arrived at the usual seasonal time" to "thinking that the world's beauty was all within himself."

15 P. 561, l. 2/11–27: OC: *Cə-lun-s ru nə tˤoŋ grˤaŋ-s, tit-s ʔ-a pˤek mʰˤe-ʔ, tˤoŋ C.men-s nə gijʔ-s, pə kˤen-s s.turʔ tˤor. (Flowing along the River, he (the Lord) travelled east until he reached the Sea of the North where, when turning his face towards the east to look out, he could not see the further edge of the water.) In my reconstruction of Old Chinese, I follow the system of Baxter and Sagart, *Old Chinese: A New Reconstruction* (Oxford: Oxford University Press, 2014).

16 P. 561, l. 2/28–l. 3/13. (Only then did the Lord of the River turn his head. Looking up to the sea, he faced the God of the North Sea, Ruo, and said, with a sigh…)

emotional state of the Lord of the River when undergoing change from self-satisfied ardour to incredulous astonishment as he goes through different stages of self-realisation. Moreover, by deploying a uniform phrase in parallel fashion where the two lines each present an opposite situation, the text makes plain the significance of perspective. The first scene portrays a world in flux where the same situation, depending on perspective, prompts very different reactions. Starting off from line 1 (於是焉河伯欣然自喜[17]), the texts presents a situation where, based on size, the Lord of the River is saturated with self-satisfaction, believing that all the world's beauty is exhausted in him. Just a few sentences further down,[18] the very same sentence pattern introduces his feelings of incredulous astonishment when he is taken aback by the size of the sea that triggers in him a sense of inferiority:

> 於是焉河伯欣然自喜，以天下之美為盡在己
> At this the Lord of the River was decidedly pleased, thinking that the world's beauty was all within himself.

He thus flows along until he reaches the sea and where he faces a vastness that dwarfs his own size, prompting a reaction as follows:

> 於是焉河伯始旋其面目，望洋向若而嘆曰
> Only then did the Lord of the River turn his head. Looking up to the sea, he faced the God of the North Sea, Ruo, and said, with a sigh: […][19]

The parallel pattern in which the statements are phrased stresses that the situation, which has triggered the two opposing sets of reactions, is in fact no different in either case. Through the literary device of uniform sets of statements that are deployed in parallel fashion but where each statement presents an opposite state of affairs, the text stresses the unchanging reality of an ever-changing world. For this insight, it would have been impossible for the authors of the "Qiushui" to use a positive assertion because this would have installed an unchanging definition, and the mere presence of such a thing would have conflicted with what the text aims to do. In such a situation, it is only through the use of a literary form that the text can deliver its message. The device for the construction of meaning discussed here is used everywhere in the "Qiushui." I call it "opposing uniformity."

---

17   P. 561, l.1/23.
18   P. 561, l. 2/28: 於是焉河伯始旋其面目.
19   The parallelism of the two sentences is not well kept in the translation, which might be rendered rather awkwardly as "at this, the Lord of the River began to turn his head…"

2.

北海若曰：
　　井蛙 不可以語 於海者， 拘 於虛也；
　　夏蟲 不可以語 於冰者， 篤 於時也；
　　曲士 不可以語 於道者， 束 於教也。
　今爾 出 於崖涘， 觀 於大海，乃 知 爾醜，爾將 可與語 大理矣。

天下之水，莫大於海，萬川歸之， 不知何時止而不盈 ；尾閭泄之， 不知何時已而不虛 ；春秋不變，水旱不知。此其過江河之流，不可為量數。而吾未嘗以此自多者，自以比形於天地，而受氣於陰陽，吾在於天地之間，猶小石小木之在大山也。方存乎見小，又奚以自多！

計四海之在天地之間也，　　　　　　　不似礨空之在大澤乎？
計中國之在海內，　　　　　　　　　　不似稊米之在太倉乎？
號物之數謂之萬，
人卒九州，穀食之所生，舟車之所通， 人處一焉 ；
此其比萬物也，　　　　　　　　　　　 人處一焉 ；
　　　　　　　　　　　　　　　　　　不似豪末之在於馬體乎？

五帝之所連，三王之所爭，
仁人之所憂，任士之所勞，盡此矣！
伯夷辭之以為名，仲尼語之以為博。此其自多也，不似爾向之自多於水乎？ [p. 563–564]

The God of the Northern Sea, Ruo, said: "that a frog in a well can tell [you] nothing about the sea is because it is captured (拘) in his hole. That a summer insect can tell [you] nothing about ice is because it is bound (篤) to its season. That a bent scholar can tell [you] nothing about the Way is because he is fettered (束) by his studies.

But now that you have *left* (出) your banks, *gazed* (觀) at the great sea and *realised* (知) your meanness, it might be possible to talk to you about the Great Principle:

> Of the waters on the earth, none is bigger than the sea, and the myriad streams [all] return to her; I don't know when this might stop—yet she never fills. At Wei Lü the waters drain out; I don't know when this might end—yet [the sea] never empties. Spring and Autumn never alter [her], and [she] neither knows floods nor droughts. It is in this that the sea surpasses the streams of the Jiang and the He immeasurably; and yet, it never happened that I have seen myself as superior because of this, since I shelter my form within Heaven and Earth and receive my spirit from the spirits[20] of light and dark; and therefore I remain between Heaven

---

20　I here follow Nathan Sivin who considers *yin* and *yang* as aspects of *qi* 氣. See Sivin, *Traditional Medicine in Contemporary China: A Partial Translation of Revised Outline of Chinese Medicine (1972): With an Introductory Study on Change in Present-day and Early Medicine* (Ann Arbor: Center for Chinese Studies, University of Michigan, 1987), esp. 59–70.

and Earth just like a small stone, or a small tree in a huge mountain—so tiny that it is only just to be seen. How could I consider myself to be great?

If you measure the Four Seas against what is between Heaven and Earth—are they not just like an ants' nest in a vast marsh? If you measure the Middle Kingdoms against what is within the sea—are they not just like a grain of rice in a vast granary?

When denoting the sum of the many things we call them "myriad"—and yet man is [only] one of them:

Man populates the nine provinces,[21] he feeds on grain and interacts with others by ship and carriage—and yet, man is only one [of the myriad things]. When comparing him to the "myriad things" from this perspective, is he not just like the tip of a hair on the body of a horse?

What the Five Emperors passed on [through abdication], what the Three Kings fought over, what benevolent ones worried about, what men in office laboured for is no more than this (the tip of a hair on the body of a horse). By declining this (all under Heaven), Boyi won himself a name, and by speaking about it, Zhongni was taken as a man of learning; but in taking themselves as so important, don't they resemble you, when just now you thought of yourself as the greatest of all the waters?"

Scene two can be subdivided into three sub-units. The first runs from the first line (北海若曰) to line five (爾將可與語大理矣), altogether 65 graphs.[22] This passage creates a duality on the lexical level of what I want to call "obstruction words," such as 'captured' (ju 拘) 'bound' (du 篤), or 'fettered' (shu 束), on the one hand, and "non-obstruction"[23] or "connecting" words, such as 'leave' (his banks) (chu 出), 'gaze' (guan 觀) and 'realise' (zhi 知), on the other, further underpinned by the division between 'can' (ke 可) and 'cannot' (bu ke 不可). It takes a bridge position with reference to the next unit where the great principle is being described, such that it is positioned between "obstruction" and "the great principle."

---

21   The *locus classicus* for the 'nine provinces' is the "Yu gong" 禹貢 (Tribute to Yu) chapter of the *Shangshu* where the Great Yu is said to divide the world into the nine provinces of Ji 冀, Yan 兗, Qing 青, Xu 徐, Yang 揚, Jing 荊, Liang 梁, Yong 雍, and Yu 豫, but different texts provide different interpretations of what constitutes the nine provinces.

22   P. 563, l. 1/1–l. 3/4: "The God of the Northern Sea, Ruo, said" to "it might be possible to talk to you about the Great Principle."

23   See also Chia-Lynne Hong on non-obstruction in the *Zhuangzi* in id., "Seeing through the *Dao*: Image Schema Related to Non-obstruction in the *Zhuangzi* 26" (Paper presented at the 19th Conference of the European Association of Chinese Studies, Paris, 5 September 2012).

The second unit of this scene contains altogether 101 graphs and runs from line six (天下之水) to the end of line nine (方存乎見小，又奚以自多).[24] It employs the water metaphor to describe the one thing that pervades the world (Dao). Parallel to the previous scene where water takes the form of a river, water here manifests as sea. But whereas water in the previous scene produces the image of constant change, it here casts light on the underlying principle of that change: the unchanging principle of the one thing that pervades the world is that it is forever changing.

The third unit of this scene explains that things are what they are in a context. The conversation between the Lord of the River and the God of the North Sea in scene 1 has confirmed the status of Kongzi (Zhongni) and Boyi as cultural heroes of the past and personae of moral integrity.[25] However, the current scene deconstructs that image by setting in parallel fashion the *zi xi* 自喜 (pleased with oneself) from scene 1[26] that ridicules the Lord of the River's self-delusion with the *zi duo* 自多 (taking oneself as great) that relates to the cultural heroes of the past,[27] indicating that they fall short in just that way by labouring for measurable achievements in the human sphere which they have mistaken for the ultimate reality but which is, as this unit makes plain, no more than just one element of the myriad things, and so just like the tip of a hair on a horse's body. The previous scene is thus put in a new context in the sense that the ideas gained from the brief conversation in scene 1 were just a fettered snippet of reality, compromised by the Lord's limited vision.

The water metaphor in this scene is placed between the two real-world descriptions from unit 1 and 3. It seems to function as a conceptual principal insertion in scene 2.[28] As is typical of the feature of a principal insertion, it delivers a passage of central importance.

---

24   P. 563, l. 3/5–l. 6/10: "Of the waters on the earth" to "just to be seen. How could I consider myself to be great?"

25   I here refer to the concept of (philosophical) personae à la Deleuze and Guattari in their work *What is Philosophy?* Translated by Hugh Tomlinson and Graham Burchill (London, New York: Verso, 1994).

26   P. 561, l. 1/30–l. 2/1.

27   P. 564, l. 4/3–4.

28   The literary device of a 'principal insertion' is discussed in full in Meyer, *Philosophy on Bamboo*, 99. Briefly, the principal insertion is an alien element cutting through an otherwise parallel figure, and so it bears some resemblance with the device of a 'double-directed parallelism' described by Joachim Gentz, "Zwischen den Argumenten lesen. Zu zweifach gerichteten Verbindungsstücken zwischen Argumenten in frühen chinesischen Texten," *Bochumer Jahrbuch fuer Ostasienforschung* 29 (2005): 35–56. The idea behind the

But this is only one feature in the construction of meaning in this scene of the "Qiushui." As in the previous scene, the "Qiushui" makes use of uniform statements to describe opposite affairs in the form of the literary device of an opposing uniformity. This allows for the insight on the part of the text recipient that one and the same situation may prompt opposing sets of perceptions, thus questioning absolute ontological truth in an ever changing world. The first instance occurs in line three (p. 563), graphs 17–24: 不知何時止而不盈 "I don't know when this might stop—yet she never fills"; and again, graphs 31–38: 不知何時已而不虛 "I don't know when this might end—yet [the sea] never empties." The two uniform statements stress the never changing principle behind everlasting change. Despite constant movement, the water level—note that when read metaphorically water can easily stand for Dao—never alters. The other instance of this recurring device of deploying uniform statements for opposing state of affairs—the literary device of an opposing uniformity—can be found just a few lines further down. It is made of just four graphs 人處一焉 "man is [only] one of them."[29] That same statement reappears in the next line (l. 2/6–9). It stresses that man—and likewise the entire human realm—is just one element among the myriad things. In the first instance (p. 564, l. 1/20–23), the line is used in the parallel context of "the Four Seas" that, when measured "against Heaven and Earth," appear "just like an ants' nest in a vast marsh." The same is true for the human realm in the context of the myriad things. It is just "one of them." At this point, the "Qiushui" zooms in on that seemingly insignificant element, which is just one (yi 一) of the myriad things (*wan wu* 萬物) and opens up a whole world of farming, trading and life, just to zoom out again immediately after, reminding the recipient of the text that this whole world, a cosmos of its own, is in fact nothing but one of the myriad things. The repetition of the same line prompts a surprise in the reading experience of the text recipient, thus slowing down the process of text reception and so helping to visualise what has just been described. It thus becomes clear how insignificant both Kongzi (aka Confucius) and Boyi were amidst the myriad things, as they just acted for this one element—the human realm—and mistook it for the whole world, the myriad things, as also conveyed so beautifully by this passage.

Scenes 1 and 2 form one larger unit as indicated through the recurring reference to the personae Zhongni (Confucius) and Boyi. Crucially, they are brought together in the form of a double-directed text segment, which features as a

---

principal insertion is to explicate the overall concern of the text passage. (See Meyer, *Philosophy on Bamboo*, 117).

29 P. 564, l. 1/20–23.

bridge between the two scenes (1: p. 561, l.1–l5/end; 2: p. 563, l. 1–p. 564, l. 4/end). That text segment is placed in scene 1 and is, at first, difficult to contextualise, reading *shi wu fu xin* 始吾弗信 "at first I did not want to believe X."[30] The question that remains is what constitutes the reference of the Lord's disbelief. One possibility would be that it refers to the voices mocking Zhongni and Boyi. The structure of the argument would thus work as follows: at first, the Lord of the River did not want to believe what he used to hear, namely that there were those mocking Zhongni and Boyi. This would imply he had thought highly of them. The problem with this reading is that the same section describes the Lord's self-esteem as he was flowing along the banks, thinking that there would be no-one like him. From such a position of absolute self-esteem, he would arguably not question the mocking of Zhongni and Boyi. It therefore seems that such disbelief on his part must relate to what was before his eyes, that is, the vastness of the sea. Accordingly, now that he realises the vastness of the sea, and thus understands his own limitations, he comprehends that the mocking of Zhongni and Boyi was questionable because it resulted from the same deluded position in which he thought of himself as great. However, scene 2 deconstructs this. It shows that Zhongni and Boyi acted from the same state of self-delusion because—just like the Lord of the River—they equally worked in a framework of misguided taxonomies by misunderstanding their context as the only thing of relevance. It therefore appears as though the mocking of Zhongni and Boyi was in the end justified due to their self-delusion. However, we will learn later on that that is just another layer of misconception.

3.
河伯曰：然則吾大天地而小豪末，　　　　可乎？
北海若曰：　　　　　　　　　　　　　　否。
夫物，
　　　　量　　無窮，
　　　　時　　無止，
　　　　分　　無常，
　　　　終始　無故。
是故
大知　觀於遠近，故小而不寡，大而不多：　知量　　無窮。
　　　證曏今故，故遙而不悶，掇而不跂：　知時　　無止；
　　　察乎盈虛，故得而不喜，失而不憂：　知分之　無常也；
　　　明乎坦塗，故生而不說，死而不禍：　知終始之　不可故也。

計　　人之所知，不若其所不知；
　　　其生之時，不若未生之時；

30　P. 561, l. 4/18–21.

TRUTH CLAIM WITH NO CLAIM TO TRUTH

以其至小,求窮其至大之域,是故迷亂而不能自得也。
由此觀之,
  又何以知毫末之足以定至細之倪,
  又何以知天地之足以窮至大之域![p. 568-569]

> The Lord of the River [then] asked: "this being so, is it then permissible that I consider Heaven and Earth as great and the tip of a hair as small?"
> The God of the Northern Sea, Ruo, said: "no, it is not. With regard to what is in the world (= the phenomenal world),
>> measures have no limit,
>> times have no endings,
>> divisions have no constancy,
>> beginnings and endings have no fixation.
>
> From this it follows that the wisest have a full vision over far and near, and so they do not make less of [what others perceive] as small, nor do they make more of [what others perceive] as big,
>> for they know that measures have no limit;
>
> They have a clear vision over past and present, and so they are not disheartened about what is far (= out of reach), nor do they go on tiptoe for what is within reach,
>> for they know that times have no endings;
>
> They discern the waxing and the waning, and so they are not rejoiced about gaining, nor are they grieved about loss,
>> for they know that divisions have no constancy;
>
> They have a clear vision about the level path, and so they are not pleased about new life, nor do they consider death a calamity,
>> for they know that [things] from their beginnings to endings cannot be kept as they were before.
>
> When considering what man knows, it does not compare with what he doesn't;
> When considering his lifespan, it does not compare with the time before he was born.
> To seek to exhaust the greatest areas by means of the smallest—that this creates confusion and cannot be achieved, is self-evident.
> When seen from this perspective,
>> how should we know whether the tip of the hair suffices to serve as a standard for defining the limits of the minute;
>> and how should we know whether Heaven and Earth suffice to serve as a realm to exhaust the vastness of the greatest?

This conversation connects directly to the previous scenes and concludes the conversation about the categories *xi* 喜 (pleased/ rejoiced), *you* 憂 (grieved), *jin* 盡 (exhaust), *yue* 說 (pleased) that find no further mention in later parts of the "Qiushui." It starts from a question by the Lord of the River showing that he mistook the contextualisation given in the previous conversation as an absolute epistemological framework, and it ends with some conclusions about the absence of absolute standards, as is clear from the men who have gained deep understanding. Just as in the previous scene, this passage about the ways of the men of deep understanding is placed between two structurally different passages and so, a conceptual principal insertion, it seems to formulate the claims of central importance in this passage. The ways of the men of deep understanding as described in the passage from "the wisest have a full vision over far and near" 大知觀於遠近 to "for they know that beginnings or endings cannot be fixed" 知終始之不可故也—comprising 76 graphs[31]—are phrased in remarkable parallel fashion, of four matching lines each. The regular patterning of this unit expresses—on the formal level of composition—the regular patterns of their ways. Even if the individual action is different in each situation, the underlying principle is forever unchanging.

The men of deep understanding have left the hermeneutical circularity that hinders understanding on our part, as is well described in this scene: when trying to encompass the greatest from the perspective of the smallest, the result is ultimately one of confusion (p. 568, l.6/14[32]). The problem is that we are inextricably bound to that perspective: just as the frog is bound to the vision gained from within the well, we cannot escape the human realm which, however, is just one of the myriad things. This scene thus describes a fundamental ontological problem that renders understanding impossible. At the same time, the text leads us through that circularity by means of the literary representation of that circularity. It thereby enables the reader to assume an all-encompassing perspective, leaving behind that limited vision. Without putting it in explicit terms, this scene thus enables the text recipient to break away from the circularity of limited vision by visualising that circularity before his or her eyes.

Following this scene, the conversation between the Lord of the River and the God of the Northern Sea moves in a different direction:

4.
河伯曰：世之議者皆曰：『至精無形，至大不可圍。』是信情乎？
北海若曰：
夫　　自細視大者不盡，
　　　自大視細者不明。
夫　　精，小之微也；
　　　垺，大之殷也：
故異便。此勢之有也。
夫　　精粗者，期於　有形者也；

31　P. 568, l. 2/23–l. 5/14.
32　以其至小，求窮其至大之域，是故迷亂而不能自得也.

無形者，數之所不能分也；
不可圍者，數之所不能窮也。
可以言論者，物之粗也；
可以意致者，物之精也；
言之所不能論，意之所不能察致者，不期精粗焉。
是故大人之行，
不出乎害人，不多仁恩；
動不為利，不賤門隸；
貨財弗爭，不多辭讓；
事焉不借人，不多食乎力，不賤貪污；
行殊乎俗，不多辟異；
為在從眾，不賤佞諂；
世之爵祿不足以為勸，戮恥不足以為辱；
知是非之不可為分，細大之不可為倪。
聞曰：『道人不聞，至德不得，大人無己。』約分之至也。[p. 572-574]

The Lord of the River said: "The debaters of our age all say, 'the most quintessential has no form, the largest cannot be encompassed.' Is this really the nature of the matter?"

The God of the North Sea, Ruo, replied:

"As a matter of principle, when looking at the great from the perspective of the minuscule, it won't be exhaustive; when looking at the minuscule from the perspective of the great, it won't be clear.

As a matter of principle, that which [the debaters of our age call] 'quintessential' refers to the minute in the small; and that which [they think of as] 'massive' refers to the chunkiness in the great. Hence, this differentiation is just for convenience; it is based on the situation.

As a matter of principle, the quintessential and the chunky both point to (期指) that which has a form; but that which has no form is something which cannot be divided through numbers (which means to say it cannot be measured); and that which cannot be encompassed is something which cannot be exhausted through numbers (which means to say it cannot be measured).

That which can be categorised through words is the chunkiness within things; and that which can be conveyed through ideas is the quintessential within things.

However, that which cannot be categorised through words, and that which cannot be investigated through ideas, does not point to anything quintessential or massive.

From this it follows that the actions of the great man do not result in harming others,[33] nor do they seek to increase good treatment and favour. When the great man acts it is not for benefit, but [at the same time] he does not despise the serv-

---

33   Because they are not directed at the material world and so have no intention of material gain.

ants and slaves (who do exactly this); he does not compete for valuables and goods, but [at the same time] he does not make much of declining and granting; when he applies himself to things he does not rely on other people, but [at the same time] he does not set great store by making a living through his own efforts or despise those who, in their greed, become impure; his actions deviate from those of the mean, but [at the same time] he does not make much of being eccentric; in his behaviour, he does not follow the masses,[34] but [at the same time], he does not despise the gossipers and sycophants; the world's ranks and riches do not suffice to stimulate him, but [at the same time], dishonour and blemish do not suffice to disgrace him; he understands that right and wrong cannot be divided [in two clear categories], and the minuscule and the big cannot be used as categories. I have heard that

'those who follow the way have no fame,'
'those of utmost virtue obtain nothing,'
'and the great man has no self.'

This is the highest form of binding oneself to one's place."

This scene works in a parallel fashion to the ultimate scene of the "Qiushui" discussed below (scene 13). The God of the North Sea is confronted with an argument based on the absolute value of language as held by current debaters and posed to him by the Lord of the River. The God of the North Sea duly engages with it and shows that it is caught in a contradiction. The God of the North Sea demonstrates that the debaters mistake categories with no intrinsic value for frameworks of ultimate reality. Because the debaters are able to categorise what they think as big and small, it must be something that has a form. As such, it refers to something that can be measured, because the debaters simply refer to material instantiations of a world in flux and not the generic ideas beyond the matrix of what surrounds us. That which has no form, however, must by definition refer to something beyond that matrix, which, therefore, cannot be categorised as such. Thus, the fact that the debaters bring those two concepts together is in itself a conflict, demonstrating the limitations of language and categorisation when mistaken for generic, and ultimately valid, frameworks.

This scene consists of two parts. The first part[35] engages with the nature of the quintessential and the chunkiness. It demonstrates that misprision is the ultimate and unavoidable result, when confusing definitions that are gained through the propositional force of language on the one hand, and real world experiences that have an intrinsic value on the other, rather than just seeing

---

34   Reading *zai* 在 as *bù* 不.
35   P. 572, l. 1/1–l. 5/end.

them as auxiliary constructions that rely on context and perspective.³⁶ The second part³⁷ portrays the implications of real comprehension with reference to the Great men, who do not confuse worldly affairs with situations that have intrinsic value.

On the whole, the text does not shy away from debate. In fact, it embraces it—as is also stressed through the repetitive use of the discourse marker *fu* 夫 'as a matter of principle' in the first part of this unit.³⁸ Just as in the Platonic dialogues, an argument is taken seriously and willingly engaged with so as to show that it is based on misguided premises. In this case, it is demonstrated that the propositional force of language is misleading because it opens up absolute categories by which situational conditions are mistaken for frameworks of ultimate value. A similar form of argument deconstruction as used in this passage reappears in the final scene of the "Qiushui."³⁹

5.
河伯曰：
若物之外，若物之內，惡至而倪貴賤？惡至而倪小大？
北海若曰：
以道觀之，物無貴賤；
以物觀之，自貴而相賤；
以俗觀之，貴賤不在己。
以差觀之，因其所大而大之，　　則萬物莫不大；因其所小而小之，則萬物莫不小。
　　　　知天地之為稊米也，
　　　　知毫末之為丘山也，　　則差數睹矣。
以功觀之，因其所有而有之，　　則萬物莫不有　；因其所無而無之，則萬物莫不無。
　　　　知東西之相反而不可以相無，則功分定矣。
以趣觀之，因其所然而然之，　　則萬物莫不然；因其所非而非之，則萬物莫不非。
　　　　知堯、桀之自然而相非，　則趣操睹矣。昔者堯、舜讓而帝之、噲讓而絕；湯、武爭而王，白公爭而滅。

---

36 It is perhaps in this context that we should read the conceptual definition constructed between 'large' (大), 'massive' (浮), and 'chunky' (粗) in this unit. On the argumentative purpose of 'conceptual definitions' in early Chinese texts, see Meyer, *Philosophy on Bamboo*, 41, 229.

37 P. 574, l. 1/1–l. 5/end.

38 On the rhetorical function of the discourse marker—overstressed in my translation of the passage—see also Wagner's contribution in this volume.

39 A brilliant analysis of that scene is given in Norman Teng, "The Relatively Happy Fish Revisited," *Asian Philosophy* 16:1 (2006): 39–47. I shall provide a discussion of that scene below.

由此觀之，
爭讓之禮，堯、桀之行，貴賤有時，未可以為常也。
梁麗可以衝城，而不可以窒穴，
言殊器也；
騏驥驊騮，一日而馳千里，捕鼠不如狸狌，
言殊技也；
鴟鵂夜撮蚤，察毫末，晝出瞋目而不見丘山，
言殊性也。
故曰，
蓋師是而無非，師治而無亂乎？
是未明天地之理，萬物之情也。
是猶師天而無地，師陰而無陽，
其不可行明矣！
然且語而不舍，非愚則誣也！
帝王殊禪，三代殊繼。
差其時，逆其俗者，謂之篡夫；
當其時，順其俗者，謂之義之徒。
默默乎河伯！女惡知貴賤之門，小大之家！[p. 577–580]

The Lord of the River said: "regardless of whether [the viewpoint] is external to things, or internal to things, what position do we need to attain to discern a standard for noble and mean, as well as for small and great?"

The God of the Northern Sea, Ruo, responded:

"When looking at it from the perspective of the Dao, things are neither noble nor mean; [but] when looking at it from the perspective of the [individual] things themselves, each considers itself as noble and the other as mean;

when looking at it from the perspective of customs, noble and mean do not lie in oneself [but depend on the judgment of others]; [but] when looking at it from the perspective of degree and difference and, going along with that which is considered as great and we call it 'great,' then none of the myriad things is not great; and when going along with that which is considered as small and we call it 'small,' then none of the myriad things is not small.

However, when you understand that Heaven and Earth are in fact like a grain of rice, and when you understand that the tip of a hair is in fact like hills and mountains, then you have assumed the position of seeing things from the perspective of degree and difference (which means to say it is a relative perspective).

When looking at it from the perspective of properties (功) and, going along with that which is considered as there and we call it 'there,' then none of the myriad things is not there; and when going along with that which is thought of as not there and we call it 'not there,' then none of the myriad things is not there.

However, when you understand that east and west are in fact opposites but cannot be without each other, then you have assumed the perspective that defines the things according to their properties.

When looking at it from the perspective of tendencies and, going along that which is thought of as so and we call it 'right,' then none of the myriad things is not right; and when going along that which is thought of as not-so and calling it 'wrong,' then none of the myriad things is not wrong. However, when you understand that Yao and Jie each considered themselves as right and the other as wrong, then you have assumed the perspective that sees the things in relation to inclinations and tendencies.

In the past, Yao and Shun abdicated but reigned as emperors; King Kuai of Yan 燕王噲 (r. 320–314) abdicated and lost everything;[40] Tang and Wu battled and reigned as kings; Duke Bo battled and perished. Looking at this from the perspective of the rituals of contending and deferring and the conduct of Yao and Jie [you see] that noble and mean each have their time and can never be seen as constancies:

A battering ram can be used to break down a city wall but not for closing up a hole, which means that there are different tools [for different things]. Fine horses (a thoroughbred piebald horse and a fine steed) may gallop up to a thousand *li* in a day, but in catching mice they cannot compare with a wildcat or weasel, which means that there are different skills [for different things]. Owls can snatch a flea at night and discern the tip of a hair, but when they come out in daytime they blink their eyes and won't see a hill or a mountain, which means that there are different natures [in different things].

This is why to say: 'why not follow that which is right instead of doing wrong; why not follow order instead of making chaos?' epitomises the fact that one hasn't understood the patterns of Heaven and Earth and the essence of the myriad things. This is like following Heaven whilst ignoring Earth, and following the spirit of *yin* whilst ignoring that of *yang*; that this cannot be done, is clear. Despite this, [people] don't give up saying such things. If this is not due to stupidity then for false pretention: the sage kings have abdicated for different reasons, and the Three Dynasties succeeded in different ways.[41] Those who stood out of their time and went against the customs are called usurpers; but those who hit on the time and went along with the customs are called men of integrity. Be silent, Lord of the River! How should you know the gates of the noble and mean, and the masters of the small and great?"

---

40 In 314 BC, King Kuai of Yan 燕王噲 (r. 320-314) resigned in favour of his minister Zi Zhi 子之. The leaders of the various states generally condemned his move as an acute violation of political propriety. The ruler of Zhongshan 中山 used this incident to invade Yan and conquer part of its territory, as recorded in a bronze vessel inscription. *Wenwu* (1995) 1: 341–369. See the discussion in Yuri Pines, "Disputers of Abdication: Zhanguo Egalitarianism and the Sovereign's Power," *T'oung Pao* 91.4–5 (2005): 243–300, 269.

41 Yao and Shun abdicated; the kings of Xia, Yin and Zhou, so this passage, were succeeded by sons.

This scene directly connects to the previous conversation by taking up the question about the guiding thread (*ni* 倪) for discerning noble and mean, great and small, that is, discerning a standard to compartmentalise the world into a known taxonomy of stable categories. Just as in the previous scenes, the answer to the Lord's question is constructed in a remarkably regular fashion of five sets of well-adjusted parallelism which, at first sight, creates a tension between the highly balanced text composition on the one hand, and its content that says that nothing is fixed and fully depends on context, on the other. Hence, the world cannot be discerned through rules and principles that determine a point of fixation from where it is possible to give an absolute value statement about a certain matter. There is no such thing as a unified standard to discern what is great or mean, big or small.

However, the regularity of text composition is on a par with the regularity of the composition of the world, whose regular pattern is the irregularity of things. Expressed through regular sentence patterns that articulate the irregularity of the things, the text composition features as a device that gives form to the regularity of flux. The non-existence of absolute standards and values therefore does not hint at chaos but at a world composition where everything is beautifully balanced and dependent on its contexts: there is no *yin* without *yang*, as there is no East without West. The literary form of this unit therefore compounds the thought of this scene to a remarkable extent and contributes to the making of the argument by means of the regularity of its formal composition. Without stating so explicitly, the world is portrayed as fully regular in its irregularity.

6.
河伯曰：
然則我何**為**乎？何**不為**乎？吾辭受趣舍，吾終奈何？
北海若曰：
以道觀之， 何貴何賤，是謂反衍；無拘而志，與道大蹇。
　　　　　 何少何多，是謂謝施；無一而行，與道參差。
　　嚴乎　　　若國之有君，其無私德；
　　繇繇乎　　若祭之有社，其無私福；
　　汎汎乎　　其若四方之無窮，其無所畛域。
　　兼懷萬物，其孰承翼？
是謂無方。
　　　　　 萬物一齊，孰短孰長？道無終始，物有死生，不恃其功。
　　　　　 一虛一滿，不位乎其形。年不可舉，時不可止。消息盈虛，終則有始。
是所以語大義之方，論萬物之理也。
　　　　　 物之生也，若驟若馳。

無動而不變,無時而不移。
何為乎,何不為乎?夫固將自化。[p. 584-585]

The Lord of the River said: "if this is so, then what should I do and what shouldn't I do? On what final consideration am I to know what to refuse or accept, and choose what to prefer or discard?"

The God of the Sea of the North, Ruo, said:
"When [you] look at it from the perspective of Dao, then

what should be noble and what should be mean when this can simply be called 'returning to the [same] source?' Don't limit your mind, so that you won't become lame with the Dao.

[When you see it from the perspective of Dao,] then

what should be [worth] less or more when this can simply be called turns come round? Don't limit your actions to one way only, so that you won't be at odds and evens with the Dao.

[Therefore:]

Be stern like a lord to his state who grants no private favours;
Be bountiful like the deity at the sacrifice who grants no private blessings;
Be endless (flowing everywhere) like the infinite in the four directions that have nothing which bounds or hedges them.
Embrace the myriad things every one—which of them would deserve special shelter?

This is what I call being without a method (無方).

When [you understand that] the myriad things even out in one, then what should be [considered as] long and what should be [considered as] short? Dao has no ending and no beginnings, but all things are bound to be born and die—you cannot rely on their achievements. One moment empty, the next moment full, you cannot take a stand on their form.

The years cannot be warded off [from coming], time cannot be stopped. Decay, growth, fullness, and emptiness—when this comes to an end it starts all over again.

This is how I describe the method of Great Meaning (大義之方) and sort the patterns of the myriad things.

The life of a thing is like a stampede, a gallop: with every movement there is a change;[42] in no time there is an alteration.

So, what is it then that we should do and that we shouldn't do, when it is in fact inherent in the things that they transform by themselves?

This scene marks a turning point in the conversation between the Lord of the River and the God of the North Sea. For the first time, there is an attempt to translate the epistemological angst of the interlocutor into a philosophy of

---

[42] Here I follow James Legge, *The Tao Te Ching, The Writings of Chuang-tzŭ, The Thai-shang Tractate of Actions and Their Retributions* (Taipei: Ch'eng wen Publishing, 1976), 431.

praxis: what is it that we should do in a world with no absolute standards and categories? The response by the God of the North Sea demonstrates the complexity of simplicity, which, as it turns out, is in fact surprisingly simple, too. For the first time in the "Qiushui," a dialectical situation is described where simplicity proves to be a complex affair, which, when taken in its full consequence, again captivates by its simplicity. And so on: our actions must be parallel to the patterns of the world with its lack of stable taxonomy clusters. However, and here we enter the realms of complexity: if seen as an absolute standard for actions, this guideline does not work either, for it implies rigidity and therefore carries the danger of "becoming lame with the Dao," that is, becoming unbending again in our actions and holding fast to a fixed pattern of irregularity. This insight with regard to the complexity of simplicity is translated into praxis as being "without a method" (無方), summing up the position one should take when looking at the things from the perspective of Dao—immediately undermined a few lines further down when the text speaks of the "method of great meaning" (大義之方). In other words, there is a method for being without a method, and this implies that one cannot live against the cycle of nature. But obviously, the 'method of great meaning' is in its implication being without a method, too, and there is a method for being without a method. Thus, a scenario of dialectical complexity is constructed that, in its full extent, is surprisingly simple: actions must be parallel to the patterns of the world with no stable taxonomy clusters, but this must not become a fixed pattern itself, for the world is in constant flux, and so, too, is the pattern of irregularity. This insight into the complexity of simplicity that, when taken to its full extent, captivates by its simplicity, was created not through the use of positive assertions—for this would contradict everything that is being said—but on the level of text composition. Interestingly, the two positions—being 'without a method' and the 'method of great meaning'—each result from what is said immediately preceding them in the text. But while being without a method sums up a form of behaviour that is expressed in two sets of rigidly parallel sentence patterns, the term 'method of great meaning' sums up something formulated in non-regular prose. The passage therefore develops concepts which, when taken together, undermine each other and so formulate an idea beyond the immediate lexicon of this passage. The strategy for producing meaning in this unit therefore carries meaning itself.

7.
河伯曰： 然則何貴於道邪？
北海若曰：
知道者必達於理，
　　　達於理者必明於權，
　　　　　明於權者不以物害己。
至德者，
　　火　　弗能熱，
　　水　　弗能溺，
　　寒暑　弗能害，
　　禽獸　弗能賊。

非謂其薄之也，言察乎安危，寧於禍福，謹於去就，莫之能害也。

故曰，
　天在內，　　人在外，
　　　　德在乎天。
　知天　　　人之行，
　本乎天，
　　　　位乎　　　　得/德：
蹢躅而屈伸，
反要而語極。

曰：
　　　　　　何謂天？　　　　何謂人？
北海若曰：
　　　　　　牛馬四足，是謂天；
　　　　　　　　　　落馬首，穿牛鼻，是謂人。
故曰，
無以人滅天，
無以故滅命，
無以得殉名。
　　謹守而勿失，
　　是謂反其真。[p. 588–591]

The Lord of the River said: "But in that case, what is there to value in the Dao?"
The God of the North Sea, Ruo, said:
"He who realises Dao is certain to reach [understanding] of the basic patterns;
　he who reaches [understanding] of the basic patterns is certain to be clear about [the right] balance;
　he who is clear about [the right] balance will not allow things to do him harm.
He who is of perfect virtue,
　fire won't burn him, water won't drown him, cold or heat won't do him harm, birds and beasts won't hurt him.

> This is not to say that he takes them lightly, but that he is perspicacious about safety and danger, peaceful about fortune and misfortune, careful in approaching and shunning, [so that] nothing can do him harm.
> That is why I say:
>> The heavenly is internal, the human is external, and virtuous power (*de*) is located in the heavenly.
>> [Therefore], when you understand the workings of the heavenly and the human [realms], you find yourself rooted in the heavenly whilst taking stance in virtuous power (*de*).[43]
>
> So, even when hastening or holding back, bending or stretching, you return to the essential to expound the supreme!"
> [The Lord of the River] said: "But what do you mean by the heavenly and the human?"
> The God of the North Sea, Ruo, said:
>> "Oxen and horses have four feet—this is what I call the heavenly; putting a halter on horses' head and piercing oxen's nose is what I call the human.
>> That is why I say:
>> Don't extinguish the heavenly through the human;
>> don't extinguish fate through reason;
>> don't let your name suffer harm through gain.
>> Embrace this carefully and without losing [it], this is what [I] call 'returning to genuine nature.'"

This unit takes the "Qiushui" to the next higher level. Based on the previous conversation about the complexity of simplicity and the dangers of becoming "lame with the Dao" when not seeing the complex in the simple and the simple in the complex, the interlocutor moves on to ask about the value of Dao. This is by far the most challenging question and this is reflected also on the level of the microstructure of this unit, which, in terms its formal composition, is the most complex of the entire "Qiushui."

This unit is the final scene where a conversation between Ruo, God of the North Sea, and the Lord of the River takes place and closes the first sub-canto of this text.[44] The strategy taken in this unit to respond to the question about

---

43 Based on the structure of the argument, I read *de* 得 'obtain' (OC *tˤək) as *de* 德 'virtue' (OC *tˤək). This change is well attested.

44 As in Meyer, *Philosophy on Bamboo*, I use 'sub-canto' to describe structurally coherent text parts. The sub-canto is the next higher unit after the pericope (Meyer, *Philosophy on Bamboo*, 56). The terminology is used for textual analysis in biblical studies. See Marjo Korpel, "Introduction to the Series Pericope," in *Delimination Criticism. Pericope 1: Scripture as Written and Read in Antiquity*, eds. Marjo Korpel and Josef Oesch (Assen: Royal Van Gorcum, 2000), 1–50. The sub-canto is a unit that should be elaborated with respect to the individual text. I want to use 'sub-canto' (as opposed to 'section') to indicate a self-contained unit at a level of meaning construction above the building block.

Dao is to construct *dao* 道 in parallel fashion to *de* 德. By taking up notions from the previous scenes and integrating them within a unified vision of reality, this unit presents a synthesis of the account so far.

This unit discusses the principles of the cosmic and the human realms, *dao* and *de*, in a conceptually parallel fashion. The two principles are also put in parallel context on the formal level of text composition, whereby the *de* chain is subordinate to the *dao* chain in that it explores the attainment of *de* in very concrete terms, while the *dao* chain moves from *dao*, and via the cosmic patterns and the varying balance, to the phenomenal world of *wu* 物 (the things in the world) in toto. Hence, whereas the *dao* chain, A, is developed on the level of cosmic entities—patterns (理), varying balance (權), as well as the phenomenal world overall (物)—the *de* chain, B, is constructed in concrete terms only. These two chains are brought together in a unifying C component that elaborates on the fact that those who understand *dao* and attain *de* will suffer no harm:

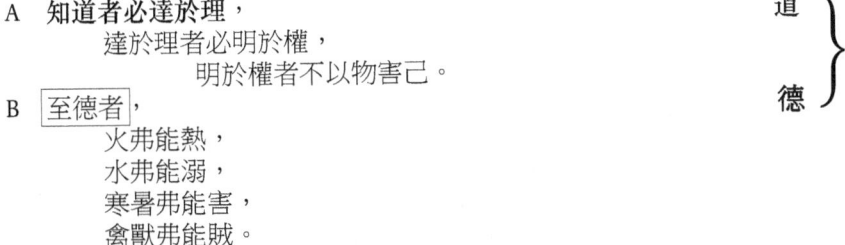

FIGURE 1   *Parallel case of* dao *and* de

Based on the formal composition of this unit, four things are clear thus far: first, the principles of *dao* and *de* work in parallel fashion; however, second, whilst it is possible to attain *de* in concrete terms, *dao* can only be grasped cognitively; third, *de* is subordinate to *dao*. It remains on the level of concrete terms while *dao* controls the cosmic principles in toto; fourth, they both lead to a level of insight on the part of the individual to the point where "he is perspicacious about safety and danger, peaceful about fortune and misfortune, careful in approaching and shunning, [so that] nothing can do him harm."[45]

---

45   This sentence will have implications for the construction of reality on the macro-level of composition. I come back to that later in this chapter.

Following these two chains of *dao* and *de* realities, a second parallel case is opened, namely that between the heavenly and the human as complementary inner and outer aspects. Just as in the two parallel chains above, the heavenly and the human are brought together in a synthesising C component that elaborates on the implications of the foregoing:

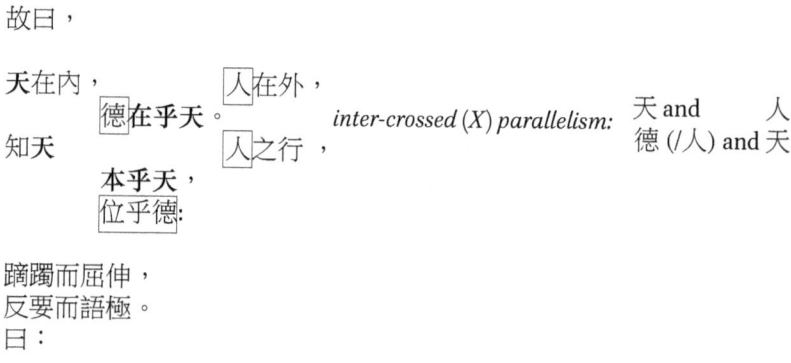

FIGURE 2 *Inter-crossed parallelism*

The figure works in the form of a chiastic parallelism that is commonly found in argument-based texts[46] beginning from the Warring States period but has not yet been well described. In the *de*-line (德在乎天 'the virtuous power resides in the heavenly'[47]), the first inter-crossed element in this figure—'human' (*ren* 人)—is replaced by *de* 德 through a conceptual definition that is typical of argument-based texts from the Warring States period, where conceptually two terms are given equal structural significance and can be substituted for each other in parallel constructions.[48] Without having to say so explicitly, this unit thus constructs a relatedness between the human and *de* 德. By so doing, the text explicates formally that *de* 德 belongs to the human realm.

The line just discussed further states that *de* 德 is located within the heavenly and so he who "understands the workings of the heavenly and of the human [realms]" is firmly "rooted in the heavenly" whilst taking a firm "stance in virtuous power (*de*)." According to the same principle of constructing a

---

46   On argument-based texts, see Meyer, *Philosophy on Bamboo*, 11 ff.
47   P. 588, l. 4/22.
48   On the composition of conceptual definitions in Warring States period philosophical texts, see Meyer, *Philosophy on Bamboo*, 40 f. Persuasive definitions with a distinction between 'emotive' and 'conceptual'—or 'descriptive'—meaning were developed by Charles Stevenson, "Ethical Judgements and Avoidability: Persuasive Definitions," *Mind* 47 (1938): 331–350 and id., *Ethics and Language* (London: Oxford University Press, 1945).

conceptual definition by substituting two conceptually related terms in the context of a parallel figure, the last line of this parallelism (位乎德[49]) substitutes *de* 德 for the human (人) which, based on its parallel context with the heavenly (天) from the previous line, is the concept one would expect to find here.

The equation of two terms works the other way round too. The figure just discussed[50] connects to the previous figure of a parallel unit within that scene[51] as indicated by the connection *gu yue* 故曰 ('that is why I say'), from where it becomes clear that a conceptual relatedness is assumed between the two parallel figures, and so, too, for the terms "heavenly" (天) and "*dao*" (道) that are substituted for one another between these two figures. This is a full circle established in this unit. Without propounding this circularity explicitly, it is shown that virtuous power (*de*) is rooted in *dao*, while *dao* is carried within; *dao* rests in the realm of the heavenly. As a result, the one who arrives at a cognitive grasp of *dao* has necessarily cultivated the heavenly within and translates this through virtuous power into worldly affairs. The figure below (figure 3) visualises this.

This complex relationship between the human and the heavenly on the one side, and *dao* and *de* on the other, recalls the *Mengzi* where self-cultivation is deemed possible (and justified!) through a connectedness between humans and heaven. The passage here demonstrates a similar connectedness between the human and the heavenly realms. However, unlike the *Mengzi*, it does so not by expounding this explicitly, but through developing this notion on the level of its formal structure and thus reduplicating the cosmic pattern, instead of defining it in categorical terms. In this passage of two parallel figures that together make a consistent pericope of text composition,[52] it is shown that by nourishing a cognitive grasp of Dao, humans realise a connectedness with heaven which translates into virtuous workings in the world that never go against the cosmic pattern around them. But this can also be established the other way round: virtuous conduct is only possible when acting according to the cosmic pattern which, in turn, requires a cognitive grasp of Dao. This most elegantly answers the initial inquiry about the value of Dao in a world where there exist no stable taxonomical values.

---

49 P. 588, l. 4/8.
50 P. 588, l. 4/16–l. 5/10.
51 P. 588, l. 2/5–l. 4/13.
52 I use the term 'pericope' to refer to structurally coherent text parts that are on the level below the sub-canto (Meyer, *Philosophy on Bamboo*, 56). Just like the sub-canto, the pericope is a unit that should be elaborated with respect to the individual text.

```
道/天          在內
    人/德      在外
 德            在乎天
知天 人 之行

              本乎天/道
              位乎    德/人
```

FIGURE 3   *Relatedness of concepts*

The subsequent dialogue where the Lord of the River further inquires about the implications of the foregoing[53] furthers the insight about the human and the heavenly with regard to *de* and *dao*. The heavenly is the natural course of things; it is carried within. The human is the man-made course of things; it is external and translates into worldly behaviour. At the same time, the human should not contradict the heavenly realm. This would disqualify one's actions and render them un-virtuous. The following holds accordingly:

> don't extinguish the heavenly through the human
> don't extinguish fate through reason
> don't let your name suffer harm through gain.

The heavenly participates in the human through *dao* and so any form of violation against the natural course of things is necessarily a violation of the human, too.

Within the "Qiushui," scene 7 appears in an environment which states that without a cognitive realisation of the unchanging cosmic pattern of everlasting change, one will always be a victim of perception: a frog, it is said in a previous scene, cannot have a conversation about the world because it is bound to its well, a summer fly can tell you nothing about the winter because it is bound to its one season. Man, in the same vein, can say nothing about Dao and the workings of heaven because he is bound to concrete affairs. Each participant is ultimately tied to the limited vision of experience, and language does little to help solve this. This proves to be a fundamental problem, a real drama of epistemological angst: the hermeneutical circularity of comprehension facilitates no insight beyond the narrow frame of understanding through immediate experience. Whatever lies beyond that horizon is by definition beyond discernment. Scene 7 is an attempt to take one step out of the hermeneutical circularity of insight that is bound to immediate vision and experience, whilst language, tied to the level of the human, proves unable to express anything beyond that

---

53   P. 590, l. 1–p. 591, l. 1/end.

level. Scene 7 does so not just by pointing out this hermeneutical circularity as was done in scene 3; it now provides a way out of this circularity: scene 7 is made up of two dialogues and three building blocks. The two dialogues are constructed in parallel fashion with regard to the strict patterns of questions and answers. Subsequent to the parallel text on *dao* and *de* there appears a rather odd insertion:

> ...蹢躅而屈伸，反要而語極[54]
> [...], when hastening or holding back, bending or stretching, you return to the essential to expound the supreme.

These lines break away from the general pattern of the text and present a somewhat alien element within this section. At first sight rather dark and ambiguous, the authors of the text felt the need to contextualise this statement through another parallel unit following that line. Situated therefore between the two parallel sections, it might be a principal insertion, if perhaps a rather vague one, and so a literary form that carries the main thought of this unit. Whilst this may well be the case, it remains that a core term of this line reappears at the end of the section: *fan* 反 'to return.' This makes the line become a recurrent text feature that contextualises the two parallel sections of this unit by looking at what has just happened: it describes movement that, in circular fashion, itself expounds the ultimate by returning to the essential. This is exactly the circle carried out in the parallel sections of the text. As a consequence, by describing the movement that the recipient of the text just undertook when engaging with this unit, it allows a vision of the hermeneutical circularity of limited understanding from outside that circular movement. Such stepping out of the circularity of limited understanding by looking at it from the outside as carrying out that circularity in oneself is in itself a way to deconstruct that circularity of limited vision. The recipient of the text is thus made to understand that she is already following the natural circle of the things—and therefore Dao—simply by virtue of reading or reciting this text. The text thus produces meaning through form. By going through the text and so carrying out that movement based on that form, the recipient of the text performs the bridge between comprehension and conduct. To recite the text may therefore become a philosophically meaningful event.[55]

---

54   P. 588, l. 5/11–20.
55   The "Qiushui" is not exceptional in this regard as becomes clear from examples such as Guodian One "Laozi" or "Tai yi sheng shui."

The "Qiushui" has now provided all the tools necessary to allow the text recipient to understand the processes by which meaning is constructed without relying on the propositional force of language. It comes as no surprise that after this unit the text moves away from the dialogic pattern of interlocutor and respondent between the God of the North Sea and the Lord of the River. Assuming that the text recipient has internalised the strategies of the "Qiushui" to invoke understanding, it now moves on to a hitherto unseen playfulness.

8.
夔憐蚿，蚿憐蛇，蛇憐風，風憐目，目憐心。
夔謂蚿曰：「吾以一足踔而行，予無如矣。今子之使萬足，獨奈何？」
蚿曰：「不然。子不見夫唾者乎？噴則大者如珠，小者如霧，雜而下者不可勝數也。今予動吾天機，而不知其所以然。」
蚿謂蛇曰：「吾以眾足行，而不及子之無足，何也？」
蛇曰：「夫天機之所動，何可易邪？吾安用足哉！」
蛇謂風曰：「予動吾脊脅而行，則有似也。今子蓬蓬然起於北海，蓬蓬然入於南海，而似無有，何也？」
風曰：「然，予蓬蓬然起於北海而入於南海也，然而指我則勝我，(鰌)我亦勝我。雖然，夫折大木，蜚大屋者，唯我能也。故以眾小不勝為大勝也。為大勝者，唯聖人能之。」[p. 591-594]

> The Kui[56] envies the millipede, the millipede envies the snake, the snake envies the wind, the wind envies the eye, and the eye envies the mind.
>
> The Kui said to the millipede: "I have one leg that I use to hop about and move along and I hardly keep up [with you]. Now that [I see] you commanding ten thousand legs—how is it that do you do that?"
>
> The millipede answered: "It is not so. Have you, sir, never seen a man spitting? As he spits, there are big bubbles like pearls and small ones like dewdrops; what drops out is in disarrangement of countless bubbles. Now that I move my natural device, I don't understand how it actually works."
>
> The millipede said to the snake: "I move by using all these legs and yet I do not keep up with you, sir, who have no feet at all, why is that?"
>
> The snake answered: "It is by means of my natural device that I move, how could it be different? What should I use feet for?
>
> The snake said to the wind: "I proceed by moving my backbone and ribs, and so I still have an appearance. But you, sir, when whirling with a blustering force you arise from the North Sea and enter into the South sea in just that way, but there is no appearance [of you]. How is that possible?"
>
> The wind answered: "It is so: I arise from the North Sea with a whirling force and enter into the South Sea in just that way; and yet, to point a finger at me

---

56 Kui is a being with only one leg. It is sometimes described as a spirit or a strange beast, sometimes as a historical personage—the Music Master Kui.

overcomes me, and to trample on me overcomes me too. Despite this, I alone have the ability to break down big trees and blow over large houses. And so, a real victory is when one is not overcome by the mass of the petty things. To achieve a real victory, only the sagacious ones are able to achieve that."

Entertaining as the scene is, I simply like to point out that it takes up notions from previous scenes, namely that of limited vision and the differences in nature as portrayed, for instance, through the frog in the well (scenes 2 and 10) or the battering ram (scene 5), and it alludes to what the "Qiushui" describes as the highest form of attaining one's lot (分) in scene 4. Through the use of parallel sentence constructions, it is stressed that for each of the natural manifestations (Kui, millipede, snake), the same situation applies. This makes it clear that despite their differences, their existence is a parallel case in point, and in each case, they are bound to their specific lot (分). By so doing, scene 8 prepares for the next scene in talking about the sagacious person and the nature of true victory:

9.
孔子游於匡，宋人圍之數匝，而弦歌不輟。
子路入見，曰：「何夫子之娛也？」孔子曰：「來，吾語女。
我　　諱窮久矣，而不免，命也；
　　　求通久矣，而不得，時也。
當堯、舜而天下無窮人，非知得也；
當桀、紂而天下無通人，非知失也：時勢適然。

夫
水行不避蛟龍者，漁父之勇也；陸行不避兕虎者，獵夫之勇也；白刃交於前，視死若生者，烈士之勇也；知窮之有命，知通之有時，臨大難而不懼者，聖人之勇也。由處矣！吾命有所制矣！」

無幾何，將甲者進，辭曰：「以為陽虎也，故圍之；今非也，請辭而退。」[p. 595-597]

Kongzi was travelling in Kuang when the men of Song encircled him with several layers of troops; nonetheless, [Kongzi] kept playing his lute and singing to it without stopping. Zi Lu entered to see him and asked: "How is it, venerated master, that you are so carefree?" Kongzi replied: "Come here, I shall tell you:

For a long time I have tried to avert hardship; the fact that I now cannot escape it is because [Heaven] has ordained it thus. For a long time I have sought to be successful; that I cannot achieve it is because the times are not right.[57] That at

---

[57] This notion is a constant in early Chinese literature. It is discussed most explicitly in the text "Qiong da yi shi" from Guodian One.

the time of Yao and Shun no men in the world suffered hardship is not because wisdom had been gained. That at the time of Jie and Zhou no [wise] men in the world were successful is not because wisdom had been lost; it was because times and circumstances coincided.

As a matter of principle:

> To travel on water yet not shrink from the sea serpent and dragon tiger—that is the courage of the fisherman. To travel on land yet not shrink from the rhinoceros and the tiger—that is the courage of the hunter. To see uncovered blades crossing just in front of the eyes and looking at death as though it was life—that is the courage of the arduous knight. But to understand that hardship depends on heavenly ordain, that be successful has its time, and to face great difficulty without fear—that is the courage of the sagacious person.[58]

Be calm, You, my destiny has been decided."

Not long afterwards, the leader of the armed men came in and apologised by saying: "We have mistaken you for Yang Hu,[59] and so we have surrounded you. Now that [I realise] you aren't, I beg to take my leave," and so he withdrew.

At a first glance, this scene seems to portray Kongzi in a very positive light: despite the obvious threat posed to him and his disciples, Kongzi stays calm and keeps on singing to his lute, fully conforming to the ways of a cultured man of learning. He is further free from distress with regard to his success in his political career, for he notes that achievements depend on heavenly commands and the right times, and so there is no way by which he can enforce success. It either happens or it does not, depending on the world around him. This notion is furthered with reference to the cases of Yao and Shun plus Jie and Zhou that are set apart through the literary device of a uniform opposition: whereas Yao and Shun flourished, Jie and Zhou perished despite the world around them being the same. Moreover, the scene makes Kongzi construct four parallel cases, each of which explains fearlessness for different types of people. This accords with the previous unit where different things are said to have different natures, each to their particular lot (分). Correspondingly, in one of the four cases developed in the unit under review, fearlessness is defined as the trait of a sagacious person: Kongzi himself. The sagacious person understands that failure depends on heavenly command whilst success relies on the times being right and so, similar to the wind in the previous unit that can uproot trees but is overcome by the pointing of a finger, the sagacious person has the power to change the course of things (through his *de* 德), but he can likewise be blocked by a random group of soldiers not letting him pass.

---

58 Cf., Burton Watson, *The Complete Works of Chuang tzu*, Translated by Burton Watson (New York: Columbia University Press, 1968), 185.

59 A contemporary of Kongzi, Yang Hu was a usurper in the state of Lu.

Kongzi is not disheartened because of this metaphorical pointing of the finger against him. By keeping his faith and singing to his lute despite hardship, he conforms to the ideal of a sagacious person as not being defeated by the multitude of petty things.

So far, so good. However, this seemingly straightforward picture dissolves under closer scrutiny. The problem is threefold. First, one of definition, second one of application, and third one of perception. First, Kongzi provides a positive definition of a sagacious person by portraying himself in such terms—beautifully exaggerated by the discourse marker *fu* 夫 'as a matter of principle.' Whereas the previous scene simply acknowledges that only a sagacious person is able to overcome the petty things of daily affairs, Kongzi translates this into a definition that requires positive action on his part, and so he restricts the notion of a 'sagacious person' to a definition of his vision and understanding. The sagacious person according to Kongzi is, secondly, just concerned with the human realm. He sought to be successful (*tong* 通), but this just applies to the 'one' (*yi* 一) of the myriad things (*wan wu* 萬物), as mentioned in scene 2. Thirdly, Kongzi confuses taxonomical realities. As previously portrayed in scene 5, an example is sought from the rulers of the past, namely Yao and Shun in comparison to Jie and Zhou. However, unlike in scene 5 where the world under Yao and Shun is different from that under Jie and Zhou with the result that Jie and Zhou are seen as usurpers whilst Yao and Shun appear as men of principle, Kongzi here portrays the world as a stable entity and the rule of Jie and Zhou as abhorrent deviations from ideal rulership. Kongzi therefore seems to misunderstand definitions of decline as absolute value categories instead of seeing them in relation to one another. Kongzi, it seems under closer scrutiny, mistakes a snapshot in time for an absolute representation and manifestation of reality.

At this point, the scene ends with an expression of misunderstanding. Kongzi was simply mistaken for someone else. He may now move on. This line therefore beautifully manifests the reading experience of this unit on the part of the text recipient by reduplicating on the textual level the expression of misunderstanding with regard to the persona of Kongzi, thus compounding on the literary level the thought of this unit. The text has its message acted out.

10.
公孫龍問於魏牟曰：
「龍少學先王之道，長而明仁義之行；合同異，離堅白；然不然，可不可；困百家之知，窮眾口之辯：吾自以為至達已。今吾聞莊子之言，茫然異之。不知論之不及與？知之弗若與？今吾無所開吾喙，敢問其方。」
公子牟隱機大息，仰天而笑曰：

「子獨不聞夫埳井之蛙乎?謂東海之鱉曰:
　『吾樂與!吾跳梁乎井幹之上,入休乎缺甃之崖。赴水則接腋持頤,蹶泥則沒足滅跗。還虷蟹與科斗,莫吾能若也。且夫擅一壑之水,而跨跱埳井之樂,此亦至矣。夫子奚不時來入觀乎?』
東海之鱉左足未入,而右膝已縶矣。於是逡巡而卻,告之海曰:
　『夫千里之遠,不足以舉其大;千仞之高,不足以極其深。禹之時,十年九潦,而水弗為加益;湯之時,八年七旱,而崖不為加損。夫不為頃久推移,不以多少進退者,此亦東海之大樂也。』
於是埳井之蛙聞之,適適然驚,規規然自失也。」

「且夫知不知是非之竟,而猶欲觀於莊子之言,是猶使蚊負山,商蚷馳河也,必不勝任矣。且夫知不知論極妙之言,而自適一時之利者,是非埳井之蛙與?且彼方跐黃泉而登大皇,無南無北,奭然四解,淪於不測;無東無西,始於玄冥,反於大通。子乃規規然而求之以察,索之以辯,是直用管闚天,用錐指地也,不亦小乎?子往矣!
且子獨不聞夫壽陵餘子之學行於邯鄲與?未得國能,又失其故行矣,直匍匐而歸耳。今子不去,將忘子之故,失子之業。」

公孫龍口呿而不合,舌舉而不下,乃逸而走。[p. 597, l. 2—p. 603, l. 1]

Gongsun Long[60] asked Wei Mou,[61] saying: "When I was a young boy, I studied the ways of the former kings; when I grew up, I gained clarity about the workings of benevolence and rightness. I harmonised alike with difference, I separated hardness from whiteness,[62] I made so what is not-so, and I permitted the non-permissible. Painfully, I mastered the knowledge of the various masters, and I exhausted the arguments of the many debaters. I considered myself to have reached the highest form of accomplishment. But now that I hear the words of Zhuangzi, I am confused in that I find them very different. I do not understand whether my theories are not as good as his, or whether my knowledge is not equal to his? Now that I have nothing about which to open my mouth, I venture to ask about his method (*fang* 方)."

Gongzi Mou leaned on [his] small table, took a long breath, looked up to heaven and said, laughingly:

"Have you, sir, alone, never heard of the frog in the old well, which said to the turtle of the Eastern Sea:

60　Gongsun is the name of the descendants of the sovereign of Zhao—one of the three successor states of Jin; Gongsun Long is known as a controversial debater infamous for his paradoxical arguments, such as that a "white horse is not a horse."
61　Wei was another successor state of Jin. Mou was one of the sons of its ruler of that time and a great admirer of Zhuangzi.
62　Gongsun Long holds that the attributes of material objects, such as hardness and whiteness, are separate existences.

'How great is my pleasure! When jumping out of the well I leap on to its parapet, when getting in, I can rest on the wall where a brick has fallen out. When diving into the water, I let it come up right under my armpits so that it supports my chin, and when slipping into the mud, I bury my feet so that [the mud] gets over my ankle. When turning around, I realise that of the mosquito larvae, crabs and tadpoles, none can possibly be my match. Moreover, to have complete control of the water in the gully and preside over all the pleasures of the well, this clearly is the best there is. Why don't you, sir, come in some time and see for yourself?'

But before the turtle of the Eastern Sea had even got her left foot into the well, her right knee already stuck fast. Upon this, she backed out and withdrew, and told the frog about the sea:

'Even the distance of a thousand miles would not suffice to measure its vastness, and the height of a thousand fathoms would not suffice to estimate its depth. At the time of the great Yu, there were [heavy] floods in nine out of ten years, and yet the level of its waters never rose; at the time of Tang, there were droughts at seven out of eight years, and yet [its waters] never ebbed away from the shores.

Thus, that no change is produced in its waters by any cause of long-term influence, and that no advance or retreat is produced in its waters by any amount of addition or subtraction; this clearly is the great pleasure of the Eastern Sea.'

Upon hearing this, the frog from the old well was at once lost in surprise and, rotating in circles, the [bloated frog] disappeared."

"Now that your knowledge does not suffice to grasp the limits of right and wrong, and still you wish to inspect the words of Zhuangzi, this is like trying to make a mosquito carry a mountain, or a pill-bug race against the River—clearly, this cannot be taken on. And now that your knowledge does not suffice to comprehend the words about the mysterious things and still you wish to appropriate them yourself for temporary gain, does this not resemble the frog in the old well [that talks about things which it doesn't understand]?

Also, that one (Zhuangzi) is at one moment putting his foot on the Yellow Springs of the underworld and mounting the heights of the great sky at another. To him, there is no north and south—in utter freedom he moves in all four directions and sinks into the immeasurable; to him, there is no east or west—he starts off from what is abysmally obscure[63] and returns to what is grandly perceptible (*da tong* 大通).

But, you, sir, whilst going in circles [like the bloated frog that is disappearing in circles], you seek to discern him, and explore [him] through disputation, this is just like using a tube to investigate the sky and using an awl to measure the

---

63 Here I follow James Legge, *The Sacred Books of China: The Writings of Kwang-sze* (Oxford: Clarendon Press, 1891), 437.

depth of the earth—surely they are too small [for this task]! Go your ways, sir! Or have you alone not heard of the young boys of Shou Ling who attempted to learn the ways of the capital of Zhao, Han Dan? Before they had even mastered [the ways] of Han Dan, they had already forgotten their old ways, and so they could only return home on their four hands and knees.[64] If you won't leave, you might forget your old acquirements, and fail in your profession."

Gongsun Long stood there, mouth open, unable to close it, his tongue right at the top; and so he turned tail and fled.

Scene 10 is one of the most amusing in the "Qiushui." The irony that comes to the fore in this unit is a literary device and important for the making of the argument.

In this scene, altogether four layers of stories are nested within one another. The conversation between the frog in the old well and the Turtle of the East Sea is one; the story about the young boys of Shou Ling is another; and this is all framed by an imagined conversation between Gongsun Long, the infamous debater of the time and known for his paradoxical claims, and Gongzi Mou, the admirer of the Zhuangzi and son of the ruler of Wei, one of the successor states of Jin. But that conversation is again written from the perspective of an outside spectator, and so nested in yet another context. That this framing conversation is again nested within yet another reality becomes especially obvious from the last line where we find a theatre-style stage direction that gives a burlesque of Gongsun Long, as he is left in utter disbelief of what is happening around him—or, in fact, to him. The distance thus created in the last line between text recipient—that is, us, the readers—and the framing conversation held between Gongsun Long and Gongzi Mou that turns the whole scene into staged theatre play puts us, the text recipient, into the role of the spectator and hence into a context providing reference. Through this device, the text makes it obvious that the foregoing is an exaggerated caricature and the 'information' to be taken with a pinch of salt. A complex reality is thus formulated where the various stories feature like Russian matryoshkas within the wider context of this scene. No such reality is to be trusted as an ultimate state of affairs but is nested within a wider, situation-specific, context. That is a clear hint as to how to approach this unit, and in fact how to approach the entire "Qiushui": a particular situation—or scene—can never be taken as the ultimate expression of reality, for there is always yet another reality to it. The literary form of this scene reduplicates this notion. Form and content are one.

---

64 It is on purpose that I keep 行 in its most generic sense rather than translating it as 'walk' to allow for its applicability to the ways of Gongsun Long.

As in Schwitzgebel's reading of the *Zhuangzi*, I should like to propose that this scene does not want to be taken at face value.[65] It talks about Zhuangzi's strategies and methods (*fang* 方), his teachings (*yan* 言) and his achievements, when there is clearly no such thing. The same is true when it is said of Zhuangzi that he disqualifies Gongsun Long for not knowing the boundaries of right and wrong, which is again clearly ironic. The *Zhuangzi* does not want to be taken seriously here; at least not in the literal sense. But as outlined above, there is a seriousness behind the non-serious, and being not serious on one level of meaning-construction means to be serious on another level. This is exactly what the text means when criticising Gongsun Long ironically for not knowing the borders (*jing* 竟) of right and wrong. The one who is criticising the other for not knowing the borders is exactly the one who claims that there is no such thing as strict boundaries. Through the irony used in this passage, Gongsun Long is criticised for taking boundaries too seriously when undermining them, thus enforcing the very concepts he intends to challenge. That this is done better in ironical terms, is clear.

Lastly, this unit parallels Gongsun Long with Kongzi as portrayed in the previous scene in that they both confuse taxonomical conventions and mistake them for ultimate realities. In both cases, it results in their belief that they have reached the ultimate (*zi yi wei zhi da yi* 自以為至達已).

11.
莊子釣於濮水。楚王使大夫二人往先焉，曰：「願以竟內累矣！」莊子持竿不顧，曰：「吾聞楚有神龜，死已三千歲矣。王巾笥而藏之廟堂之上。此龜者，寧其死為留骨而貴乎？寧其生而曳尾於塗中乎？」二大夫曰：「寧生而曳尾塗中。」莊子曰：「往矣！吾將曳尾於塗中。」[p. 603, l. 2–604/end]

> Zhuangzi was fishing in the Pu River when the King of Chu sent two great officers to him to deliver the message as follows: "I wish to entangle you with the affairs of all within my borders."
>
> Zhuangzi, holding on to his rod without looking round, said: "I have heard that in the kingdom of Chu once lived a sacred tortoise that has been dead for three thousand years now. The king keeps it in the ancestral temple inside a box wrapped with cloth. Now that tortoise, would it rather be dead and have its bones left behind and honoured? Or would it rather live and drag its tail through the mud?"
>
> The two great officers replied: "it would rather live and drag its tail through the mud."

---

65 See Eric Schwitzgebel, "Zhuangzi's Attitude Towards Language and His Skepticism," in *Essays on Skepticism*, 68–96.

Zhuangzi replied: "go your way! I, too, would rather drag my tail through the mud."

This and the next unit provide in metaphorical terms Zhuangzi's choice against prioritising the world of the one (*yi* 一) over that of the myriad things (*wanwu* 萬物). Through the repetition of border (*jing* 竟) it connects to the previous scene, while it is no longer used in the context of borders between categories but that of realms. In mention them in passing only.

12.
惠子相梁，莊子往見之。或謂惠子曰：「莊子來，欲代子相。」於是惠子恐，搜於國中三日三夜。莊子往見之，曰：「南方有鳥，其名鵷鶵，子知之乎？夫鵷鶵，發於南海而飛於北海，非梧桐不止，非練實不食，非醴泉不飲。於是鴟得腐鼠，鵷鶵過之，仰而視之曰：『嚇！』今子欲以子之梁國而嚇我邪？」 [p. 605, l. 1–606]

Huizi was minister of Liang when Zhuangzi was planning to call by to see him. Someone said to Huizi: "Zhuangzi comes in wishing to supersede you, sir, as minister." Upon this, Huizi was filled with fear and had him searched for in his realm for three days and three nights.

When Zhuangzi came by to see him, he said: "There is a bird in the south whose name is Young Phoenix; do you, sir, know of it? This Young Phoenix, when it starts out from the South Sea to fly to the North Sea, unless it is on holy Wutong trees, it does not rest; unless it is the fruit of the Lian, it does not eat; unless it is the purest springs, it does not drink. At this, an owl had just got a rotten rat when the Phoenix passed it. As the owl looked up and saw the Phoenix, fearful of its prey, it frightened it away by screaming 'He!' Do you now, sir, wish to frighten me away from your state with just that scream?"

Connecting to the topos of the choice of refusing the one (*yi* 一) over the myriad things (*wanwu* 萬物) this scene introduces Huizi, who will play a vital part in the last unit below. It thus serves as a bridge to the final unit of this text:

13.
莊子與惠子游於濠梁之上。莊子曰：「鯈魚出游從容，是魚之樂也。」惠子曰：「子非魚，安知魚之樂？」莊子曰：「子非我，安知我不知魚之樂？」惠子曰「我非子，固不知子矣；子固非魚也，子之不知魚之樂，全矣！」莊子曰：「請循其本。子曰『汝安知魚樂』云者，既已知吾知之而問我。我知之濠上也。」 [p. 606, l. 1–608]

TRUTH CLAIM WITH NO CLAIM TO TRUTH   335

> Zhuangzi and Huizi were strolling on the dam of the Hao River. Zhuangzi said, "How these minnows jump out of the water and play about at their ease! This is the joy of the fish!"
>
> Huizi said: "You, sir, are not a fish, how do you know what is the joy of fish?" Zhuangzi replied: "You, sir, are not me, how do you know that I do not know what is the joy of fish?"
>
> Huizi said: "I am not you, sir, so I inherently don't know you; but you, sir, are inherently no fish, and that you don't know what is the joy of fish, is [now] fully [established]."
>
> Zhuangzi replied: "Let's seek for the roots [of this conversation]. By asking, '*how* do you know what is the joy of fish,' you already knew that I know it, and yet you asked me; I know it by standing overlooking the Hao River."

In his brilliant analysis of this unit, Norman Teng has established the validity of Zhuangzi's argumentation. Unlike what has been argued previously, Teng holds that Zhuangzi is not dismissing Huizi's point through skilful dialecticism where a privileged position is assumed to the first person's standard of knowledge.[66] Instead of leading Huizi into a logical trap in what could be described as a dishonest way of argumentation, Zhuangzi, Teng claims, and I should like to follow him here, engages in a serious and honest way in the conversation, thus demonstrating to Huizi the flaws of disputation.

Both Huizi and Zhuangzi are paralleling each of their responses to the previous statement, thus displaying the approval—or disapproval—of what was previously said.[67] By making reference to the guidelines of argumentation as laid out in the "Lesser Pick" of the *Mozi*,[68] Teng shows that Huizi's line "I am not you, sir, so I inherently don't know you; but you, sir, are inherently no fish, and so you don't know what is the joy of fish"[69] does not improperly privilege the first person's perspective. Rather, this line suggests a reverse switch to Zhuangzi's previous response where he applies a species-specific viewpoint to the first person's perspective which, in Teng's words, proves "both elegant and powerful from an ancient Chinese dialectical viewpoint."[70] Keeping to this form of argumentation, their debate could be continued in perpetuity, thus leading to a deadlock. It is clear that both parties, Zhuangzi and Huizi, should have realised

---

66 Cf. Chad Hansen, "The Relatively Happy Fish," *Asian Philosophy* 13 (2003): 145–164, 153.
67 Norman Teng, "Revisited," 42.
68 "What is present in one's own case is not to be rejected in the other man's; what is absent from one's own case is not to be demanded of the other man's," in Graham, *Later Mohist Logic, Ethics and Science* (Hong Kong: Chinese University Press, 1978), 483. (Quoted from Teng, "Revisited," 43)
69 P. 607, l. 3/4–23.
70 Teng, "Revisited," 43.

this problem; hence Zhuangzi's proposal to go back to the roots of the conversation.[71]

With his request, "let's seek for the roots [of this conversation]," Zhuangzi invites Huizi to reorient himself to a different angle. Acknowledging Huizi's ability, Zhuangzi is "acting on behalf of his beloved philosophical partner but answering the trick from his own perspective,"[72] "I know it by standing overlooking the Hao River."[73] Zhuangzi thus proposes they go back to where they started, that is, having been on top of the dam overlooking the Hao River and "sharing all along the experience of witnessing the fish swimming easily and smoothly."[74]

History portrays Huizi as a sharp disputer who is, however, prone to pointless argumentation. By inviting him to go back to the roots of their conversation, Zhuangzi, Teng suggests, makes Huizi aware of what they both knew long ago.[75]

With this form of debate, Zhuangzi is not just seriously engaging in the conversation, he also shows, by applying the technique of paralleling and inferring, the limitations of such a debate.

Debate is shown as non-productive. In fact, it is dangerous, for it leads astray from intuitive understanding and shared, common, ground. This point has not just been made in the current scene. Scene 10 has alluded to this by ridiculing Gongsun Long, and scene 4, in a similar way to the unit under review, embraces it too, thus demonstrating that argumentation and debate, in fact, language in general when used in absolute terms, can make no claim to truth. Here, as above, an argument is engaged with seriously and on its own terms, to show that it is based on the faulty premise of language serving as a frame for categories of ultimate value by reduplicating reality. The complexity of this problem forbids expounding it in explicit terms. Instead, the text exposes the problem by carrying it out before our eyes.

Conclusion

Scene 13 ends where the "Qiushui" began: at the river. The text has come full circle. However, it has taken many turns in the meantime. Each scene offered a

---

71 Ibidem.
72 Teng, "Revisited," 45.
73 P. 607, l. 3/26–l. 4/4.
74 Teng, "Revisited," 45.
75 Teng, "Revisited," 46.

new perspective on what was previously said, either enriching it or demonstrating that the previous understanding was simply a reflection of a tainted vision of reality because it lacked yet another perspective of looking at the world. The "Qiushui" thus instructs the text recipient without instructing. It simply takes the text recipient along on its journey so that he or she undergoes the same stages of realisation where the individual stages of that journey merely reflect a tainted—that is, limited—comprehension, to the point where intuitive understanding becomes possible. It comes as no surprise that the final sentence of the text closes with exactly that: a reminder of the roots where intuitive understanding frames our comprehension of being one with the world that surrounds us.

But this is not yet the whole story. Each scene, when taken in isolation, has its own reality too, just as there is a reality for the frog in the well, for the turtle or for the summer fly. Each of these represent one of the myriad things, and each of the myriad things has its own reality and is therefore true in itself. I should like to propose that this is exactly what the text means when it talks about "the ultimate form of being bound to one's lot" (*yue fen zhi zhi* 約分之至也).[76] But this works only insofar as no reality assumes any truth claims over other realities, or perspectives, and this brings us right back to the last unit where the dispute between Zhuangzi and Huizi demonstrates exactly that: truth claims of one reality over another do not lead anywhere.

The "Qiushui" as a whole is composed such that the different scenes float smoothly one into the other, each preparing the grounds for the one to follow. It builds up slowly to the point where the text inquires into the value of Dao in scene 7. This unit is notably placed at the centre of composition, as is typical for argumentative texts from the time of the Warring States period. However, unlike argument-based texts from that period—texts such as the "Zhong xin zhi dao," the "Qiong da yi shi," the "Tai yi sheng shui," or even the "Wu xing"— the macrostructure of the "Qiushui" does not design an architecture where each unit has its necessary place in the composition of the text.[77] Instead, it creates a dramaturgy where the text recipient is taken to different stages of realisation when following the text. The composition of the text behaves like a stream, ever changing, and as such it reduplicates the image with which the text begins and with which, in fact, the text closes. In contrast to texts such as the "Zhong xin zhi dao" or the "Tai yi sheng shui," the macrostructure of the "Qiushui" does not propound a vision of the world where everything has its

---

76 See scene 4, p. 573, l. 5/2–6.
77 See Meyer, *Philosophy on Bamboo* for a discussion of the compositional structure of these texts.

given place, and I venture to say that this would in fact contradict the very concept of the "Qiushui." Instead, the structure of the text composition is such that it reduplicates the dynamics of a river, and, hence, of Dao.

This essay has cast light on the argumentative force inherent in the literary form of the "Qiushui." In the "Qiushui" thought is translated into form. The "Qiushui" does not declare, it has things performed, and such does the text recipient when following the text. The literary form is thus not only a device to express the unsayable where any kind of declaration or definition would necessarily lead to the misrepresentation of reality; rather, the literary form is part of the message. By having the message performed, in the "Qiushui" philosophy and praxis become one.

References

Allan, Sarah. *The Way of Water and Sprouts of Virtue*. Albany: SUNY Press, 1997.
Bahr, Petra. "Religious Claims of Truth Versus Critical Method—Some Western Remarks on a Complex Relationship in Western Tradition." In *Historical Truth, Historical Criticism, and Ideology: Chinese Historiography and Historical Culture from a New Comparative Perspective*, edited by Helwig Schmidt-Glintzer, Achim Mittag and Jörn Rüsen. Leiden: Brill, 2005: 1–12.
Baxter, William H., and Laurent Sagart. *Old Chinese: A New Reconstruction*. Oxford: Oxford University Press, 2014.
Birdwhistell, Anne. "Knowledge Heard and Seen: The Attempt in Early Chinese Philosophy to Analyze Experiential Knowledge." *Journal of Chinese Philosophy* 11 (1984): 67–82.
Chang, Y.M. *The Thoughts of Lao Tzu*. Taipei: Li Ming, 1977.
Cheng, Anne. "'Y a-t-il une philosophie chinoise?' Est-ce une bonne question?" *Extrême-Orient, Extrême-Occident* 27 (2005): 5–12.
Deleuze, Gilles, and Felix Guattari. *What is Philosophy?* Translated by Hugh Tomlinson and Graham Burchill. London: Verso, 1994.
Eno, Robert. "Cook Ding's Dao and the Limits of Philosophy." In *Essays on Skepticism, Relativism, and Ethics in the Zhuangzi*, edited by Paul Kjellberg and Philip J. Ivanhoe. Albany: SUNY Press, 1996: 127–151.
Gentz, Joachim. "Zwischen den Argumenten lesen. Zu zweifach gerichteten Verbindungsstücken zwischen Argumenten in frühen chinesischen Texten." In *Kunstprosa in klassischen chinesischen Texten*, edited by Wolfgang Behr and Joachim Gentz, *Bochumer Jahrbuch zur Ostasienforschung* 29 (2005): 35–56.
Graham, Angus C. *Later Mohist Logic, Ethics and Science*. Hong Kong: Chinese University Press, 1978.

———. "How much of Chuang-tzǔ did Chuang-tzǔ write?" In *Studies in Classical Chinese Thought*, edited by Henry Rosemont and Benjamin Schwartz. *Journal of the American Academy of Religions* Thematic Issue 47.3 (1979): 459-502; reprint in *Studies in Chinese Philosophy and Philosophical Literature*, by Angus C. Graham. Singapore: The Institute of East Asian Philosophies, National University of Singapore, 1986: 283–321.

Hansen, Chad. "The Relatively Happy Fish." *Asian Philosophy* 13 (2003): 145–164.

Hebei Sheng wenwu yanjiu suo 河北省文物研究所, ed. *Cuo mu—Zhanguo Zhongshanguo guowang zhi mu* CUO [壐 (玉→昔)]. 墓—戰國中山國國王之墓. *Wenwu* 1 (1995) 341–369.

Hong, Chia-Lynne. "Seeing through the *Dao*: Image Schema Related to Non-obstruction in the *Zhuangzi* 26." Paper presented at the 19th Conference of the European Association of Chinese Studies, Paris, 5 September 2012.

Klein, Esther. "Were there 'Inner Chapters' in the Warring States? A New Examination of Evidence about the *Zhuangzi*." *T'oung Pao* 96 (2011): 299–369.

Korpel, Marjo. "Introduction to the Series Pericope." In *Delimitation Criticism. Pericope 1: Scripture as Written and Read in Antiquity*, edited by Marjo Korpel and Josef Oesch. Assen: Royal Van Gorcum, 2000: 1–50.

Legge, James. *The Sacred Books of China: The Writings of Kwang-sze*. Oxford: Clarendon Press, 1891.

———. *The Tao Te Ching, The Writings of Chuang-tzǔ, The Thai-shang Tractate of Actions and Their Retributions*. Taipei: Ch'eng wen Publishing, 1976.

Liu Xiaogan. *Classifying the Zhuangzi Chapters*. Translated by William E. Savage. Ann Arbor: Center for Chinese Studies, University of Michigan, 1994.

———. *Zhuangzi zhexue ji qi yanbian* 莊子哲學及其演變. Beijing: Zhongguo Renmin Daxue, 2010.

Lloyd, Geoffrey. *The Ambitions of Curiosity*. Cambridge: Cambridge University Press, 2002.

Lloyd, Geoffrey, and Nathan Sivin. *The Way and the Word: Science and Medicine in Early China and Greece*. Yale: Yale University, 2002.

McCraw, David. *Stratifying Zhuangzi: Rhyme and Other Quantitative Evidence*. Taibei: Institute of Linguistics, Academia Sinica, 2010.

Meyer, Dirk. *Philosophy on Bamboo: Text and the Production of Meaning in Early China*. Leiden: Brill, 2012.

———. "Bamboo and the Production of Philosophy: A Hypothesis about a Shift in Writing and Thought in Early China." In *History and Material Culture in Asian Religions*, edited by Benjamin Fleming and Richard Mann. Oxford and New York: Routledge, 2014: 21–38.

Pines, Yuri. "Disputers of Abdication: Zhanguo Egalitarianism and the Sovereign's Power." *T'oung Pao* 91.4–5 (2005): 243–300.

Roetz, Heiner. *Die chinesische Ethik der Achsenzeit. Eine Rekonstruktion unter dem Aspekt des Durchbruchs zum postkonventionellen Denken.* Frankfurt: Suhrkamp, 1992.

Roth, Harold. "Who Compiled the Chuang Tzu?" in *Chinese Texts and Philosophical Contexts: Essays Dedicated to A.C. Graham*, edited by Henry J. Rosemont Jr. La Salle: Open Court, 1991: 79–128.

Schwitzgebel, Eric. "Zhuangzi's Attitude Towards Language and His Skepticism." In *Essays on Skepticism, Relativism, and Ethics in the Zhuangzi*, edited by Paul Kjellberg and Philip J. Ivanhoe. Albany: SUNY Press, 1996: 68–96.

Sivin, Nathan. *Traditional Medicine in Contemporary China: A Partial Translation of Revised Outline of Chinese Medicine (1972): With an Introductory Study on Change in Present-day and Early Medicine.* Ann Arbor: Center for Chinese Studies, University of Michigan, 1987.

Stevenson, Charles. "Ethical Judgements and Avoidability: Persuasive Definitions." *Mind* 47 (1938): 331–350.

———. *Ethics and Language.* London: Oxford University Press, 1945.

Teng, Norman. "The Relatively Happy Fish Revisited." *Asian Philosophy* 16:1 (2006): 39–47.

Wagner, Rudolf. *The Craft of a Chinese Commentator: Wang Bi on the* Laozi. Albany: SUNY Press, 2000.

Watson, Burton. *The Complete Works of Chuang tzu.* Translated by Burton Watson. New York: Columbia University Press, 1968.

Zhuangzi jishi 莊子集釋. Edited by Guo Qingfan 郭慶藩 (1894), compiled in *Xinbian Zhuzi jicheng* 新編諸子集成. Beijing: Zhonghua shuju, 1961.

Index

absolute standards, absence / non-existence of   310, 316, 318
aesthetic / aesthetics   3, 5, 10, 67–70, 76, 79, 178, 187, 196, 235
allegory   248–249; fishnet allegory ("*Zhuangzi* 26")   249, 271–277
allusion   98, 152, 207, 214, 237; and quotation, 114
ambiguity / ambiguous   1–5, 8, 11, 19, 64, 66, 203n5, 207n19, 226, 272, 325
Ames, Roger   2–3, 11
anadiplosis   116. *See also chanlian ge* 蟬聯格
Analects / Confucian *Analects*. *See Lunyu*
analogical reasoning   2, 70, 264
analogy   2, 84, 118, 139, 142, 186, 208n23, 248, 264–265, 275–276, 279; inverted, 281; with practices of craftsmanship, 139, 142
anecdote   23, 93, 102–109, 188n37, 254; historical, 26, 180
anti-structure (lack of structure)   26, 223–226.
antithetical evaluations of a single principle / policy ("*Zhuangzi* 26")   283–286, 292–293
aperçu   25, 163, 173
aphorisms   14; La Rochefoucauld's, 163; of "Yucong" 1, 161–163; orally transmitted, 130
aphoristic form   25, 166–168
apposite statements, chain of / series of   76, 81
argumentative texts, early Chinese   1, 6n29, 7, 11, 20, 38, 42, 58, 61, 116, 137, 152, 337; cultural functions of, 128; performative and structural features of, 14
argument-based texts   13, 29, 165n9, 322, 337; structural consistency in 23n92
argument deconstruction   308, 313, 325. *See also liang wang* 兩忘
Aristotle   3, 196. *See also* Poetics
assonance   8. *See also* rhyme
audience   24, 107, 173, 176–188, 192, 198, 269; anonymous, 184; general, 176; private, 107; unknown, 180; wrong, 194
author (hermeneutic term)   159, 161, 176–178, 181–187, 192–196, 224; figure of the, 177. *See also* authorship
author function   27, 177, 185

authorial figure / authorial role   176, 231. *See also* persona
authorial self   226
authorial voice   25, 60, 185, 207; individual or, 185. *See also* voice
authoritative speech   185
authorship   175–178, 185, 187, 197, 236, 246; absence of; 177, 185; concept of individual, 22, 99; question of, 175, 197. *See also* author
auto-commentaries   206. *See also* commentary

baguwen 八股文 'four-legged essay'   67n2
Bai Yulan 白於藍   168
bamboo slips / bamboo strips (*jiance* 簡冊) 119, 160, 167–168, 175, 180–181, 198, 223; *See also* bamboo texts, Beida manuscripts, Guodian, Shanghai Museum
bamboo texts / bamboo manuscripts   63, 90, 175. *See also* Beida manuscripts, Guodian, Shanghai Museum
Baxter, William H.   38n9, 88n3, 4, 99–101, 117n18, 21, 122n26, 124n31, 125n34, 302n15
Beida 北大 manuscripts   120–121. *See also Laozi*
bi 必 'invariably', 'inevitable', 'by necessity 63, 65, 136, 258, 274, 278–279, 283, 286; manner, 246, 279, 281, 285; mode of engagement, 292
Bloomfield, Leonard   16
Boltz, William   113n3, 114
Book of Songs. *See* Poetry
Book of the Way and Essential Force (Daodejing 道德經*)*. *See Laozi*
Boyarin, Daniel   227
Boyi 伯夷 (persona)   299, 304–308
bronze inscriptions   9n43, 61, 315n40; rhymed / rhyming, 89, 117
Broschat, Michael   2–3, 14–17, 113n3, 115n13, 122, 125
Buddhist writings / Buddhist texts   48, 64–65, 143n48
building block   1, 20, 113n3, 114n10, 320n44, 325
Bunkyō hifuron 文鏡秘府論   68

catechistic: nature   26, 185; procedure, 188; structure, 185
Changes of Zhou. See *Zhouyi*
chain: argument   20, 70, 80; binary, 113; complementary, 148; parallel, 52, 113, 322; of opposite statements, 76; of utterances, 69; opposite, 24, 113, 137, 142; statements, 84
chanlian ge 蟬聯格   116. See also anadiplosis
Chatman, Seymour   115n13
chengshang qixia 承上啟下 'take up a point introduced earlier and simultaneously lead in a new direction'   116n14
Chen Guying 陳鼓應   244
cheng yi 承意 'accept opinions'   268–270, 274
Chen Tongsheng 陳桐生   175n4, 176n7, 178n13, 181n21, 189, 189n40
chiasmus   70, 99
Chinese culture, modular nature of   112
Chomsky, Noam   16
chouchu 躊躇 'wavering', 'open and wavering attitude'   257–258, 267, 273, 284–287, and wandering, 292.
chronicle   202, 238, 255
Chuci 楚辭   89–93, 107, 109; "Tian wen" 天問, 92–93; "Yuan you" 遠遊, 92–93, 107
"Chu silk manuscripts" (*chu boshu* 楚帛書) 10n43; See also "Mawangdui manuscripts"
citation (rhet. device)   90–92, 114n7, 204n7; and recitation, 90; language of, 92
classical learning. See learning
classical master   202–208, 226–239. See also master
classical teachings   214. See also *jiao* 教, teachings
classicists. See, *Ru* 儒
Classic of Poetry. See Poetry
Classics. See Confucian Classics, Thirteen Classics
climactic effect   101
closed text   192
collage   114, 152–153, 298–300; strategies, 14; techniques, 153
commentary   9n38, 26, 47–48, 180, 187, 197, 202, 248 ; Buddhist writings and, 65 inner-textual, 153. See also Wang Bi
comparison. See *ni* 擬
complexity of simplicity   318–320
composite nature of early Chinese texts   114

compositional circumstances   187. See also scenes of composition
conceptual analysis   25, 162–165; abstract and de-contextualised, 173
conceptual definition   313n36, 322–323
conceptual mapping   18
condemning-opposing (*fei* 非, *fan* 反) 257–258, 284
Confucian Classics (Classics [*jing* 經], *Five Classics* [*Wu jing* 五經])   48, 50, 64, 69, 91, 96, 205, 210–215 228, 230n174, 232n185, 237; model of the, 215. See also Thirteen Classics
Confucian master. See master
Confucius. See Kongzi
constituent analysis   16, 115n13
constituents   16, 24–25, 113n3, 115n13, 128–129,
content-contrast   257, 270, 274, 277, 285.
context: dependence   316; historical, 12, 164, 178, 183; material, 178; original, 194; parallel, 307, 321, 323; pragmatic, 5; situation-specific, 332; social, 28, 243; textual   115, 249–250
context-dependent texts   13n58, 165n9, 300
contextual reading / interpretation   243, 250, 253–256, 277–278, 293
contrastive understanding   275
Cook Ding 丁 (persona)   299
correlative: classifications   113; systematic, 153; thinking, 2, 68
cosmological: conceptions   18; micro-macro correlations, 6; powers, 128; speculation, 162–164
Cratylus   8
cultivation   220–230; inner, 104, 148; personal, 104; self-, 82, 104–105, 160, 178n13, 192, 194, 323

Da Dai Liji 大戴禮記   24, 144; "Zhu yan" 主言, 24, 144–152
dao 道 'Dao', 'Way'   13, 23, 27, 45n27, 46, 62, 80–87, 92, 96, 99–103, 122–126, 130–131, 135, 141, 146–150, 171–172, 205–206, 210–216, 222, 225, 228–231, 234–235, 238–239, 248, 271, 279–280, 290n51, 297–338; cultivation of the, 205; moral and cosmic, 204; learning, 299; philosophical experience of the, 13, 297–299; praxis of, 29, 298; verbal model of the, 87, 99–107. See also *tiandao* 天道

INDEX

dao and *de* (道德): binary division into 146–147; constructed in parallel fashion 321–325

Daodejing 道德經. See *Laozi*

"Daren fu" 大人賦 107

Davis, John Francis 14–15

"Daxu" 大序. See "Great Preface"

Daxue 大學 Great Learning 72–75, 81–84, 104

dayi zhi fang 大義之方 'method of Great Meaning' 316–318

de 德 'capacity', charismatic power', 'receipt', 'virtue' 45–48, 53, 55, 59n54, 61, 75, 82, 84, 91–96, 118, 123–127, 143, 146, 190–191, 196, 213, 218–222, 229n166, 279, 288–290, 311–312, 316, 319–325, 328 ; see also *dao* 道 and *de* 德, virtues

deconstruction. See argument deconstruction, *liang wang* 兩忘

descriptive binomes 88–92, 97, 100

de yi 得意 'attract opinions', 'win over opinions' 248–249, 273–276. See also *zai yi*

diagrammatic representations of texts 114–115

dialectical: situation 318; viewpoint, 335

dialogical form 6, 152–153

dialogue (literary form) 12, 14, 144, 149, 202, 204, 208, 227–228, 230–233, 236, 266n36, 285, 300, 324–325; constructed, 211–221; contextualised, 159; mock, 55; narrative, 61; platonic, 3–6, 313; sayings and, 158–160; teaching, 20

dichotomies 22, 87; foregrounding of, 88

didactic prosimetrum 22, 88–90

direct speech 60, 185n29

discourse: 'academic' 173; analogical, 2; analytical, 20; argumentative, 11, 166; forms of, 287, 293; intertextual, 173; literary, 2; on literature, 180; on self-cultivation, 197; parabolic, 2; parallel, 69, 85; patterns of, 68; philosophical, 6, 12, 18–23, 87, 100–101, 166, 176; rhetoric of non-narrative, 37; situational, 159; specialized, 153. See also *fu* 夫 (discourse marker), *shelun* 設論

disputation / eloquent rhetoric (*bian* 辯) 159, 165, 215, 330–331; flaws of, 335

divination 47, 259–264, 267; foresight in, 261; -like patterns of judgment, 274.

Documents (*Shu* 書, *Shangshu* 尚書) 61, 179n15, 189, 221n125, 305n21; "Yaodian" 堯典, 179n15. See also *Shangshu dazhuan*

Dong Zhongshu 董仲舒 207n19, 236n198

double-directed text units / segments 19, 23, 136, 147–148, 153, 307. See also parallelism, double-directed

double voice (rhet. device) 226–227, 232, 238; creation of a, 238; employment of a, 232. See also voice

drama / dramatic / dramatization 3–5, 103, 169, 238–239, 279, 324

dui 對 'parallel' (term connoting parallelistic writing) 69, 76

dynamic mirror image writing form 266–267, 287, 293

embedded story 281

embedding 165; of verse within narrative and discursive prose, 107; a new element with a group of established elements 143, 147

enumerative catalogue 19, 23–24, 115, 144, 148–149, 151, 153; as signs of encyclopaedic completeness, 128–136; in the *Sunzi bingfa*, 129–136

epistemology / epistemological: angst 317, 324; antinomian, 84; framework, 75, 310; obstacle, 297n3;

essay (lit. form) 14, 29, 44, 58, 67n2, 92–93, 116n14, 143n48, 202, 298; expository, 238

excavated texts (*chutu wenxian* 出土文獻) 29, 118–121, 126n35, 127, 153, 158–168, 201; punctuation in, 114, 153, 173

Exemplary Figures. See *Fayan*

exostructure 26, 203

explanation. See *jie* 解

explicit verbal connections 28, 243, 246–277, 293

expository prose. See prose

extrapolative translation 45

fan 凡 'as a matter of principle' (modal particle) 59, 64, 130–131, 144, 162

fang 方 'method' 330, 333

Fayan 法言 (*Exemplary Figures*) 26–27, 202–240

figure of speech 22, 87. See also speech

Fingarette, Herbert 14

Five Classics (*Wujing* 五經). *See Confucian Classics*
Five Phases (*wuxing* 五行) 225. *See also* "Wuxing"
formal composition 29, 127, 316, 320–321
form analysis 28, 301
form and content: correlation of in Chinese philosophy 18; identity of, 332
form and thought, philosophical relevance of in early Chinese writing 12
formulaic 25, 142, 183, 185, 189, 192, 195
Foucault, Michel 159, 177n12, 185, 185n31, 187
fragments / fragmentary / fragmentation, 1, 178–181, 189, 195, 202, 244, 245n5, 249, 268n37, 272, 288n49
frame narrative. *See* narrative
framing conversation 332
fu 夫, character of: multiple uses 38–39
fu 夫, initial 'as a matter of principle' (discourse marker, phrase status marker, semantic marker of textual units) 20–21, 37–66, 268, 288, 313, 327, 329; as paragraph beginning, 40; as *xuzi* 虛字 (empty character) 38; Confucius' use of, 61; connected to *gu* 故, 59, 52, 122–123, 134–136; connected to *shiyi* 是以, 62; definition of, 39–42; demonstrative use of, 40, 58–59; in *Guanzi*, 61; history of changing uses of, 58–63; in *Huainanzi*, 41–42, 59; in *Laozi*, 62; in *Laozi weizhi lüeli*, 44; in *Laozi zhu*, 44; in *Lüshi chunqiu*, 59; in *Lunyu*, 61–62; in *Mengzi*, 41; in narrative phrases, 60; in non-narrative statements, 47; in *Shiji*, 60–61; in *Sunzi*, 60; in Wang Bi, 44–57; in Wang Chong, 58–59; in Wang Fu, 57; in *Wenyan*, 62; in *Xici*, 62; in *Xiaojing*, 40, 60–62; in *Xinshu*, 58; in Xuanxue, 44; in *Zhouyi lüeli*, 42–44; qualitative analysis of, 43–58; quantitative analysis of, 58–63; signalling principle, 47, 63; translation of, 50; use of in text layout, 57–58
fu 賦 'grand display', rhapsody (lit. genre) 107, 196, 205–208, 216, 231n178; travel, 107
fu 賦 / fu shi 賦詩 'recite verse' (rhet. device in the *Zuo zhuan* and in the *Guoyu*) 89
functionalist 18

Gabelentz, Georg von der 15
generic conventions / expectations 87, 100
Gentz, Joachim 16, 19, 23–24, 306n28
Gongsun Long 公孫龍 (author, persona) 8, 329–333, 336
Gongsunlongzi 公孫龍子, 164; "Mingshi lun" 名實論, 8
Gongzi Mou 公子牟 (persona) 329–332
Graham, Angus C., 1, 11, 41–46, 160, 165, 244–245, 273n41
Great Learning. *See Daxue*
Great Mystery. *See Taixuan*
"Great Preface" ("Daxu" 大序) 175–176, 179–180, 194
great principle (da li 大理) 304–305
gu 故 / *shi gu* 是故 'that is why' (illative conjunction, rhet. feature) 40, 46, 49, 56, 58, 61–65, 121–123, 130, 136, 143, 147–149, 166; as a deductive connector, 134. *See also fu* 夫, *shi yi* 是以
Guanzi 管子 61–63, 88n3, 93–99, 109, 159, 164; "Chi mi" 侈靡, 98; "Dizi zhi" 弟子職, 93; "Nei ye" 內業, 88n3, 104, 109
Guiguzi 鬼谷子 12, 16–17, 94n18
Guodian 郭店 29, 62n63–64, 94n18, 113n3, 118–122, 125n33, 127, 143, 160, 164, 178n13, 198, 201, 301n12, 325n25, 337n57; manuscripts, 201, *See also Laozi, Yucong*
guoduju 過渡句 'transitional sentences' 116n14
Guo Xiang 郭象 28–29, 245, 248, 298–300
Guoyu 國語 102
gu yue 故曰 'thus it is said', 'that is why it is said', 'that is why I say' 101, 108, 164, 323. *See also yue* 曰
guwen 古文 'ancient-style prose' 67–71

Hall, David 2–3, 11
Hanfei 韓非 (author, persona) 77–78, 108n56, 165
Hanfeizi 韓非子 71n7, 72, 76–77, 108, 161, 164–165, 201; "Jie Lao" 解老, 108; "Yu Lao" 喻老 (*Han Feizi*) 108
Hansen, Chad 11
Harbsmeier, Christoph 2, 24–26, 37n1
Heraclitus 161, 163, 168
hermeneutical circularity 310, 324–325; deconstruction of, 325
Hesiod 95
historical reference / historical narrative reference 148–150, 164, 183, 197, 328; as an

INDEX

exemplum of concrete action, 141;
  avoidance of / eschewal of, 88, 92, 164
historiographic authority / historiographic
  mindset 177
Holzman, Donald 158
Huainanzi 淮南子 17n75, 41–42, 48, 59, 72,
  74–75, 99, 107, 109, 145n53; "Yao lüe" 要略,
  109
Huangdi neijing Su wen 黃帝內經素問
  95–96; "*Lingshu*" 靈樞, 95
Huang Huaixin 黃懷信 92n13, 129n40–41,
  175n4, 180–183, 189–195, 198
Huang-Lao speech (*Huang Lao zhi yan* 黃老
  之言) 108
Huang-Lao thought 108
Huizi 惠子 (persona) 264–267, 334–337
Humboldt, Wilhelm von 2n8
hyperbolic imitation 255, 257, 276

illative conjunctions. *See gu* 故, *shiyi* 是以;
  false 130, 134, 152
illustration. *See yu* 喻
imitating Classics. *See ni jing* 擬經
inner cultivation. *See* cultivation
insight and intuition 27, 203, 225
institutional idiom 189
instruction 22, 90, 136, 184–189, 263;
  dialogical, 188; rhyming, 102; scenes of, 103,
  107, 188, 194
interaction. *See* linguistic interaction, social
  interaction
interlocking parallel style (IPS) 14, 16, 19, 38,
  65–66, 99–101, 122, 146, 148, 261, 268–270,
  288. *See also* parallelism
intertextuality 114, 152, 165
intuitive understanding 336–337
irony 18, 252n21, 332–333

jiance 簡冊. *See* bamboo slips
jiao 教 'teachings' 268–270, 292–293. *See
  also* teachings
Jia Yi 賈誼 58, 109n58, 207n19
jie 解 'explanation' 206. *See also shuo* 說
jigsaw puzzle, Chinese 112; Chinese texts as,
  112
jin 今 'now' (ling. marker) 60, 63, 143
Ji Zha 季札, Prince of Wu 吳 (persona) 187

Kablitz, Andreas 5

Kant, Immanuel 5, 173
Kern, Martin 23, 25, 109
Kongcongzi 孔叢子 189–191, 193n47; "Jiyi"
  記義, 189
Kongzi 孔子 (Confucius, Zhongni 仲尼)
  25–26, 46, 48, 62, 64, 90–19, 102–105,
  144–146, 149, 152, 158, 161, 164, 175–176, 181,
  188–198, 203, 205n8, n10, 208–209, 212–215,
  219–226, 229n170, 231–240, 257–261,
  269n38, 270, 274, 283–285, 294, 299,
  305–308, 327–329, 333; personal voice of,
  189, 191, 196, 198;
Kongzi jiayu 孔子家語 90, 144, 189; "Lun li"
  論理, 90; "Wang yan jie" 王言解, 143
"Kongzi shilun" 孔子詩論 (Confucius'
  Discussion of the *Poetry*). *See* "Shilun"

lack of structure. *See* anti-structure
Langer, Susanne K. 8n36
language: and meaning 8, 11, 28, 243;
  archaistic, 202; argumentative function of,
  5; artificial / artificially limited, 100; basic
  structural problem of, 8; Chinese, 2, 58;
  definitional, 56; dependency between the
  meaning and the form of, 8; inclusive /
  encompassing use of (*Zhuangzi*), 246–272;
  Indo-European, 69n6; multifunctional
  dimension of, 7; limitations of, 312;
  philosophy of, 7; poetical-rhetorical
  function of, 5; poetic self-referential
  function of (Jakobson), 5; propositional
  force of, 300, 312–313, 326; purified, 100;
  spoken, 38, 63; written, 38. *See also*
  language-tool-complex, *wang yan* 忘言,
  yan 言
language-tool-complex 271–274
Lao Dan 老聃. *See* Laozi
Lao Laizi 老萊子 (persona) 257–258, 270,
  274, 283–285
laozhe 勞者 'those straining themselves'
  251n19, 252–257, 273–277, 291–292. *See
  also* content-contrast, *yizhe-laozhe*
  distinction
Laozi 老子 (*Daodejing* 道德經) 19–25, 37,
  43n22, 58, 61, 64, 66n69, 72–77, 87–110,
  118–128, 159–166; Beida ms, 120–125;
  commentary. *See* Wang Bi; genre style, 22,
  159; Guodian ms (*Laozi* A), 62n63, 118–121;
  325n55; Mawangdui ms (*Laozi* B), 99, 121;

Laozi 老子 (*Daodejing* 道德經) (cont.)
  Laozi 41, 122–128; "Si shi" 四時, 96. *See also* Wang Bi
Laozi 老子 (author, persona) 75, 78, 80, 102, 212, 239
Laozi subgenre 88, 100, 102
"*Laozi* weizhi lüeli" 老子微指略例 44. *See also* Wang Bi
learning (*xue* 學) 21, 27, 142–143, 209–214, 225–227, 231–239, 262, 269; and practice, 210; classical, 90n10, 226–227, 232, 236–237
Ledderose, Lothar 112
li 禮 'rites', 'ritual', 'ritual decorum', 'ritual propriety' 18, 24, 62, 89–91, 98, 128, 137–138, 143–144, 152, 159, 172, 182–183, 190, 193, 196, 206n12, 212–213, 283–284, 314–315
liang wang 兩忘 'disregard on both sides', 'process or practice of deconstruction' 249, 257–28. *See also wang* 忘
Liezi 列子 103, 107, 145n53, 248
Liji 禮記 90, 91n9, 127, 130n43, 179n15; "Kongzi xianju" 孔子閑居, 90; "Yueji" 樂記, 179n15; "Ziyi" 緇衣, 127
limited lexicon 22, 87. *See also* restricted vocabulary, language
linguistic habits, socially-induced 257–258, 267, 273–276
linguistic interaction / engagement 243, 246–247, 258–263, 267, 272–276, 286–287, 292–293. *See also* linguistic habits, social interaction
Liu Rongxian 劉榮賢 245
Liu Xiang 劉向 158, 220n116
Liu Xiaogan 劉笑敢 244n5
Liu Xie 劉勰 39
Liu Xin 劉歆 158
li yi 禮義 'rites and righteousness', 'ritual and righteousness' 137–142
li yue 禮樂 'rites and music' 217
Li Xueqin 李學勤 175–176, 180–183, 189, 194, 198
literal surface 187
literary arrangement 113, 153
literary critic 205
literary form / literary form of argument 4–30, 67, 178, 243, 293–294, 300–303, 316, 325, 332, 338; argumentative silence of a, 20; as (part of the) argument, 6n29, 19, 113–154; as part of the message, 338; marking and relating textual units by means of, 130–134; of Plato's dialogues, 4; translation of into explicit linguistic forms of argument, 121
literary genres 176; philosophy of, 158–159
literary pattern 1, 18–19, 29, 178
literary techniques of textual enhancement 8, 16
literati. *See Ru*
Lloyd, Geoffrey 297n3
Logic 1, 4, 18, 71–72, 127, 169; associative, 2; formal, 2; of signs, 114; philosophical, 11
logical: analysis 2, 164, 173; capacity, 1; forms 13, 27; western techniques, 1
Lowth, Robert 14–15, 68n4
Lü Buwei 呂不韋 58
Lu Deming 陸德明 40
lun 論. *See* discourse
Lunheng 論衡 58–59
Lunyu 論語 (Analects) 27, 41n19, 62–63, 72, 79–81, 92n13, 158–159, 164–166, 176n7, 186, 188, 202, 204, 226–227, 235; genre style, 158; logia and apophthegm in, 158–159; Master's voice in, 158–159, 165
lüshi 律詩 'regulated verse' 67–70; structural paradigms of, 69–7
Lüshi chunqiu 呂氏春秋 59, 92–95, 102, 145n53, 166, 179n15; "Ren di" 任地, 9; "Zhi yi" 執一, 102

Ma Chengyuan 馬承源 182
Ma Jianzhong 馬建忠 40–41
manuscript culture 13
Mao Poetry (*Mao Shi* 毛詩). *See Classic of Poetry*
master (*zi* 子) 176, 178, 201–204, 212, 237n203, 257–258, 267, 270, 274, 280; constructed, 226–230; figure of the, 226. *See also* classical master
master of classical learning. *See* classical master
'masters' literature. *See* 'masters' texts
master-teacher (*shishi* 石師) 258, 261, 263, 267, 285–286, 292
'masters' texts 164, 178, 180, 205
Mawangdui 馬王堆 99, 121; *Laozi* A, 121; *Laozi* B, 99, 121; manuscripts, 210; texts, 62n3, 108n56. *See also Wuxing*
McCurdy, James 11

INDEX

meaning: catalogue of 195; construction of, 303, 307; contextual nature of, 294; core, 187, 195; generating, 113; level of construction, 320n44, 333; moral, 196; produced through textual form, 325; strategy of producing, 318; structures of, 201; surface, 186

Mengzi. 孟子 (Mencius) 19, 41, 72–75, 159, 161, 165, 204, 215n77, 204, 223, 323; genre style, 159

Mengzi 孟子 (Mencius [persona]) 75, 159, 202, 208n23, 213n50, 215n77, 221, 223, 236, 239

men of learning. See Ru 儒

meta-criticism of competing groups 286, 292, 293

metaphor 2–8, 18, 29, 42, 59n52, 96, 100, 115n13, 221, 235, 266n36, 291n53, 300–307; organic, 19; root, 301–302; spatial, 290; theory, 17; water / river, 300–302, 306–307

metre: rhythmical 113; tetrasyllabic, 122–123

Meyer, Dirk 16, 19–20, 23, 28–29, 113n3, 114n10, 165n9

"Minor prefaces" (xiaoxu 小序) 176, 187

ming 命 'decree', 'fate', 'mandate', ordained fate' 118, 172, 210, 213–214, 234, 319–320, 324, 327

"Min zhi fumu" 民之父母 (Shanghai Museum ms) 90–92, 102, 152

mirror structure 120

mode-contrast 257, 270, 277, 287.

model emulation 211, 216n83, 220, 237, 255, 285; critique of, 243, 293

Moeller, Hans-Georg 248–249, 271n40, 277

Mo jing 墨經 (Dialectical Chapters) / jing 經 'canons' 100, 160. See also Mozi

Moloughney, Brian 112

Montaigne, Michel de 14, 173

Mozi 墨子 97–100, 159–160; "Qin shi" 親士, 97

Mozi 墨子 (author, persona) 164, 223, 239

myth / mythical 3–4, 103–104, 177, 300

mythographic authority / mythographic mindset 177

naming 169, 287, 293

narration 301; absence of, 99; exclusion of, 100. See also narrative

narrative 60–67, 103. 107, 109, 116n14, 161–164, 173, 178, 184, 231, 249, 261, 263, 271, 286; avoidance of, 88; canonical, 49; complex, 301; frame / framework, 23, 26, 103, 109, 144–145; dialogue, 61, grand, 176; historical, 25, 148–150; illustration, 164, 256; introductory, 144; overall, 300; prologues, 6; texts, 60. See also narration

ni 擬 'comparison' (technical term of poetic rhetoric) 186

ni jing 擬經 'imitating Classics' 207

non-equivalence 71n9, 83, 276

non-obstruction 290n51, 305n23; words, 305

non-structure 27

numerical set 128–129, 148

Nylan, Michael 26–27

obstruction words 305

Odes. See Poetry

ontology / ontological: speculative 84; dramatisation of, 169; self-determination, 169; truth, 307; problem, 310

open text 192

opposing uniformity (lit. device) 303, 307, 328

oppositional pairs of positions 24, 137

orality 12–13, 22, 63, 92, 99–104

overlapping structure 14, 19

paradox 80; and dynamic mirror images 287; conscious use of in written philosophical prose, 18

paradoxical: arguments 330n60; claims, 332; expressions, 293; form, 265–267; sophistication, 163; statements, 99; truths, 103

parallel constructions / patterns / sequences 21–22, 67, 71, 81, 303, 322, 327; coordinating function of, 76; paradigmatic functioning / use of, 21, 67, 75

parallel fashion 24, 52n35, 83, 139, 306, 310, 312, 321, 325; deploying uniform sets of statements in, 303

parallel figure 306n28, 323

paralleling 335; and inferring, 336

parallelism 6, 14–24, 45–46, 49, 68, 70, 113, 116–128, 141–143, 147, 153, 159, 268, 303n19, 316, 322–323; absence of as phrase status

parallelism (cont.)
  marker, 54–55, 64; and oppositional pairs, 137–142; as an argumentative form, 16; chiastic, 322; crypto-, 68; double-directed, 23–24, 115–128, 144, 306n28; identical, 121; juxtaposition of formal, 268; negative, 147–148; non-identical, 121; of identical members / of identical lines, 117–126; partial and intermittent, 68; phonetic, 127; pseudo-, 68; quantitative, 67n2; quasi-, 68; redirected, 83; strict, 134, 151; syntactical, 127. *See also dui*, interlocking parallel style, rhyme
parallelismus membrorum 17n76
parallel prose. *See piantiwen*
parallel statements / pronouncements 49, 55, 75, 80–81, 84; multiple, 75; non-coordinate linking of 79; sequences of, 21, 72
parallel structures 134, 180
paratactic coordination 22, 69
pars pro toto construction 261–263
perception 191–192, 300, 329; opposing sets of, 307; poetic, 197; victim of, 324
performance 87, 99, 184n27, 187, 233, 275, 298; expository, 145; of tetrasyllables, 102–103, 107–110; of the *Poetry*, 187; philosophical, 299; text-, 13, 29; verbal models of the *Dao* in, 99–107
performative turn in the philosophy of language 14
pericope 320n44, 323
persona 26–27, 176, 205, 208, 229, 238, 240, 246, 306–307, 329 ; authorial, 226; constructed, 202; dual, 26, 240
personal authority / reference. *See* reference
personification 169; abstract, 169
persuasion (*shui* 說) 11, 18–29; macro modes of, 20; powers of, 219; strategies of argumentative, 29; rhetorical traditions of, 12
Phaedrus 179. *See also* Plato, Socrates
philosophical communication 13, 29, 297
philosophical masters. *See* masters
philosophical texts 1, 13, 18, 25, 43, 56, 64, 66, 100, 322n48; Daoist and Buddhist, 143n48
philosophising 18; polymorphous nature of in early China, 297n3; act of, 298

philosophy: early Chinese 1–6, 14, 18, 21, 42, 247, 293, 297–298; Daoist, 249; distinction between poetry and, 3–5; doing with words, 11; of praxis, 29, 317–318, 338; Plato's definition of 3–4; Plato's poetical, 4; political, 47, 49–50; shift in the production of, 13; Western, 3, 14
piantiwen 騈體文 'parallel prose' 69
Plato 3–8, 11, 14, 227. *See also Cratylus, Phaedrus, Republic,* Socrates
poetic: argumentation 1–2; criticism, 196; effect, 10; elements in Plato's work, 3–5; expression, 2, 190–191; language, 5n24; logic of Chinese thinking, 3; past, 189. *See also* poetry and history; perception, 197; 'principle of equivalence (Jakobson), 71; quality of Classical Chinese prose, 2–3; self-referential function of language, 5
Poetics 3n16, 196
poetry 2–5, 7n31, 92, 159, 184–186, 195–198; classical Chinese, 14, 67, 70; concept of self-referential autonomy of and rhetoric, 5; concrete or visual, 9–10; distinction between philosophy and, 3–5; Hellenistic, 4; philosophy of, 5; statements on, 179
Poetry / Classic of Poetry, (*Mao shi* 毛詩, *Shi* 詩, *Shijing* 詩經) 24–26, 54, 61, 88–91, 94–95, 101–102, 116–117, 122–125, 127, 175–198, 283; "Beifeng" 北風, 192; "Bozhou" 柏舟, 193; "Caige" 采葛, 192–193; "Datian" 大田, 193; "Didu" 杕杜, 190; "Dongfang weiming" 東方未明, 192–193; "Gantang" 甘棠, 182–183, 190; "Getan" 葛覃, 190–191; "Guanju" 關雎, 182–183, 186; "Gufeng" 鼓風, 193; "Hanguang" 漢廣, 182–183; "Haotian you chengming" 昊天有成命, 191; "Heshui" 河水, 193; interpretation of the, 184, 188n36; "Jiaozhen" 角枕, 193; "Jiumu" 樛木, 182–183; "Juan'er" 卷耳, 193; "Liao'e" 蓼莪, 193; "Liewen" 烈文, 191; "Lüyi" 綠衣, 182–183; "Mugua" 木瓜, 190; perception of the, 191; performance of the, 187; "Qiang you ci" 墻有茨, 193; "Qiangzhong" 將仲, 192–193; "Qingmiao" 清廟, 191; "Qingying" 青蠅, 193; "Qi yue" 七月, 95; "Quechao" 鵲巢, 182–183; readings of the, 187; "Sheng min" 生民, 95; "Shezhen" 涉溱, 193; "Shijiu" 鳲鳩, 191;

teaching of the, 176, 178, 180; "Wanqiu" 宛丘, 191; "Wen wang" 文王, 116–117, 191; "Xiaoming" 小明, 193; "Xia wu" 下武, 116, 122; "Xishuai" 蟋蟀, 192; "Xi you changchu" 隰有萇楚, 193; "Yang zhi shui" 揚之水, 192–193; "Yanyan" 燕燕, 182–183; "Yijie" 猗嗟, 191; "Youtu" 有兔, 193; "Zhongshi" 仲氏, 192; "Zhu'er" 箸而, 193
poetry and history 84
Prague Linguistic Circle 5, 7
praise and blame (*baobian* 襃貶) 197, 203, 219, 224, 234, 239
praising-stimulating (*yu* 譽, *dong* 動) 257–258, 284
principal insertion (lit. device) 24, 306n28, 325; conceptual, 306, 310
pronouncement (lit. form) 26, 80, 185–186, 196–197, 202, 217, 224n142, 226, 228, 285; implicit, 265; parallel. *See* parallel statements
proposition (lit. form) 47–50, 69–71, 79–83, 100, 142, 159–173, 201, 213, 227–231, 236–237; and illustration, 70; parallel 76n18, 80; programmatically enigmatic, 24. *See also fu* 夫 'discourse marker'
prose / expository prose, classical Chinese 3, 15–17, 67–85, 166, 185; and poetry criticism, 116n17; default mode of, 22, 69; parallel constructions in, 75–76; parallelism in, 15, 67n2; poetic quality of, 3
punctuation. *See* excavated texts

qi (氣) 26, 203, 225, 304n20
Qianfu lun 潛夫論 58
Qi fa 七發 (Seven stimuli) 109
"Qiong da yi shi" 窮達以時 29, 327n57, 337
"Qiu" pan 逑盤 117
quantitative matching of words 67–68
questioning (rhet. device) 94–95; and exclamation, 88, 198

reflection and doubt 262; absence of, 267, 292
ragbag hypothesis ("*Zhuangzi* 26") 28, 243–246, 277–278, 292–293. *See also* Angus C. Graham
reading experience 307, 329

reality: communicating / expressing 8, 300, 332; complex, 332–338; felt / perceived, 298n3; manifest / material, 78–80, 105, 301, 329; modes of dealing with, 256, 275–278; 292; social and political of the author, 159, 289; textual 151; ultimate, 300–302; unchanging of constant change, 301–303; vision of, 321, 337
real world experience 298, 312
reference: historical. *See* historical reference; inner-textual, 126, 147, 153; internal, 112; personal, 165; scriptural 164; to tradition 196
regulated verse. *See lüshi*
repetition 76, 91, 100–101, 117–119, 134, 148, 150, 249, 304, 334; as identity markers of position, 137–143; chain, 99; exact, 119, 142; of key terms and key verbal units, 249; of lines, 118; of programmatic clauses, 134; patterns of, 99; rhythmic, 189–190; signifiers of textual 150; verbatim 230
Republic 3
restricted vocabulary 88. *See also* limited lexicon
rhetorical theory, Western 70
rhyme 10n48, 16, 88–110, 115n13, 117–118, 122–127; closing, 97; connotations, 113; groups, 125–126; in conjunction with semantic patterning, 88n4, 99; *Laozi*, 95, 108, 161; positions, 88; repeating patterns of, 70; scheme, 123, 126; *Shijing*, 101; speak in, 96; stereotyped vocabulary of, 94; symmetrical, 14; words, 94. *See also* assonance, parallelism
rhyme-prose 91n10
rhyming 90–102, 159; patterns, 72; practices, 109; tetrasyllabic, 89, 93, 109; truisms, 103
rhythm 16, 92, 125, 302; language and, 302; non-parallel, 69; parallel, 69, 71; tetrasyllabic, 67, 92
Richter, Matthias L. 19n84, 91, 113n3, 114, 179n16, 193n49
rites . *See li, li yi*
ritual. *See li, li yi*
ritual-centred culture 177
ritual propriety. *See li*
Roth, Harold 104

Ru 儒 'classicists', ('literati', 'men of learning') 204, 215, 229n170, 232, 234–235, 283–285

sagacious person (*shengren* 聖人, term from the *Zhuangzi*) 252–253, 256n29, 257–258, 267, 270, 275, 284, 286–287, 327–329.
Saussy, Haun 117n20
scenes of composition 197. *See also* compositional circumstances
Schaberg, David 22–23
Schlegel, Gustave 15
Schwitzgebel, Eric 333
self-cultivation. *See* cultivation
self-delusion 306, 308
self-realisation 300–303
separate scenes, literary device of 300
Shanghai Museum 90, 180; arrangement of slips, 193n50; bamboo manuscripts / texts, 102, 152, 175, 178n13, 198; editors, 182. *See also* Guodian, Ma Chengyuan, Mawangdui
Shangjun shu 商君書 19
Shangshu. *See Documents*
Shangshu dazhuan 尚書大傳 189
Shaughnessy, Edward L. 116–117
shelun 設論 'hypothetical discourse' 206n12
shifa 師法 'teacher and model' 138–142, 210–211, 234. *See also* teacher, master-teacher
Shiji 史記 26, 60–61, 69, 98, 108n55–56, 109n58, 179n15, 205, 220; "Yueshu" 樂書, 179n15
Shijing. *See Poetry*
"Shilun" 詩論 (Discussion of the *Poetry*, "Kongzi shilun" 孔子詩論 [Confucius' Discussion of the *Poetry*]) 25–26, 175–198; pragmatic function of the, 178
Shi qiang *pan* 史牆盤 43n9, 117
"Shixu" 詩序 (Preface to the *Poetry*). *See* "Shilun"
shiyi 是以 (illative conjunction) 62, 66, 121, 152
shuo 說 'elaborating explanation' 160–161. *See also jie* 解
Shuoyuan 說苑 163
signifiers 112–115, 142, 150–153; formal, 122; of argumentative boundaries, 20, 23; of textual repetition, 150; positioned, 148; referential, 19, 23, 113, 115, 144, 149; repetitive, 113, 150–153

Sima Qian 司馬遷 26, 59, 207n19, 208, 213n50, 220–221, 224, 237n203. *See also Shiji*
Sima Xiangru 司馬相如 107, 205n12
siliuwen 四六文 'four-six prose' 67n2
Sivin, Nathan 304n20
social interaction 28, 89, 221n36, 229, 243, 246–247, 250–257, 268–270, 278–289, 292–293. *See also* linguistic interaction
Socrates 179–180, 194; construction of, 227. *See also Phaedrus*, Plato
song 14, 88–95, 193n47, 51; and dance, 187; forms, 69. *See also Chuci*, *Poetry*
speech (lit. form) 22, 25, 46, 89–91, 101–103, 107, 119–120, 147–150, 213, 219, 221, 263; artful, 230; idiosyncratic prose of, 103; referential, 5. *See also* direct speech, figure of speech, Huang-Lao speech, *yan* 言 (words, language)
speech vs. writing 213
status markers of phrases 20; absence of parallelism as, 54, 64; and text layout, 38; explicit and implicit, 37–38; for types of statements, 37; initial *jin* 今 as, 59; treated as *xuzi* 虛字 (empty characters), 38
stimulus. *See xing* 興
structuralist 18; post-, 5
structural linguistics 14
sub-canto 320, 323n52
subordination 22, 71, 134–136, 173, 237; hypotactic, 69n6; techniques of textual, 153
Sunzi bingfa 孫子兵法 60, 64, 129–136, 147
suoyi 所以 'that-by-which', 'tools', remedies', 'methods' 119–120, 249–257, 270–277
Supreme Mystery. *See Taixuan*
syllogisms 70
syllogistic forms 112
syntactical patterns 22, 87
syntax 275, 294; archaic, 93; Hebrew and Arabic, 71n9; Indo-European, 69; parallel 72

"Tai yi sheng shui" 太一生水 (Guodian ms) 301n12, 325, n55, 337
Taixuan 太玄 (*Supreme Mystery*) 26–27, 203, 212–215, 218, 224n141, 225, 236
Taniguchi Hiroshi 谷口洋 206–208
taxonomy of stable categories 316–318; lack of, 318

INDEX

teacher 47n30, 92, 105, 109, 186, 211–212, 220, 225–238; and model. *See shifa*. *See also* master-teacher
teaching 102, 179–180, 236n198, 275; and emulation, 237
teachings (*yan* 言) 93–95, 103, 166, 176n7, 202, 204, 209, 225n151, 268–269, 333; of the sages, 20, 50, 211, 226n151. *See also jiao*
teaching situation 185
teaching tradition 178
technopaignion (concrete poetry) 8–9
Teng, Norman 313n39, 335–336
term judgment 250, 257, 263–267, 272, 286. *See also yan*
tetrasyllables 19–23, 87–110; agricultural, 95n22; didactic, 89–99; language of, 92; *Laozi*-style / *Laozi*-verse, 22–23, 87–110, 107–110; performance of, 102–103, 107–110; rhymed, 22, 89–98, 122–123. *See also* rhyme
text-centred culture 177
text recipient 26–29, 300–302, 307, 310, 325–326, 329, 332, 337–338; as bridge between comprehension and conduct, 325
text / textual composition 15n68, 18, 28–29, 87, 114–115, 117, 137, 153, 300–302, 310, 323, 337–338; different levels of 13; formal level of, 310, 318, 321; integral structures of, 17; literary patterns of, 29, 67–70; micro-macro level of, 19, 29, 301, 321n45; non-form of, 25; textual units in, 20
textual units 20, 27, 113, 116n14, 122–123, 130, 134, 143, 150, 153
tiandao 天道 'Way of Heaven' 83, 172
tianming 天命 'ordinance of Heaven' 82. *See also ming*
The Highest order of Cultivation. *See Daxue*
Thirteen Classics (*shisan jing* 十三經) 41. *See also* Confucian Classics
traditional authority / tradition and authority 25, 177, 185, 196
transformation (*hua* 化) 57n48, 90, 92, 108, 138, 141, 182, 186, 223, 226, 317; moral, 222; of the self, 107, 262, 274
truth 12, 48, 105, 123, 190, 297–299; ahistorical, 20; and philosophy, 297; apodictic, 195; claim, 29, 43, 197, 299, 336–337; enduring, 5; experience of, 297–298; higher, 48; metaphysical, 83; ontological, 307; paradoxical, 103;

realisation of, 297; self-evident, 71; unpalatable, 228

ultimate person (*zhiren* 至人, term from the *Zhuangzi*) 268–270, 274–275, 287–291

van der Loon, Piet 258
van Ess, Hans 42n20, 59
Van Norden, Brian 11
Vergil 95
verse 10n48, 14, 21–23, 67, 70, 87–110, 119–122, 204, 209; didactic, 22, 87, 100; embedding of within narrative, 107; georgic, 95; gnomic, 22, 87; philosophical, 22, 99; satirical, 197; tetrasyllabic, 22–23, 96, 103, 109. *See also lüshi*
virtue. *See de*
virtues 96, 118, 166–167; catalogue of, 128–129; endogenic versus exogenic, 171–172
voice 4n18, 71, 158–159, 165, 192, 196, 209, 232, 235; accepted, 25; authorless, 185; didactic, 186; distinct, 158; multiple, 27, 208; non-individualized / non-authorial, 185n30; privileged, 184; stylized, 189; textual, 192, 197–198. *See also* authorial voice, double voice

Wagner, Rudolf G. 14, 16, 20–23, 99–101, 109, 113n3, 122–123, 165n9, 261n33, 297n2
wandering (*you* 遊) 247, 268–269; ability to, 291; Heaven's, 289–290; of the ideal person, 246, 292; social and internal / mental, 278, 287, 291; wavering- 292
wang 忘 'disregarding' 249–250, 267, 272–274, 277. *See also liang wang* 兩忘, *wang yan* 忘言
Wang Bi 王弼 21, 25, 28, 37, 43–64, 120–122, 247–248; *Laozi Commentary* (*Laozi zhu* 老子注), 21, 37, 44, 50; *Zhouyi Commentary* (*Zhouyi zhu* 周易注) 21, 37, 44–57, 64
Wang Chong 王充 58, 207n18
Wang Fu 王符 57
wang yan 忘言 'disregarding [ingrained] linguistic conventions' 257–258, 273–276
wan wu 萬物 'myriad things' 45, 51, 71n7, 83, 304–305, 307, 310, 313–317, 329, 334, 337
Way. *See dao*
wei yan 微言 'subtle writing' 231

Wells, Rulon 16
Wenjing mifulun. *See Bunkyō hifuron*
Wenxin diaolong 文心雕龍 68
"Wenyan" 文言 commentary. *See Zhouyi*
Wenzi 文子 99, 107, 164
Wittgenstein, Ludwig 14, 172
writing (as opposed to speech) 8–9, 99–100, 176, 181, 210, 212–213; artifact of, 194; powers of, 213; representation in, 8; visual representations of arguments in, 9
writing (composing) 158, 206–207, 211, 214–215, 225n149, 229–231; parallelistic (*dui* 對), 69
writing strategies 261n32, 286, 293–294
writing system 2, 9n38
written: argument in early Chinese texts 12, 17, 23, 29; early Chinese thought, 18; genres, 158; philosophy 1, 13; philosophical communication / discourse, 13, 20; sources of wisdom, 164; text / word, 1, 13, 104, 179, 194; versus oral argumentation, 12
wu fang 無方 'without a method' 316–318
"Wuxing" 五行 (Mawangdui ms) 186; (Guodian ms), 29, 197, 337
wu yong 無用 'useless' 261–267

Xiaojing 孝經 40–42, 60, 64
xiaoxu 小序. *See* "Minor prefaces"
"Xici" 繫辭 commentary. *See Zhouyi*
xing 興 'stimulus' (technical term of poetic rhetoric) 186
Xing Bing 邢昺 40–41
xingming 形名 'Forms and Names' 108
"Xingqing lun" 性情論 (Shanghai Museum ms) 178n13, 198
"Xing zi ming chu" 性自命出 (Guodian ms) 178n13, 198
Xinshu 新書 59
xuanxue 玄學 'Scholarly exploration of the Dark' 43–44, 50n33, 52
Xun Qing 荀卿. *See Xunzi*
Xunzi 荀子 19, 24, 72, 77, 80, 102, 137, 143, 149, 153, 159–161, 179n15, 201, 204, 239n212; "Ai gong" 哀公, 102; genre style, 159; "Xing e" 性惡, 137, 153; "Yuelun" 樂論, 179n15
Xunzi荀子 (author, persona) 78, 80, 202, 208n23, 221, 223, 225n151, 239; didactic style, 159
xuzi 虛字 (empty characters) 38

yan 言 'words', language', 'judgment' 248–250, 257–277, 286–287, 291; children mode of, 263–267, 272–273, 286–287; divination mode of, 263, 265–267, 272–274, 286–287, 293; exclusive use of, 265, 273. *See also* term judgment
Yang Xiong 揚雄 26–27, 202–240. *See also Fayan, Taixuan*
Yan Hui 顏回 (persona) 209, 210n33, 226, 230n173, 233, 238
Yantie lun 鹽鐵論 189
Yanzi chunqiu 晏子春秋 161
yi 一 'one' 307, 329, 334
yi 意 'ideas', 'meanings', 'opinions' 248–250, 268–274, 291–292
yin and *yang* (陰陽) 26, 92, 105–106, 131, 279, 304n20, 315–316
Yinque 銀雀, 164
yizhe 佚者 'person at ease' 251n19, 252–257, 273–277, 291–292. *See also* mode-contrast, *yizhe*-*laozhe* distinction
yizhe 佚者-*laozhe* 勞者 distinction 254–257. *See also laozhe, yizhe*
Yi Zhoushu 逸周書 129, 148
yong 用 'useful' 263–267
yu 喻 'illustration' (technical term of poetic rhetoric) 186–187
Yuan, Jinmei, 3
"Yucong" 1 語叢一 24–26, 160–173; as an analytically /intellectually pointilistic text, 24, 160–166, 173; internal logic of, 169; genre style, 160–161, 164
yue 曰 'it is said,' (marker of authoritative speech) 25, 92, 185; rhetorical use of, 185. *See also gu yue*
Yu Xingwu 于省吾 116–117

zai yi 在意 'catching opinions', 'getting opinions' 249, 273–276. *See also de yi*
Zengzi 曾子 (persona) 144–152
Zhanguo ce 戰國策 12, 98n28
zhi 知 'know', 'knowledge', 'realise', realisation' 136, 261, 263, 297, 307
zhi guo 治國 'governing the state' 104–105, 109
zhi shen 治身 'governing the self' 105, 109
Zhongni 仲尼. *See Kongzi*
"Zhongxin zhi dao" 忠信之道 (Guodian ms) 143

Zhongyong 中庸 (*Doctrine of the Mean*) 72, 78, 80–83
Zhou Fagao 周法高 40
Zhouguan 周官. *See Zhouli*
Zhouli 周禮 (*Zhouguan* 周官) 220
"Zhou song" 周頌 (*Classic of Poetry*) 89
Zhouyi 周易 (*Changes of Zhou*) 21, 28, 37, 44–64, 248; "Wenyan" 文言 commentary, 45, 48, 52–55, 62–64; "Xici" 繫辭 commentary, 52, 56, 62–64, 201n1, 214n68, 222n128. *See also* Wang Bi
"*Zhouyi* lüeli" 周易略例 42–44, 55–56; "Ming xiang" 名象, 56, 248n12. *See also* Wang Bi
Zhuangzi 莊子 19, 22, 27–29, 72, 84, 87, 98, 102–107, 161, 164, 166, 202, 243–295, 298–300, 305n23, 333; genre style, 161; "Qiushui" 秋水, 28–29, 297–338; "Qiwu lun" 齊物論, 84; "Renjian shi" 人間事, 102–104; "Tian Dao" 天道, 299; "Tian di" 天地, 102; "Waiwu" 外物. *See* "*Zhuangzi* 26"; "Yangsheng zhu" 養生主, 299; "Ying diwang" 應帝王, 102; "Zai you" 在宥, 102
Zhuangzi 莊子 (author, persona) 103, 173, 212, 223–224, 239–240, 264–267, 280–282, 287, 294, 330–336
"*Zhuangzi* 26" 243–295; chapter-level coherence of, 28, 243–246, 249, 264, 270, 277–278, 292, 294
Zhuang Zhou 莊周. *See Zhuangzi*
zhuzi 諸子 literature. *See* 'masters' texts
Zi Lu 子路 (persona) 327
Zixia 子夏 (persona) 90, 152, 176–178
"Ziyi" 緇衣 (Guodian ms) 127
Zuo zhuan 左傳 41, 60, 69, 89–102, 179n15, 184n27, 187–188, 197, 204, 220, 224n142

www.ingramcontent.com/pod-product-compliance
Lightning Source LLC
Chambersburg PA
CBHW052141300426

44115CB00011B/1476